Data Science with Python

Combine Python with machine learning principles to discover hidden patterns in raw data

Rohan Chopra

Aaron England

Mohamed Noordeen Alaudeen

Packt

Data Science with Python

Authors: Rohan Chopra, Aaron England and Mohamed Noordeen Alaudeen

Technical Reviewer: Santiago Riviriego Esbert

Managing Editor: Aritro Ghosh

Acquisitions Editors: Kunal Sawant and Koushik Sen

Production Editor: Samita Warang

First Published: July 2019

Production Reference: 1090719

ISBN: 978-1-83855-286-2

Published by Packt Publishing Ltd.

Livery Place, 35 Livery Street

Birmingham B3 2PB, UK

Table of Contents

Data Visualization 59

Dimensionality Reduction and Unsupervised Learning 135

Tips and Tricks of the Trade 293

Appendix 323

Index 401

Preface

About

This section briefly introduces the authors, what this book covers, the technical skills you'll need to get started, and the hardware and software requirements required to complete all of the included activities and exercises.

About the Book

Data Science with Python begins by introducing you to data science and then teaches you to install the packages you need to create a data science coding environment. You will learn three major techniques in machine learning: unsupervised learning, supervised learning, and reinforcement learning. You will also explore basic classification and regression techniques, such as support vector machines, decision trees, and logistic regression.

As you make your way through chapters, you will study the basic functions, data structures, and syntax of the Python language that are used to handle large datasets with ease. You will learn about NumPy and pandas libraries for matrix calculations and data manipulation, study how to use Matplotlib to create highly customizable visualizations, and apply the boosting algorithm XGBoost to make predictions. In the concluding chapters, you will explore convolutional neural networks (CNNs), deep learning algorithms used to predict what is in an image. You will also understand how to feed human sentences to a neural network, make the model process contextual information, and create human language processing systems to predict the outcome.

By the end of this book, you will be able to understand and implement any new data science algorithm and have the confidence to experiment with tools or libraries other than those covered in the book.

About the Authors

Rohan Chopra graduated from Vellore Institute of Technology with a bachelor's degree in Computer Science. Rohan has experience of more than 2 years in designing, implementing, and optimizing end-to-end deep neural network systems. His research is centered around using deep learning to solve computer vision-related problems and has hands-on experience of working on self-driving cars. He is a data scientist at Absolutdata.

> **Acknowledgements:**
>
> "This book was written by me, Rohan Chopra, and co-authored by Aaron England and Mohamed Noordeen Alaudeen. Big thanks to my mentor, Sanjiban Sekhar Roy, for his support; also, thanks to all the team at Packt."

Aaron England earned a PhD from the University of Utah in Exercise and Sports Science with a cognate in Biostatistics. Currently, he resides in Scottsdale, Arizona, where he works as a data scientist at Natural Partners Fullscript.

Mohamed Noordeen Alaudeen is a lead data scientist at Logitech. Noordeen has more than 7 years of experience in building and developing end-toend big data and deep neural network systems. It all started when he decided to engage in data science for the rest of his life.

He is seasoned data science and big data trainer with both Imarticus Learning and Great Learning, which are two of the renowned data science institutes in India. Apart from his teaching, he does contribute his work to open-source. He has over 90+ repositories on GitHub, which have open-sourced his technical work and data science material. He is an active influencer(with over 22,000+ connections) on Linkedin, helping the data science community.

Learning Objectives

- Pre-process data to make it ready to use for machine learning
- Create data visualizations with Matplotlib
- Use scikit-learn to perform dimension reduction using principal component analysis (PCA)
- Solve classification and regression problems
- Get predictions using the XGBoost library
- Process images and create machine learning models to decode them
- Process human language for prediction and classification
- Use TensorBoard to monitor training metrics in real time
- Find the best hyperparameters for your model with AutoML

Audience

Data Science with Python is designed for data analysts, data scientists, database engineers, and business analysts who want to move towards using Python and machine learning techniques to analyze data and predict outcomes. Basic knowledge of Python and data analytics will help you to understand the various concepts explained in this book.

Approach

Data Science with Python takes a practical approach to equip beginners and experienced data scientists with the most essential tools required to master data science and machine learning techniques. It contains multiple activities that use real-life business scenarios for you to practice and apply your new skills in a highly relevant context.

Minimum Hardware Requirements

For an optimal student experience, we recommend the following hardware configuration:

- Intel Core i5 processor or equivalent
- 4 GB RAM (8 GB preferred)
- 15 GB available hard disk space
- Internet connection

Software Requirements

You'll also need the following software installed in advance:

- OS: Windows 7 SP1 64-bit, Windows 8.1 64-bit or Windows 10 64-bit, Ubuntu Linux, or the latest version of OS X
- Browser: Google Chrome/Mozilla Firefox latest version
- Notepad++/Sublime Text as IDE (optional, as you can practice everything using Jupyter Notebook in your browser)
- Python 3.4+ (the latest version is Python 3.7) installed (https://python.org)
- Anaconda (https://www.anaconda.com/distribution/)
- Git (https://git-scm.com/)

Installation and Setup

Open Anaconda Prompt and follow these steps to get your system ready for data science. We will create a new environment on Anaconda in which we will install all the required libraries and run our code:

1. To create a new environment and install all the libraries, download the environment file from https://github.com/TrainingByPackt/Data-Science-with-Python/blob/master/environment.yml and run the following command:

   ```
   conda env create -f environment.yml
   ```

2. To activate the environment, run this command:

   ```
   conda activate DataScience
   ```

   For this book, whenever you are asked to open a terminal, you need to open Anaconda Prompt, activate the environment, and then proceed.

3. Jupyter Notebook allows us to run code and experiment in code blocks. To start Jupyter Notebook run the following inside the **DataScience** environment:

```
jupyter notebook
```

A new browser window will open with the Jupyter interface. You can then navigate to the project location and run the Jupyter Notebooks.

Using Kaggle for Faster Experimentation

The Kaggle kernel platform provides free access to GPUs, which speeds up the training of machine learning by around **10x**. GPUs are specialized chips that perform matrix calculations very quickly, much faster than a CPU. In this section, we will learn how we can make use of this free service to train our models more quickly:

1. Open https://www.kaggle.com/kernels in your browser and sign in.
2. Click on the **New Kernel** button and select **Notebook** in the popup. The screen that is loaded, which is where you can run your code, looks like this:

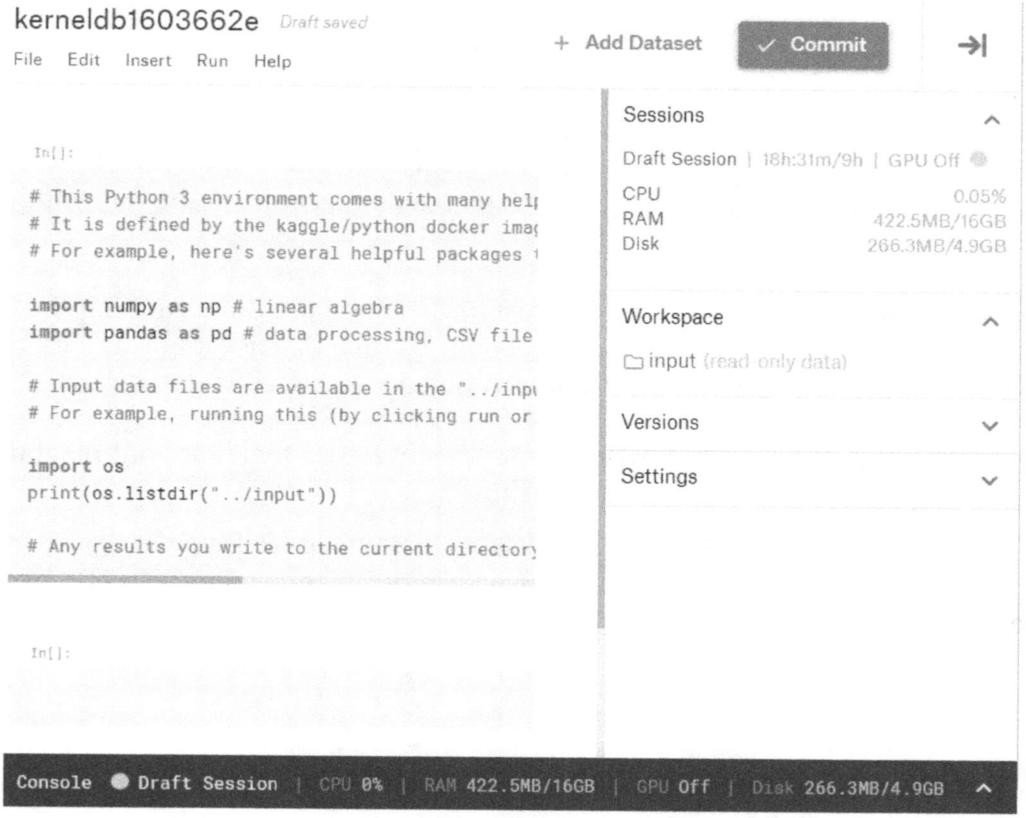

Figure 0.1: Notebook screen

In the top-left corner is the name of the notebook, which you can change.

3. Click on **Settings** and activate the GPU on this notebook. To use the internet through the notebook, you will have to authenticate with your mobile phone:

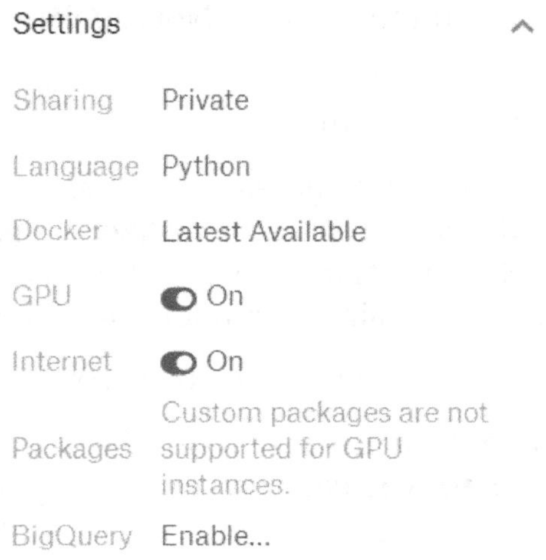

Figure 0.2: Settings screen

4. To upload a Jupyter notebook to Kaggle, click on **File** and then **Upload notebook**. To load a dataset for this notebook, click on the **Add Dataset** button in the top-right corner. From here, you can add any dataset hosted on Kaggle or upload your own dataset. You can access your uploaded dataset from the following path:

```
../input/
```

5. To download this notebook with the results after you are done running the code, click on **File** and select **Download notebook**. To save this notebook and its results in your Kaggle account, click the **Commit** button in the top-right corner.

You can make use of this Kaggle environment whenever you feel that your machine learning models are taking a lot of time to train.

This book uses datasets from UCI Machine Learning Repository [http://archive.ics.uci.edu/ml]. Irvine, CA: University of California, School of Information and Computer Science.

Conventions

Code words in text, database table names, folder names, filenames, file extensions, pathnames, dummy URLs, user input, and Twitter handles are shown as follows: "To read CSV data, you can use the **read_csv()** function by passing **filename.csv** as an argument."

A block of code is set as follows:

```
model.fit(x_train, y_train, validation_data = (x_test, y_test),
epochs=10, batch_size=512)
```

New terms and important words are shown in bold. Words that you see on the screen, for example, in menus or dialog boxes, appear in the text like this: "There are some cells that have either **NA** or are just empty."

Installing the Code Bundle

The code bundle for this book is hosted on GitHub at https://github.com/TrainingByPackt/Data-Science-with-Python.

We also have other code bundles from our rich catalog of books and videos available at https://github.com/PacktPublishing/. Check them out!

1

Introduction to Data Science and Data Pre-Processing

Learning Objectives

By the end of this chapter, you will be able to:

- Use various Python machine learning libraries
- Handle missing data and deal with outliers
- Perform data integration to bring together data from different sources
- Perform data transformation to convert data into a machine-readable form
- Scale data to avoid problems with values of different magnitudes
- Split data into train and test datasets
- Describe the different types of machine learning
- Describe the different performance measures of a machine learning model

This chapter introduces data science and covers the various processes included in the building of machine learning models, with a particular focus on pre-processing.

Introduction

We live in a world where we are constantly surrounded by data. As such, being able to understand and process data is an absolute necessity.

Data Science is a field that deals with the description, analysis, and prediction of data. Consider an example from our daily lives: every day, we utilize multiple social media applications on our phones. These applications gather and process data in order to create a more personalized experience for each user – for example, showing us news articles that we may be interested in, or tailoring search results according to our location. This branch of data science is known as **machine learning**.

Machine learning is the methodical learning of procedures and statistical representations that computers use to accomplish tasks without human intervention. In other words, it is the process of teaching a computer to perform tasks by itself without explicit instructions, relying only on patterns and inferences. Some common uses of machine learning algorithms are in email filtering, computer vision, and computational linguistics.

This book will focus on machine learning and other aspects of data science using Python. Python is a popular language for data science, as it is versatile and relatively easy to use. It also has several ready-made libraries that are well equipped for processing data.

Python Libraries

Throughout this book, we'll be using various Python libraries, including pandas, Matplotlib, Seaborn, and scikit-learn.

pandas

pandas is an open source package that has many functions for loading and processing data in order to prepare it for machine learning tasks. It also has tools that can be used to analyze and manipulate data. Data can be read from many formats using pandas. We will mainly be using CSV data throughout this book. To read CSV data, you can use the `read_csv()` function by passing `filename.csv` as an argument. An example of this is shown here:

```
>>> import pandas as pd
>>> pd.read_csv("data.csv")
```

In the preceding code, **pd** is an alias name given to pandas. It is not mandatory to give an alias. To visualize a pandas DataFrame, you can use the **head()** function to list the top five rows. This will be demonstrated in one of the following exercises.

> **Note**
>
> Please visit the following link to learn more about pandas: https://pandas.pydata.org/pandas-docs/stable/.

NumPy

NumPy is one of the main packages that Python has to offer. It is mainly used in practices related to scientific computing and when working on mathematical operations. It comprises of tools that enable us to work with arrays and array objects.

Matplotlib

Matplotlib is a data visualization package. It is useful for plotting data points in a 2D space with the help of NumPy.

Seaborn

Seaborn is also a data visualization library that is based on matplotlib. Visualizations created using Seaborn are far more attractive than ones created using matplotlib in terms of graphics.

scikit-learn

scikit-learn is a Python package used for machine learning. It is designed in such a way that it interoperates with other numeric and scientific libraries in Python to achieve the implementation of algorithms.

These ready-to-use libraries have gained interest and attention from developers, especially in the data science space. Now that we have covered the various libraries in Python, in the next section we'll explore the roadmap for building machine learning models.

Roadmap for Building Machine Learning Models

The roadmap for building machine learning models is straightforward and consists of five major steps, which are explained here:

- **Data Pre-processing**

  This is the first step in building a machine learning model. Data pre-processing refers to the transformation of data before feeding it into the model. It deals with the techniques that are used to convert unusable raw data into clean reliable data.

  Since data collection is often not performed in a controlled manner, raw data often contains outliers (for example, age = 120), nonsensical data combinations (for example, model: bicycle, type: 4-wheeler), missing values, scale problems, and so on. Because of this, raw data cannot be fed into a machine learning model because it might compromise the quality of the results. As such, this is the most important step in the process of data science.

- **Model Learning**

  After pre-processing the data and splitting it into train/test sets (more on this later), we move on to modeling. Models are nothing but sets of well-defined methods called algorithms that use pre-processed data to learn patterns, which can later be used to make predictions. There are different types of learning algorithms, including supervised, semi-supervised, unsupervised, and reinforcement learning. These will be discussed later.

- **Model Evaluation**

  In this stage, the models are evaluated with the help of specific performance metrics. With these metrics, we can go on to tune the hyperparameters of a model in order to improve it. This process is called **hyperparameter optimization**. We will repeat this step until we are satisfied with the performance.

- **Prediction**

  Once we are happy with the results from the evaluation step, we will then move on to predictions. Predictions are made by the trained model when it is exposed to a new dataset. In a business setting, these predictions can be shared with decision makers to make effective business choices.

- **Model Deployment**

  The whole process of machine learning does not just stop with model building and prediction. It also involves making use of the model to build an application with the new data. Depending on the business requirements, the deployment may be a report, or it may be some repetitive data science steps that are to be executed. After deployment, a model needs proper management and maintenance at regular intervals to keep it up and running.

This chapter will mainly focus on pre-processing. We will cover the different tasks involved in data pre-processing, such as data representation, data cleaning, and others.

Data Representation

The main objective of machine learning is to build models that understand data and find underlying patterns. In order to do so, it is very important to feed the data in a way that is interpretable by the computer. To feed the data into a model, it must be represented as a table or a matrix of the required dimensions. Converting your data into the correct tabular form is one of the first steps before pre-processing can properly begin.

Data Represented in a Table

Data should be arranged in a two-dimensional space made up of rows and columns. This type of data structure makes it easy to understand the data and pinpoint any problems. An example of some raw data stored as a CSV (**comma separated values**) file is shown here:

```
1., Avatar, 18-12-2009, 7.8
2., Titanic, 18-11-1997,
3., Avengers Infinity War, 27-04-2018, 8.5
```

Figure 1.1: Raw data in CSV format

The representation of the same data in a table is as follows:

S.No	Movie	Release Date	Ratings (IMDb)
1.	Avatar	18-12-2009	7.8
2.	Titanic	18-11-1997	*Na*
3.	Avengers Infinity War	27-04-2018	8.5

Figure 1.2: CSV data in table format

If you compare the data in CSV and table formats, you will see that there are missing values in both. We will cover what to do with these later in the chapter. To load a CSV file and work on it as a table, we use the pandas library. The data here is loaded into tables called DataFrames.

> **Note**
>
> To learn more about pandas, visit the following link: http://pandas.pydata.org/pandas-docs/version/0.15/tutorials.html.

Independent and Target Variables

The DataFrame that we use contains variables or features that can be classified into two categories. These are independent variables (also called **predictor variables**) and dependent variables (also called **target variables**). Independent variables are used to predict the target variable. As the name suggests, independent variables should be independent of each other. If they are not, this will need to be addressed in the pre-processing (cleaning) stage.

Independent Variables

These are all the features in the DataFrame except the **target variable**. They are of size (m, n), where m is the number of observations and n is the number of features. These variables must be normally distributed and should NOT contain:

- Missing or NULL values
- Highly categorical data features or high cardinality (these terms will be covered in more detail later)
- Outliers
- Data on different scales
- Human error
- Multicollinearity (independent variables that are correlated)
- Very large independent feature sets (too many independent variables to be manageable)
- Sparse data
- Special characters

Feature Matrix and Target Vector

A single piece of data is called a scalar. A group of scalars is called a vector, and a group of vectors is called a matrix. A matrix is represented in rows and columns. Feature matrix data is made up of independent columns, and the target vector depends on the feature matrix columns. To get a better understanding of this, let's look at the following table:

Car Model	Car Capacity	Car Brand	Car Price

Figure 1.3: Table containing car details

As you can see in the table, there are various columns: Car Model, Car Capacity, Car Brand, and Car Price. All columns except Car Price are independent variables and represent the feature matrix. Car Price is the dependent variable that depends on the other columns (Car Model, Car Capacity, and Car Brand). It is a target vector because it depends on the feature matrix data. In the next section, we'll go through an exercise based on features and a target matrix to get a thorough understanding.

> **Note**
>
> All exercises and activities will be primarily developed in Jupyter Notebook. It is recommended to keep a separate notebook for different assignments unless advised not to. Also, to load a sample dataset, the pandas library will be used, because it displays the data as a table. Other ways to load data will be explained in further sections.

Exercise 1: Loading a Sample Dataset and Creating the Feature Matrix and Target Matrix

In this exercise, we will be loading the **House_price_prediction** dataset into the pandas DataFrame and creating feature and target matrices. The **House_price_prediction** dataset is taken from the UCI Machine Learning Repository. The data was collected from various suburbs of the USA and consists of 5,000 entries and 6 features related to houses. Follow these steps to complete this exercise:

> **Note**
>
> The **House_price_prediction** dataset can be found at this location: https://github.com/TrainingByPackt/Data-Science-with-Python/blob/master/Chapter01/Data/USA_Housing.csv.

1. Open a Jupyter notebook and add the following code to import pandas:

```
import pandas as pd
```

2. Now we need to load the dataset into a pandas DataFrame. As the dataset is a CSV file, we'll be using the **read_csv()** function to read the data. Add the following code to do this:

```
dataset = "https://github.com/TrainingByPackt/Data-Science-with-Python/
blob/master/Chapter01/Data/USA_Housing.csv"
df = pd.read_csv(dataset, header = 0)
```

As you can see in the preceding code, the data is stored in a variable named **df**.

3. To print all the column names of the DataFrame, we'll use the **df.columns** command. Write the following code in the notebook:

```
df.columns
```

The preceding code generates the following output:

```
df.columns
```

```
Index(['Avg. Area Income', 'Avg. Area House Age', 'Avg. Area Number of Rooms',
       'Avg. Area Number of Bedrooms', 'Area Population', 'Price', 'Address'],
      dtype='object')
```

Figure 1.4: List of columns present in the dataframe

4. The dataset contains n number of data points. We can find the total number of rows using the following command:

```
df.index
```

The preceding code generates the following output:

```
df.index
```

```
RangeIndex(start=0, stop=5000, step=1)
```

Figure 1.5: Total Index in the dataframe

As you can see in the preceding figure, our dataset contains 5000 rows, from index 0 to 5000.

> **Note**
>
> You can use the **set_index()** function in pandas to convert a column into an index of rows in a DataFrame. This is a bit like using the values in that column as your row labels.
>
> ```
> Dataframe.set_index('column name', inplace = True')'
> ```

5. Let's set the **Address** column as an index and reset it back to the original DataFrame. The pandas library provides the **set_index()** method to convert a column into an index of rows in a DataFrame. Add the following code to implement this:

```
df.set_index('Address', inplace=True)
df
```

The preceding code generates the following output:

	Avg. Area Income	Avg. Area House Age	Avg. Area Number of Rooms	Avg. Area Number of Bedrooms	Area Population	Price
Address						
208 Michael Ferry Apt. 674\nLaurabury, NE 37010-5101	9545.458574	5.682861	7.009188	4.09	23086.800503	1.059034e+06
188 Johnson Views Suite 079\nLake Kathleen, CA 48958	9248.642455	6.002900	6.730821	3.09	40173.072174	1.505891e+06
9127 Elizabeth Stravenue\nDanieltown, WI 06482-3489	1287.067179	5.865890	8.512727	5.13	36882.159400	1.058988e+06
USS Barnett\nFPO AP 44820	3345.240046	7.188236	5.586729	3.26	34310.242831	1.260617e+06

Figure 1.6: DataFrame with an indexed Address column

The **inplace** parameter in the **set_index()** function is by default set to **False**. If the value is changed to **True**, then whatever operation we perform the content of the DataFrame changes directly without the copy being created.

6. In order to reset the index of the given object, we use the **reset_index()** function. Write the following code to implement this:

```
df.reset_index(inplace=True)
df
```

The preceding code generates the following output:

	Address	Avg. Area Income	Avg. Area House Age	Avg. Area Number of Rooms	Avg. Area Number of Bedrooms	Area Population	Price
0	208 Michael Ferry Apt. 674\nLaurabury, NE 3701...	79545.458574	5.682861	7.009188	4.09	23086.800503	1.059034e+06
1	188 Johnson Views Suite 079\nLake Kathleen, CA...	79248.642455	6.002900	6.730821	3.09	40173.072174	1.505891e+06
2	9127 Elizabeth Stravenue\nDanieltown, WI 06482...	61287.067179	5.865890	8.512727	5.13	36882.159400	1.058988e+06
3	USS Barnett\nFPO AP 44820	63345.240046	7.188236	5.586729	3.26	34310.242831	1.260617e+06
4	USNS Raymond\nFPO AE 09386	59982.197226	5.040555	7.839388	4.23	26354.109472	6.309435e+05

Figure 1.7: DataFrame with the index reset

> **Note**
>
> The index is like a name given to a row and column. Rows and columns both have an index. You can index by row/column number or row/column name.

7. We can retrieve the first four rows and the first three columns using a row number and column number. This can be done using the **iloc** indexer in pandas, which retrieves data using index positions. Add the following code to do this:

```
df.iloc[0:4 , 0:3]
```

```
df.iloc[0:4,0:3]
```

	Address	Avg. Area Income	Avg. Area House Age
0	208 Michael Ferry Apt. 674\nLaurabury, NE 3701...	79545.458574	5.682861
1	188 Johnson Views Suite 079\nLake Kathleen, CA...	79248.642455	6.002900
2	9127 Elizabeth Stravenue\nDanieltown, WI 06482...	61287.067179	5.865890
3	USS Barnett\nFPO AP 44820	63345.240046	7.188236

Figure 1.8: Dataset of four rows and three columns

8. To retrieve the data using labels, we use the **loc** indexer. Add the following code to retrieve the first five rows of the Income and Age columns:

```
df.loc[0:4 , ["Avg. Area Income", "Avg. Area House Age"]]
```

	Avg. Area Income	Avg. Area House Age
0	79545.458574	5.682861
1	79248.642455	6.002900
2	61287.067179	5.865890
3	63345.240046	7.188236
4	59982.197226	5.040555

Figure 1.9: Dataset of five rows and two columns

9. Now create a variable called **X** to store the independent features. In our dataset, we will consider all features except Price as independent variables, and we will use the **drop()** function to include them. Once this is done, we print out the top five instances of the **X** variable. Add the following code to do this:

```
X = df.drop('Price', axis=1)
X.head()
```

The preceding code generates the following output:

	Avg. Area Income	Avg. Area House Age	Avg. Area Number of Rooms	Avg. Area Number of Bedrooms	Area Population	Address
0	79545.458574	5.682861	7.009188	4.09	23086.800503	208 Michael Ferry Apt. 674\nLaurabury, NE 3701...
1	79248.642455	6.002900	6.730821	3.09	40173.072174	188 Johnson Views Suite 079\nLake Kathleen, CA...
2	61287.067179	5.865890	8.512727	5.13	36882.159400	9127 Elizabeth Stravenue\nDanieltown, WI 06482...
3	63345.240046	7.188236	5.586729	3.26	34310.242831	USS Barnett\nFPO AP 44820
4	59982.197226	5.040555	7.839388	4.23	26354.109472	USNS Raymond\nFPO AE 09386

Figure 1.10: Dataset showing the first five rows of the feature matrix

> **Note**
>
> The default number of instances that will be taken for the head is five, so if you don't specify the number then it will by default output five observations. The axis parameter in the preceding screenshot denotes whether you want to drop the label from rows (axis = 0) or columns (axis = 1).

10. Print the shape of your newly created feature matrix using the **X.shape** command. Add the following code to do this:

```
X.shape
```

The preceding code generates the following output:

```
(5000, 6)
```

Figure 1.11: Shape of the feature matrix

In the preceding figure, the first value indicates the number of observations in the dataset (**5000**), and the second value represents the number of features (**6**).

11. Similarly, we will create a variable called **y** that will store the target values. We will use indexing to grab the target column. Indexing allows you to access a section of a larger element. In this case, we want to grab the column named Price from the **df** DataFrame. Then, we want to print out the top 10 values of the variable. Add the following code to implement this:

```
y = df['Price']
y.head(10)
```

The preceding code generates the following output:

```
0    1.059034e+06
1    1.505891e+06
2    1.058988e+06
3    1.260617e+06
4    6.309435e+05
5    1.068138e+06
6    1.502056e+06
7    1.573937e+06
8    7.988695e+05
9    1.545155e+06
Name: Price, dtype: float64
```

Figure 1.12: Dataset showing the first 10 rows of the target matrix

12. Print the shape of your new variable using the **y.shape** command. The shape should be one-dimensional, with a length equal to the number of observations (**5000**) only. Add the following code to implement this:

```
y.shape
```

The preceding code generates the following output:

```
(5000,)
```

Figure 1.13: Shape of the target matrix

You have successfully created the feature and target matrices of a dataset. You have completed the first step in the process of building a predictive model. This model will learn the patterns from the feature matrix (columns in **X**) and how they map to the values in the target vector (**y**). These patterns can then be used to predict house prices from new data based on the features of those new houses.

In the next section, we will explore more steps involved in pre-processing.

Data Cleaning

Data cleaning includes processes such as filling in missing values and handling inconsistencies. It detects corrupt data and replaces or modifies it.

Missing Values

The concept of missing values is important to understand if you want to master the skill of successful management and understanding of data. Let's take a look at the following figure:

Customer Id	Age	Job	Credit amount	Duration	Purpose	Risk
9866746AS	67	2	1169	6	radio/TV	Low
99887589FD	22	2	5951	48	radio/TV	High
99373488WE	49	1	2096	12	education	Low
88475994YR	45			42	furniture/equipment	Low
93498765JG	53	2	4870	24	car	Low
99384766JF	35	1	9055	36	education	Low
99945949IJ		2	NA		NA	Low
98846882VC	35	3	6948	NA	car	Low
87666547AS	61	1	3059	12	NA	Low
99583999DS		3	5234	30	car	High
99348439SD	25	2	1295	NA	car	High

Figure 1.14: Bank customer credit data

As you can see, the data belongs to a bank; each row is a separate customer and each column contains their details, such as age and credit amount. There are some cells that have either **NA** or are just empty. This is missing data. Each piece of information about the customer is crucial for the bank. If any of the information is missing, then it will be difficult for the bank to predict the risk of providing a loan to the customer.

Handling Missing Data

Intelligent handling of missing data will result in building a robust model capable of handling complex tasks. There are many ways to handle missing data. Let's now look at some of those ways.

Removing the Data

Checking missing values is the first and the most important step in data pre-processing. A model cannot accept data with missing values. This is a very simple and commonly used method to handle missing values: we delete a row if the missing value corresponds to the places in the row, or we delete a column if it has more than 70%-75% of missing data. Again, the threshold value is not fixed and depends on how much you wish to fix.

The benefit of this approach is that it is quick and easy to do, and in many cases no data is better than bad data. The drawback is that you may end up losing important information, because you're deleting a whole feature based on a few missing values.

Exercise 2: Removing Missing Data

In this exercise, we will be loading the `Banking_Marketing.csv` dataset into the pandas DataFrame and handling the missing data. This dataset is related to direct marketing campaigns of a Portuguese banking institution. The marketing campaigns involved phone calls to clients to try and get them to subscribe to a particular product. The dataset contains the details of each client contacted, and whether they subscribed to the product. Follow these steps to complete this exercise:

> **Note**
>
> The `Banking_Marketing.csv` dataset can be found at this location: https://github.com/TrainingByPackt/Data-Science-with-Python/blob/master/Chapter01/Data/Banking_Marketing.csv.

1. Open a Jupyter notebook. Insert a new cell and add the following code to import pandas and fetch the **Banking_Marketing.csv** dataset:

```
import pandas as pd
dataset = 'https://github.com/TrainingByPackt/Data-Science-with-Python/
blob/master/Chapter01/Data/Banking_Marketing.csv'
#reading the data into the dataframe into the object data
df = pd.read_csv(dataset, header=0)
```

2. Once you have fetched the dataset, print the datatype of each column. To do so, use the **dtypes** attribute from the pandas DataFrame:

```
df.dtypes
```

The preceding code generates the following output:

```
age                 int64
job                object
marital            object
education          object
default            object
housing            object
loan               object
contact            object
month              object
day_of_week        object
duration            int64
campaign            int64
pdays               int64
previous            int64
poutcome           object
emp_var_rate      float64
cons_price_idx    float64
cons_conf_idx     float64
euribor3m         float64
nr_employed       float64
y                   int64
dtype: object
```

Figure 1.15: Data types of each feature

3. Now we need to find the missing values for each column. In order to do that, we use the **isna()** function provided by pandas:

```
df.isna().sum()
```

The preceding code generates the following output:

```
age                2
job                0
marital            0
education          0
default            0
housing            0
loan               0
contact            6
month              0
day of week        0
duration           7
campaign           0
pdays              0
previous           0
poutcome           0
emp_var_rate       0
cons_price_idx     0
cons_conf_idx      0
euribor3m          0
nr_employed        0
y                  0
dtype: int64
```

Figure 1.16: Missing values of each column in the dataset

In the preceding figure, we can see that there is data missing from three columns, namely **age**, **contact**, and **duration**. There are two NAs in the **age** column, six NAs in **contact**, and seven NAs in **duration**.

4. Once you have figured out all the missing details, we remove all the missing rows from the DataFrame. To do so, we use the **dropna()** function:

```
#removing Null values
data = data.dropna()
```

5. To check whether the missing vales are still present, use the **isna()** function:

```
df.isna().sum()
```

The preceding code generates the following output:

```
age               0
job               0
marital           0
education         0
default           0
housing           0
loan              0
contact           0
month             0
day_of_week       0
duration          0
campaign          0
pdays             0
previous          0
poutcome          0
emp_var_rate      0
cons_price_idx    0
cons_conf_idx     0
euribor3m         0
nr_employed       0
y                 0
dtype: int64
```

Figure 1.17: Each column of the dataset with zero missing values

You have successfully removed all missing data from the DataFrame. In the next section, we'll look at the second method of dealing with missing data, which uses imputation.

Mean/Median/Mode Imputation

In the case of numerical data, we can compute its mean or median and use the result to replace missing values. In the case of the categorical (non-numerical) data, we can compute its mode to replace the missing value. This is known as imputation.

The benefit of using imputation, rather than just removing data, is that it prevents data loss. The drawback is that you don't know how accurate using the mean, median, or mode is going to be in a given situation.

Let's look at an exercise in which we will use imputation method to solve missing data problems.

Exercise 3: Imputing Missing Data

In this exercise, we will be loading the **Banking_Marketing.csv** dataset into the pandas DataFrame and handle the missing data. We'll make use of the imputation method. Follow these steps to complete this exercise:

> **Note**
>
> The **Banking_Marketing.csv** dataset can be found at this location: https://github.com/TrainingByPackt/Data-Science-with-Python/blob/master/Chapter01/Data/Banking_Marketing.csv.

1. Open a Jupyter notebook and add a new cell. Load the dataset into the pandas DataFrame. Add the following code to do this:

```
import pandas as pd
dataset = 'https://github.com/TrainingByPackt/Data-Science-with-Python/
blob/master/Chapter01/Data/Banking_Marketing.csv'
df = pd.read_csv(dataset, header=0)
```

2. Impute the numerical data of the **age** column with its mean. To do so, first find the mean of the **age** column using the **mean()** function of pandas, and then print it:

```
mean_age = df.age.mean()
print(mean_age)
```

The preceding code generates the following output:

```
40.023812413525256
```

Figure 1.18: Mean of the age column

3. Once this is done, impute the missing data with its mean using the **fillna()** function. This can be done with the following code:

```
df.age.fillna(mean_age, inplace=True)
```

4. Now we impute the numerical data of the duration column with its median. To do so, first find the median of the duration column using the **median()** function of the pandas. Add the following code to do so:

```
median_duration = df.duration.median()
print(median_duration)
```

```
180.0
```

Figure 1.19: Median of the duration

5. Impute the missing data of the duration with its median using the **fillna()** function.

```
df. duration.fillna(median_duration,inplace=True)
```

6. Impute the categorical data of the contact column with its mode. To do so, first, find the mode of the contact column using the **mode()** function of pandas. Add the following code to do this:

```
mode_contact = df.contact.mode()[0]
print(mode_contact)
```

```
cellular
```

Figure 1.20: Mode of the contact

7. Impute the missing data of the contact column with its mode using the **fillna()** function. Add the following code to do this:

```
df.contact.fillna(mode_contact,inplace=True)
```

Unlike mean and median, there may be more than one mode in a column. So, we just take the first mode with index 0.

You have successfully imputed the missing data in different ways and made the data complete and clean.

Another part of data cleaning is dealing with outliers, which will be discussed in the next section.

Outliers

Outliers are values that are very large or very small with respect to the distribution of the other data. We can only find outliers in numerical data. Box plots are one good way to find the outliers in a dataset, as you can see in the following figure:

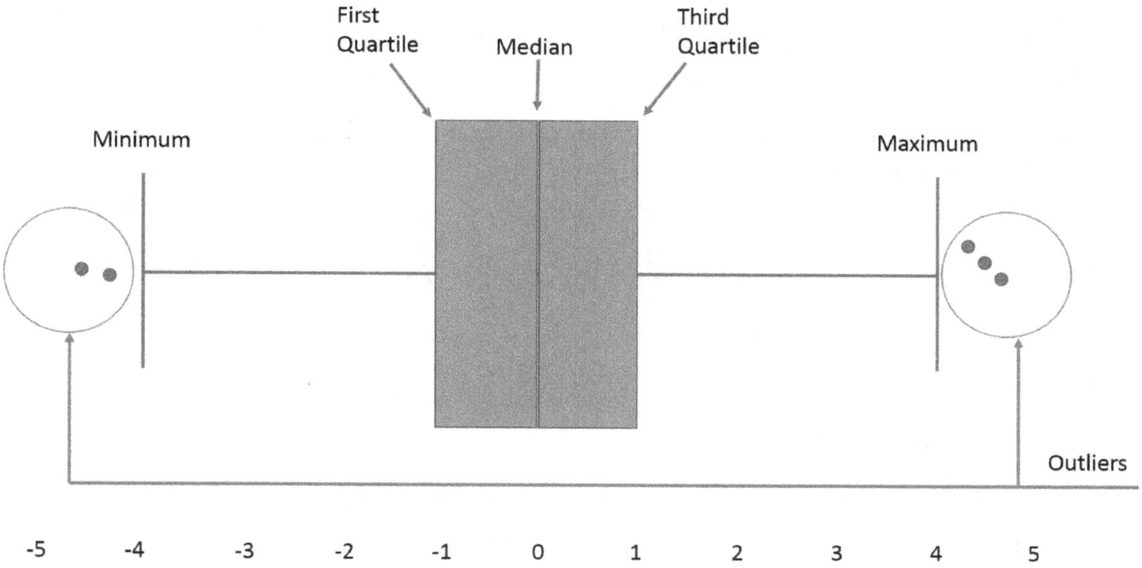

Figure 1.21: Sample of outliers in a box plot

> **Note**
>
> An outlier is not always bad data! With the help of business understanding and client interaction, you can discern whether to remove or retain the outlier.

Let's learn how to find outliers using a simple example. Consider a sample dataset of temperatures from a place at different times:

```
71, 70, 90, 70, 70, 60, 70, 72, 72, 320, 71, 69
```

We can now do the following:

1. First, we'll sort the data:

   ```
   60,69, 70, 70, 70, 70, 71, 71, 72, 72, 90, 320
   ```

2. Next, we'll calculate the median (Q2). The median is the middle data after sorting.

   Here, the middle terms are 70 and 71 after sorting the list.

   The median is (70 + 71) / 2 = 70.5

3. Then we'll calculate the lower quartile (Q1). Q1 is the middle value (median) of the first half of the dataset.

   First half of the data = **`60, 69, 70, 70, 70, 70`**

   Points 3 and 4 of the bottom 6 are both equal to 70.

   The average is (70 + 70) / 2 = 70

   Q1 = 70

4. Then we calculate the upper quartile (Q3).

   Q3 is the middle value (median) of the second half of the dataset.

   Second half of the data = **`71, 71, 72, 72, 90, 320`**

   Points 3 and 4 of the upper 6 are 72 and 72.

   The average is (72 + 72) / 2 = 72

   Q3 = 72

5. Then we find the interquartile range (IQR).

   IQR = Q3 – Q1 = 72 – 70

   IQR = 2

6. Next, we find the upper and lower fences.

   Lower fence = Q1 – 1.5 (IQR) = 70 – 1.5(2) = 67

   Upper fence = Q3 + 1.5 (IQR) = 71.5 + 1.5(2) = 74.5

   Boundaries of our fences = 67 and 74.5

Any data points lower than the lower fence and greater than the upper fence are outliers. Thus, the outliers from our example are 60, 90 and 320.

Exercise 4: Finding and Removing Outliers in Data

In this exercise, we will be loading the **german_credit_data.csv** dataset into the pandas DataFrame and removing the outliers. The dataset contains 1,000 entries with 20 categorial/symbolic attributes prepared by Prof. Hofmann. In this dataset, each entry represents a person who takes credit from a bank. Each person is classified as a good or bad credit risk according to the set of attributes. Follow these steps to complete this exercise:

> **Note**
>
> The link to the **german_credit_data.csv** dataset can be found here: https://github.com/TrainingByPackt/Data-Science-with-Python/blob/master/Chapter01/Data/german_credit_data.csv.

1. Open a Jupyter notebook and add a new cell. Write the following code to import the necessary libraries: pandas, NumPy, matplotlib, and seaborn. Fetch the dataset and load it into the pandas DataFrame. Add the following code to do this:

```
import pandas as pd
import numpy as np
%matplotlib inline
import seaborn as sbn
dataset = 'https://github.com/TrainingByPackt/Data-Science-with-Python/
blob/master/Chapter01/Data/german_credit_data.csv'
#reading the data into the dataframe into the object data
df = pd.read_csv(dataset, header=0)
```

   In the preceding code, **%matplotlib inline** is a magic function that is essential if we want the plot to be visible in the notebook.

2. This dataset contains an **Age** column. Let's plot a boxplot of the **Age** column. To do so, use the **boxplot()** function from the seaborn library:

```
sbn.boxplot(df['Age'])
```

The preceding code generates the following output:

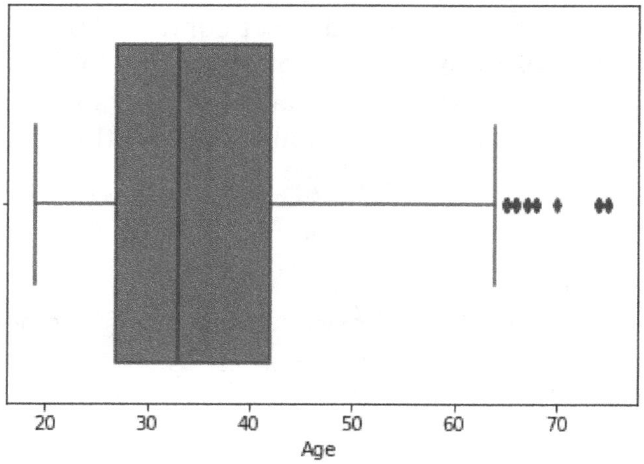

Figure 1.22: A box plot of the Age column

We can see that some data points are outliers in the boxplot.

3. The boxplot uses the IQR method to display the data and the outliers (the shape of the data). But in order to print an outlier, we use a mathematical formula to retrieve it. Add the following code to find the outliers of the **Age** column using the IQR method:

```
Q1 = df["Age"].quantile(0.25)
Q3 = df["Age"].quantile(0.75)
IQR = Q3 - Q1
print(IQR)
>>> 15.0
```

In the preceding code, Q1 is the first quartile and Q3 is the third quartile.

4. Now we find the upper fence and lower fence by adding the following code, and print all the data above the upper fence and below the lower fence. Add the following code to do this:

```
Lower_Fence = Q1 - (1.5 * IQR)
Upper_Fence = Q3 + (1.5 * IQR)
print(Lower_Fence)
print(Upper_Fence)
>>> 4.5
>>> 64.5
```

5. To print all the data above the upper fence and below the lower fence, add the following code:

```
df[((df["Age"] < Lower_Fence) |(df["Age"] > Upper_Fence))]
```

The preceding code generates the following output:

	Age	Sex	Job	Housing	Saving accounts	Checking account	Credit amount	Duration	Purpose
0	67	male	2	own	NaN	little	1169	6	radio/TV
75	66	male	3	free	little	little	1526	12	car
137	66	male	1	own	quite rich	moderate	766	12	radio/TV
163	70	male	3	free	little	moderate	7308	10	car
179	65	male	2	own	little	little	571	21	car
186	74	female	3	free	little	moderate	5129	9	car
187	68	male	0	free	little	moderate	1175	16	car

Figure 1.23: Outlier data based on the Age column

6. Filter out the outlier data and print only the potential data. To do so, just negate the preceding result using the ~ operator:

```
df = df[~((df ["Age"] < Lower_Fence) |(df["Age"] > Upper_Fence))]
df
```

The preceding code generates the following output:

	Unnamed: 0	Age	Sex	Job	Housing	Saving accounts	Checking account	Credit amount	Duration	Purpose
1	1	22	female	2	own	little	moderate	5951	48	radio/TV
2	2	49	male	1	own	little	NaN	2096	12	education
3	3	45	male	2	free	little	little	7882	42	furniture/equipment
4	4	53	male	2	free	little	little	4870	24	car
5	5	35	male	1	free	NaN	NaN	9055	36	education
6	6	53	male	2	own	quite rich	NaN	2835	24	furniture/equipment
7	7	35	male	3	rent	little	moderate	6948	36	car
8	8	61	male	1	own	rich	NaN	3059	12	radio/TV
9	9	28	male	3	own	little	moderate	5234	30	car

Figure 1.24: Potential data based on the Age column

You have successfully found the outliers using the IQR. In the next section, we will explore another method of pre-processing called data integration.

Data Integration

So far, we've made sure to remove the impurities in data and make it clean. Now, the next step is to combine data from different sources to get a unified structure with more meaningful and valuable information. This is mostly used if the data is segregated into different sources. To make it simple, let's assume we have data in CSV format in different places, all talking about the same scenario. Say we have some data about an employee in a database. We can't expect all the data about the employee to reside in the same table. It's possible that the employee's personal data will be located in one table, the employee's project history will be in a second table, the employee's time-in and time-out details will be in another table, and so on. So, if we want to do some analysis about the employee, we need to get all the employee data in one common place. This process of bringing data together in one place is called data integration. To do data integration, we can merge multiple pandas DataFrames using the **merge** function.

Let's solve an exercise based on data integration to get a clear understanding of it.

Exercise 5: Integrating Data

In this exercise, we'll merge the details of students from two datasets, namely **student.csv** and **marks.csv**. The **student** dataset contains columns such as **Age**, **Gender**, **Grade**, and **Employed**. The **marks.csv** dataset contains columns such as **Mark** and **City**. The **Student_id** column is common between the two datasets. Follow these steps to complete this exercise:

> **Note**
>
> The **student.csv** dataset can be found at this location: https://github.com/TrainingByPackt/Data-Science-with-Python/blob/master/Chapter01/Data/student.csv.
>
> The **marks.csv** dataset can be found at this location: https://github.com/TrainingByPackt/Data-Science-with-Python/blob/master/Chapter01/Data/mark.csv.

1. Open a Jupyter notebook and add a new cell. Write the following code to import pandas and load the **student.csv** and **marks.csv** datasets into the **df1** and **df2** pandas DataFrames:

```
import pandas as pd
dataset1 = "https://github.com/TrainingByPackt/Data-Science-with-Python/
blob/master/Chapter01/Data/student.csv"
dataset2 = "https://github.com/TrainingByPackt/Data-Science-with-Python/
```

```
blob/master/Chapter01/Data/mark.csv"
df1 = pd.read_csv(dataset1, header = 0)
df2 = pd.read_csv(dataset2, header = 0)
```

2. To print the first five rows of the first DataFrame, add the following code:

```
df1.head()
```

The preceding code generates the following output:

	Student_id	Mark	City
0	1	95	Chennai
1	2	70	Delhi
2	3	98	Mumbai
3	4	75	Pune
4	5	89	Kochi

Figure 1.25: The first five rows of the first DataFrame

3. To print the first five rows of the second DataFrame, add the following code:

```
df2.head()
```

The preceding code generates the following output:

	Student_id	Age	Gender	Grade	Employed
0	1	19	Male	1st Class	yes
1	2	20	Female	2nd Class	no
2	3	18	Male	1st Class	no
3	4	21	Female	2nd Class	no
4	5	19	Male	1st Class	no

Figure 1.26: The first five rows of the second DataFrame

4. **Student_id** is common to both datasets. Perform data integration on both the DataFrames with respect to the **Student_id** column using the **pd.merge()** function, and then print the first 10 values of the new DataFrame:

```
df = pd.merge(df1, df2, on = 'Student_id')
df.head(10)
```

	Student_id	Mark	City	Age	Gender	Grade	Employed
0	1	95	Chennai	19	Male	1st Class	yes
1	2	70	Delhi	20	Female	2nd Class	no
2	3	98	Mumbai	18	Male	1st Class	no
3	4	75	Pune	21	Female	2nd Class	no
4	5	89	Kochi	19	Male	1st Class	no
5	6	69	Gwalior	20	Male	2nd Class	yes
6	7	52	Bhopal	19	Female	3rd Class	yes
7	8	54	Chennai	21	Male	3rd Class	yes
8	9	55	Delhi	22	Female	3rd Class	yes
9	10	94	Mumbai	21	Male	1st Class	no

Figure 1.27: First 10 rows of the merged DataFrame

Here, the data of the **df1** DataFrame is merged with the data of the **df2** DataFrame. The merged data is stored inside a new DataFrame called **df**.

We have now learned how to perform data integration. In the next section, we'll explore another pre-processing task, data transformation.

Data Transformation

Previously, we saw how we can combine data from different sources into a unified dataframe. Now, we have a lot of columns that have different types of data. Our goal is to transform the data into a machine-learning-digestible format. All machine learning algorithms are based on mathematics. So, we need to convert all the columns into numerical format. Before that, let's see all the different types of data we have.

Taking a broader perspective, data is classified into numerical and categorical data:

- **Numerical**: As the name suggests, this is numeric data that is quantifiable.
- **Categorical**: The data is a string or non-numeric data that is qualitative in nature.

Numerical data is further divided into the following:

- **Discrete**: To explain in simple terms, any numerical data that is countable is called discrete, for example, the number of people in a family or the number of students in a class. Discrete data can only take certain values (such as 1, 2, 3, 4, etc).
- **Continuous**: Any numerical data that is measurable is called continuous, for example, the height of a person or the time taken to reach a destination. Continuous data can take virtually any value (for example, 1.25, 3.8888, and 77.1276).

Categorical data is further divided into the following:

- **Ordered**: Any categorical data that has some order associated with it is called ordered categorical data, for example, movie ratings (excellent, good, bad, worst) and feedback (happy, not bad, bad). You can think of ordered data as being something you could mark on a scale.
- **Nominal**: Any categorical data that has no order is called nominal categorical data. Examples include gender and country.

From these different types of data, we will focus on categorical data. In the next section, we'll discuss how to handle categorical data.

Handling Categorical Data

There are some algorithms that can work well with categorical data, such as decision trees. But most machine learning algorithms cannot operate directly with categorical data. These algorithms require the input and output both to be in numerical form. If the output to be predicted is categorical, then after prediction we convert them back to categorical data from numerical data. Let's discuss some key challenges that we face while dealing with categorical data:

- **High cardinality**: Cardinality means uniqueness in data. The data column, in this case, will have a lot of different values. A good example is User ID – in a table of 500 different users, the User ID column would have 500 unique values.

- **Rare occurrences**: These data columns might have variables that occur very rarely and therefore would not be significant enough to have an impact on the model.
- **Frequent occurrences**: There might be a category in the data columns that occurs many times with very low variance, which would fail to make an impact on the model.
- **Won't fit**: This categorical data, left unprocessed, won't fit our model.

Encoding

To address the problems associated with categorical data, we can use encoding. This is the process by which we convert a categorical variable into a numerical form. Here, we will look at three simple methods of encoding categorical data.

Replacing

This is a technique in which we replace the categorical data with a number. This is a simple replacement and does not involve much logical processing. Let's look at an exercise to get a better idea of this.

Exercise 6: Simple Replacement of Categorical Data with a Number

In this exercise, we will use the **student** dataset that we saw earlier. We will load the data into a pandas dataframe and simply replace all the categorical data with numbers. Follow these steps to complete this exercise:

> **Note**
>
> The **student** dataset can be found at this location: https://github.com/TrainingByPackt/Data-Science-with-Python/blob/master/Chapter01/Data/student.csv.

1. Open a Jupyter notebook and add a new cell. Write the following code to import pandas and then load the dataset into the pandas dataframe:

```
import pandas as pd
import numpy as np
dataset = "https://github.com/TrainingByPackt/Data-Science-with-Python/
blob/master/Chapter01/Data/student.csv"
df = pd.read_csv(dataset, header = 0)
```

2. Find the categorical column and separate it out with a different dataframe. To do so, use the **select_dtypes()** function from pandas:

```
df_categorical = df.select_dtypes(exclude=[np.number])
df_categorical
```

The preceding code generates the following output:

	Gender	Grade	Employed
0	Male	1st Class	yes
1	Female	2nd Class	no
2	Male	1st Class	no
3	Female	2nd Class	no
4	Male	1st Class	no

Figure 1.28: Categorical columns of the dataframe

3. Find the distinct unique values in the **Grade** column. To do so, use the **unique()** function from pandas with the column name:

```
df_categorical['Grade'].unique()
```

The preceding code generates the following output:

```
array(['1st Class', '2nd Class', '3rd Class'], dtype=object)
```

Figure 1.29: Unique values in the Grade column

4. Find the frequency distribution of each categorical column. To do so, use the **value_counts()** function on each column. This function returns the counts of unique values in an object:

```
df_categorical.Grade.value_counts()
```

The output of this step is as follows:

```
2nd Class    80
3rd Class    80
1st Class    72
Name: Grade, dtype: int64
```

Figure 1.30: Total count of each unique value in the Grade column

5. For the **Gender** column, write the following code:

```
df_categorical.Gender.value_counts()
```

The output of this code is as follows:

```
Male        136
Female       96
Name: Gender, dtype: int64
```

Figure 1.31: Total count of each unique value in the Gender column

6. Similarly, for the **Employed** column, write the following code:

```
df_categorical.Employed.value_counts()
```

The output of this code is as follows:

```
no      133
yes      99
Name: Employed, dtype: int64
```

Figure 1.32: Total count of each unique value in the Employed column

7. Replace the entries in the **Grade** column. Replace **1st class** with **1**, **2nd class** with **2**, and **3rd class** with **3**. To do so, use the **replace()** function:

```
df_categorical.Grade.replace({"1st Class":1, "2nd Class":2, "3rd
Class":3}, inplace= True)
```

8. Replace the entries in the **Gender** column. Replace **Male** with **0** and **Female** with **1**. To do so, use the **replace()** function:

```
df_categorical.Gender.replace({"Male":0,"Female":1}, inplace= True)
```

9. Replace the entries in the **Employed** column. Replace **no** with **0** and **yes** with **1**. To do so, use the **replace()** function:

```
df_categorical.Employed.replace({"yes":1,"no":0}, inplace = True)
```

10. Once all the replacements for three columns are done, we need to print the dataframe. Add the following code:

```
df_categorical.head()
```

	Gender	Grade	Employed
0	0	1	1
1	1	2	0
2	0	1	0
3	1	2	0
4	0	1	0

Figure 1.33: Numerical data after replacement

You have successfully converted the categorical data to numerical data using a simple manual replacement method. We will now move on to look at another method of encoding categorical data.

Label Encoding

This is a technique in which we replace each value in a categorical column with numbers from 0 to N-1. For example, say we've got a list of employee names in a column. After performing label encoding, each employee name will be assigned a numeric label. But this might not be suitable for all cases because the model might consider numeric values to be weights assigned to the data. Label encoding is the best method to use for ordinal data. The scikit-learn library provides **`LabelEncoder()`**, which helps with label encoding. Let's look at an exercise in the next section.

Exercise 7: Converting Categorical Data to Numerical Data Using Label Encoding

In this exercise, we will load the **`Banking_Marketing.csv`** dataset into a pandas dataframe and convert categorical data to numeric data using label encoding. Follow these steps to complete this exercise:

> **Note**
>
> The **`Banking_Marketing.csv`** dataset can be found here: https://github.com/TrainingByPackt/Master-Data-Science-with-Python/blob/master/Chapter%201/Data/Banking_Marketing.csv.

1. Open a Jupyter notebook and add a new cell. Write the code to import pandas and load the dataset into the pandas dataframe:

```
import pandas as pd
import numpy as np
dataset = 'https://github.com/TrainingByPackt/Master-Data-Science-with-Python/blob/master/Chapter%201/Data/Banking_Marketing.csv'
df = pd.read_csv(dataset, header=0)
```

2. Before doing the encoding, remove all the missing data. To do so, use the **dropna()** function:

```
df = df.dropna()
```

3. Select all the columns that are not numeric using the following code:

```
data_column_category = df.select_dtypes(exclude=[np.number]).columns
data_column_category
```

To understand how the selection looks, refer to the following screenshot:

```
Index(['job', 'marital', 'education', 'default', 'housing', 'loan', 'contact',
       'month', 'day_of_week', 'poutcome'],
      dtype='object')
```

Figure 1.34: Non-numeric columns of the dataframe

4. Print the first five rows of the new dataframe. Add the following code to do this:

```
df[data_column_category].head()
```

The preceding code generates the following output:

	job	marital	education	default	housing	loan	contact	month	day_of_week	poutcome
0	blue-collar	married	basic.4y	unknown	yes	no	cellular	aug	thu	nonexistent
1	technician	married	unknown	no	no	no	cellular	nov	fri	nonexistent
2	management	single	university.degree	no	yes	no	cellular	jun	thu	success
3	services	married	high.school	no	no	no	cellular	apr	fri	nonexistent
4	retired	married	basic.4y	no	yes	no	cellular	aug	fri	success

Figure 1.35: Non-numeric values for the columns

5. Iterate through this **category** column and convert it to numeric data using **LabelEncoder()**. To do so, import the **sklearn.preprocessing** package and use the **LabelEncoder()** class to transform the data:

```
#import the LabelEncoder class
from sklearn.preprocessing import LabelEncoder
#Creating the object instance
label_encoder = LabelEncoder()

for i in data_column_category:
    df[i] = label_encoder.fit_transform(df[i])
print("Label Encoded Data: ")
df.head()
```

The preceding code generates the following output:

Label Encoded Data:

	age	job	marital	education	default	housing	loan	contact	month	day_of_week	...	campaign	pdays	previous	pout
0	44.0	1	1	0	1	2	0	0	1	2	...	1	999	0	1
1	53.0	9	1	7	0	0	0	0	7	0	...	1	999	0	1
2	28.0	4	2	6	0	2	0	0	4	2	...	3	6	2	2
3	39.0	7	1	3	0	0	0	0	0	0	...	2	999	0	1
4	55.0	5	1	0	0	2	0	0	1	0	...	1	3	1	2

5 rows × 21 columns

Figure 1.36: Values of non-numeric columns converted into numeric form

In the preceding screenshot, we can see that all the values have been converted from categorical to numerical. Here, the original values have been transformed and replaced with the newly encoded data.

You have successfully converted categorical data to numerical data using the **LabelEncoder** method. In the next section, we'll explore another type of encoding: one-hot encoding.

One-Hot Encoding

In label encoding, categorical data is converted to numerical data, and the values are assigned labels (such as 1, 2, and 3). Predictive models that use this numerical data for analysis might sometimes mistake these labels for some kind of order (for example, a model might think that a label of 3 is "better" than a label of 1, which is incorrect). In order to avoid this confusion, we can use one-hot encoding. Here, the label-encoded data is further divided into n number of columns. Here, n denotes the total number of unique labels generated while performing label encoding. For example, say that three new labels are generated through label encoding. Then, while performing one-hot encoding, the columns will be divided into three parts. So, the value of n is 3. Let's look at an exercise to get further clarification.

Exercise 8: Converting Categorical Data to Numerical Data Using One-Hot Encoding

In this exercise, we will load the **Banking_Marketing.csv** dataset into a pandas dataframe and convert the categorical data into numeric data using one-hot encoding. Follow these steps to complete this exercise:

> **Note**
>
> The **Banking_Marketing** dataset can be found here: https://github.com/TrainingByPackt/Data-Science-with-Python/blob/master/Chapter01/Data/Banking_Marketing.csv.

1. Open a Jupyter notebook and add a new cell. Write the code to import pandas and load the dataset into a pandas dataframe:

```
import pandas as pd
import numpy as np
from sklearn.preprocessing import OneHotEncoder
dataset = 'https://github.com/TrainingByPackt/Master-Data-Science-with-Python/blob/master/Chapter%201/Data/Banking_Marketing.csv'
#reading the data into the dataframe into the object data
df = pd.read_csv(dataset, header=0)
```

2. Before doing the encoding, remove all the missing data. To do so, use the **dropna()** function:

```
df = df.dropna()
```

3. Select all the columns that are not numeric using the following code:

```
data_column_category = df.select_dtypes(exclude=[np.number]).columns
data_column_category
```

The preceding code generates the following output:

```
Index(['job', 'marital', 'education', 'default', 'housing', 'loan', 'contact',
       'month', 'day_of_week', 'poutcome'],
      dtype='object')
```

Figure 1.37: Non-numeric columns of the dataframe

4. Print the first five rows of the new dataframe. Add the following code to do this:

```
df[data_column_category].head()
```

The preceding code generates the following output:

	job	marital	education	default	housing	loan	contact	month	day_of_week	poutcome
0	blue-collar	married	basic.4y	unknown	yes	no	cellular	aug	thu	nonexistent
1	technician	married	unknown	no	no	no	cellular	nov	fri	nonexistent
2	management	single	university.degree	no	yes	no	cellular	jun	thu	success
3	services	married	high.school	no	no	no	cellular	apr	fri	nonexistent
4	retired	married	basic.4y	no	yes	no	cellular	aug	fri	success

Figure 1.38: Non-numeric values for the columns

5. Iterate through these category columns and convert them to numeric data using **OneHotEncoder**. To do so, import the **sklearn.preprocessing** package and avail yourself of the **OneHotEncoder()** class do the transformation. Before performing one-hot encoding, we need to perform label encoding:

```
#performing label encoding
from sklearn.preprocessing import LabelEncoder
label_encoder = LabelEncoder()
for i in data_column_category:
    df[i] = label_encoder.fit_transform(df[i])
print("Label Encoded Data: ")
df.head()
```

The preceding code generates the following output:

Label Encoded Data:

	age	job	marital	education	default	housing	loan	contact	month	day_of_week	...	campaign	pdays	previous	pout
0	44.0	1	1	0	1	2	0	0	1	2	...	1	999	0	1
1	53.0	9	1	7	0	0	0	0	7	0	...	1	999	0	1
2	28.0	4	2	6	0	2	0	0	4	2	...	3	6	2	2
3	39.0	7	1	3	0	0	0	0	0	0	...	2	999	0	1
4	55.0	5	1	0	0	2	0	0	1	0	...	1	3	1	2

5 rows × 21 columns

Figure 1.39: Values of non-numeric columns converted into numeric data

6. Once we have performed label encoding, we execute one-hot encoding. Add the following code to implement this:

```
#Performing Onehot Encoding
onehot_encoder = OneHotEncoder(sparse=False)
onehot_encoded = onehot_encoder.fit_transform(df[data_column_category])
```

7. Now we create a new dataframe with the encoded data and print the first five rows. Add the following code to do this:

```
#Creating a dataframe with encoded data with new column name
onehot_encoded_frame = pd.DataFrame(onehot_encoded, columns = onehot_
encoder.get_feature_names(data_column_category))
onehot_encoded_frame.head()
```

The preceding code generates the following output:

job_0.0	job_1.0	job_2.0	job_3.0	job_4.0	job_5.0	job_6.0	job_7.0	job_8.0	job_9.0	...	month_8.0	month_9.0	day_of_week_0.0
0.0	1.0	0.0	0.0	0.0	0.0	0.0	0.0	0.0	0.0	...	0.0	0.0	0.0
0.0	0.0	0.0	0.0	0.0	0.0	0.0	0.0	0.0	1.0	...	0.0	0.0	1.0
0.0	0.0	0.0	0.0	1.0	0.0	0.0	0.0	0.0	0.0	...	0.0	0.0	0.0
0.0	0.0	0.0	0.0	0.0	0.0	0.0	1.0	0.0	0.0	...	0.0	0.0	1.0
0.0	0.0	0.0	0.0	0.0	1.0	0.0	0.0	0.0	0.0	...	0.0	0.0	1.0

Figure 1.40: Columns with one-hot encoded values

8. Due to one-hot encoding, the number of columns in the new dataframe has increased. In order to view and print all the columns created, use the **columns** attribute:

```
onehot_encoded_frame.columns
```

The preceding code generates the following output:

```
Index(['job_0.0', 'job_1.0', 'job_2.0', 'job_3.0', 'job_4.0', 'job_5.0',
       'job_6.0', 'job_7.0', 'job_8.0', 'job_9.0', 'job_10.0', 'job_11.0',
       'marital_0.0', 'marital_1.0', 'marital_2.0', 'marital_3.0',
       'education_0.0', 'education_1.0', 'education_2.0', 'education_3.0',
       'education_4.0', 'education_5.0', 'education_6.0', 'education_7.0',
       'default_0.0', 'default_1.0', 'default_2.0', 'housing_0.0',
       'housing_1.0', 'housing_2.0', 'loan_0.0', 'loan_1.0', 'loan_2.0',
       'contact_0.0', 'contact_1.0', 'month_0.0', 'month_1.0', 'month_2.0',
       'month_3.0', 'month_4.0', 'month_5.0', 'month_6.0', 'month_7.0',
       'month_8.0', 'month_9.0', 'day_of_week_0.0', 'day_of_week_1.0',
       'day_of_week_2.0', 'day_of_week_3.0', 'day_of_week_4.0', 'poutcome_0.0',
       'poutcome_1.0', 'poutcome_2.0'],
      dtype='object')
```

Figure 1.41: List of new columns generated after one-hot encoding

9. For every level or category, a new column is created. In order to prefix the category name with the column name you can use this alternate way to create one-hot encoding. In order to prefix the category name with the column name, write the following code:

```
df_onehot_getdummies = pd.get_dummies(df[data_column_category],
prefix=data_column_category)
data_onehot_encoded_data = pd.concat([df_onehot_getdummies,df[data_column_
number]],axis = 1)
data_onehot_encoded_data.columns
```

The preceding code generates the following output:

```
Index(['job_admin.', 'job_blue-collar', 'job_entrepreneur', 'job_housemaid',
       'job_management', 'job_retired', 'job_self-employed', 'job_services',
       'job_student', 'job_technician', 'job_unemployed', 'job_unknown',
       'marital_divorced', 'marital_married', 'marital_single',
       'marital_unknown', 'education_basic.4y', 'education_basic.6y',
       'education_basic.9y', 'education_high.school', 'education_illiterate',
       'education_professional.course', 'education_university.degree',
       'education_unknown', 'default_no', 'default_unknown', 'default_yes',
       'housing_no', 'housing_unknown', 'housing_yes', 'loan_no',
       'loan_unknown', 'loan_yes', 'contact_cellular', 'contact_telephone',
       'month_apr', 'month_aug', 'month_dec', 'month_jul', 'month_jun',
       'month_mar', 'month_may', 'month_nov', 'month_oct', 'month_sep',
       'day_of_week_fri', 'day_of_week_mon', 'day_of_week_thu',
       'day_of_week_tue', 'day_of_week_wed', 'poutcome_failure',
       'poutcome_nonexistent', 'poutcome_success', 'age', 'duration',
       'campaign', 'pdays', 'previous', 'emp_var_rate', 'cons_price_idx',
       'cons_conf_idx', 'euribor3m', 'nr_employed', 'y'],
      dtype='object')
```

Figure 1.42: List of new columns containing the categories

You have successfully converted categorical data to numerical data using the **OneHotEncoder** method.

We will now move onto another data preprocessing step – how to deal with a range of magnitudes in your data.

Data in Different Scales

In real life, values in a dataset might have a variety of different magnitudes, ranges, or scales. Algorithms that use distance as a parameter may not weigh all these in the same way. There are various data transformation techniques that are used to transform the features of our data so that they use the same scale, magnitude, or range. This ensures that each feature has an appropriate effect on a model's predictions.

Some features in our data might have high-magnitude values (for example, annual salary), while others might have relatively low values (for example, the number of years worked at a company). Just because some data has smaller values does not mean it is less significant. So, to make sure our prediction does not vary because of different magnitudes of features in our data, we can perform feature scaling, standardization, or normalization (these are three similar ways of dealing with magnitude issues in data).

Exercise 9: Implementing Scaling Using the Standard Scaler Method

In this exercise, we will load the **Wholesale customer's data.csv** dataset into the pandas dataframe and perform scaling using the standard scaler method. This dataset refers to clients of a wholesale distributor. It includes the annual spending in monetary units on diverse product categories. Follow these steps to complete this exercise:

> **Note**
>
> The **Wholesale customer** dataset can be found here: https://github.com/TrainingByPackt/Data-Science-with-Python/blob/master/Chapter01/Data/Wholesale%20customers%20data.csv.

1. Open a Jupyter notebook and add a new cell. Write the code to import pandas and load the dataset into the pandas dataframe:

```
import pandas as pd
dataset = 'https://github.com/TrainingByPackt/Data-Science-with-Python/
blob/master/Chapter01/Data/Wholesale%20customers%20data.csv'
df = pd.read_csv(dataset, header=0)
```

2. Check whether there is any missing data. If there is, drop the missing data:

```
null_ = df.isna().any()
dtypes = df.dtypes
info = pd.concat([null_,dtypes],axis = 1,keys = ['Null','type'])
print(info)
```

The preceding code generates the following output:

	Null	type
Channel	False	int64
Region	False	int64
Fresh	False	int64
Milk	False	int64
Grocery	False	int64
Frozen	False	int64
Detergents_Paper	False	int64
Delicassen	False	int64

Figure 1.43: Different columns of the dataframe

As we can see, there are eight columns present in the dataframe, all of type **int64**. Since the null value is **False**, it means there are no null values present in any of the columns. Thus, there is no need to use the **dropna()** function.

3. Now perform standard scaling and print the first five rows of the new dataset. To do so, use the **StandardScaler()** class from **sklearn.preprocessing** and implement the **fit_transorm()** method:

```
from sklearn import preprocessing
std_scale = preprocessing.StandardScaler().fit_transform(df)
scaled_frame = pd.DataFrame(std_scale, columns=df.columns)
scaled_frame.head()
```

The preceding code generates the following output:

	Channel	Region	Fresh	Milk	Grocery	Frozen	Detergents_Paper	Delicassen
0	1.448652	0.590668	0.052933	0.523568	-0.041115	-0.589367	-0.043569	-0.066339
1	1.448652	0.590668	-0.391302	0.544458	0.170318	-0.270136	0.086407	0.089151
2	1.448652	0.590668	-0.447029	0.408538	-0.028157	-0.137536	0.133232	2.243293
3	-0.690297	0.590668	0.100111	-0.624020	-0.392977	0.687144	-0.498588	0.093411
4	1.448652	0.590668	0.840239	-0.052396	-0.079356	0.173859	-0.231918	1.299347

Figure 1.44: Data of the features scaled into a uniform unit

Using the **StandardScaler** method, we have scaled the data into a uniform unit over all the columns. As you can see in the preceding table, the values of all the features have been converted into a uniform range of the same scale. Because of this, it becomes easier for the model to make predictions.

You have successfully scaled the data using the **StandardScaler** method. In the next section, we'll have a go at an exercise in which we'll implement scaling using the **MinMax** scaler method.

Exercise 10: Implementing Scaling Using the MinMax Scaler Method

In this exercise, we will be loading the **Wholesale customers data.csv** dataset into a pandas dataframe and perform scaling using the **MinMax** scaler method. Follow these steps to complete this exercise:

> **Note**
>
> The **Whole customers data.csv** dataset can be found here: https://github.com/TrainingByPackt/Data-Science-with-Python/blob/master/Chapter01/Data/Wholesale%20customers%20data.csv.

1. Open a Jupyter notebook and add a new cell. Write the following code to import the pandas library and load the dataset into a pandas dataframe:

```
import pandas as pd
dataset = 'https://github.com/TrainingByPackt/Data-Science-with-Python/blob/master/Chapter01/Data/Wholesale%20customers%20data.csv'
df = pd.read_csv(dataset, header=0)
```

2. Check whether there is any missing data. If there is, drop the missing data:

```
null_ = df.isna().any()
dtypes = df.dtypes
info = pd.concat([null_,dtypes],axis = 1,keys = ['Null','type'])
print(info)
```

The preceding code generates the following output:

```
                   Null   type
Channel           False  int64
Region            False  int64
Fresh             False  int64
Milk              False  int64
Grocery           False  int64
Frozen            False  int64
Detergents_Paper  False  int64
Delicassen        False  int64
```

Figure 1.45: Different columns of the dataframe

As we can see, there are eight columns present in the dataframe, all of type **int64**. Since the null value is **False**, it means there are no null values present in any of the columns. Thus, there is no need to use the **dropna()** function.

3. Perform **MinMax** scaling and print the initial five values of the new dataset. To do so, use the **MinMaxScaler()** class from **sklearn.preprocessing** and implement the **fit_transorm()** method. Add the following code to implement this:

```
from sklearn import preprocessing
minmax_scale = preprocessing.MinMaxScaler().fit_transform(df)
scaled_frame = pd.DataFrame(minmax_scale,columns=df.columns)
scaled_frame.head()
```

The preceding code generates the following output:

	Channel	Region	Fresh	Milk	Grocery	Frozen	Detergents_Paper	Delicassen
0	1.0	1.0	0.112940	0.130727	0.081464	0.003106	0.065427	0.027847
1	1.0	1.0	0.062899	0.132824	0.103097	0.028548	0.080590	0.036984
2	1.0	1.0	0.056622	0.119181	0.082790	0.039116	0.086052	0.163559
3	0.0	1.0	0.118254	0.015536	0.045464	0.104842	0.012346	0.037234
4	1.0	1.0	0.201626	0.072914	0.077552	0.063934	0.043455	0.108093

Figure 1.46: Data of the features scaled into a uniform unit

Using the **MinMaxScaler** method, we have again scaled the data into a uniform unit over all the columns. As you can see in the preceding table, the values of all the features have been converted into a uniform range of the same scale. You have successfully scaled the data using the **MinMaxScaler** method.

In the next section, we'll explore another pre-processing task: data discretization.

Data Discretization

So far, we have done the categorical data treatment using encoding and numerical data treatment using scaling.

Data discretization is the process of converting continuous data into discrete buckets by grouping it. Discretization is also known for easy maintainability of the data. Training a model with discrete data becomes faster and more effective than when attempting the same with continuous data. Although continuous-valued data contains more information, huge amounts of data can slow the model down. Here, discretization can help us strike a balance between both. Some famous methods of data discretization are **binning** and using a histogram. Although data discretization is useful, we need to effectively pick the range of each bucket, which is a challenge.

The main challenge in discretization is to choose the number of intervals or bins and how to decide on their width.

Here we make use of a function called **pandas.cut()**. This function is useful to achieve the bucketing and sorting of segmented data.

Exercise 11: Discretization of Continuous Data

In this exercise, we will load the **Student_bucketing.csv** dataset and perform bucketing. The dataset consists of student details such as **Student_id**, **Age**, **Grade**, **Employed**, and **marks**. Follow these steps to complete this exercise:

> **Note**
>
> The **Student_bucketing.csv** dataset can be found here: https://github.com/TrainingByPackt/Data-Science-with-Python/blob/master/Chapter01/Data/Student_bucketing.csv.

1. Open a Jupyter notebook and add a new cell. Write the following code to import the required libraries and load the dataset into a pandas dataframe:

```
import pandas as pd
dataset = "https://github.com/TrainingByPackt/Data-Science-with-Python/
blob/master/Chapter01/Data/Student_bucketing.csv"
df = pd.read_csv(dataset, header = 0)
```

2. Once we load the dataframe, display the first five rows of the dataframe. Add the following code to do this:

```
df.head()
```

The preceding code generates the following output:

	Student_id	Age	Grade	Employed	marks
0	1	19	1st Class	yes	29
1	2	20	2nd Class	no	41
2	3	18	1st Class	no	57
3	4	21	2nd Class	no	29
4	5	19	1st Class	no	57

Figure 1.47: First five rows of the dataframe

3. Perform bucketing using the **pd.cut()** function on the **marks** column and display the top 10 columns. The **cut()** function takes parameters such as **x**, **bins**, and **labels**. Here, we have used only three parameters. Add the following code to implement this:

```
df['bucket']=pd.cut(df['marks'],5,labels=['Poor','Below_
average','Average','Above_Average','Excellent'])
df.head(10)
```

The preceding code generates the following output:

	Student_id	Age	Grade	Employed	marks	bucket
0	1	19	1st Class	yes	29	Poor
1	2	20	2nd Class	no	41	Below_average
2	3	18	1st Class	no	57	Average
3	4	21	2nd Class	no	29	Poor
4	5	19	1st Class	no	57	Average
5	6	20	2nd Class	yes	53	Average
6	7	19	3rd Class	yes	78	Above_Average
7	8	21	3rd Class	yes	70	Above_Average
8	9	22	3rd Class	yes	97	Excellent
9	10	21	1st Class	no	58	Average

Figure 1.48: Marks column with five discrete buckets

In the preceding code, the first parameter represents an array. Here, we have selected the **marks** column as an array from the dataframe. **5** represents the number of bins to be used. As we have set bins to **5**, the labels need to be populated accordingly with five values: **Poor**, **Below_average**, **Average**, **Above_average**, and **Excellent**. In the preceding figure, we can see the whole of the continuous **marks** column is put into five discrete buckets. We have learned how to perform bucketing.

We have now covered all the major tasks involved in pre-processing. In the next section, we'll look in detail at how to train and test your data.

Train and Test Data

Once you've pre-processed your data into a format that's ready to be used by your model, you need to split up your data into train and test sets. This is because your machine learning algorithm will use the data in the training set to learn what it needs to know. It will then make a prediction about the data in the test set, using what it has learned. You can then compare this prediction against the actual target variables in the test set in order to see how accurate your model is. The exercise in the next section will give more clarity on this.

We will do the train/test split in proportions. The larger portion of the data split will be the train set and the smaller portion will be the test set. This will help to ensure that you are using enough data to accurately train your model.

In general, we carry out the train-test split with an 80:20 ratio, as per the Pareto principle. The Pareto principle states that "for many events, roughly 80% of the effects come from 20% of the causes." But if you have a large dataset, it really doesn't matter whether it's an 80:20 split or 90:10 or 60:40. (It can be better to use a smaller split set for the training set if our process is computationally intensive, but it might cause the problem of overfitting – this will be covered later in the book.)

Exercise 12: Splitting Data into Train and Test Sets

In this exercise, we will load the **USA_Housing.csv** dataset (which you saw earlier) into a pandas dataframe and perform a train/test split. Follow these steps to complete this exercise:

> **Note**
>
> The **USA_Housing.csv** dataset is available here: https://github.com/TrainingByPackt/Data-Science-with-Python/blob/master/Chapter01/Data/USA_Housing.csv.

1. Open a Jupyter notebook and add a new cell to import pandas and load the dataset into pandas:

```
import pandas as pd
dataset = 'https://github.com/TrainingByPackt/Data-Science-with-Python/
blob/master/Chapter01/Data/USA_Housing.csv'
df = pd.read_csv(dataset, header=0)
```

2. Create a variable called **X** to store the independent features. Use the **drop()** function to include all the features, leaving out the dependent or the target variable, which in this case is named **Price**. Then, print out the top five instances of the variable. Add the following code to do this:

```
X = df.drop('Price', axis=1)
X.head()
```

The preceding code generates the following output:

	Avg. Area Income	Avg. Area House Age	Avg. Area Number of Rooms	Avg. Area Number of Bedrooms	Area Population	Address
0	79545.458574	5.682861	7.009188	4.09	23086.800503	208 Michael Ferry Apt. 674\nLaurabury, NE 3701...
1	79248.642455	6.002900	6.730821	3.09	40173.072174	188 Johnson Views Suite 079\nLake Kathleen, CA...
2	61287.067179	5.865890	8.512727	5.13	36882.159400	9127 Elizabeth Stravenue\nDanieltown, WI 06482...
3	63345.240046	7.188236	5.586729	3.26	34310.242831	USS Barnett\nFPO AP 44820
4	59982.197226	5.040555	7.839388	4.23	26354.109472	USNS Raymond\nFPO AE 09386

Figure 1.49: Dataframe consisting of independent variables

3. Print the shape of your new created feature matrix using the **X.shape** command:

```
X.shape
```

The preceding code generates the following output:

```
(5000, 6)
```

Figure 1.50: Shape of the X variable

In the preceding figure, the first value indicates the number of observations in the dataset (**5000**), and the second value represents the number of features (**6**).

4. Similarly, we will create a variable called **y** that will store the target values. We will use indexing to grab the target column. Indexing allows us to access a section of a larger element. In this case, we want to grab the column named Price from the **df** dataframe and print out the top 10 values. Add the following code to implement this:

```
y = df['Price']
y.head(10)
```

The preceding code generates the following output:

```
0    1.059034e+06
1    1.505891e+06
2    1.058988e+06
3    1.260617e+06
4    6.309435e+05
5    1.068138e+06
6    1.502056e+06
7    1.573937e+06
8    7.988695e+05
9    1.545155e+06
Name: Price, dtype: float64
```

Figure 1.51: Top 10 values of the y variable

5. Print the shape of your new variable using the **y.shape** command:

```
y.shape
```

The preceding code generates the following output:

```
(5000,)
```

Figure 1.52: Shape of the y variable

The shape should be one-dimensional, with a length equal to the number of observations (**5000**).

6. Make train/test sets with an 80:20 split. To do so, use the **train_test_split()** function from the **sklearn.model_selection** package. Add the following code to do this:

```
from sklearn.model_selection import train_test_split
X_train, X_test, y_train, y_test = train_test_split(X, y, test_size=0.2, 
random_state=0)
```

In the preceding code, **test_size** is a floating-point value that defines the size of the test data. If the value is 0.2, then it is an 80:20 split. **test_train_split** splits the arrays or matrices into train and test subsets in a random way. Each time we run the code without **random_state**, we will get a different result.

7. Print the shape of **X_train**, **X_test**, **y_train**, and **y_test**. Add the following code to do this:

```
print("X_train : ",X_train.shape)
print("X_test : ",X_test.shape)
print("y_train : ",y_train.shape)
print("y_test : ",y_test.shape)
```

The preceding code generates the following output:

```
X_train :  (4000, 6)
X_test :  (1000, 6)
y_train :  (4000,)
y_test :  (1000,)
```

Figure 1.53: Shape of train and test datasets

You have successfully split the data into train and test sets.

In the next section, you will complete an activity wherein you'll perform pre-processing on a dataset.

Activity 1: Pre-Processing Using the Bank Marketing Subscription Dataset

In this activity, we'll perform various pre-processing tasks on the **Bank Marketing Subscription** dataset. This dataset relates to the direct marketing campaigns of a Portuguese banking institution. Phone calls are made to market a new product, and the dataset records whether each customer subscribed to the product.

Follow these steps to complete this activity:

> **Note**
>
> The **Bank Marketing Subscription** dataset is available here: https://github.com/TrainingByPackt/Data-Science-with-Python/blob/master/Chapter01/Data/Banking_Marketing.csv.

1. Load the dataset from the link given into a pandas dataframe.
2. Explore the features of the data by finding the number of rows and columns, listing all the columns, finding the basic statistics of all columns (you can use the **describe().transpose()** function), and listing the basic information of the columns (you can use the **info()** function).

3. Check whether there are any missing (or NULL) values, and if there are, find how many missing values there are in each column.
4. Remove any missing values.
5. Print the frequency distribution of the **`education`** column.
6. The **`education`** column of the dataset has many categories. Reduce the categories for better modeling.
7. Select and perform a suitable encoding method for the data.
8. Split the data into train and test sets. The target data is in the **`y`** column and the independent data is in the remaining columns. Split the data with 80% for the train set and 20% for the test set.

> **Note**
>
> The solution for this activity can be found on page 324.

Now that we've covered the various data pre-processing steps, let's look at the different types of machine learning that are available to data scientists in some more detail.

Supervised Learning

Supervised learning is a learning system that trains using labeled data (data in which the target variables are already known). The model learns how patterns in the feature matrix map to the target variables. When the trained machine is fed with a new dataset, it can use what it has learned to predict the target variables. This can also be called predictive modeling.

Supervised learning is broadly split into two categories. These categories are as follows:

Classification mainly deals with categorical target variables. A classification algorithm helps to predict which group or class a data point belongs to.

When the prediction is between two classes, it is known as binary classification. An example is predicting whether or not a customer will buy a product (in this case, the classes are yes and no).

If the prediction involves more than two target classes, it is known as multi-classification; for example, predicting all the items that a customer will buy.

Regression deals with numerical target variables. A regression algorithm predicts the numerical value of the target variable based on the training dataset.

Linear regression measures the link between one or more predictor variables and one outcome variable. For example, linear regression could help to enumerate the relative impacts of age, gender, and diet (the predictor variables) on height (the outcome variable).

Time series analysis, as the name suggests, deals with data that is distributed with respect to time, that is, data that is in a chronological order. Stock market prediction and customer churn prediction are two examples of time series data. Depending on the requirement or the necessities, time series analysis can be either a regression or classification task.

Unsupervised Learning

Unlike supervised learning, the unsupervised learning process involves data that is neither classified nor labeled. The algorithm will perform analysis on the data without guidance. The job of the machine is to group unclustered information according to similarities in the data. The aim is for the model to spot patterns in the data in order to give some insight into what the data is telling us and to make predictions.

An example is taking a whole load of unlabeled customer data and using it to find patterns to cluster customers into different groups. Different products could then be marketed to the different groups for maximum profitability.

Unsupervised learning is broadly categorized into two types:

- **Clustering**: A clustering procedure helps to discover the inherent patterns in the data.
- **Association**: An association rule is a unique way to find patterns associated with a large amount of data, such as the supposition that when someone buys product 1, they also tend to buy product 2.

Reinforcement Learning

Reinforcement learning is a broad area in machine learning where the machine learns to perform the next step in an environment by looking at the results of actions already performed. Reinforcement learning does not have an answer, and the learning agent decides what should be done to perform the specified task. It learns from its prior knowledge. This kind of learning involves both a reward and a penalty.

No matter the type of machine learning you're using, you'll want to be able to measure how effective your model is. You can do this using various performance metrics. You will see how these are used in later chapters in the book, but a brief overview of some of the most common ones is given here.

Performance Metrics

There are different evaluation metrics in machine learning, and these depend on the type of data and the requirements. Some of the metrics are as follows:

- Confusion matrix
- Precision
- Recall
- Accuracy
- F1 score

Confusion Matrix

A **confusion matrix** is a table that is used to define the performance of the classification model on the test data for which the actual values are known. To understand this better, look at the following figure, showing predicted and actual values:

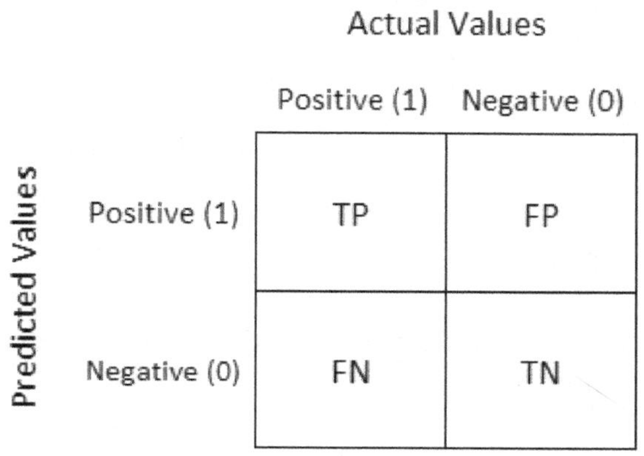

Figure 1.54: Predicted versus actual values

Let's examine the concept of a confusion matrix and its metrics, TP, TN, FP, and FN, in detail. Assume you are building a model that predicts pregnancy:

- **TP (True Positive)**: The sex is female and she is actually pregnant, and your model also predicted `True`.
- **FP (False Positive)**: The sex is male and your model predicted `True`, which cannot happen. This is a type of error called a Type 1 error.
- **FN (False Negative)**: The sex is female and she is actually pregnant, and the model predicts `False`, which is also an error. This is called a Type 2 error.

- **TN (True Negative)**: The sex is male and the prediction is `False`; that is a **True Negative**.

The Type 1 error is a more dangerous error than the Type 2 error. Depending on the problem, we have to figure out whether we need to reduce Type 1 errors or Type 2 errors.

Precision

Precision is the ratio of TP outcomes to the total number of positive outcomes predicted by a model. The precision looks at how precise our model is as follows:

$$\text{Precision} = \frac{True\ Positive}{True\ Positive + False\ Positive} = \frac{True\ Positive}{Total\ Predicted\ positive}$$

Figure 1.55: Precision equation

Recall

Recall calculates what proportion of the TP outcomes our model has predicted:

$$\text{Recall} = \frac{True\ Positive}{True\ Positive + False\ Negative} = \frac{True\ Positive}{Total\ Actual\ Positive}$$

Figure 1.56: Recall equation

Accuracy

Accuracy calculates the ratio of the number of positive predictions made by a model out of the total number of predictions made:

$$\text{Accuracy} = \frac{TP+TN}{TP+TN+FP+FN} = \frac{Number\ of\ positive\ Predictions}{Total\ number\ of\ predictions\ made}$$

Figure 1.57: Accuracy equation

F1 score

F1 score is another accuracy measure, but one that allows us to seek a balance between precision and recall:

$$\text{F1-Score} = 2 * \frac{Precision * Recall}{Precision + Recall}$$

Figure 1.58: F1-score

When considering the performance of a model, we have to understand two other important concepts of prediction error: bias and variance.

What is bias?

Bias is how far a predicted value is from the actual value. High bias means the model is very simple and is not capable of capturing the data's complexity, causing what's called underfitting.

What is variance?

High variance is when the model performs too well on the trained dataset. This causes overfitting and makes the model too specific to the train data, meaning the model does not perform well on test data.

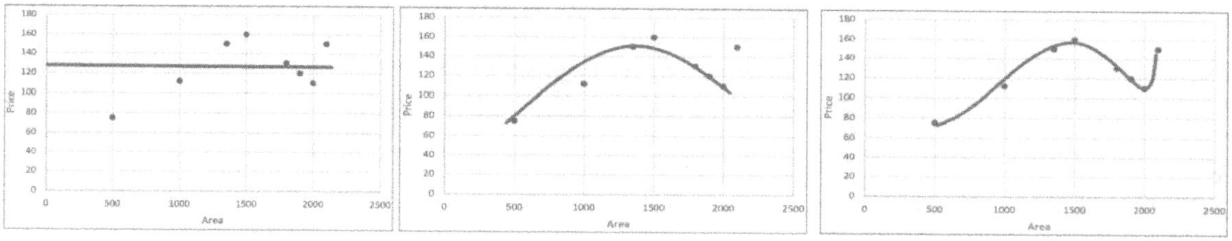

High Bias - underfit | Just Fit | High Variance – overfit

Figure 1.59: High variance

Assume you are building a linear regression model to predict the market price of cars in a country. Let's say you have a large dataset about the cars and their prices, but there are still some more cars whose prices need to be predicted.

When we train our model with the dataset, we want our model to just find that pattern within the dataset, nothing more, because if it goes beyond that, it will start to memorize the train set.

We can improve our model by tuning its hyperparameters - there is more on this later in the book. We work towards minimizing the error and maximizing the accuracy by using another dataset, called the validation set. The first graph shows that the model has not learned enough to predict well in the test set. The third graph shows that the model has memorized the training dataset, which means the accuracy score will be 100, with 0 error. But if we predict on the test data, the middle model will outperform the third.

Summary

In this chapter, we covered the basics of data science and explored the process of extracting underlying information from data using scientific methods, processes, and algorithms. We then moved on to data pre-processing, which includes data cleaning, data integration, data transformation, and data discretization.

We saw how pre-processed data is split into train and test sets when building a model using a machine learning algorithm. We also covered supervised, unsupervised, and reinforcement learning algorithms.

Lastly, we went over the different metrics, including confusion matrices, precision, recall, and accuracy.

In the next chapter, we will cover data visualization.

2

Data Visualization

Learning Objectives

By the end of this chapter, you will be able to:

- Create and customize line plots, bar plots, histograms, scatterplots, and box-and-whisker plots using a functional approach
- Develop a programmatic, descriptive plot title
- Describe the advantages of using an object-oriented approach to create Matplotlib plots
- Create a callable figure object containing a single axis or multiple axes
- Resize and save figure objects with numerous subplots
- Create and customize common plot types using Matplotlib

This chapter will cover various concepts that fall under data visualization.

Introduction

Data visualization is a powerful tool that allows users to digest large amounts of data very quickly. There are different types of plots that serve various purposes. In business, line plots and bar graphs are very common to display trends over time and compare metrics across groups, respectively. Statisticians, on the other hand, may be more interested in checking correlations between variables using a scatterplot or correlation matrix. They may also use histograms to check the distribution of a variable or boxplots to check for outliers. In politics, pie charts are widely used for comparing the total data between or among categories. Data visualizations can be very intricate and creative, being limited only by one's imagination.

The Python library Matplotlib is a well-documented, two-dimensional plotting library that can be used to create a variety of powerful data visualizations and aims to "...make easy things easy and hard things possible" (https://matplotlib.org/index.html).

There are two approaches to creating plots using Matplotlib, the **functional** and the **object-oriented approach**.

In the functional approach, one figure is created with a single plot. Plots are created and customized by a collection of sequential functions. However, the functional approach does not allow us to save the plot to our environment as an object; this is possible using the object-oriented approach. In the object-oriented approach, we create a **figure object** and assign an axis or numerous axes for one plot or multiple subplots, respectively. We can then customize the axis or axes and call that single plot or set of multiple plots by calling the figure object.

In this chapter, we will use the functional approach to create and customize line plots, bar plots, histograms, scatterplots, and box-and-whisker plots. We will then learn how to create and customize single-axis and multiple-axes plots using the object-oriented approach.

Functional Approach

The functional approach to plotting in Matplotlib is a way of quickly generating a single-axis plot. Often, this is the approach taught to beginners. The functional approach allows the user to customize and save plots as image files in a chosen directory. In the following exercises and activities, you will learn how to build line plots, bar plots, histograms, box-and-whisker plots, and scatterplots using the functional approach.

Exercise 13: Functional Approach – Line Plot

To get started with Matplotlib, we will begin by creating a line plot and go on to customize it:

1. Generate an array of numbers for the horizontal axis ranging from 0 to 10 in 20 evenly spaced values using the following code:

```
import numpy as np

x = np.linspace(0, 10, 20)
```

2. Create an array and save it as object **y**. The snippet of the following code cubes the values of **x** and saves it to the array, **y**:

```
y = x**3
```

3. Create the plot as follows:

```
import matplotlib.pyplot as plt

plt.plot(x, y)
plt.show()
```

See the resultant output here:

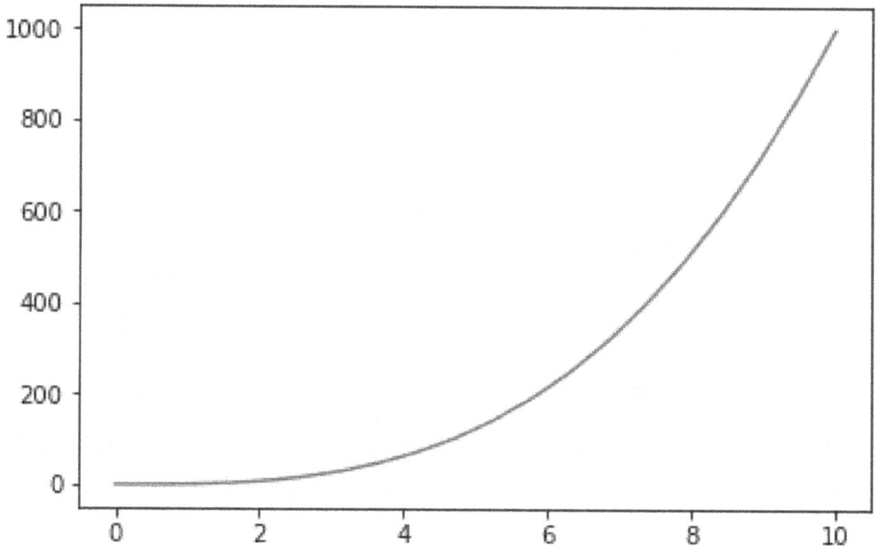

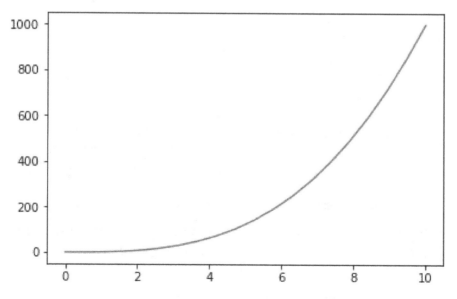

Figure 2.1: Line plot of y and x

4. Add an x-axis label that reads '**`Linearly Spaced Numbers`**' using the following:

```
plt.xlabel('Linearly Spaced Numbers')
```

5. Add a y-axis label that reads '**`y Value`**' using the following line of code:

```
plt.ylabel('y Value')
```

6. Add a title that reads '**`x by x cubed`**' using the following line of code:

```
plt.title('x by x Cubed')
```

7. Change the line color to black by specifying the color argument as **`k`** in the **`plt.plot()`** function:

```
plt.plot(x, y, 'k')
```

Print the plot to the console using plt.show().

Check out the following screenshot for the resultant output:

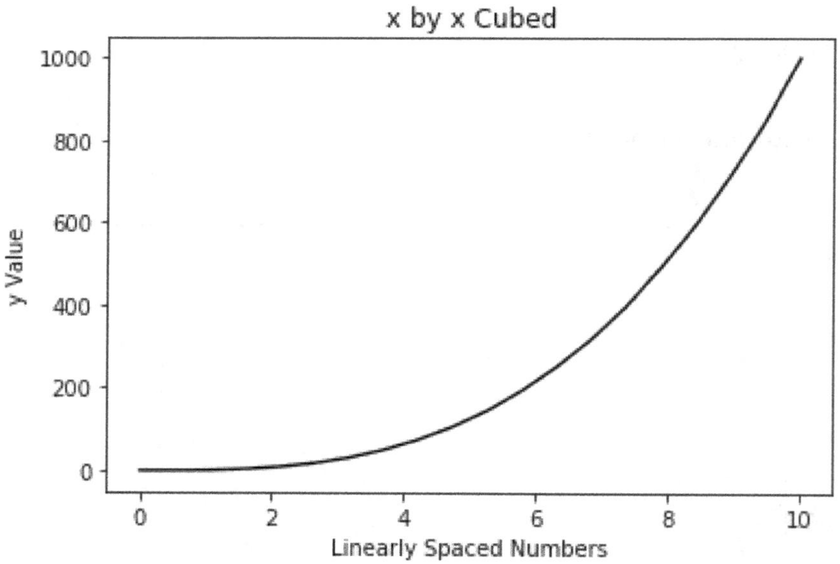

Figure 2.2: Line plot with labeled axes and a black line

8. Change the line characters into a diamond; use a character argument (that is, D) combined with the color character (that is, k) as follows:

```
plt.plot(x, y, 'Dk')
```

See the figure below for the resultant output:

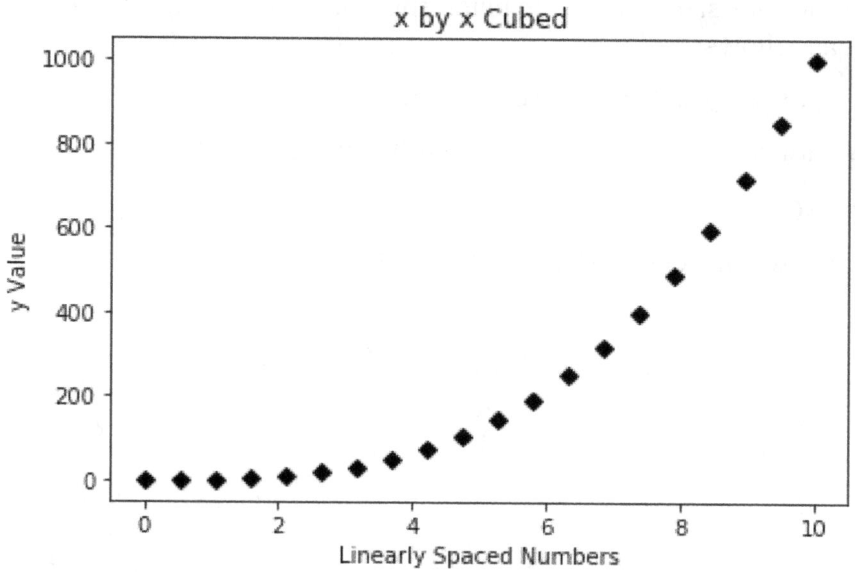

Figure 2.3: Line plot with unconnected, black diamond markers

9. Connect the diamonds with a solid line by placing '-' between 'D' and 'k' using the following:

```
plt.plot(x, y, 'D-k')
```

Refer to the following figure to see the output:

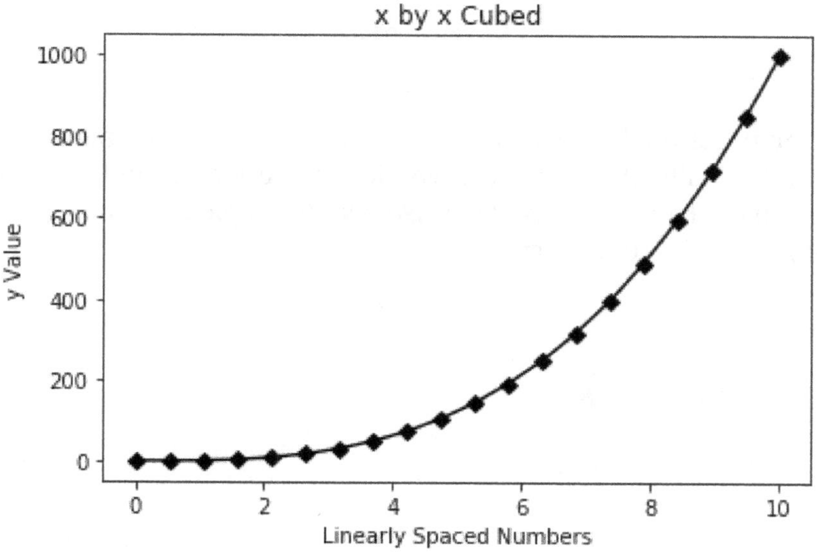

Figure 2.4: Line plot with connected, black diamond markers

10. Increase the font size of the title using the **fontsize** argument in the **plt.title()** function as follows:

```
plt.title('x by x Cubed', fontsize=22)
```

11. Print the plot to the console using the following code:

```
plt.show()
```

12. The output can be seen in the following figure:

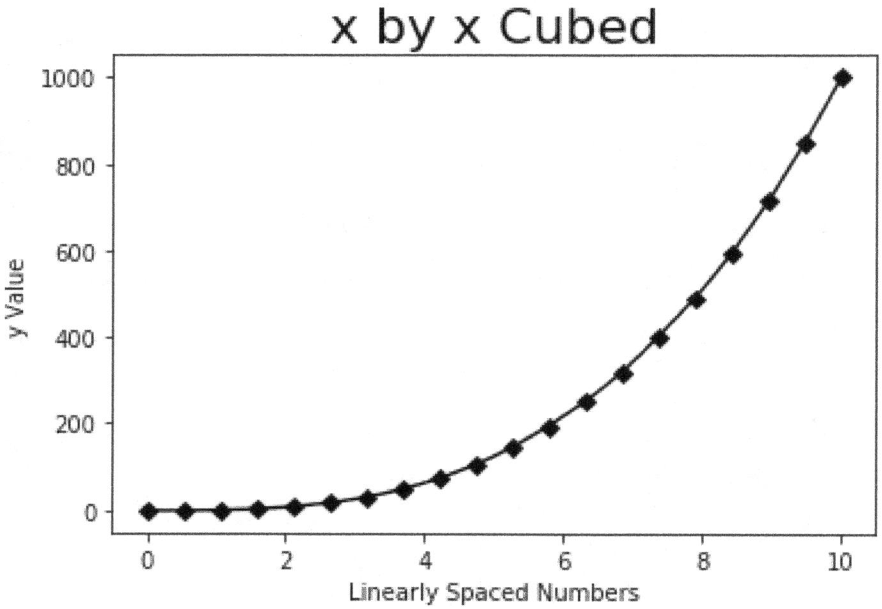

Figure 2.5: Line plot with a larger title

Here, we used the functional approach to create a single-line line plot and styled it to make it more aesthetically pleasing. However, it is not uncommon to compare multiple trends in a single plot. Thus, the next exercise will detail plotting multiple lines on a line plot and creating a legend to discern the lines.

Exercise 14: Functional Approach – Add a Second Line to the Line Plot

Matplotlib makes adding another line to a line plot very easy by simply specifying another **`plt.plot()`** instance. In this exercise, we will plot the lines for x-cubed and x-squared using separate lines:

1. Create another y object as we did for the first y object, but this time, square x rather than cubing it, as follows:

```
y2 = x**2
```

2. Now, plot **`y2`** on the same plot as y by adding **`plt.plot(x, y2)`** to the existing plot.

   Refer to the output here:

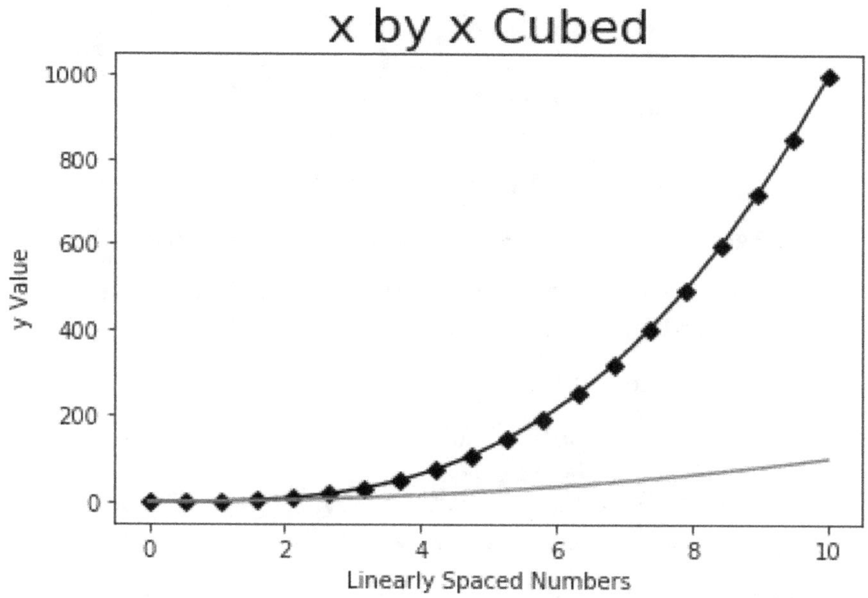

Figure 2.6: Multiple line plot of y and y2 by x

3. Change the color of **`y2`** to a dotted red line using the following code:

```
plt.plot(x, y2, '--r')
```

The output is shown in the following figure:

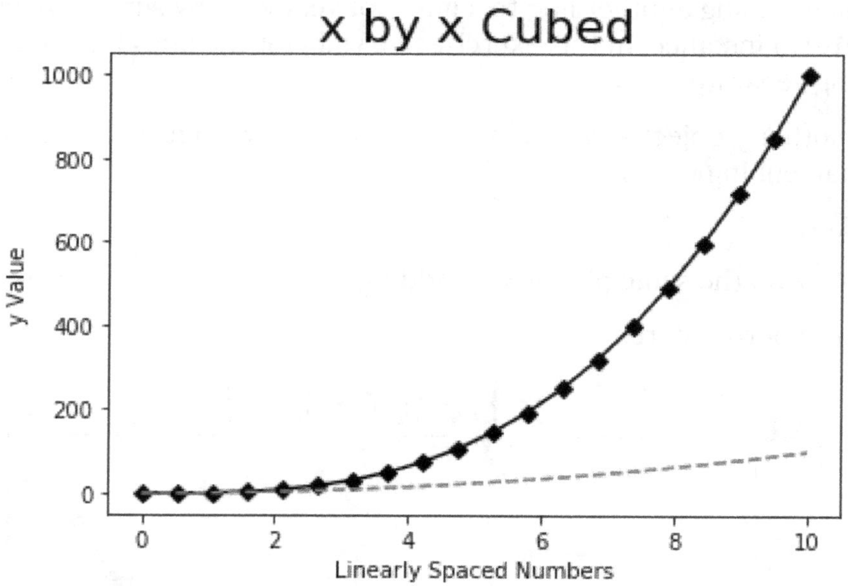

Figure 2.7: Multiple line plot with y2 as a red, dotted line

4. To create a legend, we must first create labels for our lines using the label argument inside the **plt.plot()** functions.
5. To label y as '**x cubed**', use the following:

```
plt.plot(x, y, 'D-k', label='x cubed')
```

6. Label **y2** as '**x squared**' using the following code:

```
plt.plot(x, y2, '--r', label='x squared')
```

7. Use **plt.legend(loc='upper left')** to specify the location for the legend.

   Check out the following screenshot for the resultant output:

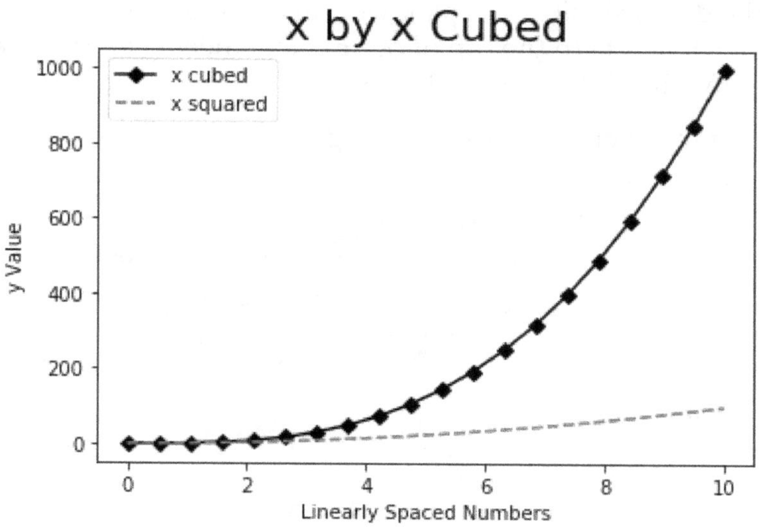

Figure 2.8: Multiple line plot with a legend

8. To break a line into new lines, we use '**\n**' at the beginning of a new line within our string. Thus, using the following code, we can create the title displayed here:

```
plt.title('As x increases, \nx Cubed (black) increases \nat a Greater Rate
than \nx Squared (red)', fontsize=22)
```

Check the output in the following screenshot:

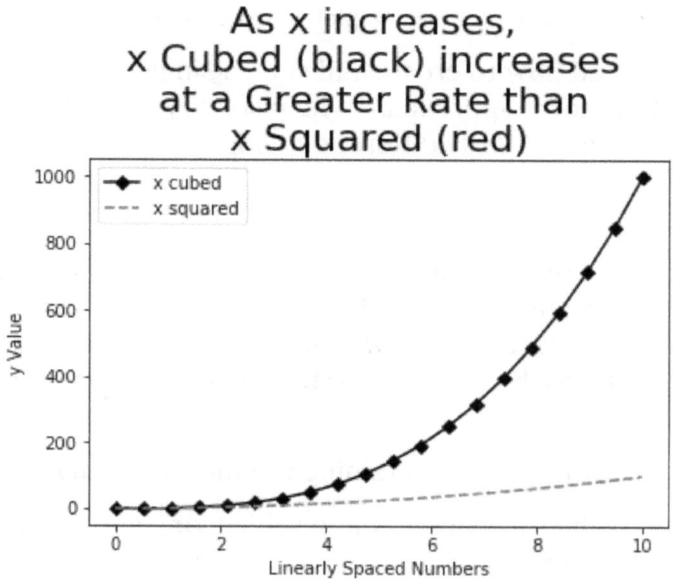

Figure 2.9: A multiple line plot with a multi-line title

9. To change the dimensions of our plot, we will need to add **`plt.figure(figsize=(10,5))`** to the top of our **`plt`** instances. The **`figsize`** arguments of 10 and 5 specify the width and height, respectively.

   To see the output, refer to the following figure:

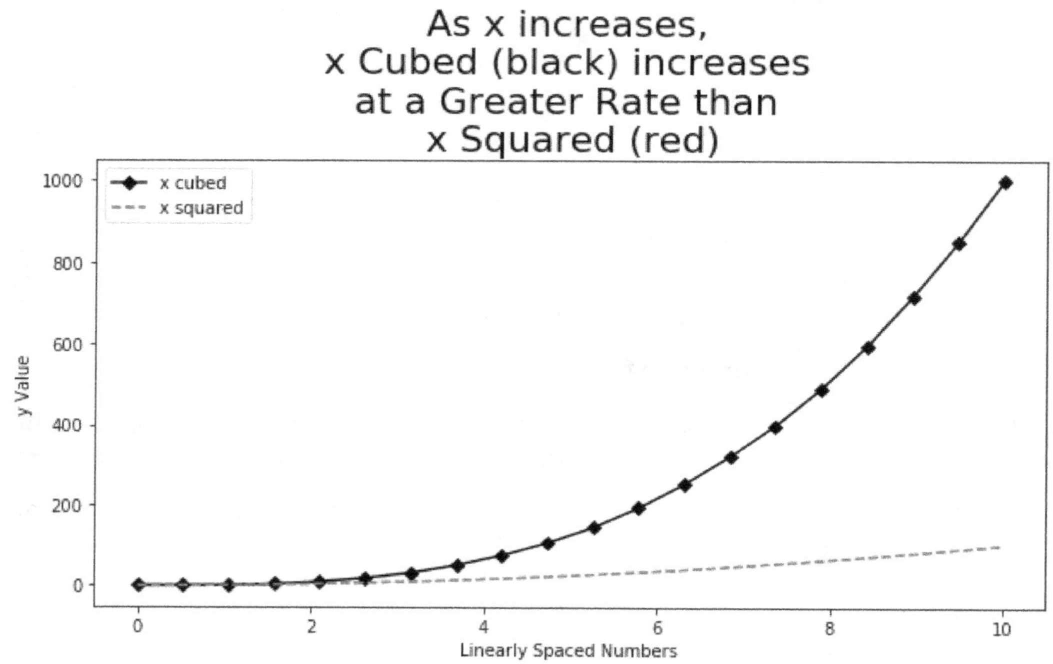

Figure 2.10: A multiple line plot with increased figure size

In this exercise, we learned how to create and style a single- and multi-line plot in Matplotlib using the functional approach. To help solidify our learning, we will plot another single-line plot with slightly different styling.

Activity 2: Line Plot

In this activity, we will create a line plot to analyze month-to-month trends for items sold in the months January through June. The trend will be positive and linear, and will be represented using a dotted, blue line, with star markers. The x-axis will be labeled '**`Month`**' and the y-axis will be labeled '**`Items Sold`**'. The title will say 'Items Sold has been Increasing Linearly:'

1. Create a list of six strings for x containing the months January through June.
2. Create a list of six values for y containing values for '**`Items Sold`**' that start at 1000 and increase by 200 in each value, so the final value is 2000.

3. Generate the described plot.

   Check out the following screenshot for the resultant output:

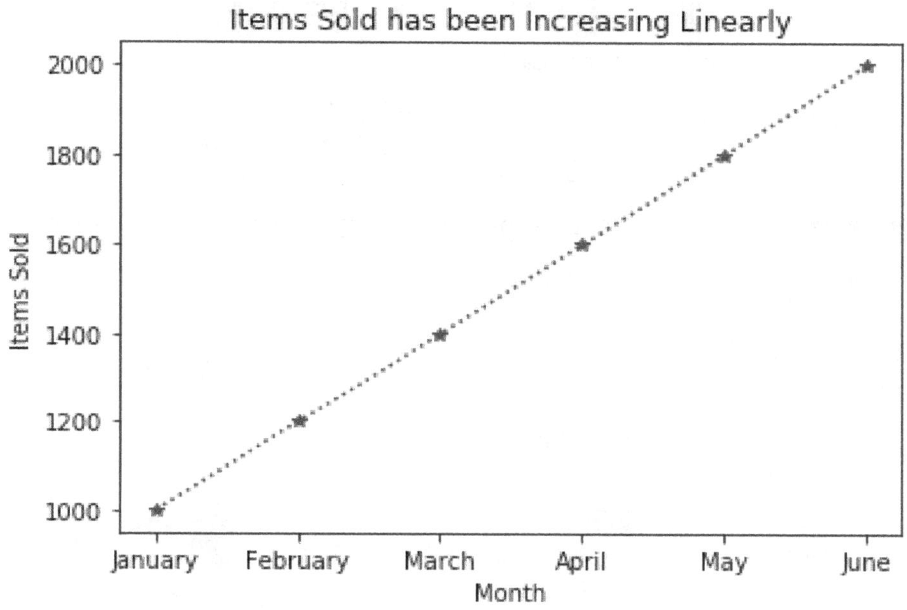

Figure 2.11: Line plot of items sold by month

> **Note**
>
> We can refer to the solution for this activity on page 333.

So far, we have gained a lot of practice creating and customizing line plots. Line plots are commonly used for displaying trends. However, when comparing values between and/or among groups, bar plots are traditionally the visualization of choice. In the following exercise, we will explore how to create a bar plot.

Exercise 15: Creating a Bar Plot

In this exercise, we will be displaying sales revenue by item type:

1. Create a list of item types and save it as **x** using the following code:

```
x = ['Shirts', 'Pants','Shorts','Shoes']
```

2. Create a list of sales revenue and save it as **y** as follows:

```
y = [1000, 1200, 800, 1800]
```

3. To create a bar plot and print it to the console, refer to the code here:

```
import matplotlib.pyplot as plt

plt.bar(x, y)
plt.show()
```

The following screenshot shows the resultant output:

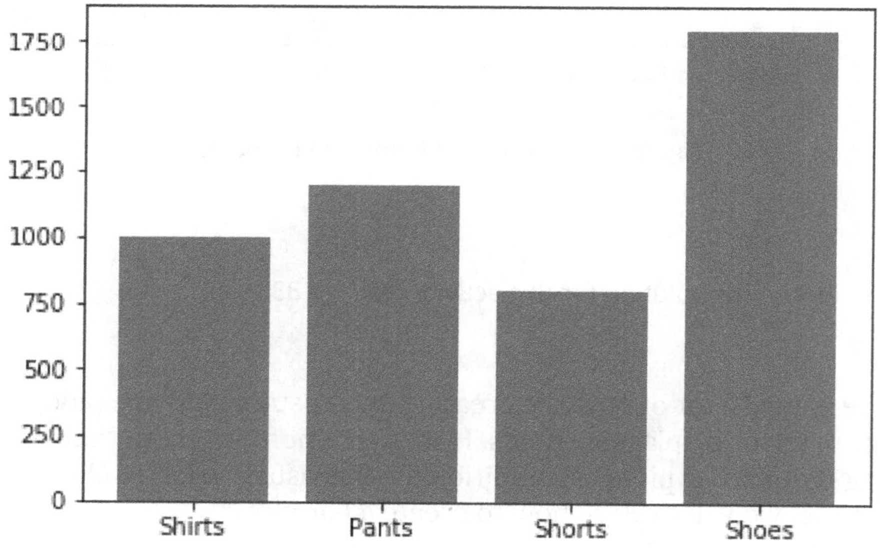

Figure 2.12: Bar plot of sales revenue by item type

4. Add a title reading '**Sales Revenue by Item Type**' using the following code:

```
plt.title('Sales Revenue by Item Type')
```

5. Create an x-axis label reading '**Item Type**' using the following:

```
plt.xlabel('Item Type')
```

6. Add a y-axis label reading '**Sales Revenue ($)**', using the following:

```
plt.ylabel('Sales Revenue ($)')
```

The following screenshot shows the output:

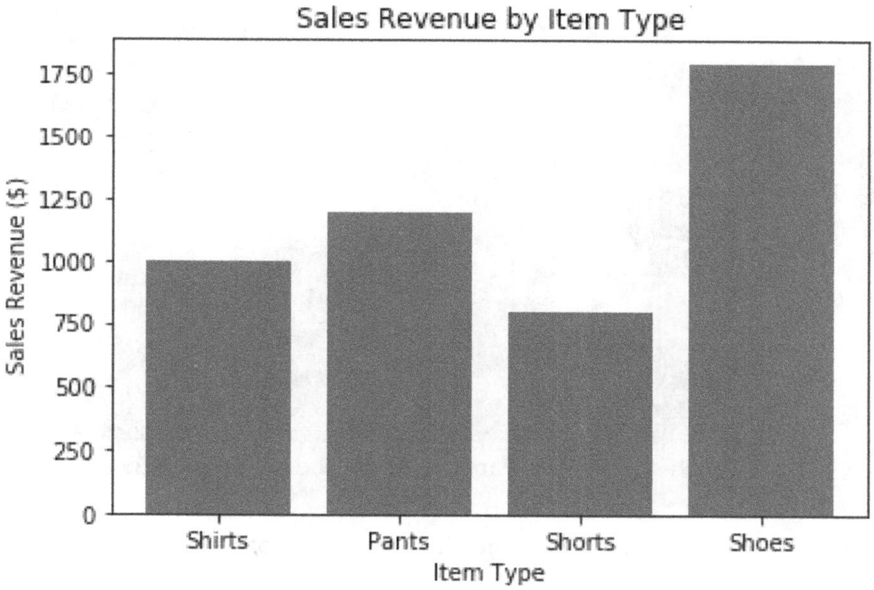

Figure 2.13: Bar plot with customized axes and title

7. We are going to create a title that will change according to the data that is plotted. For this example, it will read "**Shoes Produce the Most Sales Revenue**". First, we will find the index of the maximum value in y and save it as the **index_of_max_y** object using the following code:

```
index_of_max_y = y.index(max(y))
```

8. Save the item from list **x** with an index equaling that of **index_of_max_y** to the **most_sold_item** object using the following code:

```
most_sold_item = x[index_of_max_y]
```

9. Make the title programmatic as follows:

```
plt.title('{} Produce the Most Sales Revenue'.format(most_sold_item))
```

Check the following output:

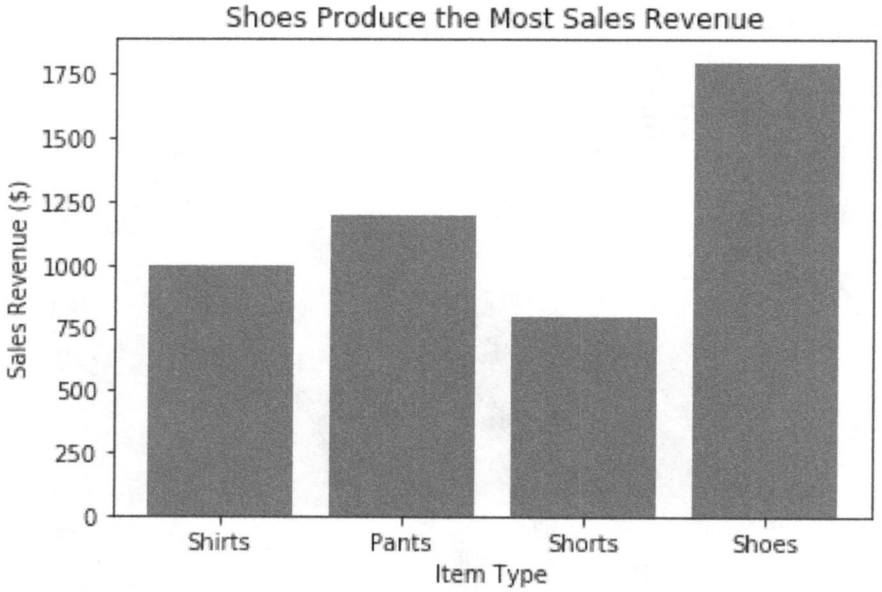

Figure 2.14: Bar plot with a programmatic title

10. If we wish to convert the plot into a horizontal bar plot, we can do so by replacing **plt.bar(x, y)** with **plt.barh(x, y)**.

The output is shown in the following screenshot:

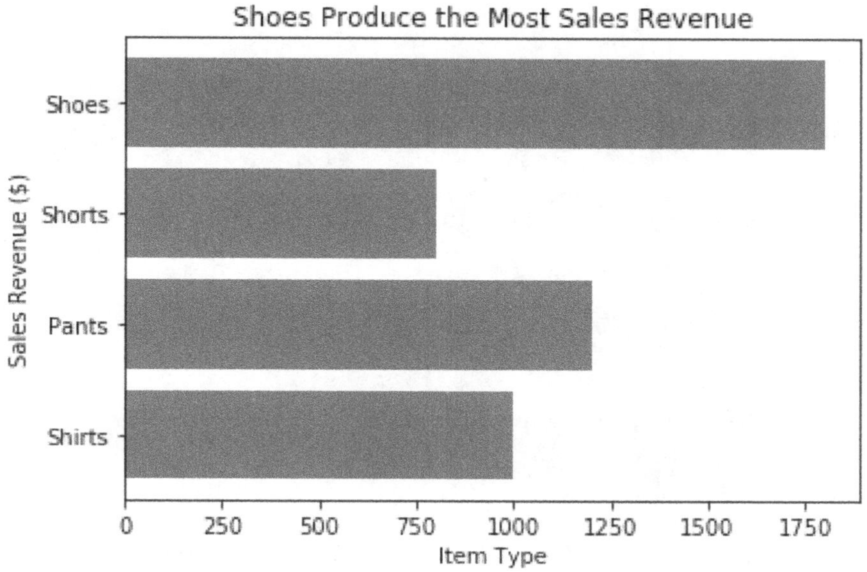

Figure 2.15: Horizontal bar plot with incorrectly labeled axes

> **Note**
>
> Remember, when a bar plot is transformed from vertical to horizontal, the x and y axes need to be switched.

11. Switch the x and y labels **`from plt.xlabel('Item Type')`** and **`plt.ylabel('Sales Revenue ($)')`**, respectively, to **`plt.xlabel('Sales Revenue ($)')`** and **`plt.ylabel('Item Type')`**.

Check out the following output for the final bar plot:

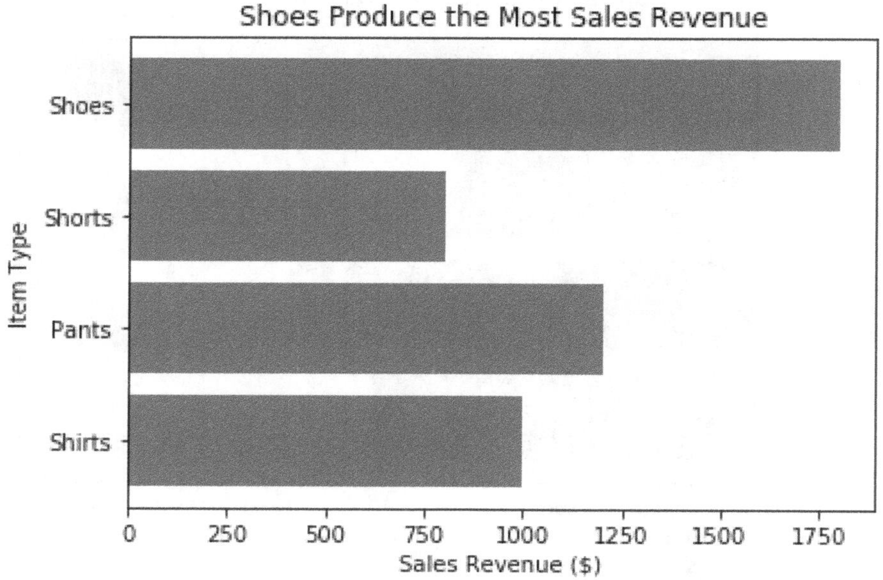

Figure 2.16: Horizontal bar plot with correctly labeled axes

In the previous exercise, we learned how to create a bar plot. Building bar plots using Matplotlib is straightforward. In the following activity, we will continue to practice building bar plots.

Activity 3: Bar Plot

In this activity, we will be creating a bar plot comparing the number of NBA championships among the five franchises with the most titles. The plot will be sorted so that the franchise with the greatest number of titles is on the left and the franchise with the least is on the right. The bars will be red, the x-axis will be titled '`NBA Franchises`', the y-axis will be titled '`Number of Championships`', and the title will be programmatic, explaining which franchise has the most titles and how many they have. Before working on this activity, make sure to research the required NBA franchise data online. Additionally, we will rotate the x tick labels 45 degrees using `plt.xticks(rotation=45)` so that they do not overlap, and we will save our plot to the current directory:

1. Create a list of five strings for `x` containing the names of the NBA franchises with the most titles.
2. Create a list of five values for `y` containing values for '`Titles Won`' that correspond with the strings in `x`.

3. Place x and y into a data frame with the column names '**Team**' and '**Titles**', respectively.
4. Sort the data frame in descending order by '**Titles**'.
5. Make a programmatic title and save it as **title**.
6. Generate the described plot.

> **Note**
>
> We can refer to the solution for this activity on page 334.

Line plots and bar plots are two very common and effective types of visualizations for reporting trends and comparing groups, respectively. However, for deeper statistical analyses, it is important to generate graphs that uncover characteristics of features not apparent with line plots and bar plots. Thus, in the following exercises, we will run through creating common statistical plots.

Exercise 16: Functional Approach – Histogram

In statistics, it is essential to be aware of the distribution of continuous variables prior to running any type of analysis. To display the distribution, we will use a histogram. Histograms display the frequency by the bin for a given array:

1. To demonstrate the creation of a histogram, we will generate an array of 100 normally distributed values with a mean of 0 and a standard deviation of 0.1, and save it as y using the following code:

```
import numpy as np

y = np.random.normal(loc=0, scale=0.1, size=100)
```

2. With Matplotlib imported, create the histogram using the following:

```
plt.hist(y, bins=20)
```

3. Create a label for the x-axis titled '**y Value**' using the following code:

```
plt.xlabel('y Value')
```

4. Title the y-axis '**Frequency**' using the following line of code:

```
plt.ylabel('Frequency')
```

5. Print it to the console using **`plt.show()`**:
6. See the output in the following screenshot:

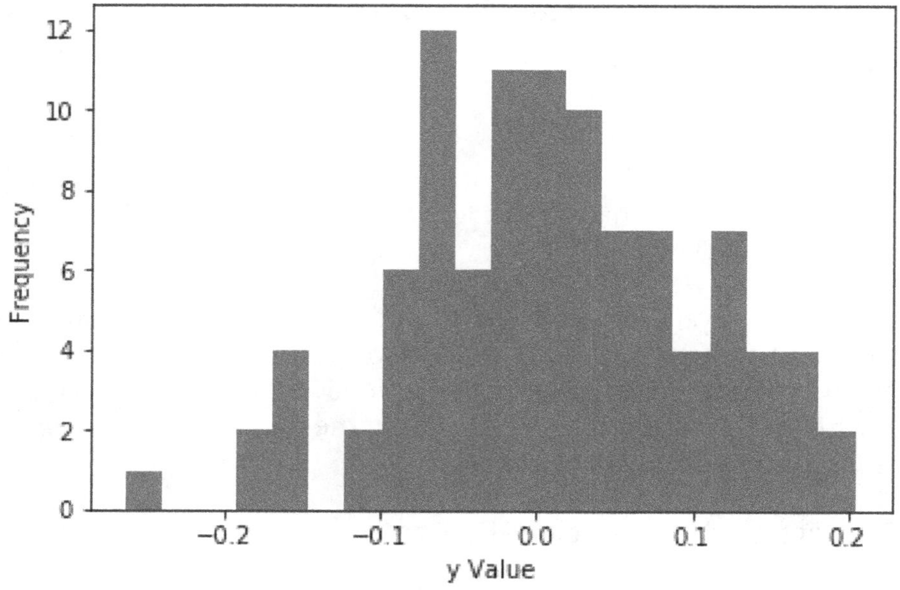

Figure 2.17: Histogram of y with labeled axes

> **Note**
>
> When we look at a histogram, we often determine whether the distribution is normal. Sometimes, a distribution may appear normal when it is not, and sometimes a distribution may appear not normal when it is normal. There is a test for normality, termed the Shapiro-Wilk test. The null hypothesis for the Shapiro-Wilk test is that data is normally distributed. Thus, a p-value < 0.05 indicates a non-normal distribution while a p-value > 0.05 indicates a normal distribution. We will use the results from the Shapiro-Wilk test to create a programmatic title communicating to the reader whether the distribution is normal or not.

7. Use tuple unpacking to save the W statistic and the p-value from the Shapiro-Wilk test into the **shap_w** and **shap_p** objects, respectively, using the following code:

```
from scipy.stats import shapiro

shap_w, shap_p = shapiro(y)
```

8. We will use an if-else statement to determine whether the data is normally distributed and store an appropriate string in a **normal_YN** object.

```
if shap_p > 0.05:
    normal_YN = 'Fail to reject the null hypothesis. Data is normally 
distributed.'
else:
    normal_YN = 'Null hypothesis is rejected. Data is not normally 
distributed.'
```

9. Assign **normal_YN** to our plot using **plt.title(normal_YN)** and print it to the console using **plt.show()**.

Check out the final output in this screenshot:

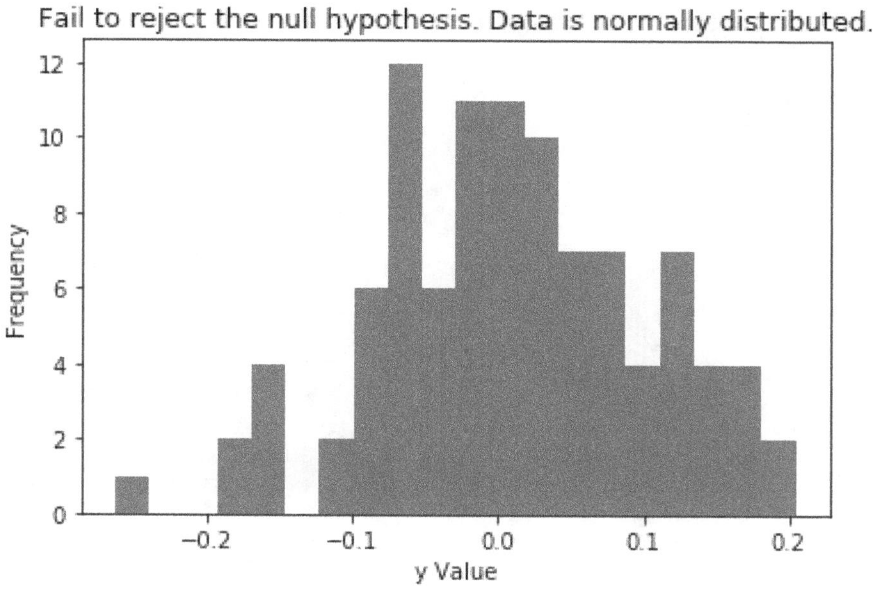

Figure 2.18: A histogram of y with a programmatic title

As mentioned previously, histograms are used for displaying the distribution of an array. Another common statistical plot for exploring a numerical feature is a box-and-whisker plot, also referred to as a boxplot.

Box-and-whisker plots display the distribution of an array based on the minimum, first quartile, median, third quartile, and maximum, but they are primarily used to indicate the skew of a distribution and to identify outliers.

Exercise 17: Functional Approach – Box-and-Whisker plot

In this exercise, we will learn how to create a box-and-whisker plot and portray information regarding the shape of the distribution and the number of outliers in our title:

1. Generate an array of 100 normally distributed numbers with a mean of 0 and a standard deviation of 0.1, and save it as y using the following code:

```
import numpy as np

y = np.random.normal(loc=0, scale=0.1, size=100)
```

2. Create and display the plot as follows:

```
import matplotlib.pyplot as plt

plt.boxplot(y)
plt.show()
```

For the output, refer to the following figure:

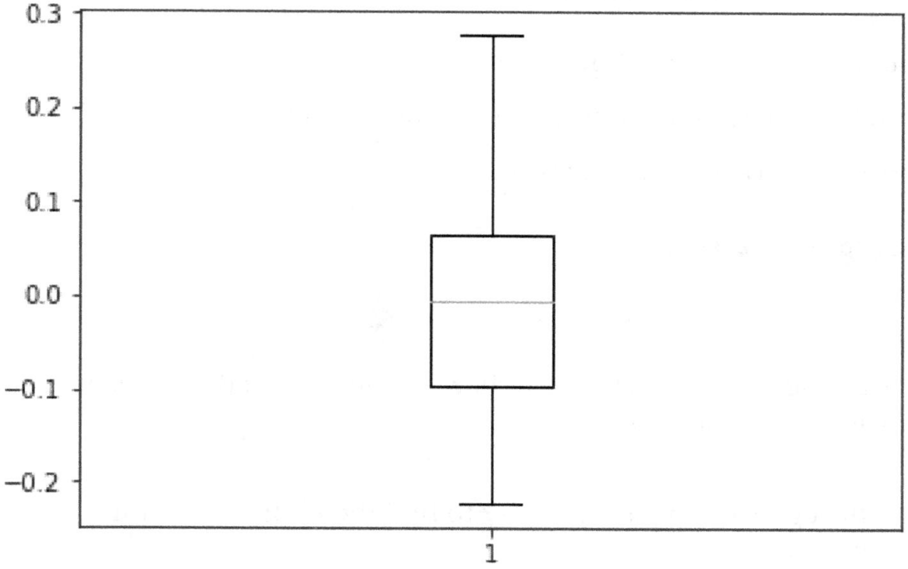

Figure 2.19: Boxplot of y

Note

The plot displays a box that represents the interquartile range (IQR). The top of the box is the 25th percentile (i.e., Q1) while the bottom of the box is the 75th percentile (that is, Q3). The orange line going through the box is the median. The two lines extending above and below the box are the whiskers. The top of the upper whisker is the "maximum" value, which is calculated using Q1 – 1.5*IQR. The bottom of the lower whisker is the "minimum" value, which is calculated using Q3 + 1.5*IQR. Outliers (or fringe outliers) are displayed as dots above the "maximum" whisker or below the "minimum" whisker.

3. Save the Shapiro W and p-value from the **shapiro** function as follows:

```
from scipy.stats import shapiro

shap_w, shap_p = shapiro(y)
```

4. Refer to the following code to convert **y** into z-scores:

```
from scipy.stats import zscore

y_z_scores = zscore(y)
```

> **Note**
>
> This is a measure of the data which shows how many standard deviations each datapoint is from the mean.

5. Iterate through the **y_z_scores** array to find the number of outliers using the following code:

```
total_outliers = 0
for i in range(len(y_z_scores)):
    if abs(y_z_scores[i]) >= 3:
        total_outliers += 1
```

> **Note**
>
> Because the array, y, was generated to be normally distributed, we can expect there to be no outliers in the data.

6. Generate a title that communicates whether the data, as well as the number of outliers, is normally distributed. If **shap_p** is greater than 0.05, our data is normally distributed. If it is not greater than 0.05, then our data is not normally distributed. We can set this up and include the number of outliers with the following logic:

```
if shap_p > 0.05:
    title = 'Normally distributed with {} outlier(s).'.format(total_
outliers)
else:
    title = 'Not normally distributed with {} outlier(s).'.format(total_
outliers)
```

7. Set our plot title as the programmatically named title using **`plt.title`** (title) and print it to the console using:

```
plt.show()
```

8. Check the final output in the following screenshot:

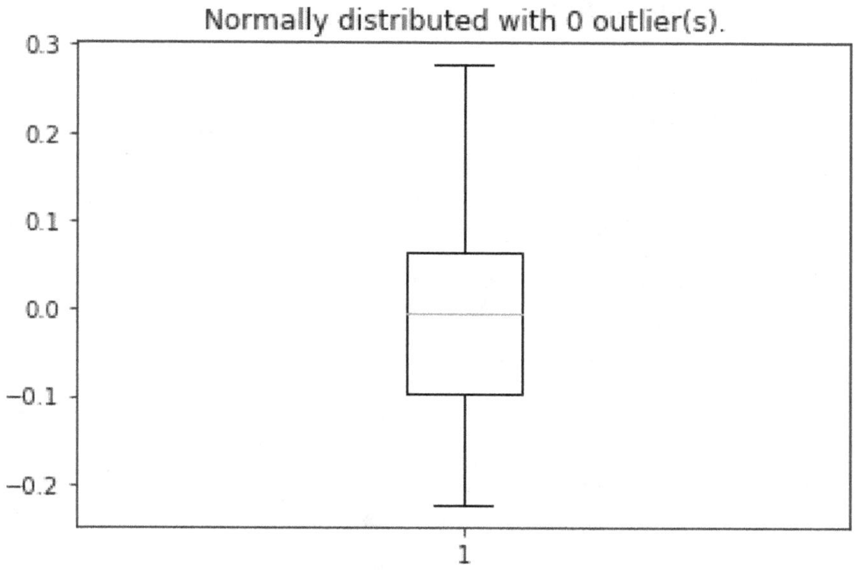

Figure 2.20: A boxplot of y with a programmatic title

Histograms and box-and-whisker plots are effective in exploring the characteristics of numerical arrays. However, they do not provide information on the relationships between arrays. In the next exercise, we will learn how to create a scatterplot – a common visualization to display the relationship between two continuous arrays.

Exercise 18: Scatterplot

In this exercise, we will be creating a scatterplot of weight versus height. We will, again, create a title explaining the message of the plot being portrayed:

1. Generate a list of numbers representing height and save it as y using the following:

```
y = [5, 5.5, 5, 5.5, 6, 6.5, 6, 6.5, 7, 5.5, 5.25, 6, 5.25]
```

2. Generate a list of numbers representing weight and save it as x using the following:

```
x = [100, 150, 110, 140, 140, 170, 168, 165, 180, 125, 115, 155, 135]
```

3. Create a basic scatterplot with weight on the x-axis and height on the y-axis using the following code:

```
import matplotlib.pyplot as plt

plt.scatter(x, y)
```

4. Label the x-axis '**Weight**' as follows:

```
plt.xlabel('Weight')
```

5. Label the y-axis '**Height**' as follows:

```
plt.ylabel('Height')
```

6. Print the plot to the console using **plt.show()**.

Our output should be similar to the following:

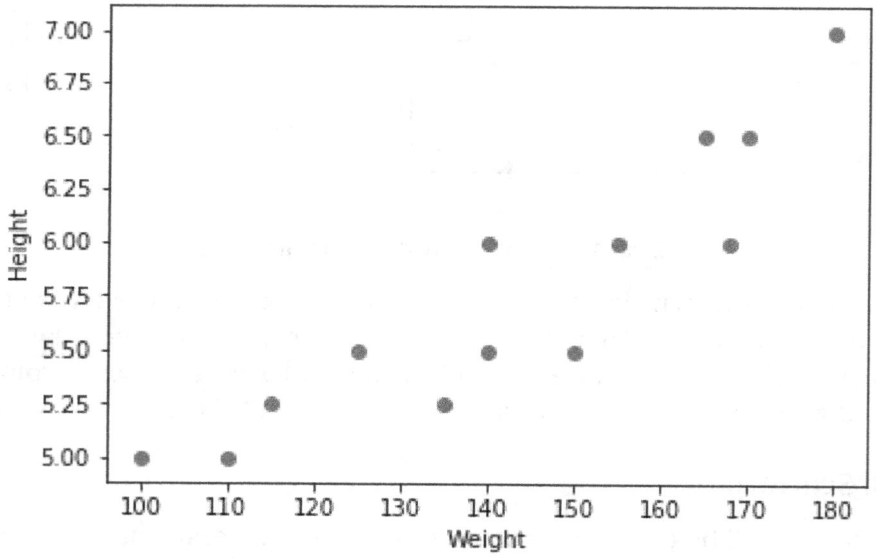

Figure 2.21: Scatterplot of height by weight

7. We want our plot title to inform the reader about the strength of the relationship and the Pearson correlation coefficient. Thus, we will calculate the Pearson correlation coefficient and interpret the value of the coefficient in the title. To compute the Pearson correlation coefficient, refer to the following code:

```
from scipy.stats import pearsonr

correlation_coeff, p_value = pearsonr(x, y)
```

8. The Pearson correlation coefficient is an indicator of the strength and direction of the linear relationship between two continuous arrays. Using if-else logic, we will return the interpretation of the correlation coefficient using the following code:

```
if correlation_coeff == 1.00:
    title = 'There is a perfect positive linear relationship (r = {0:0.2f}).'.format(correlation_coeff)
elif correlation_coeff >= 0.8:
    title = 'There is a very strong, positive linear relationship (r = {0:0.2f}).'.format(correlation_coeff)
elif correlation_coeff >= 0.6:
    title = 'There is a strong, positive linear relationship (r = {0:0.2f}).'.format(correlation_coeff)
elif correlation_coeff >= 0.4:
    title = 'There is a moderate, positive linear relationship (r = {0:0.2f}).'.format(correlation_coeff)
elif correlation_coeff >= 0.2:
    title = 'There is a weak, positive linear relationship (r = {0:0.2f}).'.format(correlation_coeff)
elif correlation_coeff > 0:
    title = 'There is a very weak, positive linear relationship (r = {0:0.2f}).'.format(correlation_coeff)
elif correlation_coeff == 0:
    title = 'There is no linear relationship (r = {0:0.2f}).'.format(correlation_coeff)
elif correlation_coeff <= -0.8:
    title = 'There is a very strong, negative linear relationship (r = {0:0.2f}).'.format(correlation_coeff)
elif correlation_coeff <= -0.6:
    title = 'There is a strong, negative linear relationship (r = {0:0.2f}).'.format(correlation_coeff)
elif correlation_coeff <= -0.4:
    title = 'There is a moderate, negative linear relationship (r = {0:0.2f}).'.format(correlation_coeff)
elif correlation_coeff <= -0.2:
    title = 'There is a weak, negative linear relationship (r = {0:0.2f}).'.format(correlation_coeff)
else:
    title = 'There is a very weak, negative linear relationship (r = {0:0.2f}).'.format(correlation_coeff)
print(title)
```

9. Now, we can use the newly created title object as our title using **`plt.title(title)`**.

   Refer to the following figure for the resultant output:

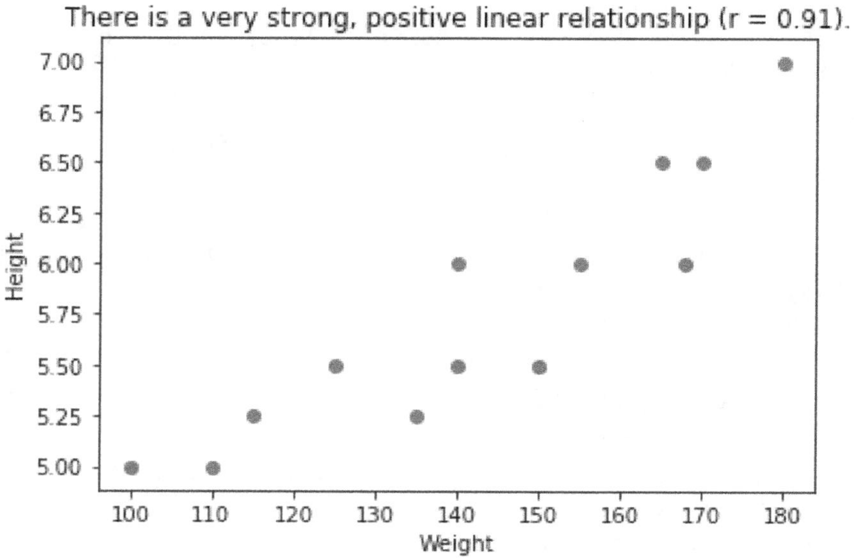

Figure 2.22: Scatterplot of height by weight with programmatic title

Up to this point, we have learned how to create and style an assortment of plots for several different purposes using the functional approach. While this approach of plotting is effective for generating quick visualizations, it does not allow us to create multiple subplots or store the plot as an object in our environment. To save the plot as an object in our environment, we must use the object-oriented approach, which will be covered in the following exercises and activities.

Object-Oriented Approach Using Subplots

Using the functional approach of plotting in Matplotlib does not allow the user to save the plot as an object in our environment. In the object-oriented approach, we create a figure object that acts as an empty canvas and then we add a set of axes, or subplots, to it. The figure object is callable and, if called, will return the figure to the console. We will demonstrate how this works by plotting the same x and y objects as we did in *Exercise 13*.

Exercise 19: Single Line Plot using Subplots

When we learned about the functional approach of plotting in Matplotlib, we began by creating and customizing a line plot. In this exercise, we will create and style a line plot using the functional plotting approach:

1. Save **x** as an array ranging from 0 to 10 in 20 linearly spaced steps as follows:

```
import numpy as np

x = np.linspace(0, 10, 20)
```

   Save **y** as x cubed using the following:

```
y = x**3
```

2. Create a figure and a set of axes as follows:

```
import matplotlib.pyplot as plt

fig, axes = plt.subplots()
plt.show()
```

   Check out the following screenshot to view the output:

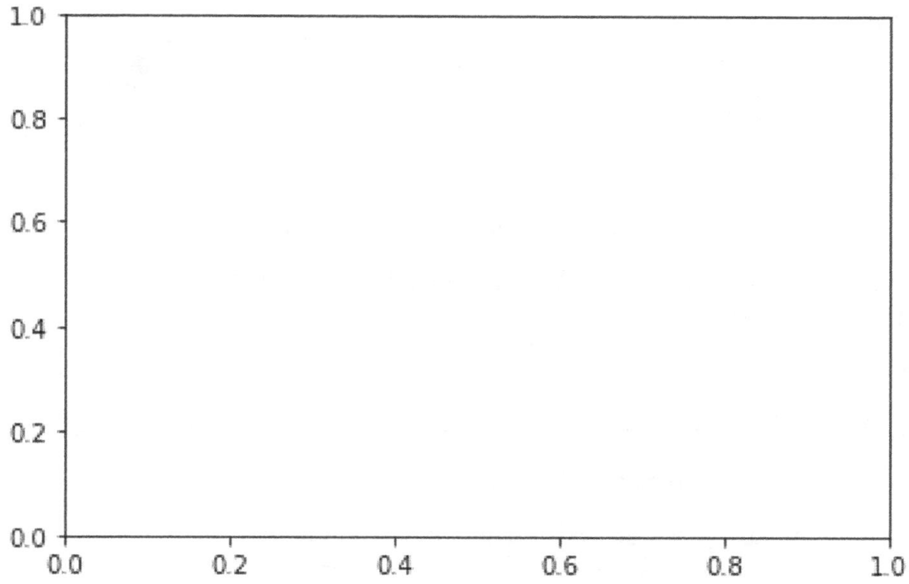

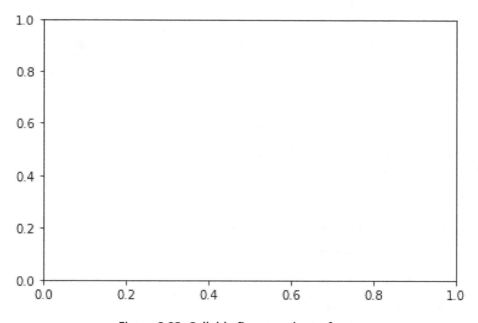

Figure 2.23: Callable figure and set of axes

> **Note**
>
> The **fig** object is now callable and returns the axis on which we can plot.

3. Plot y (that is, x squared) by x using the following:

```
axes.plot(x, y)
```

The following figure displays the output:

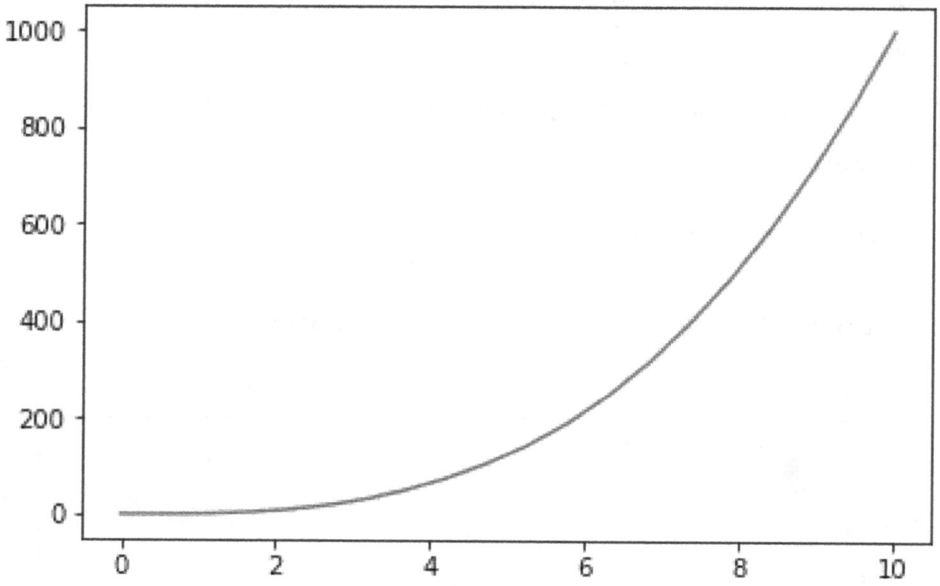

Figure 2.24: Callable line plot of y by x

4. Style the plot much the same as in *Exercise 13*. First, change the line color and markers as follows:

```
axes.plot(x, y, 'D-k')
```

5. Set the x-axis label to '`Linearly Spaced Numbers`' using the following:

```
axes.set_xlabel('Linearly Spaced Numbers')
```

6. To set the y-axis to '`y Value`' using the following code:

```
axes.set_ylabel('y Value')
```

7. Set the title to '**`As x increases, y increases by x cubed`**' using the following code:

```
axes.set_title('As x increases, y increases by x cubed')
```

The following figure displays the output:

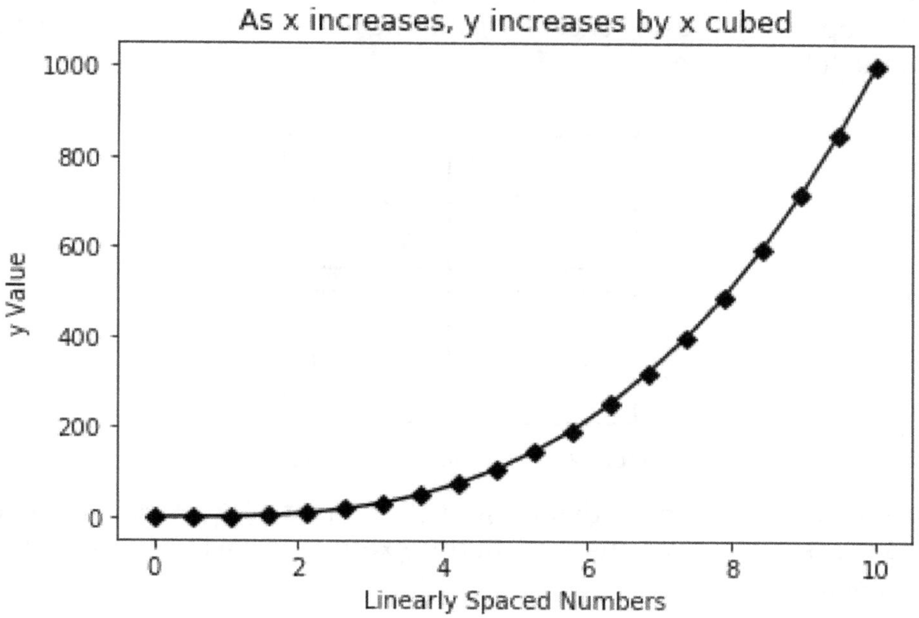

Figure 2.25: Styled, callable line plot of y by x

In this exercise, we created a plot very similar to the first plot in *Exercise 13*, but now it is a callable object. Another advantage of using the object-oriented plotting approach is the ability to create multiple subplots on a single figure object.

In some situations, we want to compare different views of data side by side. We can accomplish this in Matplotlib using subplots.

Exercise 20: Multiple Line Plots Using Subplots

Thus, in this exercise, we will plot the same lines as in Exercise 14, but we will plot them on two subplots in the same, callable figure object. Subplots are laid out using a grid format and are accessible using [row, column] indexing. For example, if our figure object contains four subplots organized in two rows and two columns, we would index reference the top-left plot using **`axes[0,0]`** and the bottom-right plot using **`axes[1,1]`**, as shown in the following figure.

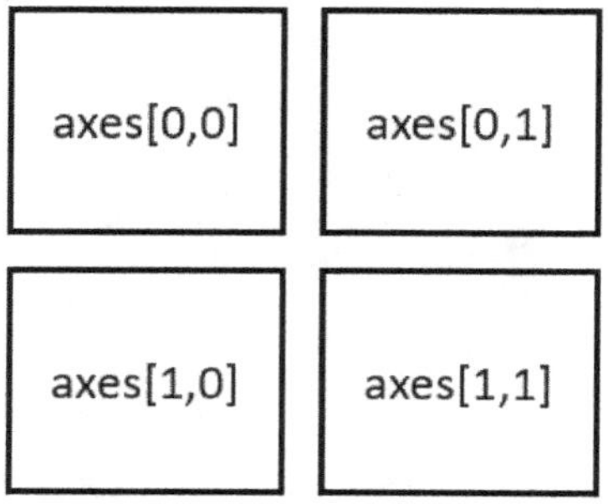

Figure 2.26: Axes index referencing

In the remaining exercises and activities, we will get a lot of practice with generating subplots and accessing the various axes. In this exercise, we will be making multiple line plots using sublots:

1. First, create **`x`**, **`y`**, and **`y2`** using the following code:

```
import numpy as np

x = np.linspace(0, 10, 20)
y = x**3
y2 = x**2
```

2. Create a figure with two axes (that is, subplots) that are side by side (that is, 1 row with 2 columns), as follows:

```
import matplotlib.pyplot as plt

fig, axes = plt.subplots(nrows=1, ncols=2)
```

The resultant output is displayed here:

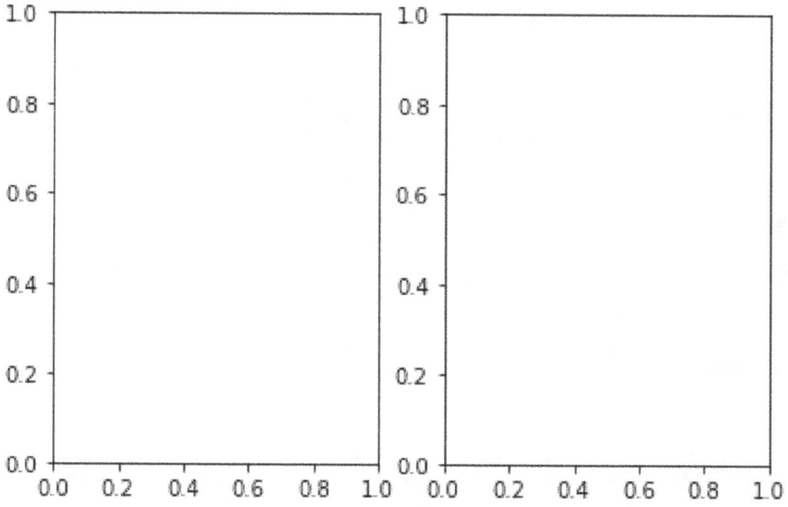

Figure 2.27: A figure with two subplots

3. To access the subplot on the left, refer to it as **axes[0]**. To access the plot on the right, refer to it as **axes[1]**. On the left axis, plot y by x using the following:

```
axes[0].plot(x, y)
```

4. Add a title using the following:

```
axes[0].set_title('x by x Cubed')
```

5. Generate an x-axis label using the following line of code:

```
axes[0].set_xlabel('Linearly Spaced Numbers')
```

6. Create a y-axis label using the following code:

```
axes[0].set_ylabel('y Value')
```

The resultant output is displayed here:

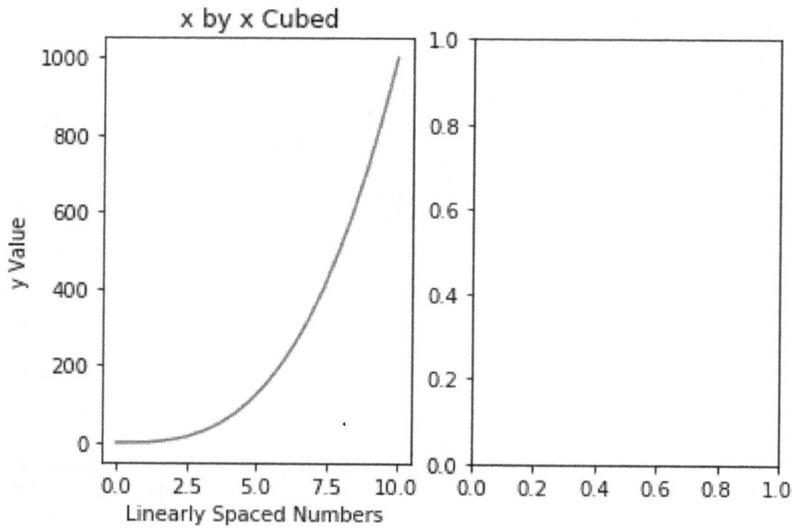

Figure 2.28: Figure with two subplots, where the left has been created

7. On the right axis, plot **y2** by **x** using the following code:

```
axes[1].plot(x, y2)
```

8. Add a title using the following code:

```
axes[1].set_title('x by x Squared')
```

9. Generate an x-axis label using the following code:

```
axes[1].set_xlabel('Linearly Spaced Numbers')
```

10. Create a y-axis label using the following code:

```
axes[1].set_ylabel('y Value')
```

The following screenshot displays the output

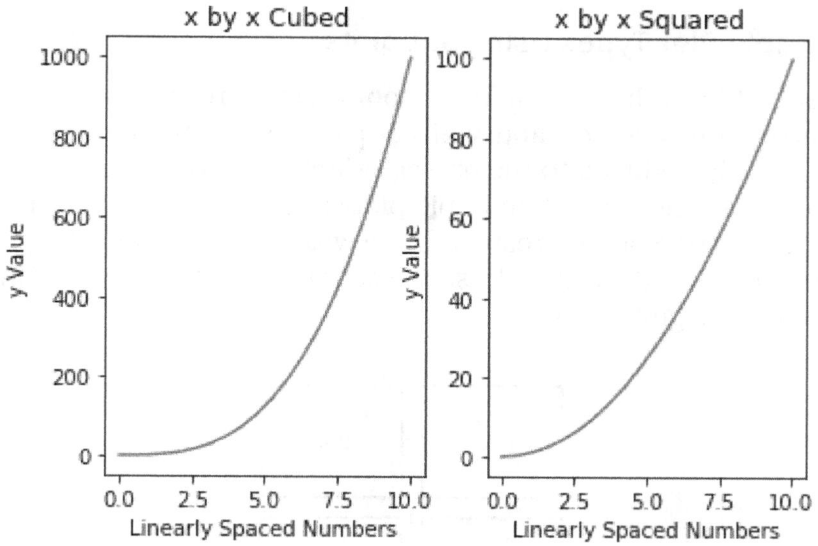

Figure 2.29: Figure with both subplots created

11. We have successfully created two subplots. However, it looks like the y-axis of the plot on the right is overlapping the left-hand plot. To prevent the overlapping of the plots, use **`plt.tight_layout()`**.

    The figure here displays the output:

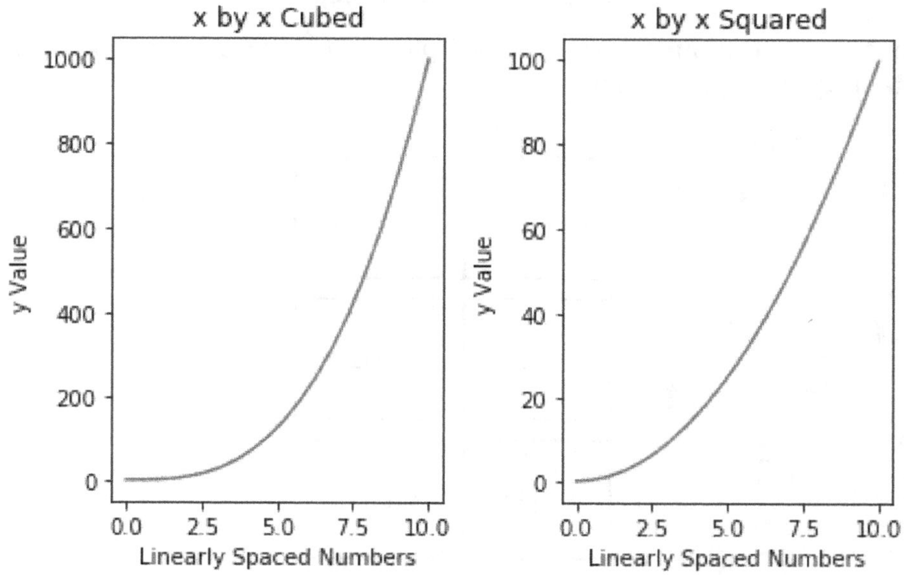

Figure 2.30: A figure with two non-overlapping subplots

Using the object-oriented approach, we can display both subplots just by calling the **fig** object. We will practice object-oriented plotting further in Activity 4.

Activity 4: Multiple Plot Types Using Subplots

We have learned uptil now how to build, customize, and program line plots, bar plots, histograms, scatterplots, and box-and-whisker plots using the functional approach. In exercise 19, we were introduced to the object-oriented approach, and in exercise 20, we learned how to create a figure with multiple plots using subplots. Thus, in this activity, we will be leveraging subplots to create a figure with multiple plots and plot types. We will be creating a figure with six subplots. The subplots will be displayed in three rows and two columns (see Figure 2.31):

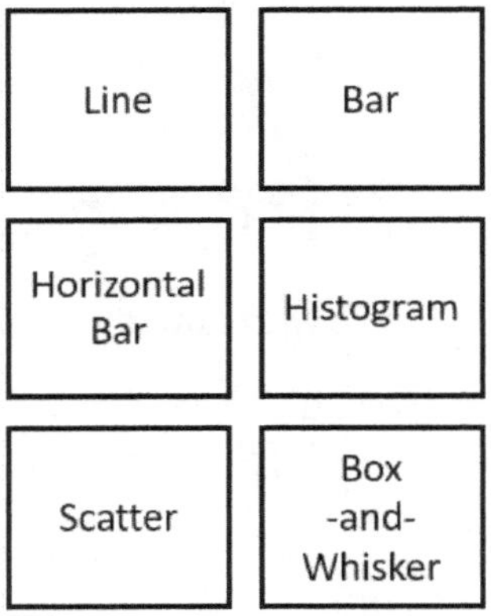

Figure 2.31: Layout for subplots

Once we have generated our figure of six subplots, we access each subplot using 'row, column' indexing (see Figure 2.32):

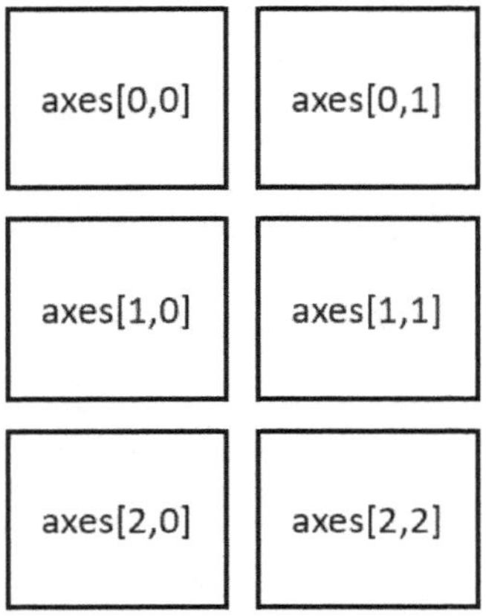

Figure 2.32: Axes index referencing

Thus, to access the line plot (that is, top-left), use **axes[0, 0]**. To access the histogram (that is, middle-right), use **axes[1, 1]**. We will be practicing this in the following activity:

1. Import **Items_Sold_by_Week.csv** and **Weight_by_Height.csv** from GitHub and generate a normally distributed array of numbers.
2. Generate a figure with six empty subplots using three rows and two columns that do not overlap.
3. Set the plot titles with six subplots organized in three rows and two columns such that do not overlap.
4. On the '**Line**', '**Bar**' and '**Horizontal Bar**' axes, plot '**Items_Sold**' by '**Week**' from '**Items_Sold_by_Week.csv**'.
5. In the '**Histogram**' and '**Box-and-Whisker**' axes, plot the array of 100 normally distributed numbers.
6. In the '**Scatter**' axis, plot weight by height with '**Weight_by_Height.csv**'.
7. Label the x- and y-axis in each subplot.
8. Increase the size of the figure and save it.

> **Note**
>
> The solution for this activity can be found on page 338.

Summary

In this chapter, we used the Python plotting library Matplotlib to create, customize, and save plots using the functional approach. We then covered the importance of a descriptive title and created our own descriptive, programmatic titles. However, the functional approach does not create a callable figure object and it does not return subplots. Thus, to create a callable figure object with the potential of numerous subplots, we created, customized, and saved our plots using the object-oriented approach. Plotting needs can vary analysis to analysis, so covering every possible plot in this chapter is not practical. To create powerful plots that meet the needs of each individual analysis, it is imperative to become familiar with the documentation and examples found on the Matplotlib documentation page.

In the subsequent chapter, we will apply some of these plotting techniques as we dive into machine learning using scikit-learn.

3

Introduction to Machine Learning via Scikit-Learn

Learning Objectives

By the end of this chapter, you will be able to:

- Prepare data for different types of supervised learning models.
- Tune model hyperparameters using a grid search.
- Extract feature importance from a tuned model.
- Evaluate performance of classification and regression models.

In this chapter, we will be covering the important concepts of handling data and making the data ready for analysis.

Introduction

scikit-learn is a free, open source library built for Python that contains an assortment of supervised and unsupervised machine learning algorithms. Additionally, scikit-learn provides functions for data preprocessing, hyperparameter tuning, and model evaluation, which we will be covering in the upcoming chapters. It streamlines the model-building process and is easy to install on a wide variety of platforms. scikit-learn started in 2007 as a Google Summer of Code project by David Corneapeau, and after a series of developments and releases, scikit-learn has evolved into one of the premier tools used by academics and professionals for machine learning.

In this chapter, we will learn to build a variety of widely used modeling algorithms, namely, linear and logistic regression, support vector machines (SVMs), decision trees, and random forests. First, we will cover linear and logistic regression.

Introduction to Linear and Logistic Regression

In regression, a single dependent, or outcome variable is predicted using one or more independent variables. Use cases for regression are included, but are not limited to predicting:

- The win percentage of a team, given a variety of team statistics
- The risk of heart disease, given family history and a number of physical and psychological characteristics
- The likelihood of snowfall, given several climate measurements

Linear and logistic regression are popular choices for predicting such outcomes due to the ease and transparency of interpretability, as well as the ability to extrapolate to values not seen in the training data. The end goal of linear regression is to draw a straight line through the observations that minimizes the absolute distance between the line and observations (that is, the line of best fit). Therefore, in linear regression, it is assumed that the relationship between the feature(s) and the continuous dependent variable follows a straight line. Lines are defined in slope-intercept form (that is, $y = a + bx$), where a is the intercept (that is, the value of y when x is 0), b is the slope, and x is the independent variable. There are two types of linear regression that will be covered in this chapter: simple linear regression and multiple linear regression.

Simple Linear Regression

Simple linear regression models define the relationship between one feature and the continuous outcome variable using $y = \alpha + \beta x$. This equation is like the slope-intercept form, where y denotes the predicted value of the dependent variable, α denotes the intercept, β (beta) represents the slope, and x is the value of the independent variable. Given x, regression models compute the values for α and β that minimize the absolute difference between predicted y values (that is, $\hat{y}$) and actual y values.

For example, if we are predicting the weight of an individual in kilograms (kg) using height in meters (m) as the lone predictor variable, and the simple linear regression model computes 1.5 as the value for α and 50 as the coefficient for β, this model can be interpreted as for every 1 m increase in height, weight increases by 50 kg. Thus, we can predict that the weight of an individual who is 1.8 m is 91.5 kg using y = 1.5 + (50 x 1.8). In the following exercises, we will demonstrate simple linear regression using scikit-learn.

Exercise 21: Preparing Data for a Linear Regression Model

To prepare our data for a simple linear regression model, we will use a random subset of the Weather in Szeged 2006-2016 dataset, which consists of hourly weather measurements from April 1, 2006, to September 9, 2016, in Szeged, Hungary. The adapted data is provided as a **.csv** file (https://github.com/TrainingByPackt/Data-Science-with-Python/blob/master/Chapter02/weather.csv) and consists of 10,000 observations of 8 variables:

- **Temperature_c**: The temperature in Celsius
- **Humidity**: The proportion of humidity
- **Wind_Speed_kmh**: The wind speed in kilometers per hour
- **Wind_Bearing_Degrees**: The wind direction in degrees clockwise from due north
- **Visibility_km**: The visibility in kilometers
- **Pressure_millibars**: The atmospheric pressure as measured in millibars
- **Rain**: rain = 1, snow = 0
- **Description**: Warm, normal, or cold

1. Import the **weather.csv** dataset using the following code:

```
import pandas as pd

df = pd.read_csv('weather.csv')
```

2. Explore the data using **df.info()**:

```
<class 'pandas.core.frame.DataFrame'>
RangeIndex: 10000 entries, 0 to 9999
Data columns (total 8 columns):
Temperature_c             10000 non-null float64
Humidity                  10000 non-null float64
Wind_Speed_kmh            10000 non-null float64
Wind_Bearing_degrees      10000 non-null int64
Visibility_km             10000 non-null float64
Pressure_millibars        10000 non-null float64
Rain                      10000 non-null int64
Description               10000 non-null object
dtypes: float64(5), int64(2), object(1)
memory usage: 625.1+ KB
```

Figure 3.1: Information describing df

3. The **Description** column is the lone categorical variable in **df**. Check the number of levels in **Description** as follows:

```
levels = len(pd.value_counts(df['Description']))
print('There are {} levels in the Description column'.format(levels))
```

The number of levels is shown in the following screenshot:

```
There are 3 levels in the Description column
```

Figure 3.2: Number of levels in the 'Description' column

> **Note**
>
> Multi-class, categorical variables must be converted into dummy variables via a process termed "dummy coding." Dummy coding a multi-class, categorical variable creates n-1 new binary features, which correspond to the levels within the categorical variable. For example, a multi-class, categorical variable with three levels will create two binary features. After the multi-class, categorical feature has been dummy coded, the original feature must be dropped.

4. To dummy code all multi-class, categorical variables, refer to the following code:

```
import pandas as pd

df_dummies = pd.get_dummies(df, drop_first=True)
```

> **Note**
>
> The original DataFrame, **df**, consisted of eight columns, one of which (that is, Description) was a multi-class, categorical variable with three levels.

5. In step 4, we transformed this feature into n-1 (that is, 2), separated dummy variables, and dropped the original feature, **Description**. Thus, **df_dummies** should now contain one more column than df (that is, 9 columns). Check this out using the following code:

```
print('There are {} columns in df_dummies'   .format(df_dummies.shape[1]))
```

```
There are 9 columns in df_dummies
```

Figure 3.3: Number of columns after dummy coding

6. To remove any possible order effects in the data, it is good practice to first shuffle the rows of the data prior to splitting the data into features (**X**) and outcome (**y**). To shuffle the rows in **df_dummies**, refer to the code here:

```
from sklearn.utils import shuffle

df_shuffled = shuffle(df_dummies, random_state=42)
```

7. Now that the data has been shuffled, we will split the rows in our data into features (**X**) and the dependent variable (**y**).

> **Note**
>
> Linear regression is used for predicting a continuous outcome. Thus, in this exercise, we will pretend that the continuous variable **Temperature_c** (the temperature in Celsius) is the dependent variable, and that we are preparing data to fit a linear regression model.

8. Split **df_shuffled** into **X** and **y** as follows:

```
DV = 'Temperature_c'
X = df_shuffled.drop(DV, axis=1)
y = df_shuffled[DV]
```

9. Split **X** and **y** into testing and training data using the code here:

```
from sklearn.model_selection import train_test_split

X_train, X_test, y_train, y_test = train_test_split(X, y, test_size=0.33,
random_state=42)
```

Now that the data has been dummy coded, shuffled, split into **X** and **y**, and further divided into testing and training datasets, it is ready to be used in a linear or logistic regression model.

The screenshot here shows the first five rows of **X_train**:

X_train - DataFrame

Index	Humidity	Wind_Speed_kmh	Wind_Bearing_degrees	Visibility_km	Pressure_millibars	Rain	Description_Normal	Description_Warm
5757	0.76	8.4525	38	14.9569	1028.63	1	1	0
7510	0.85	12.88	150	8.05	1021.9	0	0	0
55	0.47	8.0339	267	10.3523	1015.5	1	0	1
1983	0.28	20.8978	300	10.3684	1008	1	1	0
1842	1	6.2629	329	0.2254	1028.13	0	0	0

Figure 3.4: The first five rows of X_train

Exercise 22: Fitting a Simple Linear Regression Model and Determining the Intercept and Coefficient

In this exercise, we will continue using the data we prepared in Exercise 21 to fit a simple linear regression model to predict the temperature in Celsius from the humidity.

Continuing from Exercise 21, perform the following steps:

1. To instantiate a linear regression model, refer to the code here:

```
from sklearn.linear_model import LinearRegression

model = LinearRegression()
```

2. Fit the model to the **Humidity** column in the training data using this code:

```
model.fit(X_train[['Humidity']], y_train)
```

```
LinearRegression(copy_X=True, fit_intercept=True, n_jobs=None,
         normalize=False)
```

Figure 3.5: The output from fitting the simple linear regression model

3. Extract the value for the intercept using the following code:

```
intercept = model.intercept_
```

4. Extract the value for the **coefficient** as follows:

```
coefficient = model.coef_
```

5. Now, we can print a message with the formula for predicting temperature in Celsius using the code here:

```
print('Temperature = {0:0.2f} + ({1:0.2f} x Humidity)'.format(intercept,
coefficient[0]))
```

```
Temperature = 34.50 + (-30.69 x Humidity)
```

Figure 3.6: A formula to predict temperature in Celsius from humidity using simple linear regression

Great work! According to this simple linear regression model, a day with a 0.78 humidity value has a predicted a temperature of 10.56 degrees Celsius. Now that we are familiar with extracting the intercept and coefficients of our simple linear regression model, it is time to generate predictions and subsequently evaluate how the model performs on unseen, test data.

> **Teaching tip**
>
> Practice calculating temperature at various levels of humidity.

Exercise 23: Generating Predictions and Evaluating the Performance of a Simple Linear Regression Model

The very purpose of supervised learning is to use existing, labeled data to generate predictions. Thus, this exercise will demonstrate how to generate predictions on the test feature and generate model performance metrics by comparing the predictions to the actual values.

Continuing from *Exercise 22*, perform the following steps:

1. Generate predictions on the test data using the following:

```
predictions = model.predict(X_test[['Humidity']])
```

> **Note**
>
> A common way to evaluate model performance is to examine the correlation between the predicted and actual values using a scatterplot. The scatterplot displays the relationship between the actual and predicted values. A perfect regression model will display a straight, diagonal line between predicted and actual values. The relationship between the predicted and actual values can be quantified using the Pearson r correlation coefficient. In the following step, we will create a scatterplot of the predicted and actual values.

2. It is helpful if the correlation coefficient is displayed in the plot's title. The following code will show us how to do this:

```
import matplotlib.pyplot as plt
from scipy.stats import pearsonr

plt.scatter(y_test, predictions)
plt.xlabel('Y Test (True Values)')
plt.ylabel('Predicted Values')
plt.title('Predicted vs. Actual Values (r = {0:0.2f})'.format(pearsonr(y_
test, predictions)[0], 2))
plt.show()
```

Here is the resultant output:

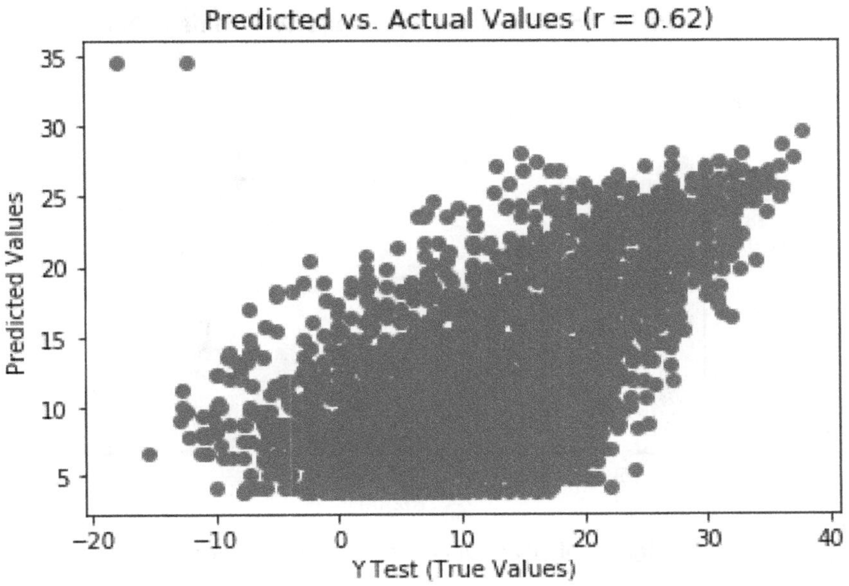

Figure 3.7: Predicted versus actual values from a simple linear regression model

> **Note**
>
> With a Pearson r value of 0.62, there is a moderate, positive, linear correlation between the predicted and actual values. A perfect model would have all points on the plot in a straight line and an r value of 1.0.

3. A model that fits the data very well will have normally distributed residuals. To create a density plot of the residuals, refer to the following code:

```
import seaborn as sns
from scipy.stats import shapiro

sns.distplot((y_test - predictions), bins = 50)
plt.xlabel('Residuals')
plt.ylabel('Density')
plt.title('Histogram of Residuals (Shapiro W p-value = {0:0.3f})'.
format(shapiro(y_test - predictions)[1]))
plt.show()
```

Refer to the resultant output here:

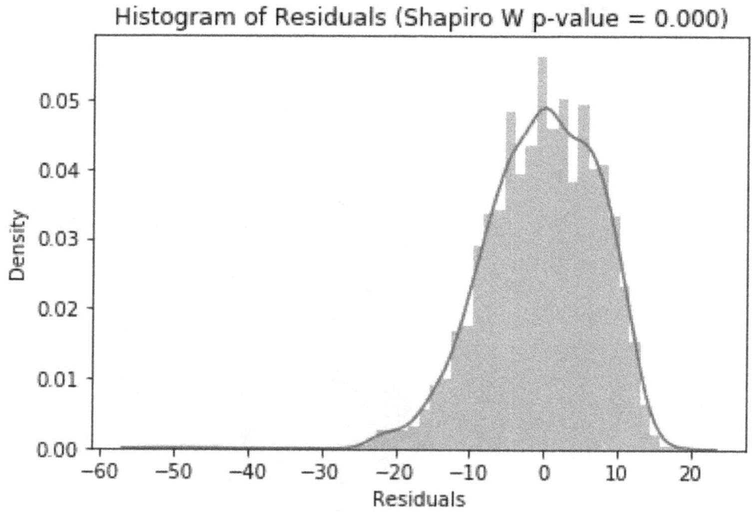

Figure 3.8: A histogram of residuals from a simple linear regression model

> **Note**
>
> The histogram shows us that the residuals are negatively skewed and the value of the Shapiro W p-value in the title tells us that the distribution is not normal. This gives us further evidence that our model has room for improvement.

4. Lastly, we will compute metrics for mean absolute error, mean squared error, root mean squared error, and R-squared, and put them into a DataFrame using the code here:

```
from sklearn import metrics
import numpy as np

metrics_df = pd.DataFrame({'Metric': ['MAE',
                                      'MSE',
                                      'RMSE',
                                      'R-Squared'],
                          'Value': [metrics.mean_absolute_error(y_test,
predictions),
                                    metrics.mean_squared_error(y_test,
predictions),
                                    np.sqrt(metrics.mean_squared_error(y_
test, predictions)),
```

```
                                        metrics.explained_variance_score(y_
    test, predictions)]}).round(3)
    print(metrics_df)
```

Please refer to the resultant output:

```
      Metric   Value
0        MAE   6.052
1        MSE  56.187
2       RMSE   7.496
3  R-Squared   0.389
```

Figure 3.9: Model evaluation metrics from a simple linear regression model

Mean absolute error (**MAE**) is the average absolute difference between the predicted values and the actual values. **Mean squared error** (**MSE**) is the average of the squared differences between the predicted and actual values. **Root mean squared error** (**RMSE**) is the square root of the MSE. R-squared tells us the proportion of variance in the dependent variable that can be explained by the model. Thus, in this simple linear regression model, humidity explained only 38.9% of the variance in temperature. Additionally, our predictions were within ± 6.052 degrees Celsius.

Here, we have successfully used scikit-learn to fit and evaluate a simple linear regression model. This is the first step in a very exciting journey to becoming a machine learning guru. Next, we will continue expanding our knowledge of regression and improving this model by exploring multiple linear regression.

Multiple Linear Regression

Multiple linear regression models define the relationship between two or more features and the continuous outcome variable using $y = \alpha + \beta_1 x_{i1} + \beta_2 x_{i2} + \ldots + \beta_{p-1} x_{i,p-1}$. Again, α represents the intercept and β denotes the slope for each feature (x) in the model. Thus, if we are predicting the weight of an individual in kg using height in m, total cholesterol in milligrams per deciliter (mg/dL), and minutes of cardiovascular exercise per day, and the multiple linear regression model computes 1.5 as the value for α, 50 as the coefficient for β_1, 0.1 as the coefficient for β_2, and -0.4 as the coefficient for β_3, this model can be interpreted as for every 1 m increase in height, weight increases by 50 kg, controlling for all other features in the model. Additionally, for every 1 mg/dL increase in total cholesterol, weight increases by 0.1 kg, controlling for all other features in the model. Lastly, for every minute of cardiovascular exercise per day, weight decreases by 0.4 kg, controlling for all other features in the model. Thus, we can predict the weight of an individual who is 1.8 m tall, with total cholesterol of 200 mg/dL, and completes 30 minutes of cardiovascular exercise per day as 99.5 kg using $y = 1.5 + (0.1 \ x\ 50) + (200 \ x\ 0.5) + (30 \ x\ -0.4)$. In the following exercise, we will demonstrate conducting multiple linear regression using scikit-learn.

Exercise 24: Fitting a Multiple Linear Regression Model and Determining the Intercept and Coefficients

In this exercise, we will continue using the data we prepared in *Exercise 21, Preparing Data for a Linear Regression Model*, to fit a multiple linear regression model to predict the temperature in Celsius from all the features in the data.

Continuing from Exercise 23, perform the following steps:

1. To instantiate a linear regression model, refer to the code here:

```
from sklearn.linear_model import LinearRegression

model = LinearRegression()
```

2. Fit the model to the training data using this code:

```
model.fit(X_train, y_train)
```

```
LinearRegression(copy_X=True, fit_intercept=True, n_jobs=None,
         normalize=False)
```

Figure 3.10: The output from fitting the multiple linear regression model

3. Extract the value for the intercept using the following code:

```
intercept = model.intercept_
```

4. Extract the value for the coefficients as follows:

```
coefficients = model.coef_
```

5. Now, we can print a message with the formula for predicting temperature in Celsius using the code here:

```
print('Temperature = {0:0.2f} + ({1:0.2f} x Humidity) + ({2:0.2f} x Wind
Speed) + ({3:0.2f} x Wind Bearing Degrees) + ({4:0.2f} x Visibility) +
({5:0.2f} x Pressure) + ({6:0.2f} x Rain) + ({7:0.2f} x Normal Weather) +
({8:0.2f} x Warm Weather)'.format(intercept,
coefficients[0],
coefficients[1],
coefficients[2],
coefficients[3],
coefficients[4],
coefficients[5],
coefficients[6],
coefficients[7]))
```

Our output should look like this:

```
Temperature = 3.54 + (-7.93 x Humidity) + (-0.07 x Wind Speed) + (0.00 x Wind Bearing Degrees) +
(0.06 x Visibility) + (0.00 x Pressure) + (5.61 x Rain) + (8.54 x Normal Weather) + (19.10 x Warm
Weather)
```

Figure 3.11: A formula to predict temperature in Celsius from humidity using multiple linear regression

Nice job! According to this multiple regression model, a day with 0.78 humidity, 5.0 km/h wind speed, wind direction at 81 degrees clockwise from due north, 3 km of visibility, 1000 millibars of pressure, no rain, and is described as normal, has a predicted temperature in Celsius of 5.72 degrees. Now that we are familiar with extracting the intercept and coefficients of our multiple linear regression model, we can generate predictions and evaluate how the model performs on the test data.

Activity 5: Generating Predictions and Evaluating the Performance of a Multiple Linear Regression Model

In *Exercise 23*, *Generating Predictions and Evaluating the Performance of a Simple Linear Regression Model*, we learned how to generate predictions and evaluate the performance of a simple linear regression model using a variety of methods. To reduce the code redundancy, we will evaluate the performance of our multiple linear regression model using the metrics in *step* 4 of *Exercise* 23, and we will determine if the multiple linear regression model performed better or worse in relation to the simple linear regression model.

Continuing from Exercise 24, perform the following steps:

1. Generate predictions on the test data using all the features.
2. Plot predictions versus actual using a scatterplot.
3. Plot the distribution of the residuals.
4. Calculate the metrics for mean absolute error, mean squared error, root mean squared error, and R-squared and put them into a DataFrame.
5. Determine if the multiple linear regression model performed better or worse in relation to the simple linear regression model.

> **Note**
>
> The solution for this activity can be found on page 343.

You should find that the multiple linear regression model performed better on every metric relative to the simple linear regression model. Most notably, in the simple linear regression model, only 38.9% of the variance in temperature was described by the model. However, in the multiple linear regression model, 86.6% of the variance in temperature was explained by the combination of features. Additionally, our simple linear regression model predicted temperatures, on average, within ± 6.052 degrees, while our multiple linear regression model predicted temperatures, on average, within ± 2.861 degrees.

The transparent nature of the intercept and beta coefficients make linear regression models very easy to interpret. In business, it is commonly requested that data scientists explain the effect of a certain feature on an outcome. Thus, linear regression provides metrics allowing a reasonable response to the business inquiry earlier.

However, much of the time, a problem requires the data scientist to predict an outcome measure that is not continuous, but categorical. For example, in insurance, given certain features of a customer, what is the probability that this customer will not renew their policy? In this case, there is not a linear relationship between the features in the data and the outcome variable, so linear regression will falter. A viable option for conducting regression analysis on a categorical dependent variable is logistic regression.

Logistic Regression

Logistic regression uses categorical and continuous variables to predict a categorical outcome. When the dependent variable of choice has two categorical outcomes, the analysis is termed binary logistic regression. However, if the outcome variable consists of more than two levels, the analysis is referred to as multinomial logistic regression. For the purposes of this chapter, we will focus our learning on the former.

When predicting a binary outcome, we do not have a linear relationship between the features and the outcome variable; an assumption of linear regression. Thus, to express a nonlinear relationship in a linear way, we must transform the data using logarithmic transformation. As a result, logistic regression allows us to predict the probability of the binary outcome occurring given the feature(s) in the model.

For logistic regression with 1 predictor, the logistic regression equation is shown here:

$$P(Y) = \frac{1}{1 + e^{-(\alpha + \beta x)}}$$

Figure 3.12: Logistic regression formula with 1 predictor

In the preceding figure, P(Y) is the probability of the outcome occurring, *e* is the base of natural logarithms, *α* is the intercept, *β* is the beta coefficient, and *x* is the value of the predictor. This equation can be extended to multiple predictors using the formula here:

$$P(Y) = \frac{1}{1 + e^{-(\alpha + \beta_1 x_{i1} + \beta_2 x_{i2} + \ldots + \beta_{p-1} x_{ip-1})}}$$

Figure 3.13: Logistic regression formula with more than one predictor

Thus, using logistic regression to model the probability of an event occurring is the same as fitting a linear regression model, except the continuous outcome variable has been replaced by the log odds (an alternate way of expressing probabilities) of success for a binary outcome variable. In linear regression, we assumed a linear relationship between the predictor variable(s) and the outcome variable. Logistic regression, on the other hand, assumes a linear relationship between the predictor variable(s) and the natural log of $p/(1-p)$, where p is the probability of the event occurring.

In the following exercise, we will use the **weather.csv** dataset to demonstrate building a logistic regression model to predict the probability of rain using all the features in our data.

Exercise 25: Fitting a Logistic Regression Model and Determining the Intercept and Coefficients

To model the probability of rain (as opposed to snow) using all the features in our data, we will use the **weather.csv** file and store the dichotomous variable **Rain** as the outcome measure.

1. Import data using the following code:

```
import pandas as pd

df = pd.read_csv('weather.csv')
```

2. Dummy code the **Description** variable as follows:

```
import pandas as pd

df_dummies = pd.get_dummies(df, drop_first=True)
```

3. Shuffle **df_dummies** using the code here:

```
from sklearn.utils import shuffle

df_shuffled = shuffle(df_dummies, random_state=42)
```

4. Split the features and outcome into **X** and **y**, respectively, as follows:

```
DV = 'Rain'
X = df_shuffled.drop(DV, axis=1)
y = df_shuffled[DV]
```

5. Split the features and outcome into training and testing data using the code here:

```
from sklearn.model_selection import train_test_split

X_train, X_test, y_train, y_test = train_test_split(X, y, test_size=0.33,
random_state=42)
```

6. Instantiate a logistic regression model using this code:

```
from sklearn.linear_model import LogisticRegression

model = LogisticRegression()
```

7. Fit the logistic regression model to the training data using **model.fit(X_train, y_train)**. We should get the following output:

```
LogisticRegression(C=1.0, class_weight=None, dual=False, fit_intercept=True,
          intercept_scaling=1, max_iter=100, multi_class='warn',
          n_jobs=None, penalty='l2', random_state=None, solver='warn',
          tol=0.0001, verbose=0, warm_start=False)
```

Figure 3.14: The output from fitting a logistic regression model

8. Get the intercept using the following:

```
intercept = model.intercept_
```

9. Extract the coefficients using the following:

```
coefficients = model.coef_
```

10. Place the coefficients into a list as follows:

```
coef_list = list(coefficients[0,:])
```

11. Match features to their coefficients, place them in a DataFrame, and print the DataFrame to the console as follows:

```
coef_df = pd.DataFrame({'Feature': list(X_train.columns),
                        'Coefficient': coef_list})
print(coef_df)
```

Refer to the resultant output here:

	Feature	Coefficient
0	Temperature_c	5.691326
1	Humidity	-0.165325
2	Wind_Speed_kmh	-0.067057
3	Wind_Bearing_degrees	-0.002367
4	Visibility_km	0.055192
5	Pressure_millibars	0.000845
6	Description_Normal	0.029056
7	Description_Warm	0.001911

Figure 3.15: Features and their coefficients from the logistic regression model

The coefficient for temperature can be interpreted as for every 1-degree increase in temperature, the log odds of rain increase by 5.69, controlling for all other features in the model. To generate predictions, we could convert the log odds to odds and the odds to probability. However, scikit-learn has functionality to generate predicted probability, as well as predicted classes.

Exercise 26: Generating Predictions and Evaluating the Performance of a Logistic Regression Model

In *Exercise* 25, we learned how to fit a logistic regression model and extract the elements necessary to generate predictions. However, scikit-learn makes our lives much easier by providing us with functions to predict the probability of an outcome, as well as the classes of an outcome. In this exercise, we will learn to generate predicted probabilities and classes, as well as evaluating a model performance using a confusion matrix and a classification report.

Continuing from Exercise 25, perform the following steps:

1. Generate predicted probabilities using the following code:

```
predicted_prob = model.predict_proba(X_test)[:,1]
```

2. Generate predicted classes using the following:

```
predicted_class = model.predict(X_test)
```

3. Evaluate a performance using a confusion matrix as follows:

```
from sklearn.metrics import confusion_matrix
import numpy as np

cm = pd.DataFrame(confusion_matrix(y_test, predicted_class))
cm['Total'] = np.sum(cm, axis=1)
```

```
cm = cm.append(np.sum(cm, axis=0), ignore_index=True)
cm.columns = ['Predicted No', 'Predicted Yes', 'Total']
cm = cm.set_index([['Actual No', 'Actual Yes', 'Total']])
print(cm)
```

Refer to the resultant output here:

```
            Predicted No  Predicted Yes  Total
Actual No            377              6    383
Actual Yes            10           2907   2917
Total                387           2913   3300
```

Figure 3.16: The confusion matrix from our logistic regression model

> **Note**
>
> From the confusion matrix, we can see that, of the 383 observations that were not classified as rainy, 377 of them were correctly classified, and of the 2917 observations that were classified as rainy, 2907 of them were correctly classified. To further inspect our model's performance using metrics such as precision, recall, and f1-score, we will generate a classification report.

4. Generate a classification report using the following code:

```
from sklearn.metrics import classification_report

print(classification_report(y_test, predicted_class))
```

Refer to the resultant output:

```
              precision    recall  f1-score   support

           0       0.97      0.98      0.98       383
           1       1.00      1.00      1.00      2917

   micro avg       1.00      1.00      1.00      3300
   macro avg       0.99      0.99      0.99      3300
weighted avg       1.00      1.00      1.00      3300
```

Figure 3.17: The classification report generated from our logistic regression model

As we can see from our confusion matrix and classification report, our model is performing very well and may be difficult to improve upon. However, machine learning models including logistic regression consist of numerous hyperparameters that can be adjusted to further improve model performance. In the next exercise, we will learn to find the optimal combination of hyperparameters to maximize model performance.

Exercise 27: Tuning the Hyperparameters of a Multiple Logistic Regression Model

In *step* 7 of *Exercise* 25, we fit a logistic regression model and the subsequent output from that model is displayed in Figure 3.14. Each of those arguments inside the **`LogisticRegression()`** function is set to a default hyperparameter. To tune the model, we will use scikit-learn's grid search function, which fits a model for every combination of possible hyperparameter values and determines the value for each hyperparameter resulting in the best model. In this exercise, we will learn how to use grid search to tune models.

Continuing from *Exercise* 26:

1. The data has already been prepared for us (see Exercise 26); thus, we can jump right into instantiating a grid of possible hyperparameter values as follows:

```
import numpy as np

grid = {'penalty': ['l1', 'l2'],
        'C': np.linspace(1, 10, 10),
        'solver': ['liblinear']}
```

2. Instantiate a grid search model to find the model with the greatest **`f1`** score (that is, the harmonic average of precision and recall) as follows:

```
from sklearn.model_selection import GridSearchCV
from sklearn.linear_model import LogisticRegression

model = GridSearchCV(LogisticRegression(solver='liblinear'), grid,
scoring='f1', cv=5)
```

3. Fit the model on the training using **model.fit(X_train, y_train)** (keep in mind, this may take a while) and find the resultant output here:

```
GridSearchCV(cv=5, error_score='raise-deprecating',
       estimator=LogisticRegression(C=1.0, class_weight=None, dual=False, fit_intercept=True,
          intercept_scaling=1, max_iter=100, multi_class='warn',
          n_jobs=None, penalty='l2', random_state=None, solver='liblinear',
          tol=0.0001, verbose=0, warm_start=False),
       fit_params=None, iid='warn', n_jobs=None,
       param_grid={'penalty': ['l1', 'l2'], 'C': array([ 1.,  2.,  3.,  4.,  5.,  6.,  7.,  8.,  9., 10.])},
       pre_dispatch='2*n_jobs', refit=True, return_train_score='warn',
       scoring='f1', verbose=0)
```

Figure 3.18: The output from our logistic regression grid search model

4. We can return the optimal combination of hyperparameters as a dictionary as follows:

```
best_parameters = model.best_params_
print(best_parameters)
```

Refer to the resultant output here:

```
{'C': 6.0, 'penalty': 'l1'}
```

Figure 3.19: The tuned hyperparameters from our logistic regression grid search model

We have found the combination of hyperparameters that maximizes the **f1** score. Remember, simply using the default hyperparameters in *Exercise* 25 resulted in a model that performed very well on the test data. Thus, in the following activity, we will evaluate how the model with tuned hyperparameters performed on the test data.

Activity 6: Generating Predictions and Evaluating Performance of a Tuned Logistic Regression Model

Once the best combination of hyperparameters has been converged upon, we need to evaluate model performance much like we did in *Exercise* 25.

Continuing from Exercise 27:

1. Generate the predicted probabilities of rain.
2. Generate the predicted class of rain.
3. Evaluate performance with a confusion matrix and store it as a DataFrame.

4. Print a classification report.

> **Note**
>
> The solution for this activity can be found on page 346.

By tuning the hyperparameters of the logistic regression model, we were able to improve upon a logistic regression model that was already performing very well. We will continue to expand upon tuning different types of models in the following exercises and activities.

Max Margin Classification Using SVMs

SVM is an algorithm for supervised learning that solves both classification and regression problems. However, SVM is most commonly used in classification problems, so, for the purposes of this chapter, we will focus on SVM as a binary classifier. The goal of SVM is to determine the best location of a hyperplane that create a class boundary between data points plotted on a multidimensional space. To help clarify this concept, refer to Figure 3.20.

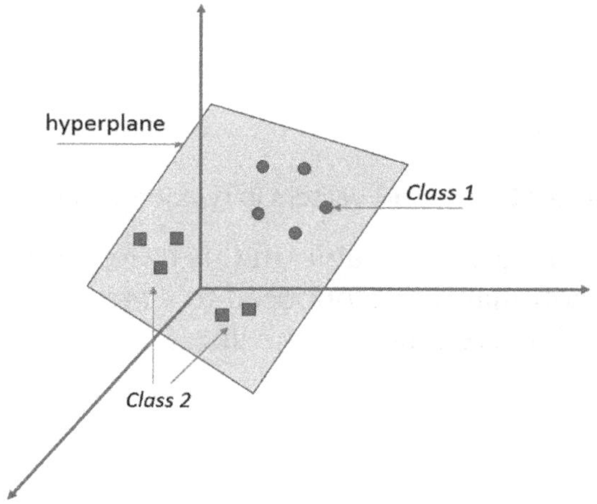

Figure 3.20: Hyperplane (blue) separating the circles from the squares in three dimensions

In Figure 3.20, the squares and circles are observations in the same DataFrame that represent different classes. In this figure, the hyperplane is depicted by a semi-transparent blue boundary lying between the circles and squares that separate the observations into two distinct classes. In this example, the observations are said to be linearly separable.

The location of the hyperplane is determined by finding the position that creates the maximum separation (that is, margin) between the two classes. Thus, this is referred to as the **Maximum Margin Hyperplane** (MMH) and improves the likelihood that the points will remain on the correct side of the hyperplane boundary. It is possible to express the MMH using the points from each class that are closest to the MMH. These points are termed support vectors and each class has at least 1. Figure 3.21 visually depicts the support vectors in relation to the MMH in 2 dimensions:

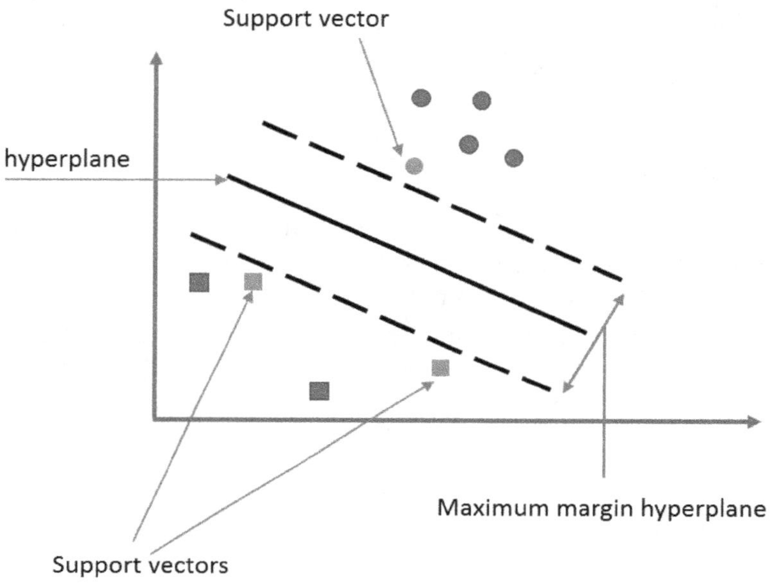

Figure 3.21: Support vectors in relation to the MMH

In reality, most data is not linearly separable. In this case, SVM makes use of a slack variable, which creates a soft margin (as opposed to a maximum margin), allowing some observations to fall on the incorrect side of the line. See the following plot:

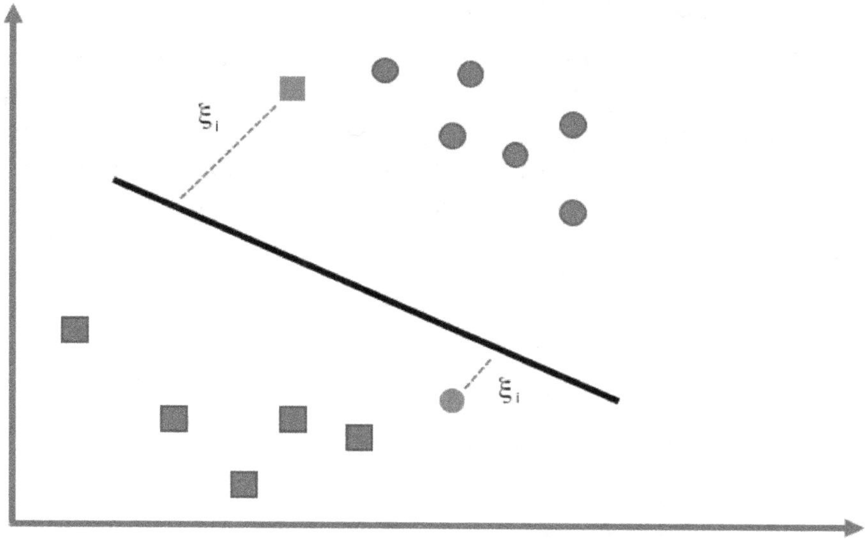

Figure 3.22: 2 observations (as denoted with grey shading and the Greek letter Xi) fall on the incorrect side of the soft margin line

A cost value is applied to the misclassified data points and, instead of finding the maximum margin, the algorithm minimizes the total cost. As the cost parameter increases, a harder SVM optimization will go for 100% separation and may overfit the training data. Conversely, lower cost parameters emphasize a wider margin and may underfit the training data. Thus, to create SVM models that perform well on the test data, it is important to determine a cost parameter that balances overfitting and underfitting.

Additionally, data that is not linearly separable can be transformed into a higher-dimension space using the kernel trick. After this mapping to a higher-dimensional space, a nonlinear relationship can appear linear. By transforming the original data, SVM can discover associations not explicitly apparent in the original features. scikit-learn uses the Gaussian RBF kernel by default, but comes equipped with common kernels such as linear, polynomial, and sigmoid as well. In order to maximize the performance of an SVM classifier model, the optimal combination of the kernel and cost function must be determined. Luckily, this can be easily achieved using grid search hyperparameter tuning, as introduced in Exercise 27. In the following exercises and activities, we will learn how this feat is accomplished.

Exercise 28: Preparing Data for the Support Vector Classifier (SVC) Model

Before fitting an SVM classifier model to predict a binary outcome variable; in this case, rain or snow, we must prepare our data. Since SVM is a black box, meaning the processes between input and output are not explicit, we do not need to worry about interpretability. Thus, we will transform the features in our data into z-scores prior to fitting the model. The following steps will show how to do this:

1. Import **weather.csv** using the following code:

```
import pandas as pd

df = pd.read_csv('weather.csv')
```

2. Dummy code the categorical feature, **Description**, as follows:

```
import pandas as pd

df_dummies = pd.get_dummies(df, drop_first=True)
```

3. Shuffle **df_dummies** to remove any ordering effects using the code here:

```
from sklearn.utils import shuffle

df_shuffled = shuffle(df_dummies, random_state=42)
```

4. Split **df_shuffled** into **X** and **y** using the following code:

```
DV = 'Rain'
X = df_shuffled.drop(DV, axis=1)
y = df_shuffled[DV]
```

5. Split **X** and **y** into testing and training data using the code here:

```
from sklearn.model_selection import train_test_split

X_train, X_test, y_train, y_test = train_test_split(X, y, test_size=0.33,
random_state=42)
```

6. To prevent any data leakage, scale **X_train** and **X_test** by fitting a scaler model to **X_train** and transforming them to z-scores separately, as follows:

```
from sklearn.preprocessing import StandardScaler

model = StandardScaler()
X_train_scaled = model.fit_transform(X_train)
X_test_scaled = model.transform(X_test)
```

Now that our data has been properly divided into features and outcome variables, split into testing and training data, and scaled separately, we can tune the hyperparameters of our SVC model using a grid search.

Exercise 29: Tuning the SVC Model Using Grid Search

Previously, we discussed the importance of determining the optimal cost function and kernel for SVM classifier models. In Exercise 27, we learned how to find the optimal combination of hyperparameters using scikit-learn's grid search function. In this exercise, we will demonstrate using grid search to find the best combination of the cost function and kernel.

Continuing from *Exercise 28*:

1. Instantiate the grid for which to search using the following code:

```
import numpy as np

grid = {'C': np.linspace(1, 10, 10),
        'kernel': ['linear', 'poly', 'rbf', 'sigmoid']}
```

2. Instantiate the **GridSearchCV** model with the **gamma** hyperparameter set to **auto** to avoid warnings, and set probability to **True** so we can extract probability of rain as follows:

```
from sklearn.model_selection import GridSearchCV
from sklearn.svm import SVC

model = GridSearchCV(SVC(gamma='auto'), grid, scoring='f1', cv=5)
```

3. Fit the grid search model using **model.fit(X_train_scaled, y_train)**:

```
GridSearchCV(cv=5, error_score='raise-deprecating',
       estimator=SVC(C=1.0, cache_size=200, class_weight=None, coef0=0.0,
  decision_function_shape='ovr', degree=3, gamma='auto', kernel='rbf',
  max_iter=-1, probability=False, random_state=None, shrinking=True,
  tol=0.001, verbose=False),
       fit_params=None, iid='warn', n_jobs=None,
       param_grid={'C': array([ 1.,  2.,  3.,  4.,  5.,  6.,  7.,  8.,  9., 10.]), 'kernel': ['linear', 'poly', 'rbf',
'sigmoid']},
       pre_dispatch='2*n_jobs', refit=True, return_train_score='warn',
       scoring='f1', verbose=0)
```

Figure 3.23: The output from fitting the SVC grid search model

4. Print the best parameters using the following code:

```
best_parameters = model.best_params_
print(best_parameters)
```

See the resultant output below:

```
{'C': 1.0, 'kernel': 'linear'}
```

Figure 3.24: Tuned hyperparameters for our SVC grid search model

Once the optimal combination of hyperparameters has been determined, it is time to generate predictions and subsequently evaluate how our model performed on the unseen test data.

Activity 7: Generating Predictions and Evaluating the Performance of the SVC Grid Search Model

In previous exercises/activities, we learned to generate predictions and evaluate classifier model performance. In this activity we will, again, evaluate the performance of our model by generating predictions, creating a confusion matrix, and printing a classification report.

Continuing from Exercise 29:

1. Extract the predicted classes.
2. Create and print a confusion matrix.
3. Generate and print a classification report.

> **Note**
>
> The solution for this activity can be found on page 348.

Here, we demonstrated how to tune the hyperparameters of an SVC model using grid search. After tuning the SVC model, it did not perform as well as the tuned logistic regression model in predicting rain/snow. Additionally, SVC models are a **black box** in that they do not provide insight into the contribution of features on the outcome measure. In the upcoming *Decision Trees* section, we will introduce a different algorithm known as a decision tree, which uses a "*divide and conquer*" approach to generate predictions and offers a feature importance attribute for determining the importance of each feature on the outcome.

Decision Trees

Imagine we are considering changing jobs. We are weighing the pros and cons of prospective job opportunities and, after a few years of being in our current position, we start to realize the things that are important to us. However, not all aspects of a career are of equal importance. In fact, after being in the job for a few years, we decide that the most important aspect of a position is our interest in the projects we will be doing, followed by compensation, then work-related stress, trailed by commute time, and, lastly, benefits. We have just created the scaffolding of a cognitive decision tree. We can go into further detail by saying that we want a job where we are very interested in the allocated projects, paying at least $55k/year, with low work-related stress, a commute of under 30 minutes, and good dental insurance. Creating mental decision trees is a decision-making process we all utilize by nature and is one of the reasons why decision trees are one of the most widely used machine learning algorithms today.

In machine learning, decision trees use either *gini* impurity or *entropy* information gain as the criterion to measure the quality of a split. First, the decision tree algorithm determines the feature that maximizes the value indicating quality of a split. This becomes referred to as the root node, as it is the most important feature in the data. In the job offer mentioned earlier, being very interested in the prospective projects would be considered the root node. Taking into consideration the root node, the job opportunities are divided into those with very interesting projects and those without very interesting projects.

Next, each of these two categories are divided into the next most important feature, given the previous feature(s), and so on and so forth, until the potential jobs are identified as being of interest or not.

This approach is termed recursive partitioning, or "*divide and conquer*", because it continues the process of splitting and subsetting the data until the algorithm determines the subsets in the data as sufficiently homogenous, or:

- Nearly all the observations at the corresponding node have the same class (that is, purity).
- There are no further features in the data for which to split.
- The tree has reached the size limit decided upon a priori.

For example, if purity is determined by entropy, we must understand that entropy is a measure of randomness within a set of values. Decision trees operate by choosing the splits that minimize entropy (randomness) and, in turn, maximize information gain. Information gain is calculated as the difference in entropy between the split and all other following splits. The total entropy is then computed by taking the sum of the entropy in each partition, weighted by the proportion of observations in the partition. Luckily, scikit-learn provides us with a function that does all of this for us. In the following exercises and activities, we will implement the decision tree classifier model to predict whether it is raining or snowing, using the familiar **weather.csv** dataset.

Activity 8: Preparing Data for a Decision Tree Classifier

In this activity, we will prepare our data for a decision tree classifier model. Perform the following steps to complete the activity:

1. Import **weather.csv** and store it as a DataFrame
2. Dummy code the multi-level, categorical feature **Summary**
3. Shuffle the data to remove any possible order effects
4. Split the data into features and outcome
5. Further divide the features and outcome into testing and training data
6. Scale **X_train** and **X_test** using the following code:

```
from sklearn.preprocessing import StandardScaler
model = StandardScaler()
X_train_scaled = model.fit_transform(X_train)
X_test_scaled = model.transform(X_test)
```

> **Note**
>
> The solution for this activity can be found on page 349

In the following exercise, we will learn to tune and fit a decision tree classifier model..

Exercise 30: Tuning a Decision Tree Classifier Using Grid Search

In the current exercise, we will instantiate a hyperparameter space and tune the hyperparameters of a decision tree classifier using a grid search.

Continuing from *Activity* 8, perform the following steps:

1. Specify the hyperparameter space as follows:

```
import numpy as np

grid = {'criterion': ['gini', 'entropy'],
        'min_weight_fraction_leaf': np.linspace(0.0, 0.5, 10),
        'min_impurity_decrease': np.linspace(0.0, 1.0, 10),
        'class_weight': [None, 'balanced'],
'presort': [True, False]}Instantiate the GridSearchCV model
```

2. Instantiate a grid search model using the code here:

```
from sklearn.model_selection import GridSearchCV
from sklearn.tree import DecisionTreeClassifier

model = GridSearchCV(DecisionTreeClassifier(), grid, scoring='f1', cv=5)
```

3. Fit to the training set using the following:

```
model.fit(X_train_scaled, y_train)
```

See the resultant output displayed here:

```
GridSearchCV(cv=5, error_score='raise-deprecating',
       estimator=DecisionTreeClassifier(class_weight=None, criterion='gini', max_depth=None,
            max_features=None, max_leaf_nodes=None,
            min_impurity_decrease=0.0, min_impurity_split=None,
            min_samples_leaf=1, min_samples_split=2,
            min_weight_fraction_leaf=0.0, presort=False, random_state=None,
            splitter='best'),
       fit_params=None, iid='warn', n_jobs=None,
       param_grid={'criterion': ['gini', 'entropy'], 'min_weight_fraction_leaf': array([0.     , 0.05556, 0.11111,
0.16667, 0.22222, 0.27778, 0.33333,
       0.38889, 0.44444, 0.5    ]), 'min_impurity_decrease': array([0.     , 0.11111, 0.22222, 0.33333, 0.44444,
0.55556, 0.66667,
       0.77778, 0.88889, 1.     ]), 'class_weight': [None, 'balanced'], 'presort': [True, False]},
       pre_dispatch='2*n_jobs', refit=True, return_train_score='warn',
       scoring='f1', verbose=0)
```

Figure 3.25: The output from fitting our decision tree classifier grid search model

4. Print the tuned parameters:

```
best_parameters = model.best_params_
print(best_parameters)
```

See the resultant output below:

```
{'class_weight': None, 'criterion': 'gini', 'min_impurity_decrease': 0.0, 'min_weight_fraction_leaf': 0.0, 'presort': True}
```

Figure 3.26: The tuned hyperparameters for our decision tree classifier grid search model

We can see from Figure 3.26 that it used **gini** impurity as the criterion to measure the quality of a split. Further explanations of the hyperparameters are outside the scope of this chapter but can be found in the decision tree classifier scikit-learn documentation.

Remember, in practice, it is common for decision makers to ask how various features are affecting the predictions. In linear and logistic regression, the intercept and coefficient(s) make model predictions very transparent.

> **Note**
>
> Decision trees can also be very easy to interpret, as we can see where the decisions were made, but this requires an installation and proper configuration of Graphviz, as well as unscaled features.

Instead of plotting the tree in the following exercise, we will explore an attribute found in scitkit-learn's tree-based model algorithms, '`feature_importances_`', which returns an array containing values of relative feature importance for each feature. It is important to note that this attribute is unavailable from a grid search model. As a result, in the next exercise, we will learn to programmatically extract values from the `best_parameters` dictionary and re-fit the tuned decision tree model, allowing us to access the attributes provided by the decision tree classifier function.

Exercise 31: Programmatically Extracting Tuned Hyperparameters from a Decision Tree Classifier Grid Search Model

In the previous exercise, we saved the tuned hyperparameters as key value pairs in the `best_parameters` dictionary. This allows us to programmatically access the values and assign them to the appropriate hyperparameters of a decision tree classifier model. By fitting the tuned decision tree model, we will be able to access the attributes made available from the scikit-learn decision tree classifier function.

Continuing from *Exercise* 30, perform the following steps:

1. Prove that we can access the value for '**Tree_criterion**' using:

```
print(best_parameters['criterion'])
```

See the resultant output here:

```
gini
```

Figure 3.27: The value assigned to the 'Tree_criterion' key in the best_parameters dictionary

2. Instantiate decision tree classifier model and assign the values to the corresponding hyperparameters as follows:

```
from sklearn.tree import DecisionTreeClassifier

model = DecisionTreeClassifier(class_weight=best_parameters['class_
weight'],
                               criterion=best_parameters['criterion'],
                        min_impurity_decrease=best_parameters['min_impurity_
decrease'],
                  min_weight_fraction_leaf=best_parameters['min_weight_
fraction_leaf'],
                               presort=best_parameters['presort'])
```

3. Fit the grid search model to the scaled training data using the following:

```
model.fit(X_train_scaled, y_train)
```

```
DecisionTreeClassifier(class_weight=None, criterion='gini', max_depth=None,
            max_features=None, max_leaf_nodes=None,
            min_impurity_decrease=0.0, min_impurity_split=None,
            min_samples_leaf=1, min_samples_split=2,
            min_weight_fraction_leaf=0.0, presort=True, random_state=None,
            splitter='best')
```

Figure 3.28: The output from fitting the decision tree classifier model with tuned hyperparameters

4. Extract **feature_importances** attribute using:

```
print(model.feature_importances_)
The resultant output is shown below:
```

```
[1. 0. 0. 0. 0. 0. 0. 0.]
```

Figure 3.29: An array of feature importance from our tuned decision tree classifier model

From the array in Figure 3.29, we can see that the first feature completely dominated the other variables in terms of feature importance.

5. Visualize this using the following code:

```
import pandas as pd
import matplotlib.pyplot as plt

df_imp = pd.DataFrame({'Importance': list(model.feature_importances_)},
index=X.columns)
df_imp_sorted = df_imp.sort_values(by=('Importance'), ascending=True)
df_imp_sorted.plot.barh(figsize=(5,5))
plt.title('Relative Feature Importance')
plt.xlabel('Relative Importance')
plt.ylabel('Variable')
plt.legend(loc=4)
plt.show()
```

See the resultant output here:

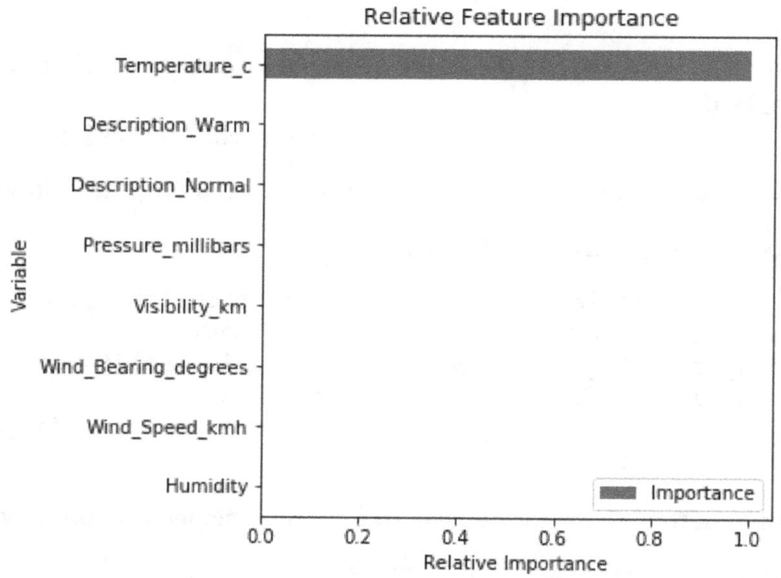

Figure 3.30: Feature importance from a tuned decision tree classifier model

It looks like temperature in Celsius was the sole driver in this classification problem. With the outcome measure being **rain ('Rain'=1)** or **snow ('Rain'=0)** and the way in which decision trees make split decisions via "*divide and conquer*," it makes sense that the algorithm used temperature to determine if there was rainfall or snowfall at the time of measurement. In the upcoming activity, we will evaluate how the model performed.

Activity 9: Generating Predictions and Evaluating the Performance of a Decision Tree Classifier Model

We have generated predictions and evaluated the model performance in previous exercises and activities. We will be taking the same approach in this activity to evaluate the performance of our tuned decision tree classifier model.

Continuing from Exercise 31, perform the following steps:

1. Generate the predicted probabilities of rain.
2. Generate the predicted classes of rain.
3. Generate and print a confusion matrix.
4. Print a classification report.

> **Note**
>
> The solution for this activity can be found on page 350.

You should find that there was only one misclassified observation. Thus, by tuning a decision tree classifier model on our `weather.csv` dataset, we were able to predict rain (or snow) with great accuracy. We can see that the sole driving feature was temperature in Celsius. This makes sense due to the way in which decision trees use recursive partitioning to make predictions.

Sometimes, after evaluation, a single model is a weak learner and does not perform well. However, by combining weak learners, we create a stronger learner. The approach of combining numerous weak learners to create a stronger learner is termed ensemble. Random forest models combine numerous decision tree models to create a stronger ensemble model. Random forests can be used for classification or regression problems.

Random Forests

As briefly mentioned earlier, random forests are ensembles of decision trees that can be used to solve classification or regression problems. Random forests use a small portion of the data to fit each tree, so they can handle very large datasets, and they are less prone to the "*curse of dimensionality*" relative to other algorithms. The curse of dimensionality is a situation in which an abundance of features in the data diminishes the performance of the model. Predictions of the random forest are then determined by combining the predictions of each tree. Like SVM, random forests are a **black box** with inputs and outputs which cannot be interpreted.

In the upcoming exercises and activities, we will tune and fit a random forest regressor using grid search to predict the temperature in Celsius. Then, we will evaluate the performance of the model.

Exercise 32: Preparing Data for a Random Forest Regressor

First, we will prepare the data for the random forest regressor with '**Temperature_c**' as the dependent variable, just as we did in Exercise 21:

1. Import '**weather.csv**' and save it as **df** using the following code:

```
import pandas as pd

df = pd.read_csv('weather.csv')
```

2. Dummy code the multi-class, categorical variable, Description, as follows:

```
import pandas as pd

df_dummies = pd.get_dummies(df, drop_first=True)
```

3. Remove any possible ordering effects by shuffling **df_dummies** using the following code:

```
from sklearn.utils import shuffle

df_shuffled = shuffle(df_dummies, random_state=42)
```

4. Split **df_shuffled** into **X** and **y** using the following code:

```
DV = 'Temperature_c'
X = df_shuffled.drop(DV, axis=1)
y = df_shuffled[DV]
```

5. Split **X** and **y** into testing and training data as follows:

```
from sklearn.model_selection import train_test_split

X_train, X_test, y_train, y_test = train_test_split(X, y, test_size=0.33,
random_state=42)
```

6. Scale **X_train** and **X_test** using the code here:

```
from sklearn.preprocessing import StandardScaler

scaler = StandardScaler()
X_train_scaled = scaler.fit_transform(X_train)
X_test_scaled = scaler.transform(X_test)
```

Now that we have imported, shuffled, separated our data into features (**X**) and dependent variable (**y**), split **X** and **y** into testing and training data, and scaled **X_train** and **X_test**, we will tune a random forest regressor model using grid search.

Activity 10: Tuning a Random Forest Regressor

The data has been prepared for inclusion in a random forest regressor. Now, we must set up the hyperparameter space and find the optimal combination of hyperparameters using a grid search.

Continuing from Exercise 32, perform the following steps:

1. Specify the hyperparameter space.
2. Instantiate the **GridSearchCV** model optimizing the explained variance.
3. Fit the grid search model to the training set.
4. Print the tuned parameters.

> **Note**
>
> The solution for this activity can be found on page 351.

After performing a grid search of our random forest regressor hyperparameters, we need to fit a random forest regressor model with the tuned hyperparameters. We will programmatically extract the values in the **best_parameters** dictionary and assign them to the corresponding hyperparameters in the random forest regressor function, so we can access the attributes from the random forest regressor function.

Exercise 33: Programmatically Extracting Tuned Hyperparameters and Determining Feature Importance from a Random Forest Regressor Grid Search Model

By extracting the value from the key-value pairs in the **best_parameters** dictionary, we eliminate the possibility of manual errors, as well as make our code more automated. In this exercise, we will replicate the steps from *Exercise 31*, but will adapt our code for the random forest regressor model.

Continuing from *Activity 10*, perform the following steps:

1. Instantiate a random forest regressor model with the values for each key from the **best_parameters** dictionary assigned to the corresponding hyperparameter:

```
from sklearn.ensemble import RandomForestRegressor

model = RandomForestRegressor(criterion=best_parameters['criterion'],
                              max_features=best_parameters['max_
features'],
                              min_impurity_decrease=best_parameters['min_
impurity_decrease'],
                              bootstrap=best_parameters['bootstrap'],
                              warm_start=best_parameters['warm_start'])
```

2. Fit the model on the training data using the following:

```
model.fit(X_train_scaled, y_train)
```

Find the resultant output here:

```
RandomForestRegressor(bootstrap=True, criterion='mae', max_depth=None,
           max_features=None, max_leaf_nodes=None,
           min_impurity_decrease=0.0, min_impurity_split=None,
           min_samples_leaf=1, min_samples_split=2,
           min_weight_fraction_leaf=0.0, n_estimators=10, n_jobs=None,
           oob_score=False, random_state=None, verbose=0, warm_start=True)
```

Figure 3.31: The output from fitting the random forest regressor model with tuned hyperparameters

3. Plot feature importance in descending order using the following code:

```
import pandas as pd
import matplotlib.pyplot as plt

df_imp = pd.DataFrame({'Importance': list(model.feature_importances_)},
index=X.columns)
df_imp_sorted = df_imp.sort_values(by=('Importance'), ascending=True)
```

```
df_imp_sorted.plot.barh(figsize=(5,5))
plt.title('Relative Feature Importance')
plt.xlabel('Relative Importance')
plt.ylabel('Variable')
plt.legend(loc=4)
plt.show()
```

See the resultant output here:

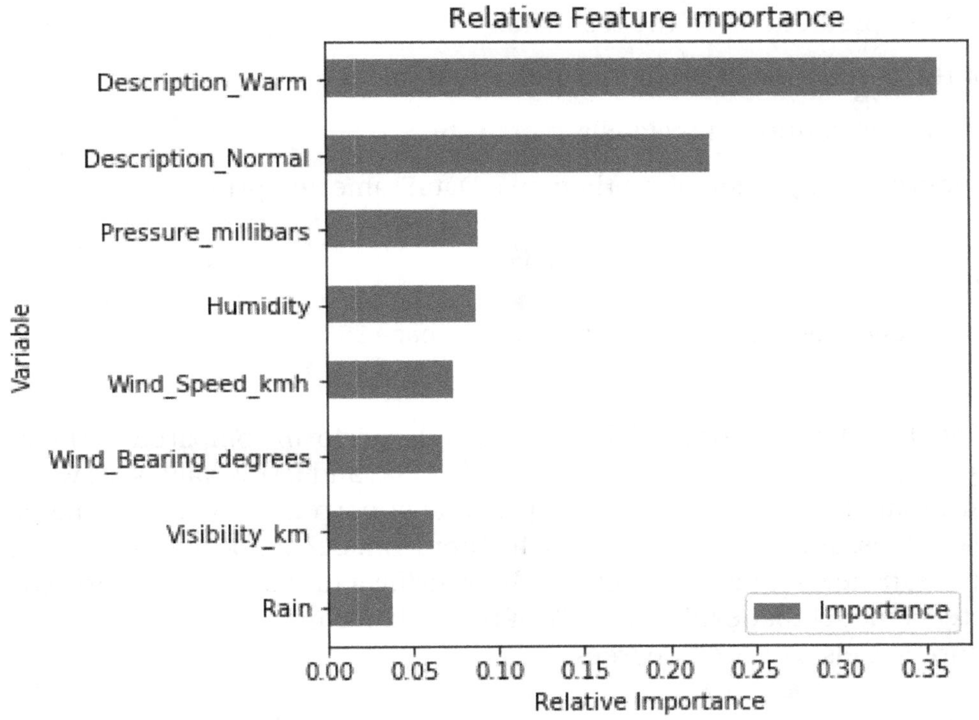

Figure 3.32: Feature importance from a random forest regressor model with tuned hyperparameters

From Figure 3.32, we can see that the '**Description_Warm**' dummy variable and '**Humidity**' are the main drivers of temperature in Celsius. Meanwhile, '**Visibility_km**' and '**Wind_Bearing_degrees**' have a small effect on the temperature. Let's now check to see how our model performs on the test data.

Activity 11: Generating Predictions and Evaluating the Performance of a Tuned Random Forest Regressor Model

In *Exercise* 23 and *Activity* 5, we learned to generate predictions and evaluate the performance of regression models that predict a continuous outcome. In this activity, we will be taking the same approach to evaluate the performance of our random forest regressor model to predict temperature in Celsius.

Continuing from *Exercise* 33, perform the following steps:

1. Generate predictions on the test data.
2. Plot the correlation of predicted and actual values.
3. Plot the distribution of residuals.
4. Compute metrics, then place them in a DataFrame and print it.

> **Note**
>
> The solution for this activity can be found on page 352.

The random forest regressor model seems to underperform compared to the multiple linear regression, as evidenced by greater MAE, MSE, and RMSE values, as well as less explained variance. Additionally, there was a weaker correlation between the predicted and actual values, and the residuals were further from being normally distributed. Nevertheless, by leveraging ensemble methods using a random forest regressor, we constructed a model that explains 75.8% of the variance in -temperature and predicts temperature in Celsius ± 3.781 degrees.

Summary

In this chapter, we were introduced to the open source machine learning library for Python, scikit-learn. You learned to preprocess data, as well as how to tune and fit a few different regression and classification algorithms. Lastly, you learned how to quickly and effectively evaluate the performance of classification and regression models. This was a very comprehensive introduction to the scikit-learn library, and the strategies employed here can be applied to building numerous additional algorithms provided by scikit-learn.

In the next chapter, you will learn about dimensionality reduction and unsupervised learning.

4

Dimensionality Reduction and Unsupervised Learning

Learning Objectives

By the end of this chapter, you will be able to:

- Compare hierarchical cluster analysis (HCA) and k-means clustering
- Conduct an HCA and interpret the output
- Tune a number of clusters for k-means clustering
- Select an optimal number of principal components for dimension reduction
- Perform supervised dimension compression using linear discriminant function analysis (LDA)

This chapter will cover various concepts that fall under dimensionality reduction and unsupervised learning.

Introduction

In unsupervised learning, **descriptive models** are used for exploratory analysis to uncover patterns in unlabeled data. Examples of unsupervised learning tasks include algorithms for **clustering** and those for **dimension reduction**. In clustering, observations are assigned to groups in which there is high within-group homogeneity and between-group heterogeneity. Simply put, observations are placed into clusters of samples with other observations that are very similar. Use cases for clustering algorithms are vast. For example, analysts seeking to elevate sales by targeting selected customers for marketing advertisements and promotions separate customers by their shopping behavior.

> **Note**
>
> Additionally, hierarchical clustering has been implemented in academic neuroscience and motor behavior research (https://www.researchgate.net/profile/Ming-Yang_Cheng/project/The-Effect-of-SMR-Neurofeedback-Training-on-Mental-Representation-and-Golf-Putting-Performance/attachment/57c8419808aeef0362ac36a5/AS:401522300080128@1472741784217/download/Schack+-+2012+-+Measuring+mental+representations.pdf?context=ProjectUpdatesLog) and k-means clustering has been used in fraud detection (https://www.semanticscholar.org/paper/Fraud-Detection-in-Credit-Card-by-Clustering-Tech/3e98a9ac78b5b89944720c2b428ebf3e46d9950f).

However, when building descriptive or predictive models, it can be a challenge to determine which features to include in a model to improve it, and which features to exclude because they diminish a model. Too many features can be troublesome because the greater the number of variables in a model, the higher the probability of multicollinearity and subsequent overfitting of a model. Additionally, numerous features expand the complexity of a model and increase the time for model tuning and fitting.

This becomes troublesome with larger datasets. Fortunately, another use case for unsupervised learning is to reduce the number of features in a dataset by creating combinations of the original features. Reducing the number of features in data helps eliminate multicollinearity and converges on a combination of features to best produce a model that performs well on unseen test data.

> **Note**
>
> Multicollinearity is a situation in which at least two variables are correlated. It is a problem in linear regression models because it does not allow the isolation of the relationship between each independent variable and the outcome measure. Thus, coefficients and p-values become unstable and less precise.

In this chapter, we will be covering two widely used unsupervised clustering algorithms: *Hierarchical Cluster Analysis* (HCA) and *k-means clustering*. Additionally, we will explore dimension reduction using *principal component analysis* (PCA) and observe how reducing dimensionality can improve model performance. Lastly, we will implement linear discriminant function analysis (LDA) for supervised dimensionality reduction.

Hierarchical Cluster Analysis (HCA)

Hierarchical cluster analysis (HCA) is best implemented when the user does not have a priori number of clusters to build. Thus, it is a common approach to use HCA as a precursor to other clustering techniques where a predetermined number of clusters is recommended. HCA works by merging observations that are similar into clusters and continues merging clusters that are closest in proximity until all observations are merged into a single cluster.

HCA determines similarity as the Euclidean distance between and among observations and creates links at the distance in which the two points lie.

With the number of features indicated by n, the Euclidean distance is calculated using the formula:

$$\mathrm{dist}(\mathrm{x},\mathrm{y}) = \sqrt{\sum_{i=1}^{n} (x_i - y_i)^2}$$

Figure 4.1: The Euclidean distance

After the distance between observations and cluster have been calculated, the relationships between and among all observations are displayed using a dendrogram. Dendrograms are tree-like structures displaying horizontal lines as the distance between links.

Dr. Thomas Schack (https://www.researchgate.net/profile/Ming-Yang_Cheng/project/The-Effect-of-SMR-Neurofeedback-Training-on-Mental-Representation-and-Golf-Putting-Performance/attachment/57c8419808aeef0362ac36a5/AS:401522300080128@1472741784217/download/Schack+-+2012+-+Measuring+mental+representations.pdf?context=ProjectUpdatesLog) relates this structure to the human brain in which each observation is a node and the links between observations are neurons.

This creates a hierarchical structure in which items that are closely related are "chunked" together into clusters. An example dendrogram is displayed here:

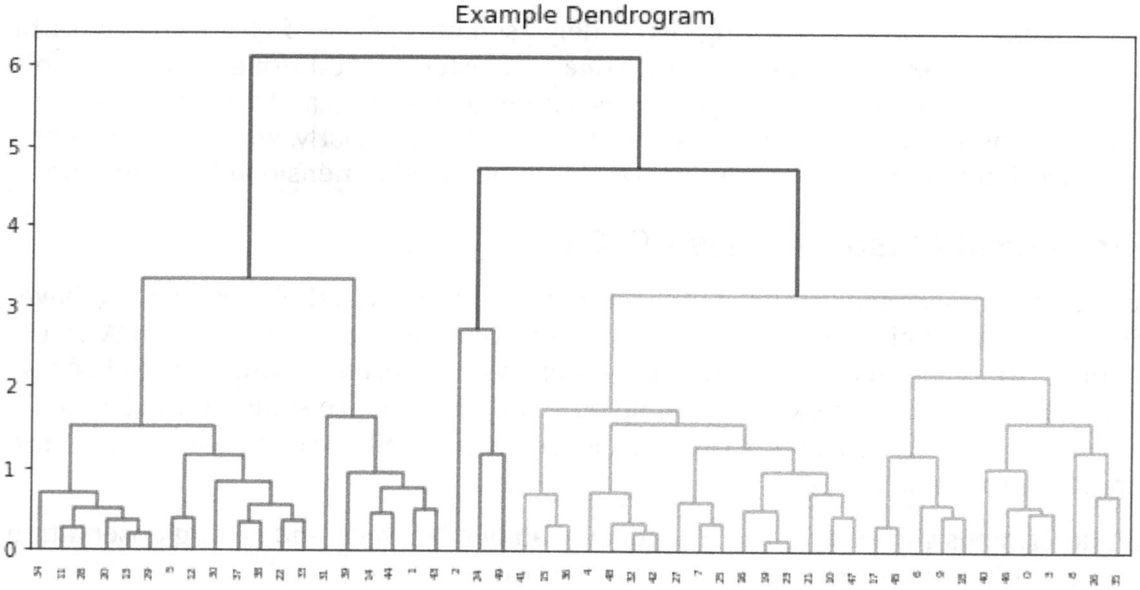

Figure 4.2: An example dendrogram

The y-axis indicates the Euclidean distance, while the x-axis indicates the row index for each observation. Horizontal lines denote links between observations; links closer to the x-axis indicate shorter distance and a subsequent closer relationship. In this example, there appear to be three clusters. The first cluster includes observations colored in green, the second cluster includes observations colored in red, and the third cluster includes observations colored in turquoise.

Exercise 34: Building an HCA Model

To demonstrate HCA, we will be use an adapted version of the glass dataset from the University of California – Irvine (https://github.com/TrainingByPackt/Data-Science-with-Python/tree/master/Chapter04). This data contains 218 observations and 9 features corresponding to the percent weight of various oxides found in glass:

- RI: refractive index
- Na: weight percent in sodium
- Mg: weight percent in magnesium
- Al: weight percent in aluminum
- Si: weight percent in silicon
- K: weight percent in potassium
- Ca: weight percent in calcium
- Ba: weight percent in barium
- Fe: weight percent in iron

In this exercise, we will use the refractive index (RI) and weight percent in each oxide to segment the glass type.

1. To get started, we will import pandas and read the **glass.csv** file using the following code:

```
import pandas as pd

df = pd.read_csv('glass.csv')
```

2. Look for some basic data frame information by printing **df.info()** to the console using the following code:

```
print(df.info()):
```

```
<class 'pandas.core.frame.DataFrame'>
RangeIndex: 218 entries, 0 to 217
Data columns (total 9 columns):
RI     218 non-null float64
Na     218 non-null float64
Mg     218 non-null float64
Al     218 non-null float64
Si     218 non-null float64
K      218 non-null float64
Ca     218 non-null float64
Ba     218 non-null float64
Fe     218 non-null float64
dtypes: float64(9)
memory usage: 15.4 KB
None
```

Figure 4.3: DataFrame information

3. To remove any possible order effects in the data, we will shuffle the rows prior to building any models and save it as a new data frame object, as follows:

```
from sklearn.utils import shuffle

df_shuffled = shuffle(df, random_state=42)
```

4. Transform each observation into a z-score by fitting and transforming shuffled data using:

```
from sklearn.preprocessing import StandardScaler

scaler = StandardScaler()
scaled_features = scaler.fit_transform(df_shuffled)
```

5. Perform hierarchical clustering using the linkage function on **scaled_features**. The following code will show you how:

```
from scipy.cluster.hierarchy import linkage
model = linkage(scaled_features, method='complete')
```

Congratulations! You've successfully built an HCA model.

Exercise 35: Plotting an HCA Model and Assigning Predictions

Now that the HCA model has been built, we will continue with the analysis by visualizing clusters using a dendrogram and using the visualization to generate predictions.

1. Display the dendrogram by plotting the linkage model as follows:

```
import matplotlib.pyplot as plt
from scipy.cluster.hierarchy import dendrogram


plt.figure(figsize=(10,5))
plt.title('Dendrogram for Glass Data')
dendrogram(model, leaf_rotation=90, leaf_font_size=6)
plt.show()
```

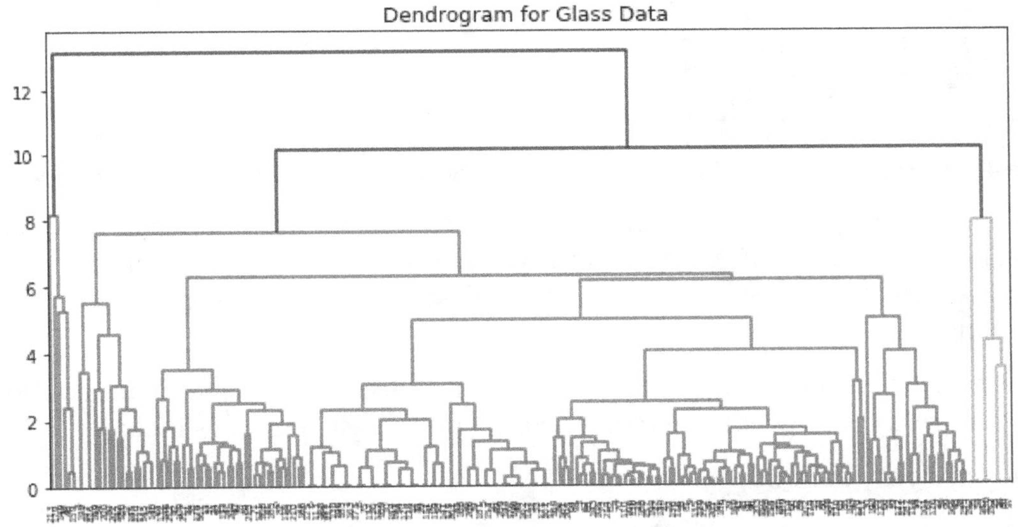

Figure 4.4: Dendogram for glass data

> **Note**
>
> The index for each observation or row in a dataset is on the x-axis. The Euclidean distance is on the y-axis. Horizontal lines are links between and among observations. By default, scipy will color code the different clusters that it finds.

Now that we have the predicted clusters of observations, we can use the **fcluster** function to generate an array of labels that correspond to rows in **df_shuffled**.

2. Generate predicted labels of the cluster which an observation belongs to using the following code:

```
from scipy.cluster.hierarchy import fcluster

labels = fcluster(model, t=9, criterion='distance')
```

3. Add the labels array as a column in the shuffled data and preview the first five rows using the following code:

```
df_shuffled['Predicted_Cluster'] = labels
print(df_shuffled.head(5))
```

4. Check the output in the following figure:

	RI	Na	Mg	...	Ba	Fe	Predicted_Cluster
100	1.51655	12.75	2.85	...	0.11	0.22	2
215	1.51640	14.37	0.00	...	0.54	0.00	2
139	1.51674	12.87	3.56	...	0.00	0.00	2
178	1.52247	14.86	2.20	...	0.00	0.00	2
15	1.51761	12.81	3.54	...	0.00	0.00	2

Figure 4.5: The first five rows of df_shuffled after predictions have been matched to observations.

We have successfully learned the difference between supervised and unsupervised learning, how to build an HCA model, how to visualize and interpret the HCA dendrogram, and how to assign the predicted cluster label to the appropriate observation.

Here, we have utilized HCA to cluster our data into three groups and matched the observations with their predicted cluster. Some pros of HCA models include:

- They are easy to build
- There is no need to specify the number of clusters in advance
- Visualizations are easy to interpret

However, some drawbacks of HCA include:

- Vagueness in terms of the termination criteria (that is, when to finalize the number of clusters)
- The algorithm cannot adjust once the clustering decisions have been made
- Can be very computationally expensive to build HCA models on large datasets with many features

Next, we will introduce you to another clustering algorithm, k-means clustering. This algorithm addresses some of the HCA shortcomings by having the ability to adjust when the clusters have been initially generated. It is more computationally frugal than HCA.

K-means Clustering

Like HCA, K-means also uses distance to assign observations into clusters not labeled in data. However, rather than linking observations to each other as in HCA, k-means assigns observations to *k* (user-defined number) clusters.

To determine the cluster to which each observation belongs, k cluster centers are randomly generated, and observations are assigned to the cluster in which its Euclidean distance is closest to the cluster center. Like the starting weights in artificial neural networks, cluster centers are initialized at random. After cluster centers have been randomly generated there are two phases:

- Assignment phase
- Updating phase

> **Note**
>
> The randomly generated cluster centers are important to remember, and we will be visiting it later in this chapter. Some refer to this random generation of cluster centers as a weakness of the algorithm, because results vary between fitting the same model on the same data, and it is not guaranteed to assign observations to the appropriate cluster. We can turn it into an advantage by leveraging the power of loops.

In the assignment phase, observations are assigned to the cluster from which it has the smallest Euclidean distance, as shown in the following figure:

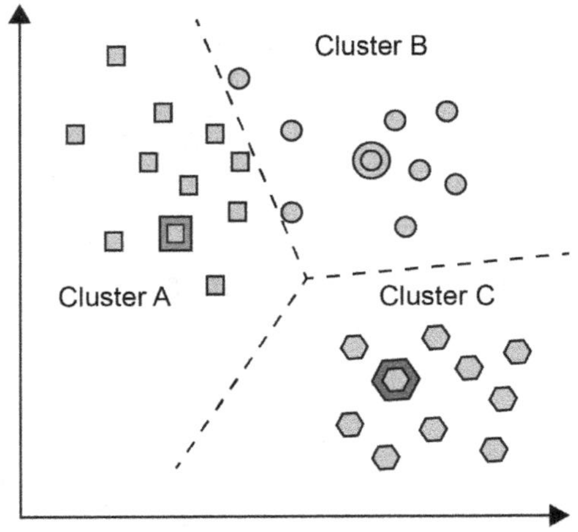

Figure 4.6: A scatterplot of observations and the cluster centers as denoted by the star, triangle, and diamond.

Next, in the updating phase, cluster centers are shifted to the mean position of the points in that cluster. These cluster means are known as the centroids, as shown in the following figure:

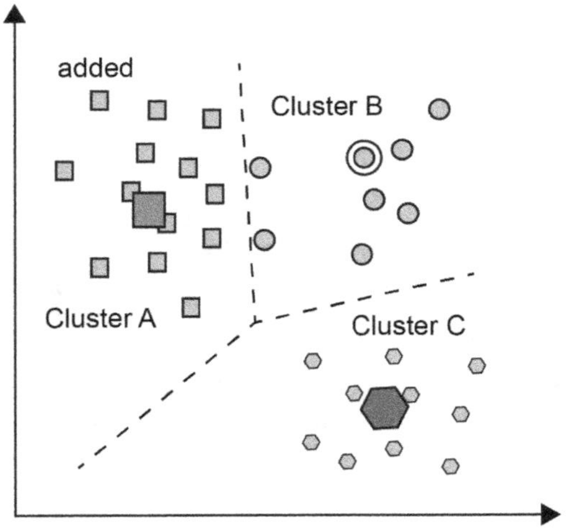

Figure 4.7: Shifting of the cluster centers to the cluster centroid.

However, once the centroids have been calculated, some of the observations are reassigned to a different cluster due to being closer to the new centroid than the previous cluster center. Thus, the model must update its centroids once again. This is shown in the following figure:

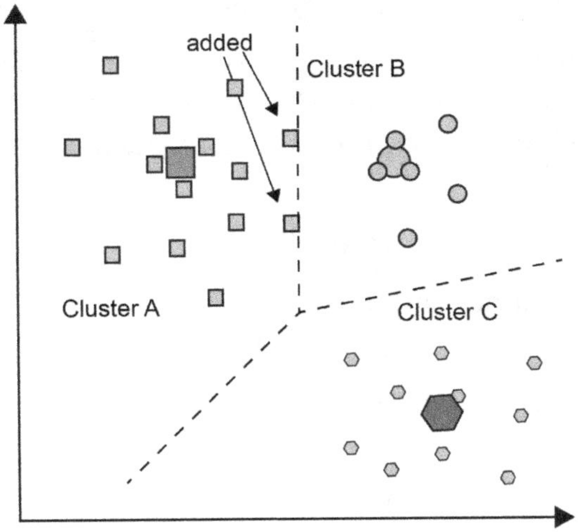

Figure 4.8: Updating of the centroids after observation reassignment.

This process of updating centroids continues until there are no further observation reassignments. The final centroid is shown in the following figure:

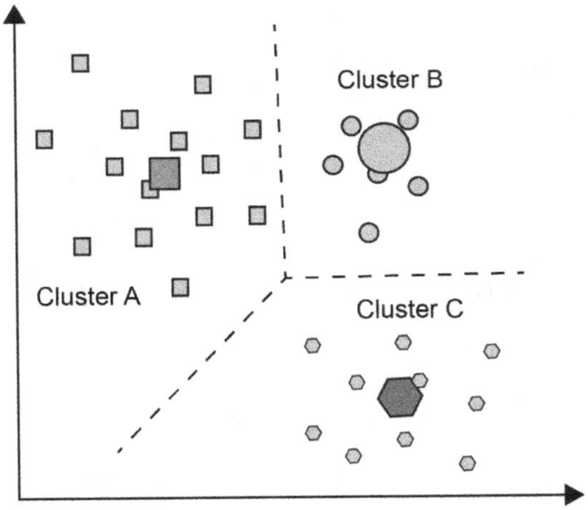

Figure 4.9: The final centroid position and cluster assignments.

Using the same glass dataset from *Exercise* 34, *Building an* HCA *Model*, we will fit a k-means model with user-defined number of clusters. Next, because of the randomness in which group centroids are chosen, we will increase the confidence in our predictions by building an ensemble of k-means models with a given number of clusters and assigning each observation to the mode of the predicted clusters. After that, we will tune the optimal number of clusters by monitoring the mean *inertia*, or within-cluster sum of squares, by number of clusters, and finding the point at which there are diminishing returns in inertia by adding more clusters.

Exercise 36: Fitting k-means Model and Assigning Predictions

Since our data has already been prepared (see *Exercise 34, Building an HCA Model*), and we understand concepts behind the k-Means algorithm, we will learn how easy it is to fit a k-means model, generate predictions, and assign these predictions to the appropriate observation.

After the glass dataset has been imported, shuffled, and standardized:

1. Instantiate a KMeans model with an arbitrary number of, in this case, two clusters, as follows:

    ```
    from sklearn.cluster import KMeans

    model = KMeans(n_clusters=2)
    ```

2. Fit the model to **scaled_features** using the following line of code:

    ```
    model.fit(scaled_features)
    ```

3. Save the cluster labels from our model into the array, labels, using the following:

    ```
    labels = model.labels_
    ```

4. Generate a frequency table of the labels:

    ```
    import pandas as pd

    pd.value_counts(labels)
    ```

    To get a better idea, refer to the following screenshot:

    ```
    1    157
    0     61
    dtype: int64
    ```

    Figure 4.10: Frequency table of two clusters

    Using two clusters, 61 observations were placed into the first cluster and 157 observations were grouped into the second cluster.

5. Add the labels array as the '**Predicted Cluster**' column into the **df_shuffled** data frame and preview the first five rows using the following code:

    ```
    df_shuffled['Predicted_Cluster'] = labels
    print(df_shuffled.head(5))
    ```

6. Check the output in the following figure:

```
          RI     Na    Mg      ...       Ba    Fe  Predicted_Cluster
100  1.51655  12.75  2.85      ...     0.11  0.22                  1
215  1.51640  14.37  0.00      ...     0.54  0.00                  0
139  1.51674  12.87  3.56      ...     0.00  0.00                  1
178  1.52247  14.86  2.20      ...     0.00  0.00                  1
15   1.51761  12.81  3.54      ...     0.00  0.00                  1
```

Figure 4.11: First five rows of df_shuffled

Activity 12: Ensemble k-means Clustering and Calculating Predictions

When algorithms use randomness as part of their method for finding the optimal solution (that is, in artificial neural networks and k-means clustering), running identical models on the same data may result in different conclusions, limiting the confidence we have in our predictions. It is advised to run these models many times and generate predictions using a summary measure across all models (that is, mean, median, and mode). In this activity, we will build an ensemble of 100 k-means clustering models.

After the glass dataset has been imported, shuffled, and standardized (see *Exercise 34*, *Building an HCA Model*):

1. Instantiate an empty data frame to append the labels for each model and save it as the new data frame object **labels_df**.
2. Using a for loop, iterate through 100 models, appending the predicted labels to **labels_df** as a new column at each iteration. Calculate the mode for each row in **labels_df** and save it as a new column in **labels_df**. The output should be as follows:

```
   Model_1_Labels  Model_2_Labels     ...      Model_100_Labels  row_mode
0               0               0     ...                     0         0
1               1               1     ...                     1         1
2               0               0     ...                     0         0
3               0               0     ...                     0         0
4               0               0     ...                     0         0

[5 rows x 101 columns]
```

Figure 4.12: First five rows of labels_df

> **Note**
>
> The solution for this activity can be found on page 356.

We have drastically increased the confidence in our predictions by iterating through numerous models, saving the predictions at each iteration, and assigning the final predictions as the mode of these predictions. However, these predictions were generated by models using a predetermined number of clusters. Unless we know the number of clusters a priori, we will want to discover the optimal number of clusters to segment our observations.

Exercise 37: Calculating Mean Inertia by n_clusters

The k-means algorithm groups observations into clusters by minimizing the within-cluster sum of squares, or inertia. Thus, to improve our confidence in the tuned number of clusters for our k-means model, we will place the loop we created in *Activity 12, Ensemble k-means Clustering and Calculating Predictions* (with a few minor adjustments) inside of another loop which will iterate through a range of **`n_clusters`**. This creates a nested loop which iterates through 10 possible values for **`n_clusters`** and builds 100 models at each iteration. At each of the 100 inner iterations, model inertia will be calculated. For each of the 10 outer iterations, mean inertia over the 100 models will be computed, resulting in the mean inertia value for each **`n_clusters`** value.

After the glass dataset has been imported, shuffled, and standardized (see *Exercise 34, Building an HCA Model*):

1. Import the packages we need outside of the loop as shown here:

```
from sklearn.cluster import KMeans
import numpy as np
```

2. It is easier to build and comprehend nested loops by working from the inside-out. First, instantiate an empty list, **`inertia_list`**, for which we will append inertia values after each iteration of the inside loop as shown here:

```
inertia_list = []
```

3. In the for loop, we will iterate through 100 models using the following code:

```
for i in range(100):
```

4. Inside the loop, build a **`KMeans`** model with **`n_clusters=x`**, as follows:

```
model = KMeans(n_clusters=x)
```

> **Note**
>
> The value for x is determined by the outer for loop, which we have not covered yet, but we will cover in detail very shortly.

5. Fit the model to **scaled_features** as shown here:

```
model.fit(scaled_features)
```

6. Get the inertia value and save it to the object inertia as follows:

```
inertia = model.inertia_
```

7. Append inertia to **inertia_list** using the following code:

```
inertia_list.append(inertia)
```

8. Move to the outside loop, instantiate another empty list to store the average inertia values, as shown here:

```
mean_inertia_list = []
```

9. Iterate through the values 1 through 10 for **n_clusters** using the following code:

```
for x in range(1, 11):
```

10. After the inside for loop has run through 100 iterations, and the inertia value for each of the 100 models have been appended to **inertia_list**, compute the mean of this list and save as the object, **mean_inertia** as follows:

```
mean_inertia = np.mean(inertia_list)
```

11. Append **mean_inertia** to **mean_inertia_list** as shown here:

```
mean_inertia_list.append(mean_inertia)
```

12. After 100 iterations have been completed 10 times for a total of 1000 iterations, **mean_inertia_list** contains 10 values that are the average inertia values for each value of **n_clusters**.

13. Print **mean_inertia_list** as shown in the following code. The values are shown in the following figure:

```
print(mean_inertia_list)
```

```
[1961.9999999999998, 1341.158072686119, 1013.183469500984, 856.6385685772449, 722.9110960360813,
603.1272461641258, 498.57219149636114, 450.03610411899103, 409.1821381484066, 373.0986488183049]
```

Figure 4.13: mean_inertia_list

Exercise 38: Plotting Mean Inertia by n_clusters

Continuing from Exercise 38:

Now that we have generated mean inertia over 100 models for each value of **n_clusters**, we will plot mean inertia by **n_clusters**. Then, we will discuss how to visually assess the best value to use for **n_clusters**.

1. First, import matplotlib as follows:

```
import matplotlib.pyplot as plt
```

2. Create a list of numbers and save it as the object x, so we can plot it on the x-axis as shown here:

```
x = list(range(1, len(mean_inertia_list)+1))
```

3. Save **mean_inertia_list**, as the object y as shown here:

```
y = mean_inertia_list
```

4. Plot the mean inertia by number of clusters, as follows:

```
plt.plot(x, y)
```

5. Set the plot title to read '**Mean Inertia by n_clusters**' using the following:

```
plt.title('Mean Inertia by n_clusters')
```

6. Label the x-axis '**n_clusters**' using **plt.xlabel('n_clusters')**, and label the y-axis '**Mean Inertia**' using the following code:

```
plt.ylabel ('Mean Inertia')
```

7. Set the tick labels on the x-axis as the values in x using the following:

```
plt.xticks(x)
```

8. Display the plot used in **plt.show()**. To better understand, refer to the following code:

```
plt.plot(x, y)
plt.title('Mean Inertia by n_clusters')
plt.xlabel('n_clusters')
plt.xticks(x)
plt.ylabel('Mean Inertia')
plt.show()
```

For the resultant output, refer to the following screenshot:

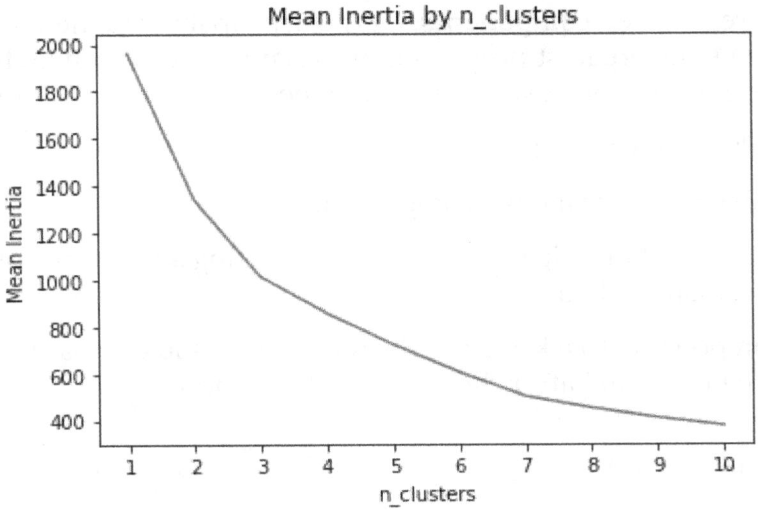

Figure 4.14: Mean inertia by n_clusters

To determine the best number of **n_clusters**, we will use the "elbow method." That is, the point in the plot where there are diminishing returns for the added complexity of more clusters. From Figure 4.14, we can see that there are rapid decreases in mean inertia from **n_clusters** 1 to 3. After **n_clusters** equals 3, the decreases in mean inertia seem to become less rapid and the decrease in inertia may not be worth the added complexity of adding additional clusters. Thus, the appropriate number of **n_clusters** in this situation is 3.

However, if the data has too many dimensions, the k-means algorithm can fall subject to the curse of dimensionality by inflated Euclidean distances and subsequent erroneous results. Thus, before fitting a k-Means model, using a dimension reduction strategy is encouraged.

Reducing the number of dimensions helps to eliminate multicollinearity and decreases the time to fit the model. **Principal component analysis** (**PCA**) is a common method to reduce the number of dimensions by discovering a set of underlying linear variables in the data.

Principal Component Analysis (PCA)

At a high level, PCA is a technique for creating uncorrelated linear combinations from the original features termed **components**. Of the principal components, the first component explains the greatest proportion of variance in data, while the following components account for progressively less variance.

To demonstrate PCA, we will:

- Fit PCA model with all principal components
- Tune the number of principal components by setting a threshold of explained variance to remain in data
- Fit those components to a k-means cluster analysis and compare k-means performance before and after the PCA transformation

Exercise 39: Fitting a PCA Model

In this exercise, you will learn to fit a generic PCA model using data we prepared in *Exercise 34, Building an HCA Model* and the brief explanation of PCA.

1. Instantiate a PCA model as shown here:

```
from sklearn.decomposition import PCA

model = PCA()
```

2. Fit the PCA model to **scaled_features**, as shown in the following code:

```
model.fit(scaled_features)
```

3. Get the proportion of explained variance in the data for each component, save the array as the object **explained_var_ratio**, and print the values to the console as follows:

```
explained_var_ratio = model.explained_variance_ratio_
print(explained_var_ratio)
```

4. For the resultant output, refer to the following screenshot:

```
[3.53143625e-01 2.50532563e-01 1.25244721e-01 9.69358544e-02
 9.26479607e-02 4.62631534e-02 2.77498886e-02 7.37245537e-03
 1.09779199e-04]
```

Figure 4.15: Explained variance in the data for each principal component

Each principal component explains a proportion of the variance in data. In this exercise, the first principal component explained .35 of the variance in data, the second explained. 25, the third .13%, and so on. Altogether, these nine components explain 100% of the variance in data. The goal of dimensionality reduction is to decrease the number of dimensions in data with the objectives of limiting overfitting and time to fit the subsequent model. Thus, we will not keep all nine components. However, if we retain too few components, the percent of explained variance in the data will be low and the subsequent model will under fit. Therefore, a challenge for data scientists exists in determining the number of **n_components** that minimize over fitting and under fitting.

Exercise 40: Choosing n_components using Threshold of Explained Variance

In *Exercise* 39, *Fitting* PCA *Model*, you learned to fit a PCA model with all available principal components. However, keeping all of the principal components does not reduce the number of dimensions in data. In this exercise, we will reduce the number of dimensions in data by retaining the components that explain a threshold of variance in it.

1. Determine the number of principal components in which a minimum of 95% of the variance in the data is explained by calculating the cumulative sum of explained variance by the principal component. Let's look at the following code, to see how it's done:

   ```
   import numpy as np


   cum_sum_explained_var = np.cumsum(model.explained_variance_ratio_)
   print(cum_sum_explained_var)
   ```

   For the resultant output, refer to the following screenshot:

   ```
   [0.35314362 0.60367619 0.72892091 0.82585676 0.91850472 0.96476788
    0.99251777 0.99989022 1.        ]
   ```

   Figure 4.16: The cumulative sum of the explained variance for each principal component

2. Set the threshold for the percent of variance to keep in data as 95%, as follows:

   ```
   threshold = .95
   ```

3. Using this threshold, we will loop through the list of cumulative explained variance and see where they explain no less than 95% of the variance in data. Since we will be looping through the indices of **cum_sum_explained_var**, we will instantiate our loop using the following:

   ```
   for i in range(len(cum_sum_explained_var)):
   ```

4. Check to see if the item in **cum_sum_explained_var** is greater than or equal to 0.95, as shown here:

```
if cum_sum_explained_var[i] >= threshold:
```

5. If that logic is met, then we will add 1 to that index (because we cannot have 0 principal components), save the value as an object, and break the loop. To do this, we will use **best_n_components = i+1** inside of the if statement and break in the next line. Look at the following code to get an idea:

```
best_n_components = i+1
break
```

The last two lines in the if statement instruct the loop not to do anything if the logic is not met:

```
else:
pass
```

6. Print a message detailing the best number of components using the following code:

```
print('The best n_components is {}'.format(best_n_components))
```

View the output from the previous line of code:

```
The best n_components is 6
```

Figure 4.17: The output message displaying number of components

The value for **best_n_components** is 6. We can refit another PCA model with **n_components = 6**, transform the data into principal components, and use these components in a new k-means model to lower the inertia values. Additionally, we can compare the inertia values across **n_clusters** values for the models built using PCA transformed data to those using data that was not PCA transformed.

Activity 13: Evaluating Mean Inertia by Cluster after PCA Transformation

Now that we know the number of components to retain at least 95% of the variance in the data, how to transform our features into principal components, and a way to tune the optimal number of clusters for k-means clustering with a nested loop, we will put them all together in this activity.

Continuing from *Exercise* 40:

1. Instantiate a PCA model with the value for the **n_components** argument equal to **best_n_components** (that is, remember, **best_n_components = 6**).

2. Fit the model to **scaled_features** and transform it into the first six principal components
3. Using a nested loop, calculate the mean inertia over 100 models at values 1 through 10 for **n_clusters** (see *Exercise 40*, *Choosing n_components using Threshold of Explained Variance*).

```
[1892.8745743658694, 1272.0635708451114, 945.9585011131066, 792.9280542109909, 660.6137294703674, 542.2679610880247,
448.0582942646142, 402.0775746619672, 363.76887622845425, 330.43291214440774]
```

Figure 4.18: mean_inertia_list_PCA

Now, much like in *Exercise 38*, *Plotting Mean Inertia by n_clusters*, we have a mean inertia value for each value of **n_clusters** (1 through 10). However, **mean_inertia_list_PCA** contains the mean inertia value for each value of **n_clusters** after PCA transformation. But, how do we know if the k-means model performs better after PCA transformation? In the next exercise, we will visually compare the mean inertia values before and after PCA transformation at each value of **n_clusters**.

> **Note**
>
> The solution for this activity can be found on page 357.

Exercise 41: Visual Comparison of Inertia by n_clusters

To visually compare mean inertia by **n_clusters** before and after PCA transformation, we will slightly modify the plot created in *Exercise 38*, *Plotting Mean Inertia by n_clusters*, by:

- Adding a second line to the plot showing mean inertia by **n_clusters** after PCA transformation
- Creating a legend distinguishing the lines
- Changing the title

> **Note**
>
> For this visualization to work properly, **mean_inertia_list** from *Exercise 38, Plotting Mean Inertia by n_clusters*, must still be in the environment.

Continuing from *Activity* 13:

1. Import Matplotlib using the following code:
   ```
   import matplotlib.pyplot as plt
   ```
2. Create a list of numbers and save it as the object x, so we can plot it on the x-axis as follows:
   ```
   x = list(range(1,len(mean_inertia_list_PCA)+1))
   ```
3. Save **`mean_inertia_list_PCA`** as the object y using the following code:
   ```
   y = mean_inertia_list_PCA
   ```
4. Save **`mean_inertia_list`** as the object y2 using the following:
   ```
   y2 = mean_inertia_list
   ```
5. Plot mean inertia after a PCA transformation by number of clusters using the following code:
   ```
   plt.plot(x, y, label='PCA')
   ```
   Add our second line of mean inertia before a PCA transformation by number of clusters using the following:
   ```
   plt.plot(x, y2, label='No PCA)
   ```
6. Set the plot title to read '**`Mean Inertia by n_clusters for Original Features and PCA Transformed Features`**' as follows:
   ```
   plt.title('Mean Inertia by n_clusters for Original Features and PCA
   Transformed Features')
   ```
7. Label the x-axis '**`n_clusters`**' using the following code:
   ```
   plt.xlabel('n_clusters')
   ```
8. Label the y-axis '**`Mean Inertia`**' using:
   ```
   plt.ylabel('Mean Inertia')
   ```
9. Set the tick labels on the x-axis as the values in x using **`plt.xticks(x)`**.
10. Show a legend using and display the plot as follows:
    ```
    plt.legend()
    plt.show()
    ```

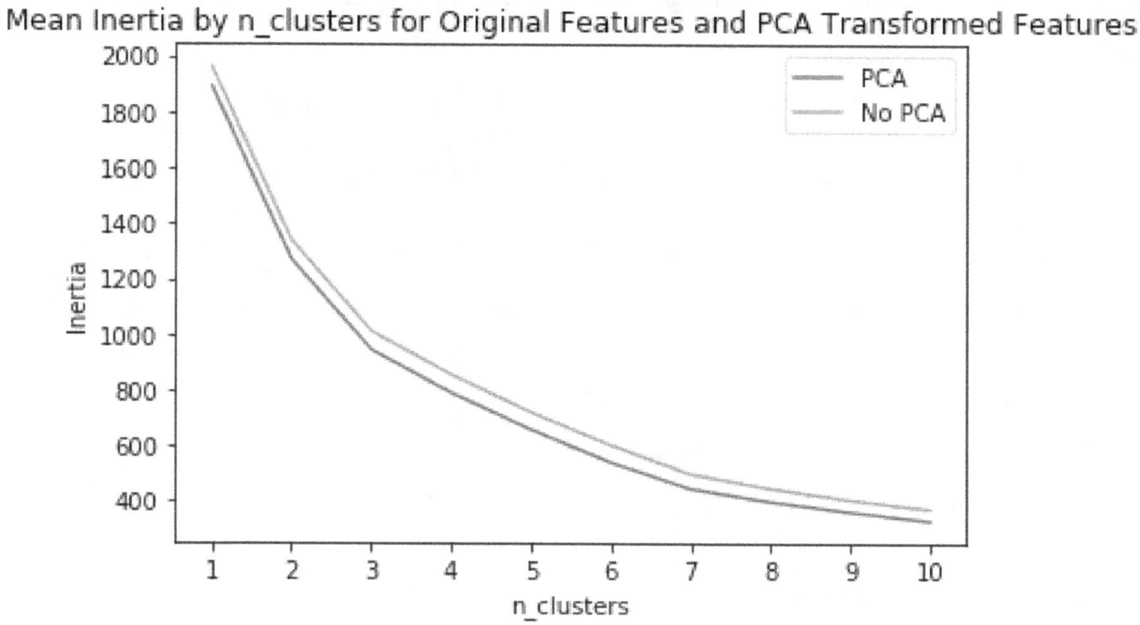

Figure 4.19: Mean inertia by n_clusters for original features (orange) and PCA transformed features (blue)

From the plot, we can see that inertia is lower at every number of clusters in the model using the PCA transformed features. This indicates that there was less distance between the group centroids and observations in each cluster after the PCA transformation relative to before the transformation. Thus, using a PCA transformation on the original features, we were able to decrease the number of features and simultaneously improve our model by decreasing the within-cluster sum of squares (that is, inertia).

HCA and k-means clustering are two widely-used unsupervised learning techniques used for segmentation. PCA can be used to help reduce the number of dimensions in our data and improve models in an unsupervised fashion. Linear discriminant function analysis (LDA), on the other hand, is a supervised method for reducing the number of dimensions via data compression.

Supervised Data Compression using Linear Discriminant Analysis (LDA)

As discussed previously, PCA transforms features into a set of variables to maximize the variance among the features. In PCA, the output labels are not considered when fitting the model. Meanwhile, LDA uses the dependent variable to help compress data into features that best discriminate the classes of the outcome variable. In this section, we will walk through how to use LDA as a supervised data compression technique.

To demonstrate using LDA as supervised dimensionality compression technique, we will:

- Fit an LDA model with all possible **n_components**
- Transform our features to **n_components**
- Tune the number of **n_components**

Exercise 42: Fitting LDA Model

To fit the model as a supervised learner using the default parameters of the LDA algorithm we will be using a slightly different glass data set, **glass_w_outcome.csv**. (https://github.com/TrainingByPackt/Data-Science-with-Python/tree/master/Chapter04) This dataset contains the same nine features as glass, but also an outcome variable, Type, corresponding to the type of glass. Type is labeled 1, 2, and 3 for building windows float processed, building windows non float processed, and headlamps, respectively.

1. Import the **glass_w_outcome.csv** file and save it as the object df using the following code:

```
import pandas as pd


df = pd.read_csv('glass_w_outcome.csv')
```

2. Shuffle the data to remove any ordering effects and save it as the data frame **df_shuffled** as follows:

```
from sklearn.utils import shuffle
df_shuffled = shuffle(df, random_state=42)
```

3. Save '**Type**' as **DV** (I.e., dependent variable) as follows:

```
DV = 'Type'
```

4. Split the shuffled data into features (i.e., X) and outcome (i.e., y) using **`X = df_shuffled.drop(DV, axis=1)`** and **`y = df_shuffled[DV]`**, respectively.

5. Split X and y into testing and training as follows:

```
from sklearn.model_selection import train_test_split
X_train, X_test, y_train, y_test = train_test_split(X, y, test_size=0.33,
random_state=42)
```

6. Scale **`X_train`** and **`X_test`** separately using the following code:

```
from sklearn.preprocessing import StandardScaler


scaler = StandardScaler()
X_train_scaled = scaler.fit_transform(X_train)
X_test_scaled = scaler.fit_transform(X_test)
```

7. Instantiate the LDA model and save it as model. The following will show you how.

```
from sklearn.discriminant_analysis import LinearDiscriminantAnalysis


-model = LinearDiscriminantAnalysis()
```

> **Note**
>
> By instantiating an LDA model with no argument **`for n_components`** we will return all possible components.

8. Fit the model to the training data using the following:

```
model.fit(X_train_scaled, y_train)
```

9. See the resultant output below:

```
array([0.95863843, 0.04136157])
```

Figure 4.20: Output from fitting linear discriminant function analysis

10. Much like in PCA, we can return the percentage of variance explained by each component.

```
model.explained_variance_ratio_
```

The output is shown in the following figure.

```
array([0.95863843, 0.04136157])
```

Figure 4.21: Explained variance by component.

> **Note**
>
> The first component explains 95.86% of the variance in the data and the second component explains 4.14% of the variance in the data for a total of 100%.

We have successfully fit an LDA model to compress our data from nine features to two features. Decreasing the features to two cuts the time to tune and fit machine learning models. However, prior to using these features in a classifier model we must transform the training and testing features into their two components. In the next exercise, we will show how this is done.

Exercise 43: Using LDA Transformed Components in Classification Model

Using supervised data compression, we will transform our training and testing features (i.e., **X_train_scaled** and **X_test_scaled**, respectively) into their components and fit a **RandomForestClassifier** model on them.

Continuing from *Exercise 42*:

1. Compress **X_train_scaled** into its components as follows:

```
X_train_LDA = model.transform(X_train_scaled)
```

2. Compress **X_test** into its components using:

```
X_test_LDA = model.transform(X_test_scaled)
```

3. Instantiate a **RandomForestClassifier** model as follows:

```
from sklearn.ensemble import RandomForestClassifier
model = RandomForestClassifier()
```

> **Note**
>
> We will be using the default hyperparameters of the **RandomForestClassifier** model because tuning hyperparameters is beyond the scope of this chapter.

4. Fit the model to the compressed training data using the following code:

```
model.fit(X_train_LDA, y_train)
```

See the resultant output below:

```
RandomForestClassifier(bootstrap=True, class_weight=None, criterion='gini',
            max_depth=None, max_features='auto', max_leaf_nodes=None,
            min_impurity_decrease=0.0, min_impurity_split=None,
            min_samples_leaf=1, min_samples_split=2,
            min_weight_fraction_leaf=0.0, n_estimators=10, n_jobs=None,
            oob_score=False, random_state=None, verbose=0,
            warm_start=False)
```

Figure 4.22: Output after fitting random forest classifier model

5. Generate predictions on **X_test_LDA** and save them as the array, predictions using the following code:

```
predictions = model.predict(X_test_LDA)
```

6. Evaluate model performance by comparing predictions to **y_test** using a confusion matrix. To generate and print a confusion matrix see the code below:

```
from sklearn.metrics import confusion_matrix
import pandas as pd
import numpy as np

cm = pd.DataFrame(confusion_matrix(y_test, predictions))
cm['Total'] = np.sum(cm, axis=1)
cm = cm.append(np.sum(cm, axis=0), ignore_index=True)
cm.columns = ['Predicted 1', 'Predicted 2', 'Predicted 3', 'Total']
cm = cm.set_index([['Actual 1', 'Actual 2', 'Actual 3', 'Total']])
print(cm)
```

The output is shown in the following figure:

	Predicted 1	Predicted 2	Predicted 3	Total
Actual 1	14	8	0	22
Actual 2	5	16	2	23
Actual 3	1	3	23	27
Total	20	27	25	72

Figure 4.23: 3x3 confusion matrix for evaluating RandomForestClassifier model performance using the LDA compressed data

Summary

This chapter introduced you to two widely used unsupervised, clustering algorithms, HCA and k-means clustering. While learning about k-means clustering, we leveraged the power of loops to create ensembles of models for tuning the number of clusters and to gain more confidence in our predictions. During the PCA section, we determined the number of principal components for dimensionality reduction and fit the components to a k-means model. Additionally, we compared the differences in k-means model performance before and after PCA transformation. We were introduced to an algorithm, LDA, which reduces dimensionality in a supervised manner. Lastly, we tuned the number of components in LDA by iterating through all possible values for components and programmatically returning the value resulting in the best accuracy score from a Random Forest classifier model. You should now feel comfortable with dimensionality reduction and unsupervised learning techniques.

We were briefly introduced to creating plots in this chapter; however, in the next chapter, we will learn about structured data and how to work with XGboost and Keras libraries

5

Mastering Structured Data

Learning Objectives

By the end of this chapter, you will be able to:

- Work with structured data to create highly accurate models
- Use the XGBoost library to train boosting models
- Use the Keras library to train neural network models
- Fine-tune model parameters to get the best accuracy
- Use cross-validation
- Save and load your trained models

This chapter will cover the basics on how to create highly accurate structured data models.

Introduction

There are two main types of data, structured and unstructured. Structured data refers to data that has a defined format and is usually shaped as a table, such as data stored in an Excel sheet or a relational database. Unstructured data does not have a predefined schema. Anything that cannot be stored in a table falls under this category. Examples include voice files, images, and PDFs.

In this chapter, we will focus on structured data and creating machine learning models using XGBoost and Keras. The XGBoost algorithm is widely used by industry experts and researchers due to the speed at which it delivers high-precision models, and also due to its distributed nature. The distributed nature refers to the ability to process data and train models in parallel; this enables faster training and much shorter turnaround time for data scientists. Keras on the other hand lets us create neural network models. Neural networks work much better than boosting algorithms in some cases, but finding the right network and the right configuration of the network is tough. The following topics will help you get familiar with both libraries, making sure that you can tackle any structured data in your data science journey.

Boosting Algorithms

Boosting is a way to improve the accuracy of any learning algorithm. Boosting works by combining rough, high-level rules into a single prediction that is more accurate than any single rule. Iteratively, a subset of the training dataset is ingested into a "weak" algorithm to generate a weak model. These weak models are then combined to form the final prediction. Two of the most effective boosting algorithms are gradient boosting machine and XGBoost.

Gradient Boosting Machine (GBM)

GBM makes use of classification trees as the weak algorithm. The results are generated by improving estimations from these weak models using a differentiable loss function. The model fits consecutive trees by considering the net loss of the previous trees; therefore, each tree is partially present in the final solution. Hence, boosting trees decreases the speed of the algorithm, and the transparency that they provide gives much better results. The GBM algorithm has a lot of parameters and it is sensitive to noise and extreme values. At the same time, GBM overfits the data, and thus a proper stopping point is required, but it is often the best possible model.

XGBoost (Extreme Gradient Boosting)

XGBoost is the algorithm of choice for researchers across the world when modelling structured data. XGBoost also uses trees as the weak algorithm. So, why is it the first algorithm that comes to mind when data scientists see structured data? XGBoost is portable and distributed, which means that it can be easily used in different architectures and can use multiple cores (single machine) or multiple machines (clusters). As a bonus, the XGBoost library is written in C++, which makes it fast. It is also useful when working with a huge dataset, as it allows you to store data on an external disk and not load all the data on to the memory.

> **Note**
>
> You can read more about XGBoost here: https://arxiv.org/abs/1603.02754

Exercise 44: Using the XGBoost library to Perform Classification

In this exercise, we will perform classification on the wholesale customer dataset (https://github.com/TrainingByPackt/Data-Science-with-Python/tree/master/Chapter05/data) using XGBoost library for Python. The dataset contains purchase data for clients of a wholesale distributor. It includes the annual spending on diverse range of product categories. We will predict the channel based on the annual spend on various products. The channel here describes whether the client is either a horeca (hotel/restaurant/café) or a retail customer.

1. Open the Jupyter Notebook from your virtual environment.
2. Import XGBoost, Pandas, and sklearn for the function that we will use to calculate the accuracy. The accuracy is required to understand how our model is performing.

```
import pandas as pd
import xgboost as xgb
from sklearn.metrics import accuracy_score
```

3. Read the wholesale customer dataset using pandas and check to see if it was loaded successfully using the following command:

```
data = pd.read_csv("data/wholesale-data.csv")
```

4. Check the first five entries of the dataset using the **head()** command. The output is shown in the following screenshot:

```
data.head()
```

Out[7]:

	Channel	Region	Fresh	Milk	Grocery	Frozen	Detergents_Paper	Delicassen
0	2	3	12669	9656	7561	214	2674	1338
1	2	3	7057	9810	9568	1762	3293	1776
2	2	3	6353	8808	7684	2405	3516	7844
3	1	3	13265	1196	4221	6404	507	1788
4	2	3	22615	5410	7198	3915	1777	5185

Figure 5.1: Screenshot showing first five elements of dataset

5. Now the "**data**" dataframe has all the data. It has the target variable, which is "**Channel**" in our case, and it has the predictor variables. So, we split the data into features (predictor) and labels (target).

```
X = data.copy()
X.drop("Channel", inplace = True, axis = 1)
Y = data.Channel
```

6. Create training and test sets as discussed in previous chapters. Here, we use an 80:20 split as the number of data points in the dataset is less. You can experiment with different splits.

```
X_train, X_test = X[:int(X.shape[0]*0.8)].values, X[int(X.shape[0]*0.8):].
values
Y_train, Y_test = Y[:int(Y.shape[0]*0.8)].values, Y[int(Y.shape[0]*0.8):].
values
```

7. Convert the pandas dataframe into a DMatrix, an internal data structure that is used by XGBoost to store training and testing datasets.

```
train = xgb.DMatrix(X_train, label=Y_train)
test = xgb.DMatrix(X_test, label=Y_test)
```

8. Specify the training parameters and train the model.

> **Note**
>
> We will go over these parameters in depth in the next section.

```
param = {'max_depth':6, 'eta':0.1, 'silent':1,
'objective':'multi:softmax', 'num_class': 3}
num_round = 5
model = xgb.train(param, train, num_round)
```

> **Note**
>
> By default, XGBoost uses all threads available to it for multiprocessing. To limit this, you can use the nthread parameter. Refer the next section for more information.

9. Predict the "**`Channel`**" values of the test set using the model that we just created.

   ```
   preds = model.predict(test)
   ```

10. Get the accuracy of the model that we have trained for the test dataset.

    ```
    acc = accuracy_score(Y_test, preds)
    print("Accuracy: %.2f%%" % (acc * 100.0))
    ```

    The output screenshot is as follows:

```
Accuracy: 89.77%
```

Figure 5.2: Final accuracy

Congratulations! You just made your first XGBoost model with approximately 90% accuracy without much fine-tuning!

XGBoost Library

The library we used to perform the above classification is named XGBoost. The library enables a lot of customization using the many parameters it has. In the following sections, we will dive in and understand the different parameters and functions of the XGBoost library.

> **Note**
>
> For more information about XGBoost, refer the website: https://xgboost.readthedocs.io

Training

Parameters that affect the training of any XGBoost model are listed below.

- `booster`: Even though we mentioned in the introduction that the base learner of XGBoost is a regression tree, using this library, we can use linear regression as the weak learner as well. Another weak learner, DART booster, is a new method to tree boosting, which drops trees at random to prevent overfitting. To use tree boosting, pass "`gbtree`" (default); for linear regression, pass "`gblinear`"; and for tree boosting with dropout, pass "`dart`".

> **Note**
>
> You may learn more about DART from this paper: http://www.jmlr.org/proceedings/papers/v38/korlakaivinayak15.pdf

- `silent`: 0 prints the training logs, whereas 1 is the silent mode.
- `nthread`: This signifies the number of parallel threads to be used. It defaults to the maximum number of threads available in the system.

> **Note**
>
> The parameter silent has been deprecated and has been replaced with verbosity, which takes any of the following values: 0 (silent), 1 (warning), 2 (info), 3 (debug).

- `seed`: This is the seed value for the random number generator. Set a constant value here to get reproducible results. The default value is 0.
- `objective`: This is a function that the model tries to minimize. The next few points cover the objective functions.

  `reg:linear`: Linear regression should be used with continuous target variables (regression problem). (Default)

  `binary:logistic`: logistic regression to be used in case of binary classification. It outputs probability and not classes.

  `binary:hinge`: This is binary classification that outputs predictions of 0 or 1, rather than the probabilities. Use this when you are not concerned about the probabilities.

`multi:softmax`: If you want to do a multiclass classification, use this to perform the classification using the softmax objective. It is mandatory to set the `num_class` parameter to the number of classes for this.

`multi:softprob`: This works the same as softmax, but the outputs predict the probability of each data point instead of predicting a class.

- `eval_metric`: The performance of a model needs to be observed on the validation set (as discussed in *Chapter 1, Introduction to Data Science and Data Preprocessing*). This parameter takes the evaluation metric for the validation data. The default metric is chosen according to the objective function (`rmse` for regression and `logloss` for classification). You can use multiple evaluation metrics.

  `rmse`: Root mean square error (RMSE) penalizes large errors more. So, it is appropriate when being off by 1 is more than three times as bad as being off by 3.

  `mae`: Mean absolute error (MAE) can be used in cases where being off by 1 is similar to being off by 3.

  The following graph shows the increase in the error with the increase in difference between the actual and predicted values. Here, it would be the following:

$$X = Actual\ Value - Predicted\ Value$$

Figure 5.3: Difference between actual and predicted value

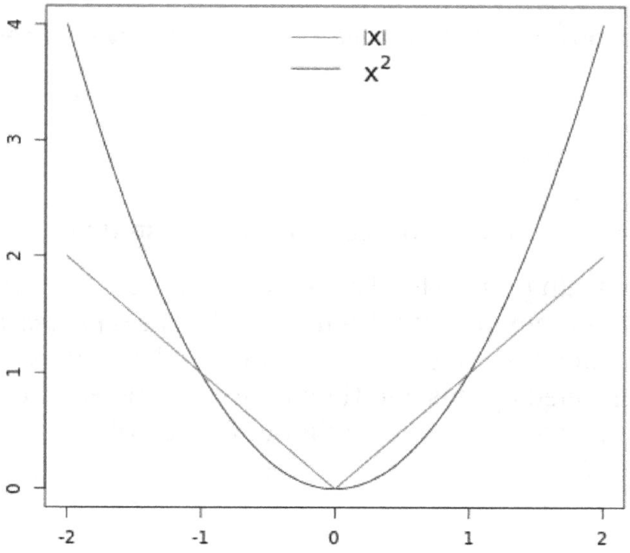

Figure 5.4: Variation of penalty with variation in error; |X| is mae and X2 is rmse

`logloss`: The negative log-likelihood, **logloss** is a classification loss function. Minimising the `logloss` of a model is equivalent to maximising the model's accuracy. It is defined mathematically as:

$$-\frac{1}{N}\sum_{i=1}^{N}\sum_{j=1}^{M} y_{ij} \log p_{ij}$$

Figure 5.5: Logloss equation diagram

Here, N is the number of data points, M is the number of classes and is either 1 or 0 depending on whether the prediction was correct or not, is the probability of predicting label j for data point i.

AUC: **Area under the curve** is used widely for binary classification. You should always use this if your dataset has a **class imbalance problem**. A class imbalance problem occurs when your data is not split up into classes of similar sizes; for example, if class A makes up 90% of the data and class B makes up 10% of the data. We will talk more about the class imbalance problem in the Handling Imbalanced Datasets section.

aucpr: Area under the **precision-recall** (**PR**) curve is the same as the AUC curve, but should be preferred in case of a highly imbalanced dataset. We shall discuss this too in the Handling Imbalanced Datasets section.

> **Note**
>
> AUC or AUCPR should be used as a rule of thumb whenever you are working with a binary dataset.

Tree Booster

Parameters that are specific to tree-based models are listed below:

- **eta**: This is the learning rate. Modify this value to prevent overfitting as discussed in *Chapter 1, Introduction to Data Science and Data Preprocessing*. The learning rate decides by how much the weights will get updated in each step. The gradient of weights gets multiplied by this and then added to the weight. This defaults to 0.3 and has a maximum value of 1 and a minimum value of 0.

- `gamma`: This is the minimum loss reduction to make a partition. The larger gamma is, the more conservative the algorithm will be. Being more conservative prevents overfitting. The value depends on the dataset and other parameters used. It ranges from 0 to infinity and the default value is 0. A lower value leads to shallow trees and larger values give rise to deeper trees.

> **Note**
>
> Gamma values above 1 usually do not give good results.

- `max_depth`: This is the maximum depth of any tree as discussed in *Chapter 3, Introduction to ML via Sklearn*. Increasing the max depth will make the model more likely to overfit. 0 means no limit. It defaults to 6.
- `subsample`: Setting this to 0.5 will cause the algorithm to randomly sample half of the training data before growing the trees. This prevents overfitting. Subsampling occurs once every boosting iteration and defaults to 1, which makes the model take the complete dataset and not a sample.
- `lambda`: This is the L2 regularization term. L2 regularization adds a squared magnitude of the coefficient as the penalty term to the loss function. Increasing this value prevents overfitting. Its default value is 1.
- `alpha`: This is the L1 regularization term. L1 regularization adds an absolute magnitude of the coefficient as the penalty term to the loss function. Increasing this value prevents overfitting. Its default value is 0.
- `scale_pos_weight`: This is useful when the classes are highly imbalanced. We will learn more about imbalanced data in the following sections. A typical value to consider introducing: the sum of negative instances / the sum of positive instances. Its default value is 1.
- `predictor`: There are two predictors. `cpu_predictor` uses CPU for prediction. It is the default. `gpu_predictor` uses GPU for prediction.

> **Note**
>
> Get a list of all the parameters here: https://xgboost.readthedocs.io/en/latest/parameter.html

Controlling Model Overfitting

If you observe high accuracy on the training dataset but a low accuracy on the test dataset, your model has overfit to the training data, as seen in *Chapter 1, Introduction to Data Science and Data Preprocessing*. There are two main ways to limit overfitting in XGBoost:

- **Control model complexity**: Modify `max_depth`, `min_child_weight`, and `gamma` while monitoring the training and test metrics to get the best model without overfitting to the training dataset. You will learn more about this in the following sections.
- **Add randomness to the model to make training it robust to noise**: Use the subsample parameter to get a subsample of the training data. Setting the parameter subsample to 0.5 will make the library randomly sample half of the training dataset before creating the weak models. `colsample_bytree` does the same thing as subsampling but with columns instead of rows.

To understand better, see the training and accuracy graphs in the following figure:

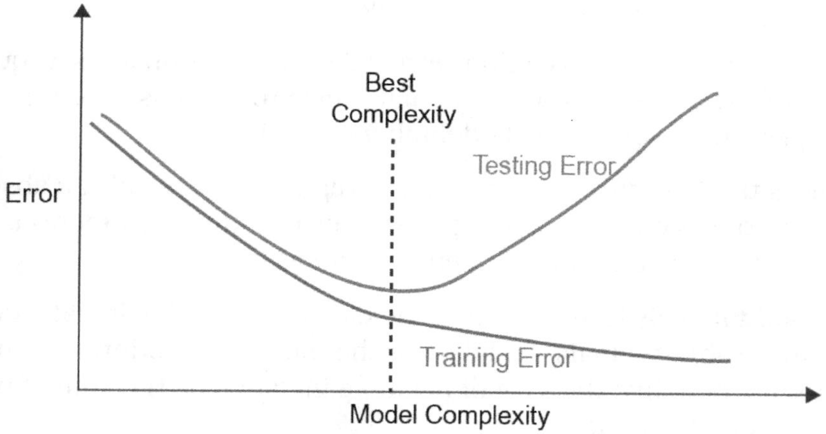

Figure 5.6: Training and accuracy graphs

To understand the conceptualization of a dataset with overfit and proper-fit models, refer to the following figure:

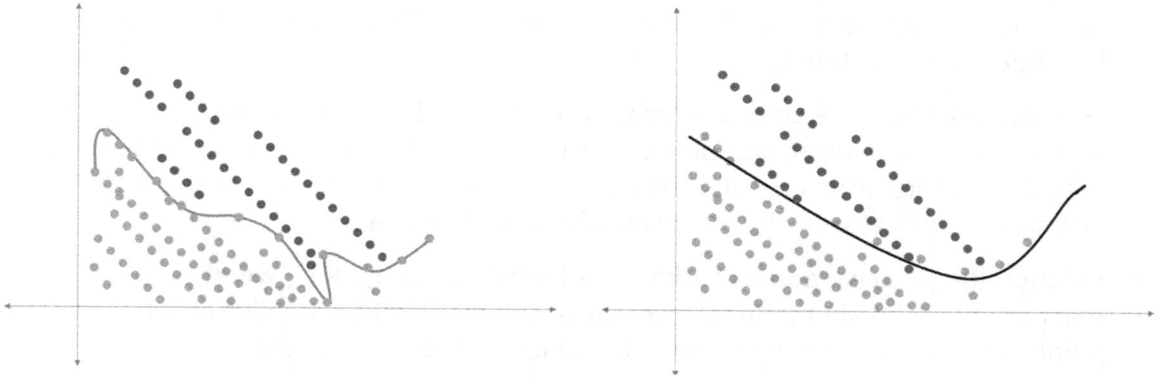

Figure 5.7: Illustration of a dataset with overfit and proper-fit models

> **Note**
>
> The black line represents the model that has a proper fit, whereas the model represented by the red line has overfit the dataset.

Handling Imbalanced Datasets

Imbalanced datasets cause a lot of problems to data scientists. One example of an imbalanced dataset is credit card fraud data. Here, about 95% of transactions will be legitimate and only 5% will be fraudulent. In this case, a model that predicts every transaction to be a correct transaction will get 95% accuracy, but, it is a very bad model. To see the distribution of your classes, you can use the following function:

```
data['target_variable'].value_counts()
```

The output would be as follows:

```
0     298
1     142
Name: target_variable, dtype: int64
```

Figure 5.8: Class distribution

To handle imbalanced datasets, you can use the following methods:

- **Undersample the class that has a higher number of records**: In the case of credit card fraud, you can randomly sample legitimate transactions to get records equal to the fraudulent records. This will result in equal distribution of the two classes, fraudulent and legitimate.
- **Oversample the class that has lesser records**: In the case of credit card fraud, you can introduce more samples of the fraudulent transactions by adding either new data points or by copying the existing data points. This will result in equal distribution of the two classes, **fraudulent** and **legitimate**.
- **Balance the positive and negative weights with scale_pos_weight**: You can use this parameter to allot a higher weight to the class with a smaller number of data points and thus artificially balance the classes. The value of the parameter can be:

$$\frac{Number\ of\ negative\ data\ points}{Number\ of\ positive\ data\ points}$$

Figure 5.9: Value parameter equation

You can check the distribution of the classes using the following code:

```
positive = sum(Y == 1)
negative = sum(Y == 0)
scale_pos_weight = negative/positive
```

- **Use AUC or AUCPR for evaluation**: As mentioned earlier, the AUC and AUCPR metrics are sensitive to imbalanced dataset, unlike accuracy, which gives you a high value for a bad model that predicts the majority class most of the time. AUC can be plotted only for binary classification problems. It is a representation of the **True Positive Rate vs. the False Positive Rate** at different thresholds (0, 0.01, 0.02... 1) of the predicted value. It is shown in the following figure:

$$TPR = \frac{True\ Positives}{True\ Positives + False\ Negatives}$$

$$FPR = \frac{False\ Positives}{False\ Positives + True\ Negatives}$$

Figure 5.10: TPR and FPR equations

The metric is the area under the curve that we get after plotting **TPR** and **FPR**. When dealing with highly skewed datasets, AUCPR gives a better picture and is thus preferred. AUCPR is the representation of precision and recall at different thresholds

$$Precision = \frac{True\ Positives}{True\ Positives + False\ Positives}$$

$$Recall = \frac{True\ Positives}{True\ Positives + False\ Negatives}$$

Figure 5.11: Precision and recall equations

As a rule of thumb, you should use AUC or AUCPR as the evaluation metric when dealing with imbalanced classes as it gives a clearer picture of the model.

> **Note**
>
> Machine learning algorithms cannot easily process strings or categorical variables represented as strings, so we have to convert them into numbers.

Activity 14: Training and Predicting the Income of a Person

In this activity, we will attempt to predict whether or not the income of an individual exceeds $50,000. The adult income dataset (https://github.com/TrainingByPackt/Data-Science-with-Python/tree/master/Chapter05/data) has its data sourced from the 1994 census dataset (https://archive.ics.uci.edu/ml/datasets/adult) and contains information such as income, education qualification of a person, and their occupation. Let's look at the following scenario: You work at a car company and you need to create a system by which the sales representatives of your firm can figure out what kind of car to sell to which person.

To do this, you create a machine learning model that predicts the income of a prospective buyer and thus provides the salesperson with the right information to sell the right car.

1. Load the income dataset (**`adult-data.csv`**) using pandas.
2. The data should look like this:

	age	workclass	education-num	occupation	capital-gain	capital-loss	hours-per-week	income
32556	27	Private	12	Tech-support	0	0	38	<=50K
32557	40	Private	9	Machine-op-inspct	0	0	40	>50K
32558	58	Private	9	Adm-clerical	0	0	40	<=50K
32559	22	Private	9	Adm-clerical	0	0	20	<=50K
32560	52	Self-emp-inc	9	Exec-managerial	15024	0	40	>50K

Figure 5.12: Screenshot showing five elements of census dataset

Use the following code to specify column names:

```
data = pd.read_csv("../data/adult-data.csv", names=['age',
'workclass','education-num', 'occupation', 'capital-gain', 'capital-loss',
'hoursper-week', 'income'])
```

3. Convert all the categorical variables from strings to integers using sklearn.
4. Perform prediction using the XGBoost library and perform parameter tuning to improve the accuracy to be more than 80%.

We have successfully predicted the income using the dataset with around 83% accuracy.

> **Note**
>
> The solution for this activity can be found on page 360.

External Memory Usage

When you have an exceptionally large dataset that you can't load on to your RAM, the external memory feature of the XGBoost library will come to your rescue. This feature will train XGBoost models for you without loading the entire dataset on the RAM.

Using this feature requires minimal effort; you just need to add a cache prefix at the end of the filename.

```
train = xgb.DMatrix('data/wholesale-data.dat.train#train.cache')
```

This feature supports only **libsvm** file. So, we will now convert a dataset loaded in pandas into a **libsvm** file to be used with the external memory feature.

> **Note**
>
> You might have to do this in batches depending on how big your dataset is.

```
from sklearn.datasets import dump_svmlight_file

dump_svmlight_file(X_train, Y_train, 'data/wholesale-data.dat.train', zero_
based=True, multilabel=False)
```

Here, **X_train** and **Y_train** are the predictor and target variables respectively. The **libsvm** file will get saved into the data folder.

Cross-validation

Cross-validation is a technique that helps data scientists evaluate their models on unseen data. It is helpful when your dataset isn't large enough to create three splits (training, testing, and validation). Cross-validation helps the model avoid overfitting by presenting it with different partitions of the same data. It works by feeding different training and validation sets of the dataset for every pass of cross-validation. 10-fold cross-validation is the most used, where the dataset is divided into 10 completely different subsets and is trained on each one of them, and finally, the metrics are averaged out to obtain the accurate prediction performance of the model. In every round of cross-validation, we do the following:

1. Shuffle the dataset and split it into k different groups (k=10 for 10-fold cross-validation).
2. Train the model on k-1 groups and test it on 1 group.
3. Evaluate the model and store the results.
4. Repeat steps 2 and 3 with different groups until all k combinations are trained.
5. The final metric is the mean of the metrics generated in the different rounds.

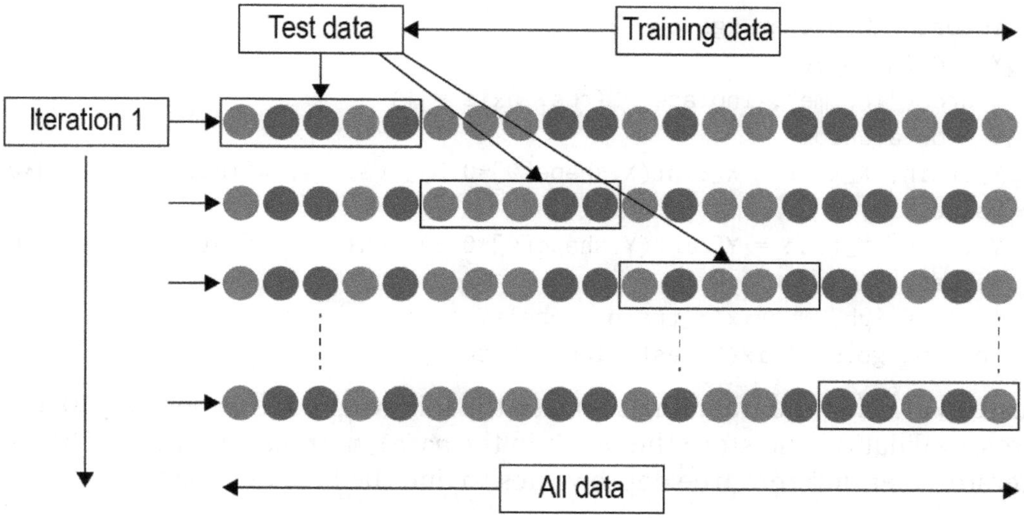

Figure 5.13: Illustration of a cross-validation dataset

The XGBoost library has an inbuilt function to perform cross-validation. This section will help you get you familiar using it.

Exercise 45: Using Cross-validation to Find the Best Hyperparameters

In this exercise, we will find the best hyperparameters for the adult dataset from the previous activity using the XGBoost library for Python. To do this, we will make use of the cross-validation feature of the library.

1. Load the census dataset from *Activity 14* and perform all the preprocessing steps.

```
import pandas as pd
import numpy as np
data = pd.read_csv("../data/adult-data.csv", names=['age', 'workclass',
'fnlwgt', 'education-num', 'occupation', 'capital-gain', 'capital-loss',
'hours-per-week', 'income'])
```

   Use Label Encoder from sklearn to encode strings. First, import Label Encoder, then encode all the string categorical columns one by one.

```
from sklearn.preprocessing import LabelEncoder
data['workclass'] = LabelEncoder().fit_transform(data['workclass'])
data['occupation'] = LabelEncoder().fit_transform(data['occupation'])
data['income'] = LabelEncoder().fit_transform(data['income'])
```

2. Make train and test sets from the data and convert the data into Dmatrix.

```
import xgboost as xgb
X = data.copy()
X.drop("income", inplace = True, axis = 1)
Y = data.income
X_train, X_test = X[:int(X.shape[0]*0.8)].values, X[int(X.shape[0]*0.8):].
values
Y_train, Y_test = Y[:int(Y.shape[0]*0.8)].values, Y[int(Y.shape[0]*0.8):].
values
train = xgb.DMatrix(X_train, label=Y_train)
test = xgb.DMatrix(X_test, label=Y_test)
```

3. Instead of using the train function, use the following code to perform 10-fold cross-validation and store the result in the **model_metrics** dataframe. The for loop iterates over different tree depth values to find the best one for our dataset.

```
test_error = {}
for i in range(20):
    param = {'max_depth':i, 'eta':0.1, 'silent':1,
'objective':'binary:hinge'}
    num_round = 50
    model_metrics = xgb.cv(param, train, num_round, nfold = 10)
    test_error[i] = model_metrics.iloc[-1]['test-error-mean']
```

4. Visualize the results using Matplotlib.

```
import matplotlib.pyplot as plt
plt.scatter(test_error.keys(),test_error.values())
plt.xlabel('Max Depth')
plt.ylabel('Test Error')
plt.show()
```

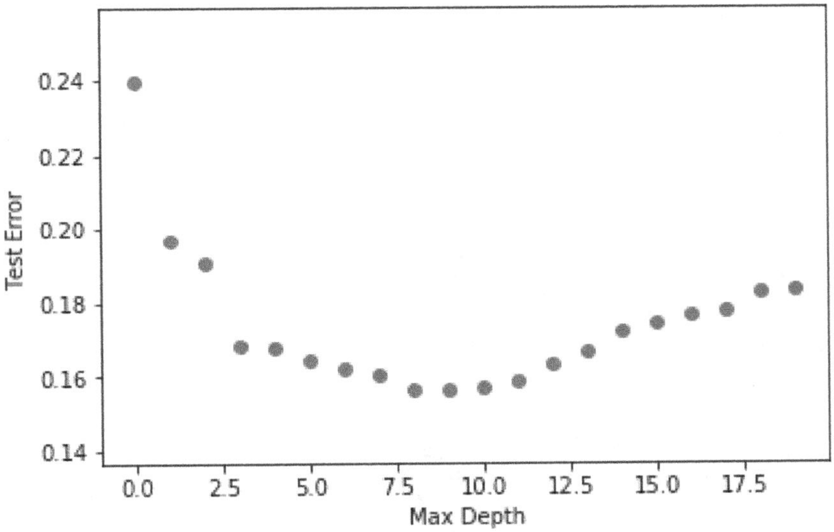

Figure 5.14: Graph of max depth with test error

From the graph, we understand that the max depth of 9 works best for our dataset as it has the lowest test error.

5. Find the best learning rate. Running this piece of code will take a while as it iterates over a lot of learning rates for 500 rounds each.

```
for i in range(1,100,5):
    param = {'max_depth':9, 'eta':0.001*i, 'silent':1,
'objective':'binary:hinge'}
    num_round = 500
    model_metrics = xgb.cv(param, train, num_round, nfold = 10)
    test_error[i] = model_metrics.iloc[-1]['test-error-mean']
```

6. Visualize the results.

```
lr = [0.001*(i) for i in test_error.keys()]
plt.scatter(temp,test_error.values())
plt.xlabel('Learning Rate')
plt.ylabel('Error')
plt.show()
```

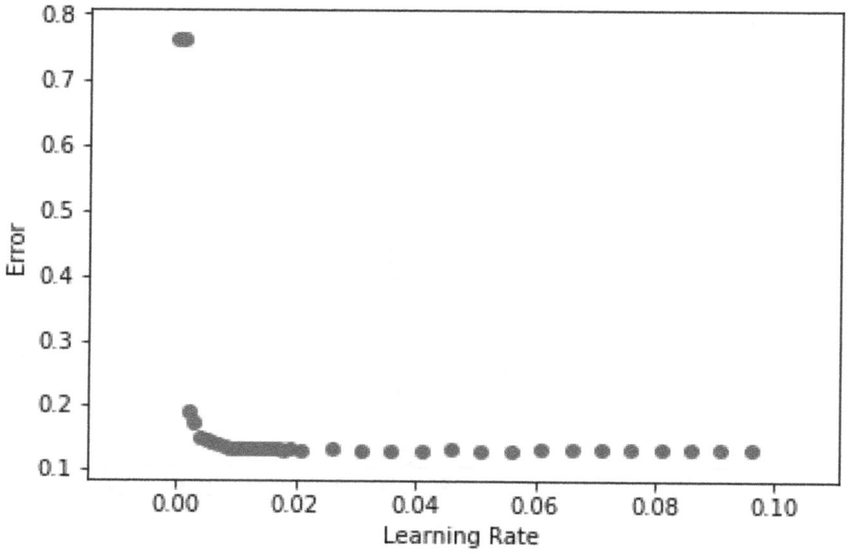

Figure 5.15: Graph of learning rate with test error

From the graph, we can see that a learning rate of about 0.01 works best for our model as it has the lowest error.

7. Let us visualize the training and testing errors for each round for the learning rate 0.01.

```
param = {'max_depth':9, 'eta':0.01, 'silent':1,
'objective':'binary:hinge'}
num_round = 500
model_metrics = xgb.cv(param, train, num_round, nfold = 10)

plt.scatter(range(500),model_metrics['test-error-mean'], s = 0.7, label =
'Test Error')
plt.scatter(range(500),model_metrics['train-error-mean'], s = 0.7, label =
'Train Error')
plt.legend()
plt.show()
```

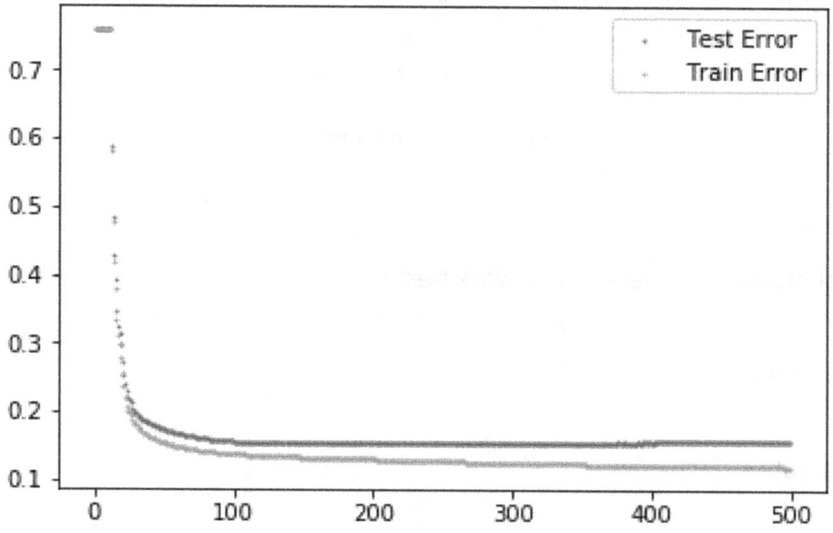

Figure 5.16: Graph of training and testing errors with respect to number of rounds

> **Note**
>
> From this graph, we can see that we get the least error around round 490. This means that our model performs the best when the number of rounds is around 490. Creating this curve helps us create more accurate models.

To check the least error, use the following code:

```
list(model_metrics['test-error-mean']).index(min(model_metrics['test-
error-mean']))
```

8. To understand, check out the output.

```
492
```

Figure 5.17: Least error

> **Note**
>
> The final model parameters that work best for this dataset:
>
> Max depth = 9
>
> Learning rate = 0.01
>
> Number of rounds = 496

Saving and Loading a Model

The last piece in mastering structured data is the ability to save and load the models that you have trained and fine-tuned. Training a new model every time we need a prediction will waste a lot of time, so being able to save a trained model is imperative for data scientists. The saved model allows us to replicate the results and to create apps and services that make use of the machine learning model. The steps are as follows:

1. To save an XGBoost model, you need to call the **`save_model`** function.

   ```
   model.save_model('wholesale-model.model')
   ```

2. To load a previously saved model, you have to call load_model on an initialized XGBoost variable.

   ```
   loaded_model = xgb.Booster({'nthread': 2})
   loaded_model.load_model('wholesale-model.model')
   ```

> **Note**
>
> If you give XGBoost access to all the threads it can get, your computer might become slow while training or predicting.

You are now ready to get started on modeling your structured dataset using the XGBoost library!

Exercise 46: Creating a Python Pcript that Predicts Based on Real-time Input

In this exercise, we will first create a model and save it. We will then create a Python script that will make use of this saved model to perform predictions on the data input by the user.

1. Load the income dataset from Activity 14 as a pandas dataframe.

```
import pandas as pd
import numpy as np
data = pd.read_csv("../data/adult-data.csv", names=['age', 'workclass',
'education-num', 'occupation', 'capital-gain', 'capital-loss', 'hours-per-
week', 'income'])
```

2. Strip away all trailing spaces.

```
data[['workclass', 'occupation', 'income']] = data[['workclass',
'occupation', 'income']].apply(lambda x: x.str.strip())
```

3. Convert all the categorical variables from strings to integers using scikit.

```
from sklearn.preprocessing import LabelEncoder
from collections import defaultdict
label_dict = defaultdict(LabelEncoder)
data[['workclass', 'occupation', 'income']] = data[['workclass',
'occupation', 'income']].apply(lambda x: label_dict[x.name].fit_
transform(x))
```

4. Save the label encoder in a pickle file for future use. A pickle file stores Python objects so that we can access them later when we need them.

```
import pickle
with open( 'income_labels.pkl', 'wb') as f:
        pickle.dump(label_dict, f, pickle.HIGHEST_PROTOCOL)
```

5. Split the dataset into training and testing and create the model.

6. Save the model to a file.

```
model.save_model('income-model.model')
```

7. In a Python script, load the model and the label encoder.

```
import xgboost as xgb
loaded_model = xgb.Booster({'nthread': 8})
loaded_model.load_model('income-model.model')
def load_obj(file):
     with open(file + '.pkl', 'rb') as f:
          return pickle.load(f)
label_dict = load_obj('income_labels')
```

8. Read the input from the user.

```
age = input("Please enter age: ")
workclass = input("Please enter workclass: ")
education_num = input("Please enter education_num: ")
occupation = input("Please enter occupation: ")
capital_gain = input("Please enter capital_gain: ")
capital_loss = input("Please enter capital_loss: ")
hours_per_week = input("Please enter hours_per_week: ")
```

9. Create a dataframe to store this data.

```
data_list = [age, workclass, education_num, occupation, capital_gain,
capital_loss, hours_per_week]
data = pd.DataFrame([data_list])
data.columns = ['age', 'workclass', 'education-num', 'occupation',
'capital-gain', 'capital-loss', 'hours-per-week']
```

10. Preprocess the data.

```
data[['workclass', 'occupation']] = data[['workclass', 'occupation']].
apply(lambda x: label_dict[x.name].transform(x))
```

11. Convert into Dmatrix and perform prediction using the model.

```
data = data.astype(int)
data_xgb = xgb.DMatrix(data)
pred = loaded_model.predict(data_xgb)
```

12. Perform inverse transformation to get the results.

```
income = label_dict['income'].inverse_transform([int(pred[0])])
```

The output is as follows:

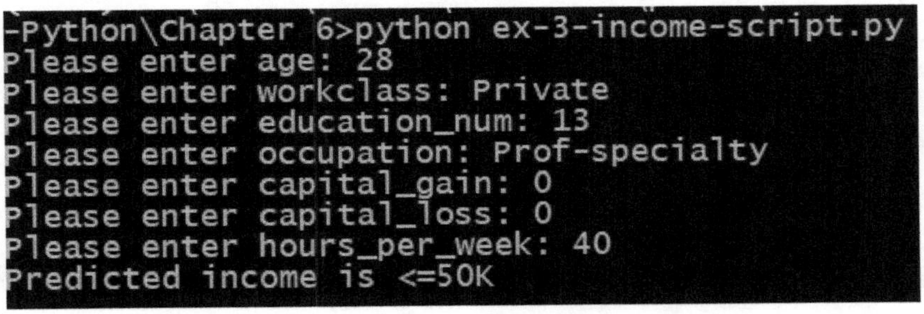

-Python\Chapter 6>python ex-3-income-script.py
Please enter age: 28
Please enter workclass: Private
Please enter education_num: 13
Please enter occupation: Prof-specialty
Please enter capital_gain: 0
Please enter capital_loss: 0
Please enter hours_per_week: 40
Predicted income is <=50K

Figure 5.18: Inverse transformation output

> **Note**
>
> Make sure that the values of **`workclass`** and **`occupation`** that you enter as input are present in the training data, otherwise the script will throw an error. This error occurs when the **`LabelEncoder`** encounters a new value it has not seen before.

Congratulations! You built a script that predicts the outcome using user input data. You will now be able to deploy your models anywhere you want to.

Activity 15: Predicting the Loss of Customers

In this activity, we will attempt to predict whether a customer will move to another telecom provider. The data is sourced from IBM sample datasets. Let's look at the following scenario: You work at a telecom company, and recently, a lot of your users have started moving to other providers. Now, to be able to give defecting customers a price cut, you need to predict which customer is the most likely to defect before they do so. To do this, you need to create a machine learning model that predicts which customer will defect.

1. Load the telecom churn (**`telco-churn.csv`**) dataset (https://github.com/TrainingByPackt/Data-Science-with-Python/tree/master/Chapter05/data) using pandas. This dataset contains information about the customers of a telecom provider. The original source of the dataset is at: https://www.ibm.com/communities/analytics/watson-analytics-blog/predictive-insights-in-the-telco-customer-churn-data-set/. It contains multiple fields such as charges, tenure, and streaming information, along with a variable that tells us if the customer churned or not. The first few rows should look like this:

	customerID	gender	SeniorCitizen	Partner	Dependents	tenure	PhoneService	MultipleLines	InternetService	OnlineSecurity	...	DeviceProtection	TechSup
0	7590-VHVEG	Female	0	Yes	No	1	No	No phone service	DSL	No	...	No	
1	5575-GNVDE	Male	0	No	No	34	Yes	No	DSL	Yes	...	Yes	
2	3668-QPYBK	Male	0	No	No	2	Yes	No	DSL	Yes	...	No	
3	7795-CFOCW	Male	0	No	No	45	No	No phone service	DSL	Yes	...	Yes	
4	9237-HQITU	Female	0	No	No	2	Yes	No	Fiber optic	No	...	No	

Figure 5.19: Screenshot showing first five elements of telecom churn dataset

2. Remove unnecessary variables.
3. Convert all the categorical variables from strings to integers using scikit. You can use the following code: `data.TotalCharges = pd.to_numeric(data.TotalCharges, errors='coerce')`
4. Fix the data type mismatch when loading with pandas.
5. Perform prediction using the XGBoost library and perform parameter tuning using cross-validation to improve accuracy to be more than 80%.
6. Save your model for future use.

> **Note**
>
> The solution for this activity can be found on page 361.

Neural Networks

A neural network is one of the most popular machine learning algorithms available to data scientists. It has consistently outperformed traditional machine learning algorithms in problems where images or digital media are required to find the solution. Given enough data, it outperforms traditional machine learning algorithms in structured data problems. Neural networks that have more than 2 layers are referred to as deep neural networks and the process of using these "deep" networks to solve problems is referred to as deep learning. Two handle unstructured data there are two main types of neural networks: a **convolutional neural network** (**CNN**) can be used to process images and a **recurrent neural network** (**RNN**) can be used to process time series and natural language data. We will talk more about CNNs and RNNs in *Chapter 6, Decoding Images* and *Chapter 7, Processing Human Language*. Let us now see how a vanilla neural network really works. In this section, we will go over the different parts of a neural network in brief. We will explain each topic in detail in the following chapters.

What Is a Neural Network?

The basic unit of a neural network is a neuron. The inspiration for neural networks was taken from the biological brain, which is where the name neuron was inspired from. All connections in the neural network, like the synapses in the brain, can transmit information from one neuron to another. In a neural network, a weighted combination of the input signal is aggregated, and the output signal is then transmitted forward after passing it through a function. This function is a nonlinear activation function and is the neuron's activation threshold. Multiple layers of these interconnected neurons form a neural network. Only the non-output layers of a neural network include bias units. The weights associated with every neuron along with these biases determine the output of the entire network; hence, these are the parameters we modify to fit the data during training.

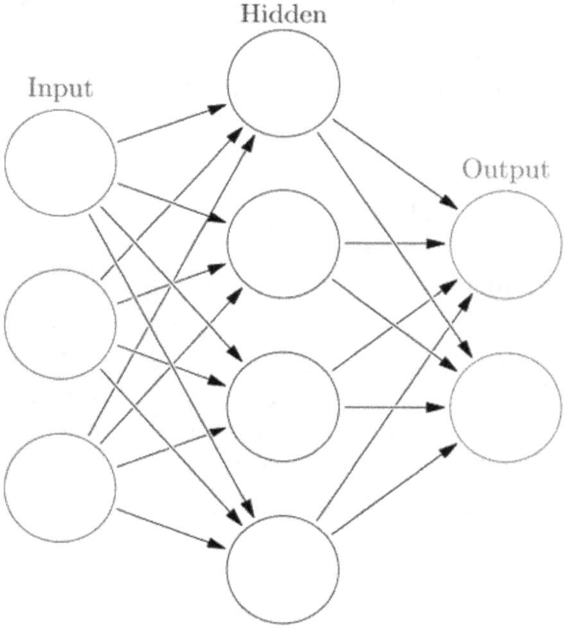

Figure 5.20: Representation of single layer neural network

The first layer of the neural network has nodes equal to the number of independent variables in the dataset. This layer is thus called the input layer, which is followed by multiple hidden layers, at the end of which is the output layer. Each neuron of the input layer takes in one independent variable of the dataset. The output layer outputs the final prediction. These outputs can be continuous (such as 0.2, 0.6, 0.8) if it is a regression problem or categorical (such as 2, 4, 5) if it is a classification problem. The training of a neural network modifies the weights and biases of the network to minimize the error, which is the difference between the expected and the output values. Weights are multiplied with the input to the neuron and then the bias value is added to the combination of these weights to get the output.

$$y = f\left(\sum w_i x_i + b\right)$$

Figure 5.21: Neuron output

Here, *y* is the output of the neuron and *x* the input, *w* and *b* are the weights and bias respectively, and *f* is the activation function, which we will learn more about later.

Optimization Algorithms

To minimize the error of the model, we train the neural network to minimize a predefined loss function using an optimization algorithm. There are many choices for this optimization algorithm, and you can choose one depending on your data and model. For most of this book, we will work with **stochastic gradient descent** (**SGD**), which works well in most cases, but we will explain other optimizers as and when they are required. SGD works by iteratively finding out the gradient, which is the change in the weights with respect to the error. In mathematical terms, it is the partial derivative with respect to the inputs. It finds the gradient that would help it minimize a given function, which in our case is called the loss function. As we get closer to the solution, this gradient reduces in magnitude, thus preventing us from overshooting the optimal solution.

The most intuitive way to understand SGD is the act of descending the bottom of a valley. Initially, we take steep descents, and then when we are close to the bottom, the slope reduces.

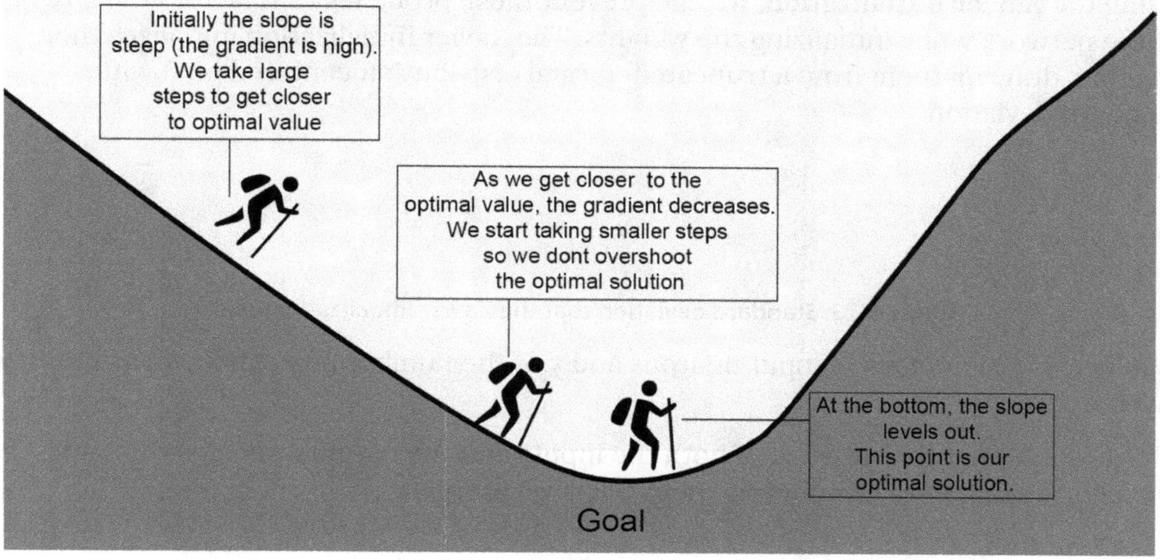

Initially the slope is steep (the gradient is high). We take large steps to get closer to optimal value
As we get closer to the optimal value, the gradient decreases. We start taking smaller steps so we dont overshoot the optimal solution
At the bottom, the slope levels out. This point is our optimal solution.
Goal

Figure 5.22: Intuition of gradient descent (k represents magnitude of gradient)

Hyperparameters

A big parameter that determines the time required to train a model is called the **learning rate**, which essentially is the size of the step that we take to perform the descent. Too small a step, and it will take the model a long time to get to the optimal solution; too big, and it will overshoot the optimal solution. To circumvent this, we start with a large learning rate and reduce the learning rate after a few steps. This helps us reach the minimum point faster, and due to the reduction in step size, prevents the model from overshooting the solution.

Next is the initialization of the weights. We need to perform initialization of the weights of a neural network to have a starting point from where we can then modify the weights to minimize the error. Initialization plays a major role in preventing the **vanishing** and **exploding gradient** problems.

Vanishing gradient problem refers to the reducing gradients with every layer as the product of any number smaller than 1 is even smaller, so over multiple layers, this value becomes 0.

Exploding gradient problem occurs when large error gradients add up and result in a very large update to the model. If the model loss goes to NaN, this could be a problem.

Using the **Xavier initialization**, we can prevent these problems as it factors the size of the network while initializing the weights. The Xavier initialization initializes the weights, drawing them from a truncated normal distribution centered on 0 with standard deviation

$$\sqrt{\frac{2}{x_i + y_i}}$$

Figure 5.23: Standard deviation that the Xavier initialization uses.

Where x_i is the number of input neurons and y_i is the number of output neurons for that layer

This ensures that the variance of both the inputs and the outputs remains the same even if the number of layers in the network is very large.

Loss Function

Another hyperparameter to consider is the loss function. Different loss functions are used depending on the type of the problem, classification or regression. For classification, we choose loss functions such as cross entropy and hinge. For regression, we use loss functions such as mean squared error, mean absolute error (MAE), and Huber. Different functions work well with different datasets. We will go over them as we use them.

Activation Function

While creating the neural network layers, you will have to define an activation function, which depends on whether the layer is a hidden layer or an output layer. In the case of a hidden layer, we will use the ReLU or the tanh activation functions. Activation functions help the neural network model non-linear functions. Almost no real-life situation can be solved using a linear model. Now, apart from this, different activation functions have different features. Sigmoid output has values between 0 and 1, whereas tanh centers the output around 0, which enables better learning. ReLU on the other hand prevents the vanishing gradient problem and is computationally efficient. This is the representation of a ReLU graph.

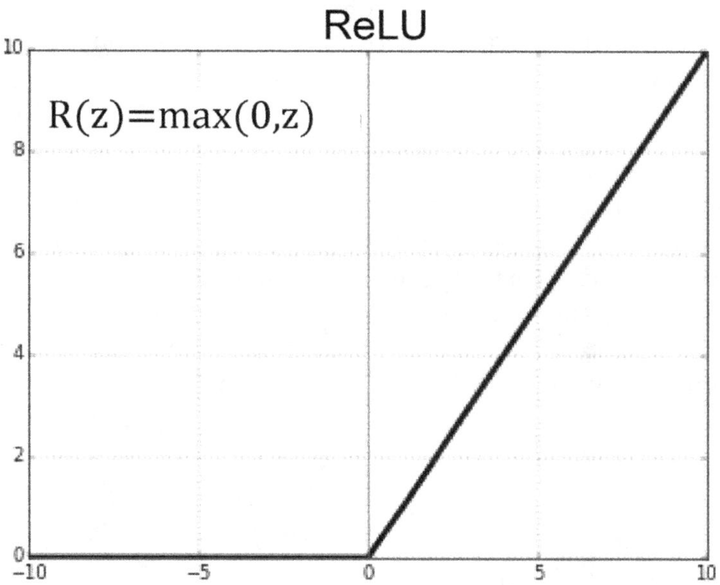

Figure 5.24: Representation of ReLU activation function

Softmax outputs probabilities and is used when multiclass classification is being performed, whereas sigmoid outputs a value between 0 and 1 and is used only for binary classification. Linear activation is mostly used for models that solve the regression problem. A representation of the sigmoid activation function is shown in the following figure:

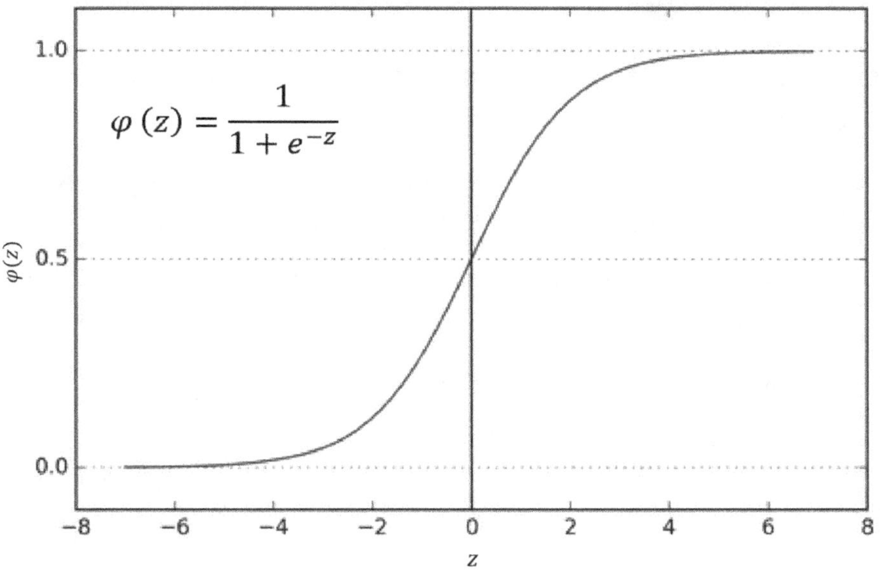

Figure 5.25: Representation of sigmoid activation function

The previous section had a lot of new information; if you are confused, do not worry. We will apply all these concepts practically in the rest of the chapters, which will reinforce all these topics.

Keras

Keras is an open-source, high-level neural network API written in Python. It is capable of running on top of TensorFlow, Microsoft Cognitive Toolkit (CNTK), or Theano. Keras was developed to enable fast experimentation and thus help in rapid application development. Using Keras, one can get from idea to result with the least possible delay. Keras supports almost all the latest data science models relating to neural networks due to the huge community support. It contains multiple implementations of commonly used building blocks such as layers, batch normalization, dropout, objective functions, activation functions, and optimizers. Also, Keras allows users to create models for smartphones (Android and iOS), the web, or for the **Java Virtual Machine** (**JVM**). With Keras, you can train your models on your GPU without any change in code.

Given all these features of Keras, it is imperative for data scientists to learn how to use all the different aspects of the library. Mastering the use of Keras will help you tremendously in your journey as a data scientist. To demonstrate the power of Keras, we will now install it and create a single layer neural network model.

> **Note**
>
> You can read more about Keras here: https://keras.io/

Exercise 47: Installing the Keras library for Python and Using it to Perform Classification

In this exercise, we will perform classification on the wholesale customer dataset (which we used in *Exercise 44*), using the Keras library for Python.

1. Run the following command in your virtual environment to install Keras.

   ```
   pip3 install keras
   ```

2. Open Jupyter Notebook from your virtual environment.

3. Import Keras and other required libraries.

```
import pandas as pd
from keras.models import Sequential
from keras.layers import Dense
import numpy as np
from sklearn.metrics import accuracy_score
```

4. Read the wholesale customer dataset using pandas and check to see if it was loaded successfully using the following command:

```
data = pd.read_csv("data/wholesale-data.csv")
data.head()
```

The output should look like this:

Out[7]:

	Channel	Region	Fresh	Milk	Grocery	Frozen	Detergents_Paper	Delicassen
0	2	3	12669	9656	7561	214	2674	1338
1	2	3	7057	9810	9568	1762	3293	1776
2	2	3	6353	8808	7684	2405	3516	7844
3	1	3	13265	1196	4221	6404	507	1788
4	2	3	22615	5410	7198	3915	1777	5185

Figure 5.26: Screenshot showing first five elements of dataset

5. Split the data into features and labels.

```
X = data.copy()
X.drop("Channel", inplace = True, axis = 1)
Y = data.Channel
```

6. Create training and test sets.

```
X_train, X_test = X[:int(X.shape[0]*0.8)].values, X[int(X.shape[0]*0.8):].
values
Y_train, Y_test = Y[:int(Y.shape[0]*0.8)].values, Y[int(Y.shape[0]*0.8):].
values
```

7. Create the neural network model.

```
model = Sequential()
model.add(Dense(units=8, activation='relu', input_dim=7))
model.add(Dense(units=16, activation='relu'))
model.add(Dense(units=1, activation='sigmoid'))
```

Here, we create a four-layer network, with one input layer, two hidden layers, and one output layer. The hidden layers have ReLU activation and the output layer has softmax activation.

8. Compile and train the model. We use the binary cross-entropy loss function, which is the same as the logloss we discussed before; we have chosen the optimizer to be stochastic gradient descent. We run the training for five epochs with a batch size of eight.

```
model.compile(loss='binary_crossentropy',
              optimizer='sgd',
              metrics=['accuracy'])
model.fit(X_train, Y_train, epochs=5, batch_size=8)
```

> **Note**
>
> You will see the model training log. Epoch refers to the training iteration, and 352 refers to the size of the dataset divided by the batch size. After the progress bar, you can see the time taken for one iteration. Next to that, you see the average time taken to train each batch. Next comes the loss of the model, which over here is the binary cross-entropy loss, followed by the accuracy after the iteration. A few of these terms are new, but we will understand each of them in the following sections.

```
Epoch 1/5
352/352 [==============================] - 1s 4ms/step - loss: -5.6614 - acc: 0.6449
Epoch 2/5
352/352 [==============================] - 0s 233us/step - loss: -5.6614 - acc: 0.6449
Epoch 3/5
352/352 [==============================] - 0s 221us/step - loss: -5.6614 - acc: 0.6449
Epoch 4/5
352/352 [==============================] - 0s 213us/step - loss: -5.6614 - acc: 0.6449
Epoch 5/5
352/352 [==============================] - 0s 216us/step - loss: -5.6614 - acc: 0.6449
```

Figure 5.27: Screenshot of model training logs

9. Predict the values of the test set.

```
preds = model.predict(X_test, batch_size=128)
```

10. Obtain the accuracy of the model.

```
accuracy = accuracy_score(Y_test, preds.astype(int))
print("Accuracy: %.2f%%" % (accuracy * 100.0))
```

The output is as follows:

```
Accuracy: 80.68%
```

Figure 5.28: Output accuracy

Congratulations! You just made your first neural network model with around 81% accuracy, without any fine-tuning! You will notice that this accuracy is quite low when compared with XGBoost. In the following sections, you will figure out how to improve this accuracy. A major reason for the low accuracy is the size of the data. For a neural network model to really shine, it must have a large dataset to train on; otherwise, it overfits the data.

Keras Library

Keras enables modularity. All initializers, cost functions, optimizers, layers, regularizers, and activation functions are standalone modules that can be used for any type of data and network architecture. You will find almost all the latest functions already implemented in Keras. This allows reusability of code and enables fast experimentation. You as a data scientist are not limited by the inbuilt modules; it is extremely easy to create your own custom modules and use them with other inbuilt modules. This enables research and helps with different use cases. For example, you might have to write a custom loss function to maximize the volume of cars sold, giving more weight to cars that have bigger margins, leading to higher profits.

All the different kinds of layers that you would need to create a neural network are defined in Keras. We will investigate them as we use them. There are two main ways to create neural models in Keras, the sequential model and the functional API.

Sequential: The **sequential model** is a linear stack of layers. This is the easiest way to create neural network models with Keras. A snippet of this model is given below:

```
model = Sequential()
model.add(Dense(128, input_dim=784))
model.add(Activation('relu'))

model.add(Dense(10))
model.add(Activation('softmax'))
```

Functional API: **Functional API** is the way to go for complex models. Due to the linear nature of the sequential model, creating a complex model is not possible. The functional API lets you create multiple parts of the model and then merge them together. The same model in the functional API is given below:

```
inputs = Input(shape=(784,))
x = Dense(128, activation='relu')(inputs)
prediction = Dense(10, activation='softmax')(x)
model = Model(inputs=inputs, outputs=prediction)
```

A powerful feature of Keras is callback. Callbacks allow you to use a function at any stage of the training process. This proves to be useful to get the statistics and save the model at different stages. It can be used to apply a custom decay to the learning rate and also to perform early stopping.

```
filepath="model-weights-{epoch:02d}-{val_loss:.2f}.hdf5"
model_ckpt = ModelCheckpoint(filepath, monitor='val_loss', verbose=1, save_
best_only=True, mode='auto')
callbacks = [model_ckpt]
```

To save models you trained on Keras, you need to just use the following line of code:

```
model.save('Path to model')
```

To load the model from a file, use the following code:

```
keras.models.load_model('Path to model')
```

Early stopping is a useful feature that can be implemented using callbacks. Early stopping helps you save time when training models. It stops the training process if the change in the metric specified is less than the set threshold.

```
EarlyStopping(monitor='val_loss', min_delta=0.01, patience=5, verbose=1,
mode='auto')
```

The callback mentioned above stops training if the change in the validation loss is less than 0.01 for five epochs.

> **Note**
>
> Always use **`ModelCheckpoint`** to store the model state. This is especially important for larger datasets and larger networks.

Exercise 48: Predicting Avocado Price Using Neural Networks

Let us apply the knowledge that we received in this section to create an excellent neural network model that will predict the price of different kinds of avocados. The dataset (https://github.com/TrainingByPackt/Data-Science-with-Python/tree/master/Chapter05/data) contains information such as average price of the produce, volume of the produce, region where the avocado was produced, and size of the bags that were used. It also has a few unknown variables that might help us with the model.

> **Note**
>
> Original source site: www.hassavocadoboard.com/retail/volume-and-price-data

1. Import the avocado dataset and observe the columns. You will see something like this:

```
import pandas as pd
import numpy as np
data = pd.read_csv('data/avocado.csv')
data.T
```

	0	1	2	3	4	5	6	7
Unnamed: 0	0	1	2	3	4	5	6	7
Date	27-12-2015	20-12-2015	13-12-2015	06-12-2015	29-11-2015	22-11-2015	15-11-2015	08-11-2015
AveragePrice	1.33	1.35	0.93	1.08	1.28	1.26	0.99	0.98
Total Volume	64236.6	54877	118220	78992.1	51039.6	55979.8	83453.8	109428
4046	1036.74	674.28	794.7	1132	941.48	1184.27	1368.92	703.75
4225	54454.8	44638.8	109150	71976.4	43838.4	48068	73672.7	101815
4770	48.16	58.33	130.5	72.58	75.78	43.61	93.26	80
Total Bags	8696.87	9505.56	8145.35	5811.16	6183.95	6683.91	8318.86	6829.22
Small Bags	8603.62	9408.07	8042.21	5677.4	5986.26	6556.47	8196.81	6266.85
Large Bags	93.25	97.49	103.14	133.76	197.69	127.44	122.05	562.37
XLarge Bags	0	0	0	0	0	0	0	0
type	conventional	conventional	conventional	conventional	conventional	conventional	conventional	conventional
year	2015	2015	2015	2015	2015	2015	2015	2015
region	Albany	Albany	Albany	Albany	Albany	Albany	Albany	Albany

Figure 5.29: Screenshot showing avocado dataset

2. Look through the data and split the date column into days and months. This will help us catch the seasonality while ignoring the year. Now, drop the date and unnamed columns.

```
data['Day'], data['Month'] = data.Date.str[:2], data.Date.str[3:5]
data = data.drop(['Unnamed: 0', 'Date'], axis = 1)
```

3. Encode the categorical variables using the **LabelEncoder** so that Keras can use it to train the model.

```
from sklearn.preprocessing import LabelEncoder
from collections import defaultdict
label_dict = defaultdict(LabelEncoder)
data[['region', 'type', 'Day', 'Month', 'year']] = data[['region',
'type', 'Day', 'Month', 'year']].apply(lambda x: label_dict[x.name].fit_
transform(x))
```

4. Split the data into training and testing sets.

```
from sklearn.model_selection import train_test_split
X = data
y = X.pop('AveragePrice')
X_train, X_test, y_train, y_test = train_test_split(X, y, test_size=0.3,
random_state=9)
```

5. Use callbacks to save the model whenever the loss improves and for early stopping of the model if it starts performing poorly.

```
from keras.callbacks import ModelCheckpoint, EarlyStopping
filepath="avocado-{epoch:02d}-{val_loss:.2f}.hdf5"
model_ckpt = ModelCheckpoint(filepath, monitor='val_loss', verbose=1, save_
best_only=True, mode='auto')
es = EarlyStopping(monitor='val_loss', min_delta=1, patience=5, verbose=1)
callbacks = [model_ckpt, es]
```

6. Create a neural network model. Here, we make use of the same model as before.

```
from keras.models import Sequential
from keras.layers import Dense
model = Sequential()
model.add(Dense(units=16, activation='relu', input_dim=13))
model.add(Dense(units=8, activation='relu'))
model.add(Dense(units=1, activation='linear'))
model.compile(loss='mse', optimizer='adam')
```

7. Train and evaluate the model to get the MSE of the model.

```
model.fit(X_train, y_train, validation_data = (X_test, y_test), epochs=40,
batch_size=32)
model.evaluate(X_test, y_test)
```

8. Check the final output in the following screenshot:

```
5475/5475 [==============================] - 0s 26us/step

11.995191503812189
```

Figure 5.30: MSE of model

Congratulations! You have just trained your neural network to get a reasonable error on the avocado dataset. The value shown above is the mean square error of the model. Modify some hyperparameters and use the rest of the data to see if you can get a better error score. Make use of the information provided in the previous sections.

> **Note**
>
> A decrease in MSE is favorable. The most optimal value will depend on the situation. For example, while predicting the speed of a car, values less than 100 are ideal, whereas when predicting the GDP of a country, an MSE of 1000 is good enough.

Categorical Variables

A categorical variable is one whose values can be represented in different categories. Examples are colours of a ball, breed of dogs, and zip codes. Mapping these categorical variables in a single dimension creates a sort of dependence on each other, which is incorrect. Even though these categorical variables do not have an order or dependence, inputting them to a neural network as a single feature makes the neural network create dependence between these variables depending on the order, whereas in reality, the order does not mean anything. In this section, we will learn about the ways in which can fix this issue and train effective models.

One-hot Encoding

The easiest and the most widely used method of mapping categorical variables is to use one-hot encoding. Using this method, we convert a categorical feature into features equal to the number of categories in the feature.

Gender		Male	Female
Male	→	1	0
Female		0	1
Male		1	0

Figure 5.31: Categorical feature conversion

Use the following steps to convert categorical variables into one-hot encoded variables:

1. Convert the data into a number if represented as a data type other than int. There are two ways to do this
2. You can directly use the `LabelEncoder` method of sklearn.
3. Create bins to reduce the number of categories. The higher the number of categories, the more difficult it is for the model. You can choose an integer to represent each bin. Do keep in mind that doing this will lead to a loss in information and might result in a bad model. You can perform histogram binning using the following rule:

   If the number of categorical columns is less than 25, use 5 bins.

   If it is between 25 and 100, use n/5 bins, where n is the number of categorical columns, and if it is more than 100, use 10 * log (n) bins.

> **Note**
>
> You can combine the categories with frequencies smaller than 5% into one category.

4. Convert the numerical array from Step 1 into a one-hot vector using the `get_dummies` function of pandas.

```
pd.get_dummies(data,columns=['type'])
```

Date	AveragePrice	Total Volume	4046	4225	4770	Total Bags	Small Bags	Large Bags	XLarge Bags	year	region	type_conventional	type_organic
-2015	1.33	64236.62	1036.74	54454.85	48.16	8696.87	8603.62	93.25	0.00	2015	Albany	1	0
-2015	1.35	54876.98	674.28	44638.81	58.33	9505.56	9408.07	97.49	0.00	2015	Albany	1	0
-2015	0.93	118220.22	794.70	109149.67	130.50	8145.35	8042.21	103.14	0.00	2015	Albany	1	0
-2015	1.08	78992.15	1132.00	71976.41	72.58	5811.16	5677.40	133.76	0.00	2015	Albany	1	0
-2015	1.28	51039.60	941.48	43838.39	75.78	6183.95	5986.26	197.69	0.00	2015	Albany	1	0

Figure 5.32: Output of get_dummies function

There are two main reasons why one-hot encoding isn't the best way to use categorical data:

- Different values of the categorical variables are assumed to be completely independent of each other. This leads to a loss of information about the relationship between them.
- Categorical variables with many categories result in a very computationally expensive model. Wider datasets require more data points to make meaningful models. This is known as the curse of dimensionality.

To work through these issues, we will use entity embedding.

Entity Embedding

Entity embedding represents categorical features in a multidimensional space. This ensures that the network learns the correct relationship between the different categories of a feature. The dimensions of this multidimensional space do not represent anything specific; it could be anything that the model deems fit to learn. For example, in the case of the days of a week, one dimension could be whether the day is a weekday or not and another could be the distance from a weekday. This method has been inspired from word embedding that is used in natural language processing to learn the semantic similarities between words and phrases. Creating an embedding can help teach the neural networks how Friday is different from Wednesday or how a puppy and a dog are different. For example, a four-dimensional embedding matrix for the days of the week will look something like this:

Thursday	[0.1, 0.2, 0.8, 0.95]
Friday	[0.1, 0.7, 0.2, 0.76]
Saturday	[0.8, 0.8, 0.1, 0.52]
Sunday	[0.7, 0.7, 0.2, 0.55]

Figure 5.33: Four-dimensional embedding matrix

From the above matrix, you can see that the embedding learns the dependence between the categories: it knows that Saturday and Sunday are more similar than Thursday and Friday, as the vectors for Saturday and Sunday are similar. Entity embedding gives a big edge when you have a lot of categorical variables in your dataset. To create entity embedding in Keras, you can use the embedding layer.

> **Note**
>
> Always try to use word embedding as it gives the best result.

Exercise 49: Predicting Avocado Price Using Entity Embedding

Let us use the knowledge of entity embedding to predict the avocado price by creating a better neural network model. We will use the same avocado dataset from before.

1. Import the avocado price dataset and check for null values. Split the date column into month and day columns.

```
import pandas as pd
import numpy as np
data = pd.read_csv('data/avocado.csv')
data['Day'], data['Month'] = data.Date.str[:2], data.Date.str[3:5]
data = data.drop(['Unnamed: 0', 'Date'], axis = 1)
data = data.dropna()
```

2. Encode the categorical variables.

```
from sklearn.preprocessing import LabelEncoder
from collections import defaultdict
label_dict = defaultdict(LabelEncoder)
data[['region', 'type', 'Day', 'Month', 'year']] = data[['region',
'type', 'Day', 'Month', 'year']].apply(lambda x: label_dict[x.name].fit_
transform(x))
```

3. Split the data into training and testing sets.

```
from sklearn.model_selection import train_test_split
X = data
y = X.pop('AveragePrice')
X_train, X_test, y_train, y_test = train_test_split(X, y, test_size=0.3,
random_state=9)
```

4. Create a dictionary that maps categorical column names to the unique values in them.

```
cat_cols_dict = {col: list(data[col].unique()) for col in ['region',
'type', 'Day', 'Month', 'year'] }
```

5. Next, get the input data in the format that the embedding neural network will accept.

```
train_input_list = []
test_input_list = []

for col in cat_cols_dict.keys():
    raw_values = np.unique(data[col])
    value_map = {}
    for i in range(len(raw_values)):
        value_map[raw_values[i]] = i
    train_input_list.append(X_train[col].map(value_map).values)
    test_input_list.append(X_test[col].map(value_map).fillna(0).values)

other_cols = [col for col in data.columns if (not col in cat_cols_dict.
keys())]
train_input_list.append(X_train[other_cols].values)
test_input_list.append(X_test[other_cols].values)
```

Here, what we are doing is creating a list of arrays of all the variables.

6. Next, create a dictionary that will store the output dimensions of the embedding layers. This is the number of values the variable will be denoted by. You must get to the right number with trial and error.

```
cols_out_dict = {
    'region': 12,
    'type': 1,
    'Day': 10,
    'Month': 3,
    'year': 1
}
```

7. Now, create the embedding layers for the categorical variables. In each iteration of the loop, we create one embedding layer for the categorical variable.

```
from keras.models import Model
from keras.layers import Input, Dense, Concatenate, Reshape, Dropout
from keras.layers.embeddings import Embedding
inputs = []
embeddings = []
for col in cat_cols_dict.keys():

    inp = Input(shape=(1,), name = 'input_' + col)
    embedding = Embedding(cat_cols_dict[col], cols_out_dict[col], input_
length=1, name = 'embedding_' + col)(inp)
    embedding = Reshape(target_shape=(cols_out_dict[col],))(embedding)
    inputs.append(inp)
    embeddings.append(embedding)
```

8. Now, add the continuous variable to the network and complete the model.

```
input_numeric = Input(shape=(8,))
embedding_numeric = Dense(16)(input_numeric)
inputs.append(input_numeric)
embeddings.append(embedding_numeric)

x = Concatenate()(embeddings)
x = Dense(16, activation='relu')(x)
x = Dense(4, activation='relu')(x)
output = Dense(1, activation='linear')(x)

model = Model(inputs, output)
model.compile(loss='mse', optimizer='adam')
```

9. Train the model with the train_input_list, which we created in Step 5 for 50 epochs.

```
model.fit(train_input_list, y_train, validation_data = (test_input_list,
y_test), epochs=50, batch_size=32)
```

10. Now, get the weights from the embedding layers to visualize the embedding.

```
embedding_region = model.get_layer('embedding_region').get_weights()[0]
```

11. Perform PCA and plot the output using the region labels (which you can get by performing inverse transform on the dictionary that we created earlier). PCA displays similar data points closer, by reducing the dimensionality to two dimensions. Here, we plot only the first 25 regions.

You can plot all of them if you want.

```
import matplotlib.pyplot as plt
from sklearn.decomposition import PCA
pca = PCA(n_components=2)
Y = pca.fit_transform(embedding_region[:25])
plt.figure(figsize=(8,8))
plt.scatter(-Y[:, 0], -Y[:, 1])
for i, txt in enumerate((label_dict['region'].inverse_transform(cat_cols_
dict['region']))[:25]):
    plt.annotate(txt, (-Y[i, 0],-Y[i, 1]), xytext = (-20, 8), textcoords =
'offset points')
plt.show()
```

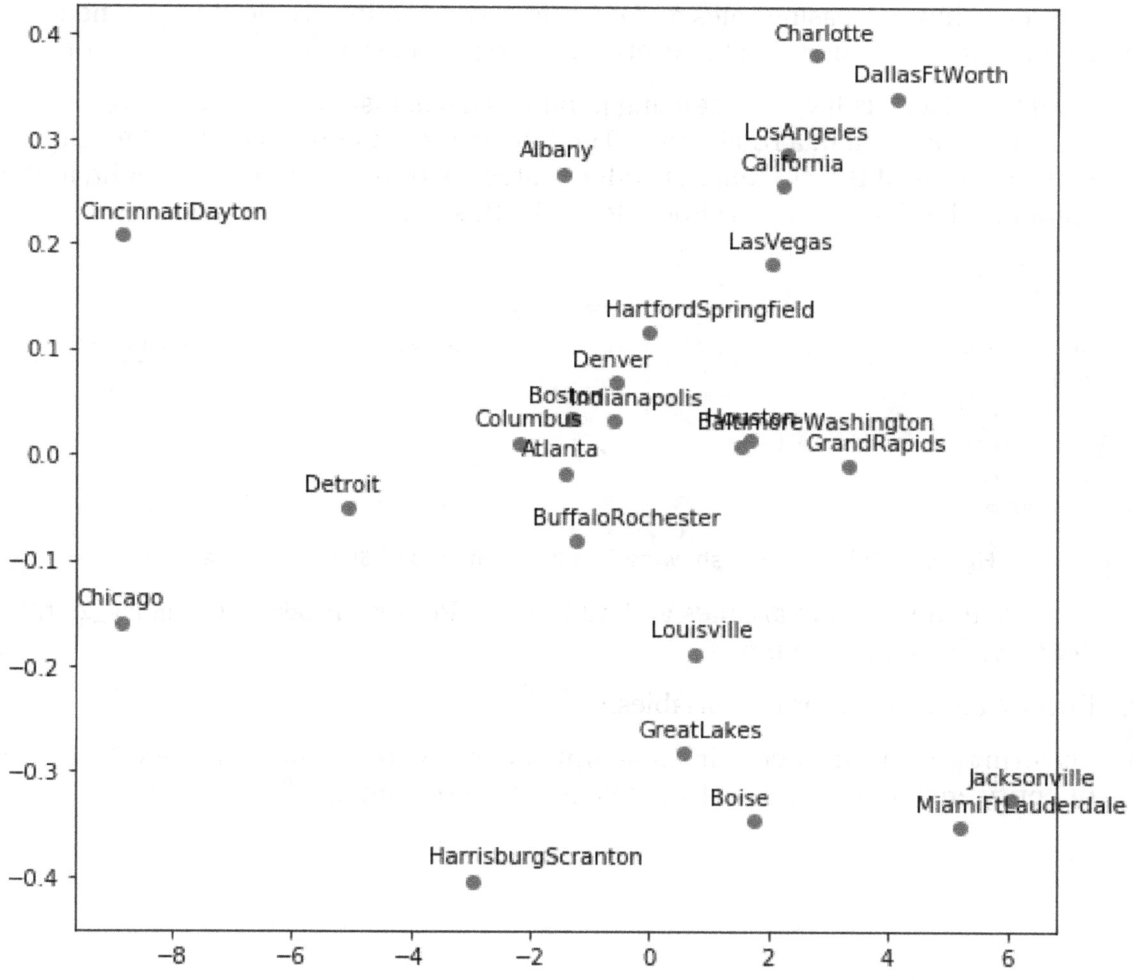

Figure 5.34: Graphical representation of avocado growing region using entity embedding

Congratulations! You improved the accuracy of your model by using entity embedding. As you can see from the embedding plot, the model was able to figure out the regions with high and low average prices. You can plot the embedding of other variables to see what relationships the network makes from the data. Also, try to improve the accuracy of this model through hyperparameter tuning.

Activity 16: Predicting a Customer's Purchase Amount

In this activity, we will attempt to predict the amount a customer will spend on a product category. The dataset (https://github.com/TrainingByPackt/Data-Science-with-Python/tree/master/Chapter05/data) contains transactions made in a retail store. Let's look at the following scenario: You work at a big retail chain and want to predict which kind of customer will spend how much money on a particular product category. Doing this will help your frontline staff recommend the right kind of products to customers, thus increasing sales and customer satisfaction. To do this, you need to create a machine learning model that predicts the purchase value of a transaction.

1. Load the Black Friday dataset using pandas. This dataset is a collection of transactions made in a retail store. The information it contains is the age, city, marital status of the customer, product category of the item being bought, and bill amount. The first few rows should look like this:

```
data.head()
```

	User_ID	Product_ID	Gender	Age	Occupation	City_Category	Stay_In_Current_City_Years	Marital_Status	Product_Category_1	Product_Category_2
0	1000001	P00069042	F	0-17	10	A	2	0	3	NaN
1	1000001	P00248942	F	0-17	10	A	2	0	1	6.0
2	1000001	P00087842	F	0-17	10	A	2	0	12	NaN
3	1000001	P00085442	F	0-17	10	A	2	0	12	14.0
4	1000002	P00285442	M	55+	16	C	4+	0	8	NaN

Figure 5.35: Screenshot showing first five elements of Black Friday dataset

Remove unnecessary variables and null values. Remove **Product_Category_2** and **Product_Category_3** columns.

2. Encode all the categorical variables.

3. Perform prediction by creating a neural network with the Keras library. Make use of entity embedding and perform hyperparameter tuning.

4. Save your model for future use.

> **Note**
>
> The solution for this activity can be found on page 364.

Summary

In this chapter, we learnt how to create highly accurate structured data models and understood what XGBoost is and how to use the library to train models, Before we started, we were wondering what neural networks are and how to use the Keras library to train models. After learning about neural networks, we moved to handling categorical data. Finally, we learned what cross-validation is and how to use it.

Now that you have completed this chapter, you can handle any kind of structured data and creating machine learning models with it. In the next chapter, you will learn how to create neural network models for image data.

6

Decoding Images

Learning Objectives

By the end of this chapter, you will be able to:

- Create models that can classify images into different categories
- Use the Keras library to train neural network models for images
- Utilize concepts of image augmentation in different business scenarios
- Extract meaningful information from images

This chapter will cover various concepts on how to read and process images.

Introduction

So far, we have only been working with numbers and text. In this chapter, we will learn how to use machine learning to decode images and extract meaningful information, such as the type of object present in an image, or the number written in an image. Have you ever stopped to think about how our brains interpret the images they receive from our eyes? After millions of years of evolution, our brains have become highly efficient and accurate at recognizing objects and patterns from the images they get from our eyes. We have been able to replicate the function of our eyes using cameras, but making computers recognize patterns and objects in images is a really tough job. The field associated with understanding what is present in images is known as computer vision. The field of computer vision has witnessed tremendous research and advancements in the past few years. The introduction of Convoluted Neural Networks (CNNs) and the ability to train neural networks on GPUs were the biggest of these breakthroughs. Today, CNNs are used anywhere we have a computer vision problem, for example, self-driving cars, facial recognition, object detection, object tracking, and creating fully autonomous robots. In this chapter, we will learn how these CNNs work and how big an improvement they are compared to traditional methods.

Images

The digital cameras that we have today store images as a big matrix of numbers. These are what we call digital images. A single number on this matrix refers to a single pixel in the image. Individual numbers refer to the intensity of the color at that pixel. For a grayscale image, these values vary from 0 to 255, where 0 is black and 255 is white. For a colored image, this matrix is three-dimensional, where each dimension has values for red, green, and blue. The values in the matrices refer to the intensities of the respective colors. We use these values as input to our computer vision programs or data science models to perform predictions and recognitions.

Now, there are two ways for us to create machine learning models using these pixels:

- Input individual pixels as different input variables to the neural network
- Use a convolutional neural network

Creating a fully connected neural network that takes individual pixel values as input variables is the easiest and the most intuitive way for us right now, so we will start by creating this model. In the next section, we will learn about CNNs and see how much better they are at dealing with images.

Exercise 50: Classify MNIST Using a Fully Connected Neural Network

In this exercise, we will perform classification on the **Modified National Institute of Standards and Technology database** (**MNIST**) dataset. MNIST is a dataset of handwritten digits that have been normalized to fit into a 28 x 28 pixel bounding box. There are 60,000 training images and 10,000 testing images in this dataset. In case of the fully connected network, we feed the individual pixels as features to the network, and then train it as a normal neural network, much like the first neural network we trained in *Chapter 5, Mastering Structured Data.*

To complete this exercise, complete the following steps:

1. Load the required libraries, as illustrated here:

```
import numpy as np
import matplotlib.pyplot as plt
from sklearn.preprocessing import LabelBinarizer

from keras.datasets import mnist
from keras.models import Sequential
from keras.layers import Dense
```

2. Load the MNIST dataset using the Keras library:

```
(x_train, y_train), (x_test, y_test) = mnist.load_data()
```

3. From the shape of the dataset, you can figure out that the data is available in 2D format. The first element is the number of images available, whereas the next two elements are the width and height of the images:

```
x_train.shape
```

The output is as follows:

```
(60000, 28, 28)
```

Figure 6.1: Width and height of images

4. Plot the first image to see what kind of data you are dealing with:

```
plt.imshow(x_test[0], cmap=plt.get_cmap('gray'))
plt.show()
```

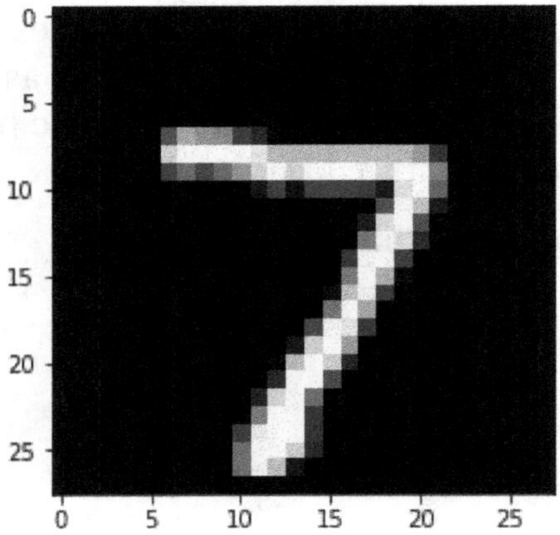

Figure 6.2: Sample image of the MNIST dataset

5. Convert the 2D data into 1D data so that our neural network can take it as input (28 x 28 pixels = 784):

```
x_train = x_train.reshape(60000, 784)
x_test = x_test.reshape(10000, 784)
```

6. Convert the target variable to a one-hot vector so that our network does not form unnecessary connections between the different target variables:

```
label_binarizer = LabelBinarizer()
label_binarizer.fit(range(10))
y_train = label_binarizer.transform(y_train)
y_test = label_binarizer.transform(y_test)
```

7. Create the model. Make a small two-layer network; you can experiment with other architectures. You will learn more about cross-entropy loss in the following section:

```
model = Sequential()
model.add(Dense(units=32, activation='relu', input_dim=784))
model.add(Dense(units=32, activation='relu'))
model.add(Dense(units=10, activation='softmax'))

model.compile(loss='categorical_crossentropy', optimizer='adam', metrics =
['acc'])
model.summary()
```

```
model.summary()
```

```
Layer (type)                 Output Shape              Param #
=================================================================
dense_8 (Dense)              (None, 32)                25120
_________________________________________________________________
dense_9 (Dense)              (None, 32)                1056
_________________________________________________________________
dense_10 (Dense)             (None, 10)                330
=================================================================
Total params: 26,506
Trainable params: 26,506
Non-trainable params: 0
_________________________________________________________________
```

Figure 6.3: Model architecture of the dense network

8. Train the model and check the final accuracy:

```
model.fit(x_train, y_train, validation_data = (x_test, y_test), epochs=40,
batch_size=32)
score = model.evaluate(x_test, y_test)
print("Accuracy: {0:.2f}%".format(score[1]*100))
```

The output is as follows:

```
Accuracy: 93.57%
```

Figure 6.4: Model accuracy

Congratulations! You have now created a model that can predict the number on an image with 93.57% accuracy. You can plot different test images and see your network's result using the following code. Change the value of the image variable to get different images:

```
image = 6
plt.imshow(x_test[image].reshape(28,28),
cmap=plt.get_cmap('gray'))
plt.show()
y_pred = model.predict(x_test)
print("Prediction: {0}".format(np.argmax(y_pred[image])))
```

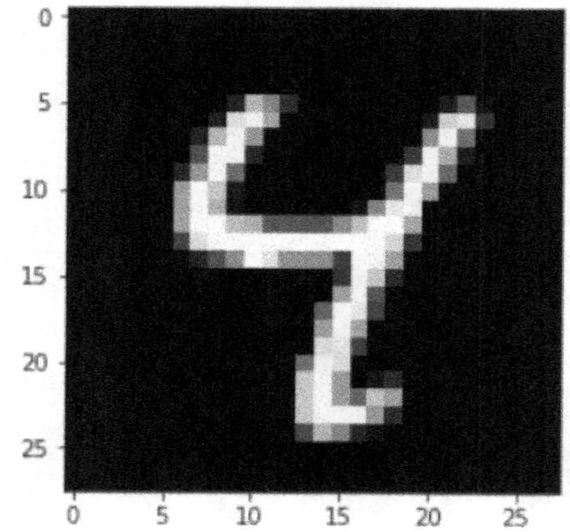

```
Prediction: 4
```

Figure 6.5: An MNIST image with prediction from dense network

You can visualize only the incorrect predictions to understand where your model fails:

```
incorrect_indices = np.nonzero(np.argmax(y_pred,axis=1) != np.argmax(y_
test,axis=1))[0]
image = 4
plt.imshow(x_test[incorrect_indices[image]].reshape(28,28),
cmap=plt.get_cmap('gray'))
plt.show()
print("Prediction: {0}".format(np.argmax(y_pred[incorrect_indices[image]])))
```

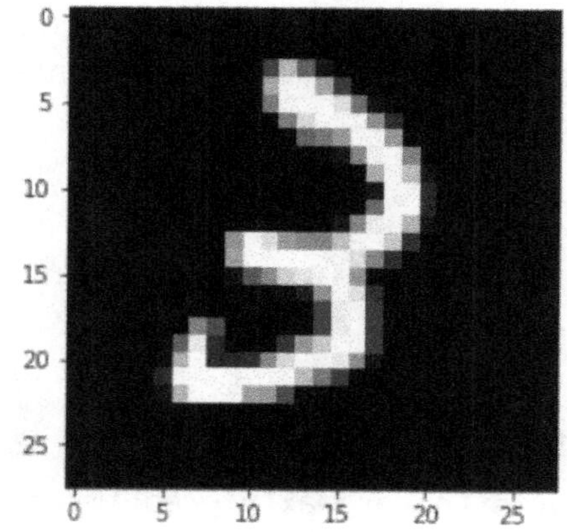

```
Prediction: 2
```

Figure 6.6: Incorrectly classified example from the dense network

As you can see in the previous screenshot, the model failed because we predicted the class to be 2 whereas the correct class was 3.

Convolutional Neural Networks

Convolutional Neural Network (**CNN**) is the name given to a neural network that has convolutional layers. These convolutional layers handle the high dimensionality of raw images efficiently with the help of convolutional filters. CNNs allow us to recognize highly complex patterns in images, which would be impossible with a simple neural network. CNNs can also be used for natural language processing.

The first few layers of a CNN are convolutional, where the network applies different filters to the image to find useful patterns in the image; then there's the pooling layers, which help down-sample the output of the convolutional layers. The activation layer controls which signal flows from one layer to the next, emulating the neurons in our brain. The last few layers in the network are dense layers; these are the same layers we used for the previous exercise.

Convolutional Layer

The convolutional layer consists of multiple filters that learn to activate when they see a certain feature, edge, or color in the initial layers, and eventually faces, honeycombs, and wheels. These filters are exactly like the Instagram filters that we are all so used to. Filters change the appearance of the image by altering the pixels in a certain manner. Let's take a filter that detects horizontal edges as an example.

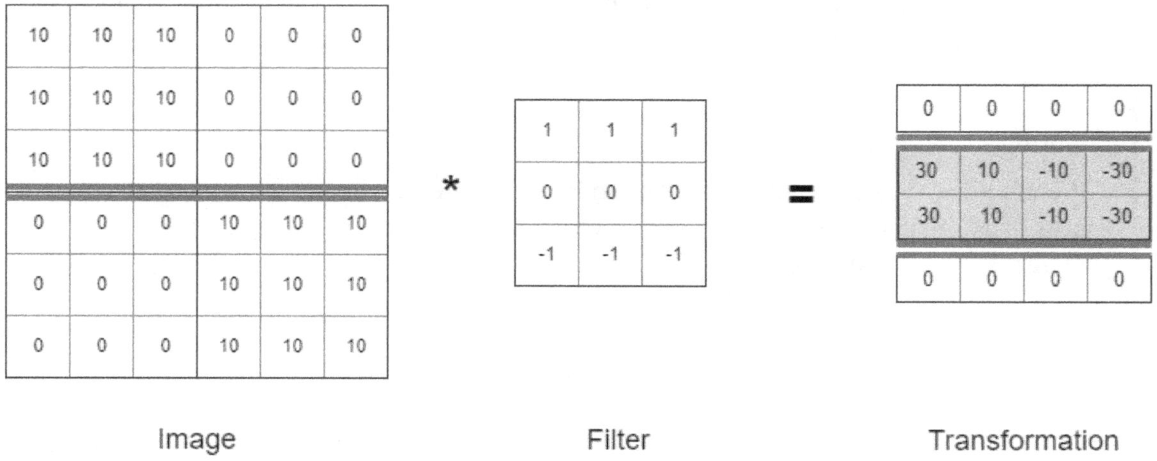

Figure 6.7: Horizontal edge detection filter

As you can see in the preceding screenshot, the filter transforms the image into another image that has the horizontal line highlighted. To get the transformation, we multiply parts of the image by the filter one by one. First, we take the top-left 3 x 3 cross section of the image and perform matrix multiplication with the filter to get the first top-left pixel of the transformation. Then we move the filter one pixel to the right and get the second pixel of the transformation, and so on. The transformation is a new image that has only the horizontal line section of the image highlighted. The values of the filter parameters, 9 in this case, are the weights or parameters that a convolutional layer learns while training. Some filters might learn to detect horizontal lines, some vertical lines, and some lines at a 45-degree angle. The subsequent layers learn more complex structures, such as the pattern of a wheel or a human face.

Some hyperparameters of the convolutional layer are listed here:

- **Filters**: This is the count of filters in each layer of the network. This number also reflects the dimension of the transformation, because each filter will result in one dimension of the output.
- **Filter size**: This is the size of the convolutional filter that the network will learn. This hyperparameter will determine the size of the output transformation.
- **Stride**: In the preceding horizontal edge example, we moved the filter by one pixel every pass. This is the stride. It refers to how much the filter will move every pass. This hyperparameter also determines the size of the output transformation.
- **Padding**: This hyperparameter makes the network pad the image with zeros on all the sides. This helps preserve edge information in some cases and helps us keep the input and output of the same size.

> **Note**
>
> If you perform padding, then you get an image of the same or larger size as the output of the convolution operation. If you do not perform padding, then the image will decrease in size.

Pooling Layer

Pooling layers reduce the size of the input image to reduce the amount of computation and parameters in the network. Pooling layers are inserted periodically between convolutional layers to control overfitting. The most common variant of pooling is 2 x 2 max pooling with a stride of 2. This variant performs down-sampling of the input to keep only the maximum value of the four pixels in the output. The depth dimension remains unchanged.

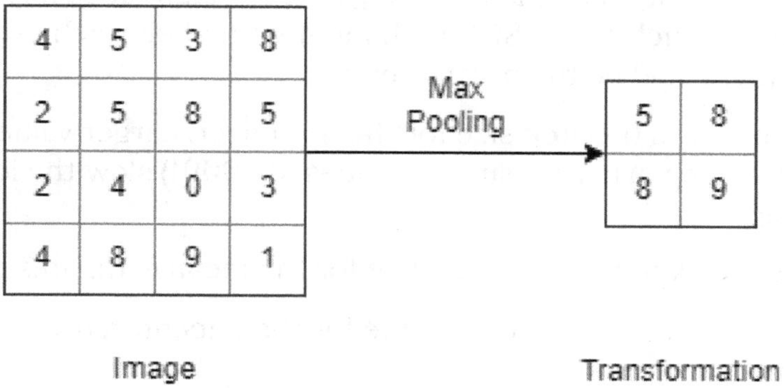

Figure 6.8: Max pooling operation

in the past, we used to perform average pooling as well, but max pooling is used more often nowadays because it has proven to work better in practice. Many data scientists do not like using pooling layers, simply due to the information loss that accompanies the pooling operation. There has been some research on this topic, and it has been found that simple architectures without pooling layers outperform state-of-the-art models at times. To reduce the size of the input, it is suggested to use larger strides in the convolutional layer every once in a while.

> **Note**
>
> The research paper *Striving for Simplicity: The All Convolutional Net* evaluates models with pooling layers to find that pooling layers do not always improve the performance of the network, mostly when enough data is available. For more information, read the *Striving for Simplicity: The All Convolutional Net* paper: https://arxiv.org/abs/1412.6806

Adam Optimizer

Optimizers update weights with the help of loss functions. Selecting the wrong optimizer or the wrong hyperparameter for the optimizer can lead to a delay in finding the optimal solution for the problem.

The name Adam is derived from adaptive moment estimation. Adam has been designed specifically for training deep neural networks. The use of Adam is widespread in the data science community due to its speed in getting close to the optimal solution. Thus, if you want fast convergence, use the **Adam optimizer**. Adam does not always lead to the optimal solution; in such cases, SGD with momentum helps achieve state-of-the-art results. The following would be the parameters:

- **Learning rate**: This is the step size for the optimizer. Larger values (0.2) result in faster initial learning, whereas smaller values (0.00001) slow the learning down during training.
- **Beta 1**: This is the exponential decay rate for the mean estimates of the gradient.
- **Beta 2**: This is the exponential decay rate for the uncentered variance estimates of the gradient.
- **Epsilon**: This is a very small number to prevent division by zero.

A good starting point for deep learning problems are learning rate = 0.001, beta 1 = 0.9, beta 2 = 0.999, and epsilon = 10^{-8}.

> **Note**
>
> For more information, read the Adam paper: https://arxiv.org/abs/1412.6980v8

Cross-entropy Loss

Cross-entropy loss is used when we are working with a classification problem where the output of each class is a probability value between 0 and 1. The loss here increases as the model deviates from the actual value; it follows a negative log graph. This helps when the model predicts probabilities that are far from the actual value. For example, if the probability of the true label is 0.05, we penalize the model with a huge loss. On the other hand, if the probability of the true label is 0.40, we penalize it with a smaller loss.

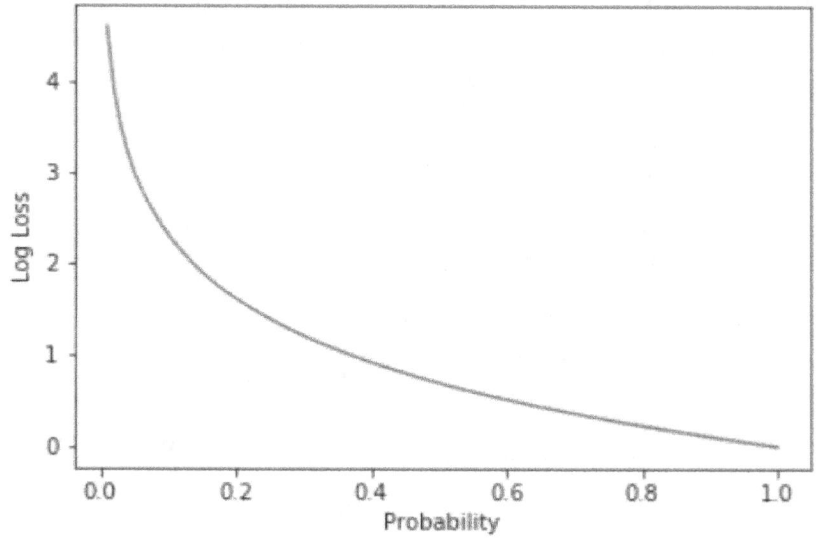

Figure 6.9: Graph of log loss versus probability

The preceding graph shows that the loss increases exponentially as the predictions get further from the true label. The formula that the cross-entropy loss follows is as follows:

$$Loss = -\sum_{c=1}^{M} y_c \log(p_c)$$

Figure 6.10: Cross entropy loss formula

M is number of classes in the dataset (10 in the case of MNIST), y is the true label, and p is the predicted probability of the class. We prefer cross-entropy loss for classification since the weight update becomes smaller as we get closer to the ground truth. Cross-entropy loss penalizes the probability of the correct class only.

Exercise 51: Classify MNIST Using a CNN

In this exercise, we will perform classification on the **Modified National Institute of Standards and Technology (MNIST)** dataset using a CNN instead of the fully connected layers used in *Exercise 50*. We feed the network the complete image as input and get the number on the image as output:

1. Load the MNIST dataset using the Keras library:

```
from keras.datasets import mnist
(x_train, y_train), (x_test, y_test) = mnist.load_data()
```

2. Convert the 2D data into 3D data with the third dimension having only one layer, which is how Keras requires the input:

```
x_train = x_train.reshape(-1, 28, 28, 1)
x_test = x_test.reshape(-1, 28, 28, 1)
```

3. Convert the target variable to a one-hot vector so that our network does not form an unnecessary connection between the different target variables:

```
from sklearn.preprocessing import LabelBinarizer
label_binarizer = LabelBinarizer()
label_binarizer.fit(range(10))
y_train = label_binarizer.transform(y_train)
y_test = label_binarizer.transform(y_test)
```

4. Create the model. Here, we make a small CNN. You can experiment with other architectures:

```
from keras.models import Model, Sequential
from keras.layers import Dense, Conv2D, MaxPool2D, Flatten
model = Sequential()
```

Add the convolutional layers:

```
model.add(Conv2D(32, kernel_size=3,
padding="same",input_shape=(28, 28, 1),    activation = 'relu'))
model.add(Conv2D(32, kernel_size=3, activation = 'relu'))
```

Add the pooling layer:

```
model.add(MaxPool2D(pool_size=(2, 2)))
```

5. Flatten the 2D matrices into 1D vectors:

```
model.add(Flatten())
```

6. Use dense layers as the final layers for the model:

```
model.add(Dense(128, activation = "relu"))
model.add(Dense(10, activation = "softmax"))

model.compile(loss='categorical_crossentropy', optimizer='adam',
metrics = ['acc'])
model.summary()
```

To understand this fully, look at the output of the model in the following screenshot:

```
model.summary()
```

```
_________________________________________________________________
Layer (type)                 Output Shape              Param #
=================================================================
conv2d_34 (Conv2D)           (None, 28, 28, 32)        320
_________________________________________________________________
conv2d_35 (Conv2D)           (None, 26, 26, 32)        9248
_________________________________________________________________
max_pooling2d_20 (MaxPooling (None, 13, 13, 32)        0
_________________________________________________________________
flatten_10 (Flatten)         (None, 5408)              0
_________________________________________________________________
dense_24 (Dense)             (None, 128)               692352
_________________________________________________________________
dense_25 (Dense)             (None, 10)                1290
=================================================================
Total params: 703,210
Trainable params: 703,210
Non-trainable params: 0
_________________________________________________________________
```

Figure 6.11: Model architecture of the CNN

7. Train the model and check the final accuracy:

```
model.fit(x_train, y_train, validation_data = (x_test, y_test),
epochs=10, batch_size=1024)
score = model.evaluate(x_test, y_test)
print("Accuracy: {0:.2f}%".format(score[1]*100))
```

The output is as follows:

```
Accuracy: 98.62%
```

Figure 6.12: Final model accuracy

Congratulations! You have now created a model that can predict the number on an image with 98.62% accuracy. You can plot different test images and see your network's result using the code given in *Exercise* 50. Also, plot the incorrect predictions to see where the model went wrong:

```
import numpy as np
import matplotlib.pyplot as plt
incorrect_indices = np.nonzero(np.argmax(y_pred,axis=1) != np.argmax(y_
test,axis=1))[0]
image = 4
plt.imshow(x_test[incorrect_indices[image]].reshape(28,28),
cmap=plt.get_cmap('gray'))
plt.show()
print("Prediction: {0}".format(np.argmax(y_pred[incorrect_indices[image]])))
```

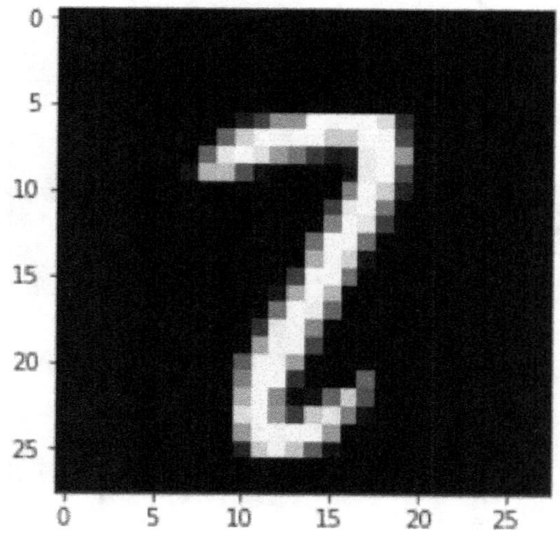


```
Prediction: 7
```

Figure 6.13: Incorrect prediction of the model; the true label is 2

As you can see, the model is having difficulty predicting images that are ambiguous. You can play around with the layers and hyperparameters to see if you can get a better accuracy. Try substituting the pooling layers with convolutional layers with a higher stride, as suggested in the previous section.

Regularization

Regularization is a technique that helps machine learning models generalize better by making modifications in the learning algorithm. This helps prevent overfitting and helps our model work better on data that it hasn't seen during training. In this section, we will learn about the different regularizers available to us.

Dropout Layer

Dropout is a regularization technique that we use to prevent overfitting in our neural network models. We ignore randomly selected neurons from the network while training. This prevents the activations of those neurons continuing down the line, and the weight updates are not applied to them during back propagation. The weights of neurons are tuned to identify specific features; neurons that neighbor them become dependent on this, which can lead to overfitting because these neurons can get specialized to the training data. When neurons are randomly dropped, the neighboring neurons step in and learn the representation, leading to multiple different representations being learned by the network. This make the network generalize better and prevents the model from overfitting. One import thing to keep in mind is that dropout layers should not be used when you are performing predictions or testing your model. This would make the model lose valuable information and would lead to a loss in performance. Keras takes care of this by itself.

When using the dropout layer, it is recommended to create larger networks because it gives the model more opportunities to learn. We generally use a dropout probability between 0.2 and 0.5. This probability refers to the probability by which a neuron will be dropped from training. A dropout layer after every layer is found to give good results, so you can start by placing dropout layers with a probability of 0.2 after every layer and then fine-tune from there.

To create a dropout layer in Keras with a probability of 0.5, you can use the following function:

```
keras.layers.Dropout(0.5)
```

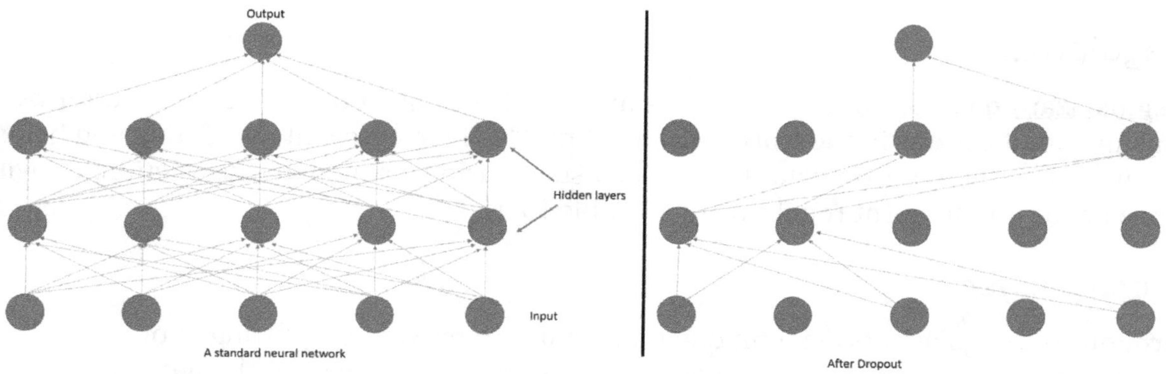

Figure 6.14: Visualizing dropout in a dense neural network

L1 and L2 Regularization

L2 is the most common type of regularization, followed by **L1**. These regularizers work by adding a term to the loss of the model to get the final cost function. This added term leads to a decrease in the weights of the model. This in turn leads to a model that generalizes well.

The cost function of L1 regularization looks like this:

$$Cost\ function = Loss + \frac{\lambda}{2m}\sum |w|$$

Figure 6.15: Cost function of L1 regularization

Here, λ is the regularization parameter. L1 regularization leads to weights that are very close to zero. This makes the neurons with L1 regularization become dependent only on the most important inputs and ignore the noisy inputs.

The cost function of L2 regularization looks like this:

$$Cost\ function = Loss + \frac{\lambda}{2m}\sum w^2$$

Figure 6.16: Cost function of L2 regularization

L2 regularization heavily penalizes high-weight vectors and prefers weights that are diffused. L2 regularization is also known as weight decay because it forces the weights of a network to decay towards zero but, unlike L1 regularization, not exactly to zero. We can combine L1 and L2 and implement them together. To implement these regularizers, you can use the following functions in Keras:

```
keras.regularizers.l1(0.01)

keras.regularizers.l2(0.01)

keras.regularizers.l1_l2(l1=0.01, l2=0.01)
```

Batch Normalization

In *Chapter 1, Introduction to Data Science and Data Pre processing* we learned how to perform normalization and how it helped speed up the training of our machine learning models. Here, we will extend that same normalization to the individual layers of the neural network. **Batch normalization** allows layers to learn independently of other layers. It does this by normalizing the inputs to a layer to have a fixed mean and variance; this prevents the changes in parameters of previous layers from affecting the input of the layer too much. It also has a slight regularization effect; much like dropout, it prevents overfitting, but it does that by introducing noise into the values of the mini batches. When using batch normalization, make sure to use a lower dropout, which is better because dropout leads to a loss of information. However, do not remove dropout and rely completely on batch normalization, because a combination of the two has been seen to work better. While using batch normalization, a higher learning rate can be used because it makes sure that no action is too high or too low.

$$\hat{x}_i = \frac{x_i + \mu}{\sqrt{\sigma^2 + \epsilon}}$$

$$\hat{y} = \gamma \hat{x}_i + \beta$$

Figure 6.17: Batch normalization equation

Here, (x_i) is the input to the layer and y is the normalized input. μ is the batch mean and σ^2 is the batch's standard deviation. Batch normalization introduces two new (x_i)^the loss.

To create a batch normalization layer in Keras, you can use the following function:

```
keras.layers.BatchNormalization()
```

Exercise 52: Improving Image Classification Using Regularization Using CIFAR-10 images

In this exercise, we will perform classification on the Canadian Institute for Advanced Research (CIFAR-10) dataset. It consists of 60,000 32 x 32 color images in 10 classes. The 10 different classes represent birds, airplanes, cats, cars, frogs, deer, dogs, trucks, ships, and horses. It is one of the most widely used datasets for machine learning research, mainly in the field of CNNs. Due to the low resolution of the images, models can be trained much quicker on these images. We will use this dataset to implement some of the regularization techniques we learned in the previous section:

> **Note**
>
> To get the raw CIFAR-10 files and CIFAR-100 dataset, visit https://www.cs.toronto.edu/~kriz/cifar.html.

1. Load the CIFAR-10 dataset using the Keras library:

```
from keras.layers import Dense, Conv2D, MaxPool2D, Flatten, Dropout, BatchNormalization
from keras.datasets import cifar10
(x_train, y_train), (x_test, y_test) = cifar10.load_data()
```

2. Check the dimensions of the data:

```
x_train.shape
```

The output is as follows:

(50000, 32, 32, 3)

Figure 6.18: Dimensions of x

Similar dimensions, for **y**:

```
y_train.shape
```

The output is as follows:

(50000, 1)

Figure 6.19: Dimensions of y

As these are color images, they have three channels.

3. Convert the data to the format that Keras requires:

```
x_train = x_train.reshape(-1, 32, 32, 3)
x_test = x_test.reshape(-1, 32, 32, 3)
```

4. Convert the target variable to a one-hot vector so that our network does not form unnecessary connections between the different target variables:

```
from sklearn.preprocessing import LabelBinarizer
label_binarizer = LabelBinarizer()
label_binarizer.fit(range(10))
y_train = label_binarizer.transform(y_train)
y_test = label_binarizer.transform(y_test)
```

5. Create the model. Here, we make a small CNN without regularization first:

```
from keras.models import Sequential
model = Sequential()
```

Add the convolutional layers:

```
model.add(Conv2D(32, (3, 3), activation='relu', padding='same', input_
shape=(32,32,3)))
model.add(Conv2D(32, (3, 3), activation='relu'))
```

Add the pooling layer:

```
model.add(MaxPool2D(pool_size=(2, 2)))
```

6. Flatten the 2D matrices into 1D vectors:

```
model.add(Flatten())
```

7. Use dense layers as the final layers for the model and compile the model:

```
model.add(Dense(512, activation='relu'))

model.add(Dense(10, activation='softmax'))
model.compile(loss='categorical_crossentropy', optimizer='adam',
metrics = ['acc'])
```

8. Train the model and check the final accuracy:

```
model.fit(x_train, y_train, validation_data = (x_test, y_test),
epochs=10, batch_size=512)
```

9. Now check the accuracy of the model:

```
score = model.evaluate(x_test, y_test)
print("Accuracy: {0:.2f}%".format(score[1]*100))
```

The output is as follows:

```
10000/10000 [==============================] - 21s 2ms/step
Accuracy: 10.00%
```

Figure 6.20: Accuracy of model

10. Now create the same model, but with regularization. You can experiment with other architectures as well:

```
model = Sequential()
```

Add the convolutional layers:

```
model.add(Conv2D(32, (3, 3), activation='relu', padding='same', input_
shape=(32,32,3)))
model.add(Conv2D(32, (3, 3), activation='relu'))
```

Add the pooling layer:

```
model.add(MaxPool2D(pool_size=(2, 2)))
```

11. Add the batch normalization layer along with a dropout layer:

```
model.add(BatchNormalization())
model.add(Dropout(0.10))
```

12. Flatten the 2D matrices into 1D vectors:

```
model.add(Flatten())
```

13. Use dense layers as the final layers for the model and compile the model:

```
model.add(Dense(512, activation='relu'))
model.add(Dropout(0.5))

model.add(Dense(10, activation='softmax'))
model.compile(loss='categorical_crossentropy', optimizer='adam',
metrics = ['acc'])
model.summary()
```

```
model.summary()
```

```
_________________________________________________________________
Layer (type)                 Output Shape              Param #
=================================================================
conv2d_11 (Conv2D)           (None, 32, 32, 32)        896
_________________________________________________________________
conv2d_12 (Conv2D)           (None, 30, 30, 32)        9248
_________________________________________________________________
max_pooling2d_4 (MaxPooling2 (None, 15, 15, 32)        0
_________________________________________________________________
batch_normalization_4 (Batch (None, 15, 15, 32)        128
_________________________________________________________________
dropout_7 (Dropout)          (None, 15, 15, 32)        0
_________________________________________________________________
flatten_4 (Flatten)          (None, 7200)              0
_________________________________________________________________
dense_7 (Dense)              (None, 512)               3686912
_________________________________________________________________
dropout_8 (Dropout)          (None, 512)               0
_________________________________________________________________
dense_8 (Dense)              (None, 10)                5130
=================================================================
Total params: 3,702,314
Trainable params: 3,702,250
Non-trainable params: 64
_________________________________________________________________
```

Figure 6.21: Architecture of the CNN with regularization

14. Train the model and check the final accuracy:

```
model.fit(x_train, y_train, validation_data = (x_test, y_test),
epochs=10, batch_size=512)
score = model.evaluate(x_test, y_test)
print("Accuracy: {0:.2f}%".format(score[1]*100))
```

The output is as follows:

```
Accuracy: 69.32%
```

Figure 6.22: Final accuracy output

Congratulations! You made use of regularization to make your model work better than before. If you do not see an improvement in your model, train it for longer, so set it for more epochs. You will also see that you can train for a lot more epochs without worrying about overfitting.

You can plot different test images and see your network's result using the code given in *Exercise* 50. Also, plot the incorrect predictions to see where the model went wrong:

```
import numpy as np
import matplotlib.pyplot as plt
y_pred = model.predict(x_test)
incorrect_indices = np.nonzero(np.argmax(y_pred,axis=1) != np.argmax(y_
test,axis=1))[0]
labels = ['airplane', 'automobile', 'bird', 'cat', 'deer', 'dog', 'frog',
'horse', 'ship', 'truck']
image = 3
plt.imshow(x_test[incorrect_indices[image]].reshape(32,32,3))
plt.show()
print("Prediction: {0}".format(labels[np.argmax(y_pred[incorrect_
indices[image]])]))
```

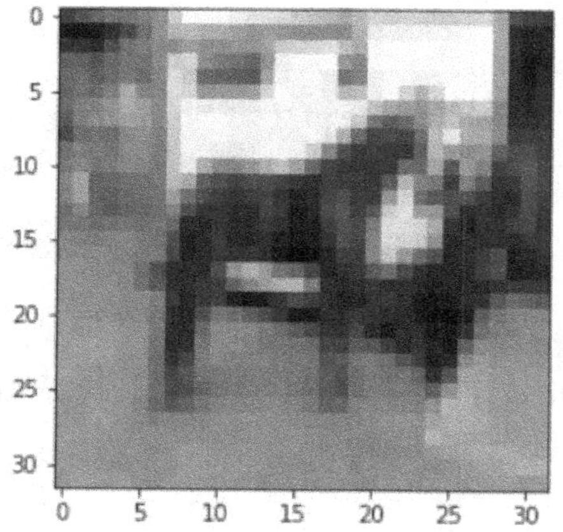


```
Prediction: deer
```

Figure 6.23: Incorrect prediction of the model

As you can see, the model is having difficulty in predicting images that are ambiguous. The true label is *horse*. You can play around with the layers and hyperparameters to see if you can get a better accuracy. Try creating more complex models with regularization and train them for longer.

Image Data Preprocessing

In this section, we go over a few techniques that you can use as a data scientist to preprocess images. First, we look at image normalization, and then we learn how we can convert a color image into a greyscale image. Finally, we look at ways in which we can bring all images in a dataset to the same dimensions. Preprocessing images is needed because datasets do not contain images that are the same size; we need to convert them into a standard size to train machine learning models on them. Some image preprocessing techniques help by reducing the model's training time by either making the important features easier to identify for the model or by reducing the dimensions as in the case of a greyscale image.

Normalization

In the case of images, the scale of the pixels is of the same order and in the range 0 to 255. Therefore, this normalization step is optional, but it might help speed up the learning process. To reiterate, centering the data and scaling it to the same order helps the network by ensuring that the gradients do not go out of control. A neural network shares parameters (neurons). If inputs are not scaled to the same order, it would make it difficult for the network to learn.

Converting to Grayscale

Depending on the kind of dataset and problem you have, you can convert your images from RGB to greyscale. This helps the network work much more quickly because it has a lot fewer parameters to learn. Depending on the type of problem, you might not want to do this because it leads to a loss in information provided by the colors of the image. To convert an RGB image to a grayscale image, use the **Pillow** library:

```
from PIL import Image
image = Image.open('rgb.png').convert('LA')
image.save('greyscale.png')
```

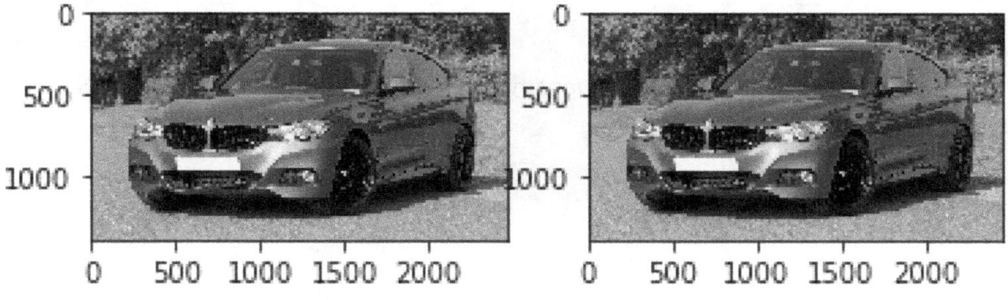

Figure 6.24: Image of a car converted to grayscale

Getting All Images to the Same Size

When working with real-life datasets, you will often come across a major challenge in that not all the images in your dataset will be the same size. You can perform one of the following steps depending on the situation to get around the issue:

- **Upsampling**: You can upsample smaller images to fix a specific size. If the aspect ratio doesn't match the size that you have decided upon, you can crop the image. There will be some loss of information, but you can get around this by taking different centers while cropping and introducing these new images to the dataset. This will make the model more robust. To do this, utilize the following code:

```
from PIL import Image
img = Image.open('img.jpg')
scale_factor = 1.5
new_img = img.resize((int(img.size[0]* scale_factor),int(img.size[1]*
scale_factor)), Image.BICUBIC)
```

  The second parameter of the **resize** function is the algorithm that will be used to get new pixels of the resized image. The bicubic algorithm is fast and is one of the best pixel resampling algorithms for upsampling.

Figure 6.25: Upsampled image of a car

- **Downsampling**: Similar to upsampling, you can perform downsampling on large images to make then smaller and then crop to fit the size that you have selected. You can use the following code to downsample images:

```
scale_factor = 0.5
new_img = img.resize(
(int(img.size[0]* scale_factor ),
 int(img.size[1]* scale_factor)),
Image.ANTIALIAS)
```

The second parameter of the **`resize`** function is the algorithm that will be used to get the new pixels of the resized image, as mentioned previously. The antialiasing algorithm helps smoothen out the pixelated images. It works better than bicubic but is much slower. Antialiasing is one of the best pixel resampling algorithms for downsampling.

Figure 6.26: Down sampled image of a car

- **Crop**: This is another method to make all images of the same size is to crop them. As mentioned before, you can use different centers to prevent the loss of information. You can use the following code to crop your images:

```
area = (1000, 500, 2500, 2000)
cropped_img = img.crop(area)
```

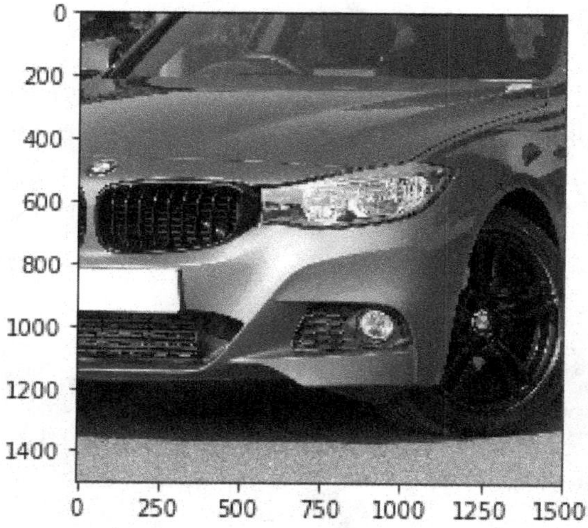

Figure 6.27: Cropped image of a car

- **Padding**: Padding adds a layer of zeros or ones around the image to increase the size of the image. To perform padding, use the following code:

```
size = (2000,2000)
back = Image.new("RGB", size, "white")
offset = (250, 250)
back.paste(cropped_img, offset)
```

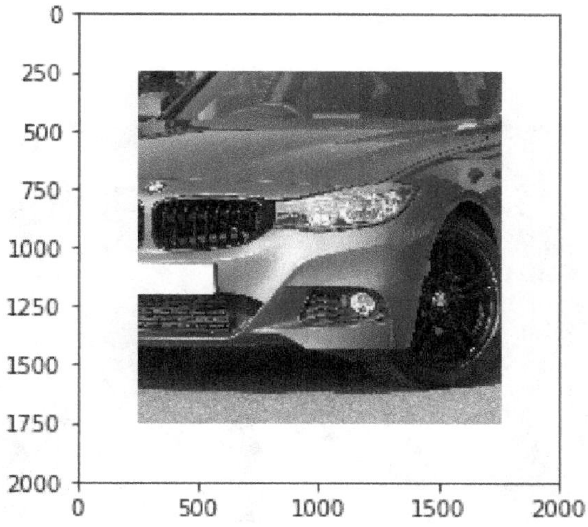

Figure 6.28: Padded image of a cropped car

Other Useful Image Operations

The **Pillow** library has many functions for modifying and creating new images. These will be helpful for creating new images from our existing training data.

To flip an image, we can use the following code:

```
img.transpose(Image.FLIP_LEFT_RIGHT)
```

Figure 6.29: Flipped image of a cropped car

To rotate an image by 45 degrees, we can use the following code:

```
img.rotate(45)
```

Figure 6.30: The cropped car image rotated 45 degrees

To shift an image by 1,000 pixels, we can use the following code:

```
import PIL
width, height = img.size
image = PIL.ImageChops.offset(img, 1000, 0)
image.paste((0), (0, 0, 1000, height))
```

Figure 6.31: Rotated image of the cropped car

Activity 17: Predict if an Image Is of a Cat or a Dog

In this activity, we will attempt to predict if the provided image is of a cat or a dog. The cats and dogs dataset (https://github.com/TrainingByPackt/Data-Science-with-Python/tree/master/Chapter06) from Microsoft contains 25,000 color images of cats and dogs. Let's look at the following scenario: You work at a veterinary clinic with two vets, one that specializes in dogs and one in cats. You want to automate the appointments of the doctors by figuring out if the next client is a dog or a cat. To do this, you create a CNN model:

1. Load the dog versus cat dataset and preprocess the images.
2. Use the image filenames to find the cat or dog label for each image. The first images should look like this:

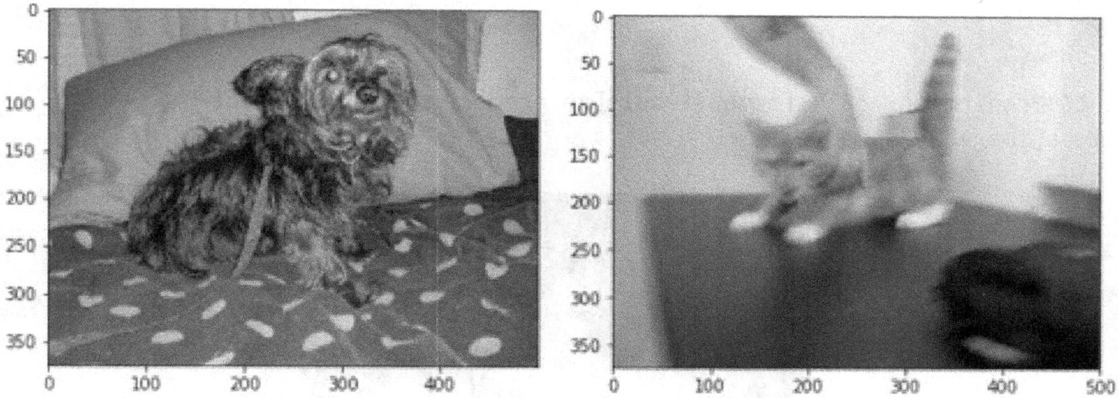

Figure 6.32: First images of the dog and cat class

3. Get the images in the correct shape to be trained.
4. Create a CNN that makes use of regularization.

> **Note**
>
> The solution for this activity can be found on page 369.

You should find that the test set accuracy for this model is 70.4%. The training set accuracy is really high, around 96. This means that the model has started to overfit. Improving the model to get the best possible accuracy is left for you as an exercise. You can plot the incorrectly predicted images using the code from previous exercises to get a sense of how well the model performs:

```
import matplotlib.pyplot as plt

y_pred = model.predict(x_test)

incorrect_indices = np.nonzero(np.argmax(y_pred,axis=1) != np.argmax(y_
test,axis=1))[0]

labels = [‘dog', ‘cat']

image = 5

plt.imshow(x_test[incorrect_indices[image]].reshape(50,50),  cmap=plt.get_
cmap(‘gray'))

plt.show()

print(“Prediction: {0}”.format(labels[np.argmax(y_pred[incorrect_
indices[image]])]))
```

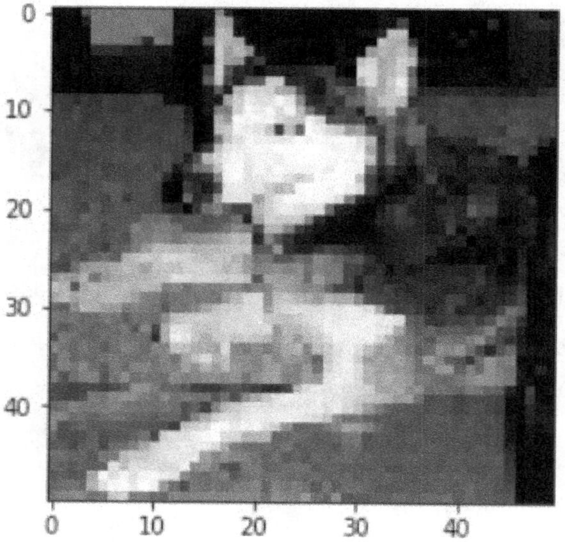


```
Prediction: cat
```

Figure 6.33: Incorrect prediction of a dog by the regularized CNN model

Data Augmentation

While training machine learning models, we data scientists often run into the problem of imbalanced classes and a lack of training data. This leads to sub-par models that perform poorly when deployed in real-life scenarios. One easy way to deal with these problems is data augmentation. There are multiple ways of performing data augmentation, such as rotating the image, shifting the object, cropping an image, shearing to distort the image, and zooming in to a part of the image, as well as more complex methods such as using Generative Adversarial Networks (GANs) to generate new images. GANs are simply two neural networks that are competing with each other. A generator network tries to make images that are similar to the already existing images, while a discriminator network tries to determine if the image was generated or was part of the original data. After the training is complete, the generator network is able to create images that are not a part of the original data but are so similar that they can be mistaken for images that were actually captured by a camera.

> **Note**
> You can learn more about GANs in this paper: https://arxiv.org/abs/1406.2661.

Figure 6.34: On the left is a fake image generated by a GAN, whereas the one on the right is an image of a real person

> **Note**
> Credits: http://www.whichfaceisreal.com

Coming back to the traditional methods of performing image augmentation, we perform the operations mentioned previously, such as flipping images, and then train our model on both the original and the transformed image. Let's say we have the following flipped image of a cat on the left:

Figure 6.35: Normal picture of the cat on the right and flipped image on the left

Now, a machine learning model trained on this left image would have a hard time recognizing the flipped image on the right as that of a cat because it is facing the other way. This is because the convolutional layers are trained to detect images of cats looking to the left only. It has created rules about the position of the different features of a body.

Thus, we train our model on all the augmented images. Data augmentation is the key to getting the best results from a CNN model. We make use of the **`ImageDataGenerator`** class in Keras to perform image augmentations easily. You will learn more about generators in the next section.

Generators

In the previous chapter, we discussed how big datasets could lead to problems in training due to the limitations in RAM. This problem is a bigger issue when working with images. Keras has implemented generators that help us get batches of input images and their corresponding labels while training on the fly. These generators also help us perform data augmentation on images before using them for training. First, we will see how we can make use of the **`ImageDataGenerator`** class to generate augmented images for our model.

To implement data augmentation, we just need to change our *Exercise* 3 code a little bit. We will substitute **model.fit()** with the following:

```
BATCH_SIZE = 32


aug = ImageDataGenerator(rotation_range=20,
width_shift_range=0.2, height_shift_range=0.2,
shear_range=0.15, zoom_range=0.15,
horizontal_flip=True, vertical_flip=True,
fill_mode=”nearest”)


log = model.fit_generator(
aug.flow(x_train, y_train, batch_size= BATCH_SIZE),
validation_data=( x_test, y_test), steps_per_epoch=len(x_train) // BATCH_
SIZE, epochs=10)
```

Let's now look at what **ImageDataGenerator** is actually doing:

- **rotation_range**: This parameter defines the maximum degrees by which the image can be rotated. This rotation is random and can be of any value less than the amount mentioned. This ensures that no two images are the same.
- **width_shift_range/height_shift_range**: This value defines the amount by which the image can be shifted. If the value is less than 1, then the value is assumed to be a fraction of the total width. If it is more than 1, it is taken as pixel. The range will be in the interval (**-shift_range**, **+ shift_range**).
- **shear_range**: This is the shearing angle in degrees (counter-clockwise direction).
- **zoom_range**: The value here can either be [**lower_range**, **upper_range**] or be a float, in which case the range would be [**1-zoom_range**, **1+zoom_range**]. This is the range for the random zooming.
- **horizontal_flip** / **vertical_flip**: A true value here makes the generator randomly flip the image horizontally or vertically.
- **fill_mode**: This helps us decide what to put in the whitespaces created by the rotation and searing process.

constant: This fills the white space with a constant value that has to be defined using the **cval** parameter.

nearest: This fills the whitespace with the nearest pixel.

reflect: This causes a reflection effect, much like a mirror.

wrap: This causes the image to wrap around and fill the whitespace.

The generator is applying the preceding operations randomly on all the images it encounters. This ensures that the model does not see the same image twice and mitigates overfitting. We have to use the **fit_generator()** function instead of the **fit()** function when working with generators. We pass a suitable batch size to the generator depending on the amount of free RAM we have for training.

The default Keras generator has a bit of memory overhead; to remove this, you can create your own generator. To do this, you will have to make sure you implement these four parts of the generator:

1. Read the input image (or any other data).
2. Read or generate the label.
3. Preprocess or augment the image.

> **Note**
>
> Make sure to augment the images randomly.

4. Generate output in the form that Keras expects.

An example code to help you create your own generator is given here:

```
def custom_image_generator(images, labels, batch_size = 128):

    while True:
        # Randomly select images for the batch
        batch_images = np.random.choice(images,
                                        size = batch_size)
        batch_input = []
        batch_output = []

        # Read image, perform preprocessing and get labels
```

```
        for image in batch_images:

            # Function that reads and returns the image
            input = get_input(image)

            # Function that gets the label of the image
            output = get_output(image,labels =labels)

            # Function that pre-processes and augments the image
            input = preprocess_image(input)

            batch_input += [input]
            batch_output += [output]



        batch_x = np.array( batch_input )
        batch_y = np.array( batch_output )

        # Return a tuple of (images,labels) to feed the network
        yield(batch_x, batch_y)
```

Implementing **get_input**, **get_output**, and **preprocess_image** is left as an exercise.

Exercise 53: Classify CIFAR-10 Images with Image Augmentation

In this exercise, we will perform classification on the CIFAR-10 (Canadian Institute for Advanced Research) dataset, similar to *Exercise 52*. Here, we will make use of generators to augment the training data. We will rotate, shift, and flip the images randomly:

1. Load the CIFAR-10 dataset using the Keras library:

```
from keras.datasets import cifar10
(x_train, y_train), (x_test, y_test) = cifar10.load_data()
```

2. Convert the data to the format that Keras requires:

```
x_train = x_train.reshape(-1, 32, 32, 3)
x_test = x_test.reshape(-1, 32, 32, 3)
```

3. Convert the target variable to a one-hot vector so that our network does not form unnecessary connections between the different target variables:

```
from sklearn.preprocessing import LabelBinarizer
label_binarizer = LabelBinarizer()
label_binarizer.fit(range(10))
y_train = label_binarizer.transform(y_train)
y_test = label_binarizer.transform(y_test)
```

4. Create the model. We will use the network from *Exercise 3*:

```
from keras.models import Sequential
model = Sequential()
```

   Add the convolutional layers:

```
from keras.layers import Dense, Dropout, Conv2D, MaxPool2D, Flatten, BatchNormalization
model.add(Conv2D(32, (3, 3), activation='relu', padding='same', input_shape=(32,32,3)))
model.add(Conv2D(32, (3, 3), activation='relu'))
```

   Add the pooling layer:

```
model.add(MaxPool2D(pool_size=(2, 2)))
```

   Add the batch normalization layer, along with a dropout layer:

```
model.add(BatchNormalization())
model.add(Dropout(0.10))
```

5. Flatten the 2D matrices into 1D vectors:

```
model.add(Flatten())
```

6. Use dense layers as the final layers for the model:

```
model.add(Dense(512, activation='relu'))
model.add(Dropout(0.5))

model.add(Dense(10, activation='softmax'))
```

7. Compile the model using the following code:

```
model.compile(loss='categorical_crossentropy', optimizer='adam', metrics = ['acc'])
```

8. Create the data generator and pass it the augmentations you want on the data:

```
from keras.preprocessing.image import ImageDataGenerator
datagen = ImageDataGenerator(
    rotation_range=45,
    width_shift_range=0.2,
    height_shift_range=0.2,
    horizontal_flip=True)
```

9. Train the model:

```
BATCH_SIZE = 128
model_details = model.flow(datagen.flow(x_train, y_train, batch_size =
BATCH_SIZE),
                    steps_per_epoch = len(x_train) // BATCH_SIZE,
                    epochs = 10,
                    validation_data= (x_test, y_test),
                    verbose=1)
```

10. Check the final accuracy of the model:

```
score = model.evaluate(x_test, y_test)
print("Accuracy: {0:.2f}%".format(score[1]*100))
```

The output is shown as follows:

Accuracy: 60.35%

Figure 6.36: Model accuracy output

Congratulations! You have made use of data augmentation to make your model recognize a wider range of images. You must have noticed that the accuracy of your model decreased. This is due to the low number of epochs we trained the model on. Models in which we use data augmentatio n need to be trained for more epochs. You will also see that you can train for a lot more epochs without worrying about overfitting. This is because every epoch, the model is seeing a new image from the dataset. Images are rarely repeated, if ever. You will definitely see an improvement if you run the model for more epochs. Experiment with more architectures and augmentations.

Here you can see an incorrectly classified image. By checking the incorrectly identified images, you can gauge the performance of the model and can figure out where it is performing poorly.

```
y_pred = model.predict(x_test)

incorrect_indices = np.nonzero(np.argmax(y_pred,axis=1) != np.argmax(y_test,axis=1))[0]

labels = ['airplane', 'automobile', 'bird', 'cat', 'deer', 'dog', 'frog', 'horse', 'ship', 'truck']


image = 2

plt.imshow(x_test[incorrect_indices[image]].reshape(32,32,3))

plt.show()

print("Prediction: {0}".format(labels[np.argmax(y_pred[incorrect_indices[image]])]))
```

See the following screenshot to check the incorrect prediction:

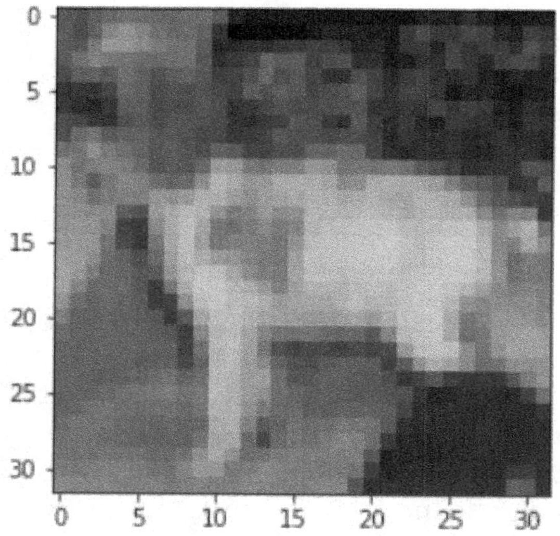

Prediction: horse

Figure 6.37: Incorrect prediction from the CNN model that was trained on augmented data

Activity 18: Identifying and Augmenting an Image

In this activity, we will attempt to predict if an image is of a cat or a dog, like in *Activity 17*. However, this time we will make use of generators to handle images and perform data augmentation on them to get better results:

1. Create functions to get each image and each image label. Then, create a function to preprocess the loaded images and augment them. Finally, create a data generator (as shown in the **Generators** section) to make use of the aforementioned functions to feed data to Keras during training.
2. Load the test dataset that will not be augmented. Use the functions from *Activity 17*.
3. Create a CNN that will identify if the image provided is of a cat or a dog. Make sure to make use of regularization.

> **Note**
>
> The solution for this activity can be found on page 373.

You should find that the test set accuracy for this model is around 72%, which is an improvement on the model in *Activity 17*. You will observe that the training accuracy is really high, at around 98%. This means that this model has started to overfit, much like the one in *Activity 17*. This could be due to a lack of data augmentation. Try changing the data augmentation parameters to see if there is any change in accuracy. Alternatively, you can modify the architecture of the neural network to get better results. You can plot the incorrectly predicted images to get a sense of how well the model performs.

```
import matplotlib.pyplot as plt
y_pred = model.predict(validation_data[0])
incorrect_indices = np.nonzero(np.argmax(y_pred,axis=1) !=
np.argmax(validation_data[1],axis=1))[0]
labels = ['dog', 'cat']

image = 7
```

```
plt.imshow(validation_data[0][incorrect_indices[image]].reshape(50,50),
cmap=plt.get_cmap('gray'))
plt.show()
print("Prediction: {0}".format(labels[np.argmax(y_pred[incorrect_
indices[image]])]))
```

An example is shown in the following screenshot:

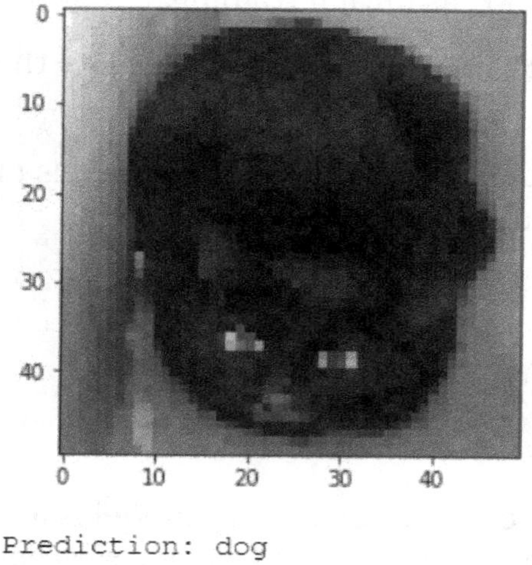

Figure 6.38: Incorrect prediction of a cat by the data augmentation CNN model

Summary

In this chapter, we learned what digital images are and how to create machine learning models with them. We then covered how to use the Keras library to train neural network models for images. We also covered what regularization is, how to use it with neural networks, what image augmentation is, and how to use it was our focus. We covered what CNNs are and how to implement them. Lastly, we discussed various image preprocessing techniques.

Now that you have completed this chapter, you will be able to handle any kind of data to create machine learning models. In the next chapter, we shall learn how to process human language.

7

Processing Human Language

Learning Objectives

By the end of this chapter, you will be able to:

- Create machine learning models for textual data
- Use the NLTK library to preprocess text
- Utilize regular expressions to clean and analyze strings
- Create word embedding using the Word2Vec model

This chapter shall cover the concepts on processing human language.

Introduction

One of the most important goals of artificial intelligence (AI) is to understand the human language to perform tasks. Spellcheck, sentiment analysis, question answering, chat bots, and virtual assistants (such as Siri and Google Assistant) all have a natural language processing (NLP) module. The NLP module enables virtual assistants to process human language and perform actions based on it. For example, when we say, "OK Google, set an alarm for 7 A.M.", the speech is first converted to text and then this text is processed by the NLP module. After this processing, the virtual assistant calls the appropriate API of the Alarm/Clock application. Processing human language has its own set of challenges because it is ambiguous, with words meaning different things depending on the context in which they are used. This is the biggest pain point of language for AI.

Another big reason is the unavailability of complete information. We tend to leave out most of the information while communicating; information that is common sense or things that are universally true or false. For example, the sentence "I saw a man on a hill with a telescope" can have different meanings depending on the contextual information. For example, it could mean that "I saw a man who had a telescope on a hill," but it could also mean that "I saw a man on a hill through a telescope." It is very difficult for computers to keep track of this information as most of it is contextual. Due to the advances in deep learning, NLP today works much better than when we used traditional methods such as clustering and linear models. This is the reason we will use deep learning on text corpora to solve NLP problems. NLP, like any other machine learning problem, has two main parts, data processing and model creation. In the next topic, we will learn how to process textual data, and later, we will learn how to use this processed data to create machine learning models to solve our problems.

Text Data Processing

Before we start building machine learning models for our textual data, we need to process the data. First, we will learn the different ways in which we can understand what the data comprises. This helps us get a sense of what the data really is and decide on the preprocessing techniques to be used in the next step. Next, we will move on to learn the techniques that will help us preprocess the data. This step helps reduce the size of the data, thus reducing the training time, and also helps us transform the data into a form that would be easier for machine learning algorithms to extract information from. Finally, we will learn how to convert the textual data to numbers so that machine learning algorithms can actually use it to create models. We do this using word embedding, much like the entity embedding we performed in *Chapter 5: Mastering Structured Data.*

Regular Expressions

Before we start working on textual data, we need to learn about regular expressions (RegEx). RegEx is not really a preprocessing technique, but a sequence of characters that defines a search pattern in a string. RegEx is a powerful tool when dealing with textual data as it helps us find sequences in a collection of text. A RegEx consists of metacharacters and regular characters.

<table>
<tr><th>Metacharacter</th><th>Use</th><th>Example</th></tr>
<tr><td>^ and $</td><td>^ = Match to the start
$ = Match to the end</td><td>"^The" matches any string that starts with The
"you$" matches any string that ends with you</td></tr>
<tr><td>*</td><td>Match the preceding character with zero or more character</td><td>"Hello*" matches strings with Hell followed by any number of 'o's</td></tr>
<tr><td>+</td><td>Match the preceding character with one or more character</td><td>"Hello+" matches strings with Hello followed by any number of 'o's</td></tr>
<tr><td>?</td><td>Match the preceding character with zero or one character</td><td>"Hello?" matches with either "Hell" or "Hello"</td></tr>
<tr><td>{a,b}</td><td>Matches the preceding character with a minimum of a and maximum of b times</td><td>"Hello{2,5}" matches strings with Hell followed by any 2 to 5 'o's. It will match "Helloo" and not "Hello"</td></tr>
<tr><td>.</td><td>Matches any character</td><td>"e." Matches any character after e. It will match "ello world" in the string "Hello world"</td></tr>
<tr><td>| and []</td><td>| = Matches either preceding or following character
[] = matches any of the characters inside the brackets</td><td>"a|b" matches strings with either a or b
"[ab]" same as above
In the string "bat" regex will first match b and the match a.</td></tr>
<tr><td>\w, \d and \s</td><td>\w = Single alphanumeric character
\d = Single digit
\s = Single white space
(Capital versions match where these do not exist)</td><td>"\w\s\d" matches a string which starts with a character then has a space and then ends with a digit. It will match "d 9" in the string "winners scored 90"</td></tr>
</table>

Figure 7.1: Tables containing metacharacters used in RegEx, and some examples

Using RegEx, we can search for complex patterns in a text. For example, we can use it to remove URLs from a text. We can use the **re** module in Python to remove a URL as follows:

```
re.sub(r"https?\://\S+\s", '', "https://www.asfd.com hello world")
```

re.sub accepts three parameters: the first is RegEx, the second is the expression you want to substitute in place of the matched pattern, and the third is the text in which it should search for the pattern.

The output of the command is as follows:

```
'hello world'
```

Figure 7.2: Output command

> **Note**
>
> It is difficult to remember all the RegEx conventions, so when working with RegEx, refer to a cheat sheet, such as: (http://www.pyregex.com/).

Exercise 54: Using RegEx for String Cleaning

In this exercise, we will use the **re** module of Python to modify and analyze a string. We will simply learn how to use RegEx in this exercise, and in the following section, we will see how we can use RegEx to preprocess our data. We will use a single review from the IMDB Movie Review dataset (https://github.com/TrainingByPackt/Data-Science-with-Python/tree/master/Chapter07), which we shall also work on later in the chapter to create sentiment analysis models. This dataset is already processed, and some words have been removed. This will be the case sometimes when dealing with prebuilt datasets, so it is important to analyze the dataset you are working on before you start working.

1. In this exercise, we will use a movie review from IMDB. Save the review text into a variable, as in the following code. You can use any other paragraph of text for this exercise:

```
string = "first think another Disney movie, might good, it's kids
movie. watch it, can't help enjoy it. ages love movie. first saw movie 10
8 years later still love it! Danny Glover superb could play part better.
Christopher Lloyd hilarious perfect part. Tony Danza believable Mel Clark.
can't help, enjoy movie! give 10/10!<br /><br />- review Jamie Robert Ward
(http://www.invocus.net)"
```

2. Calculate the length of the review to know by how much we should reduce the size. We will use **len(string)** and get the output, as shown in the following code:

```
len(string)
```

The output length is as follows:

```
344
```

Figure 7.3: Length of the string

3. Sometimes, when you scrape data from websites, hyperlinks get recorded as well. Most of the times, hyperlinks do not provide us any information. Remove any hyperlink from the data using a complex regex string, as in "**https?\://\S+**". This selects any substring with **https://** in it:

```
import re
string = re.sub(r"https?\://\S+", '', string)
string
```

The string with hyperlinks is removed as follows:

```
"first think another Disney movie, might good, it's kids movie. watch it,
can't help enjoy it. ages love movie. first saw movie 10 8 years later still
love it! Danny Glover superb could play part better. Christopher Lloyd
hilarious perfect  part. Tony Danza believable Mel Clark. can't help,
enjoy movie! give 10/10!<br /><br />- review Jamie Robert Ward ("
```

Figure 7.4: The string with hyperlinks removed

4. Next, we will remove the **br** HTML tags from the text, which we observed while reading the string. Sometimes, these HTML tags get added to the scrapped data:

```
string = re.sub(r'<br />', ' ', string)
string
```

The string without the **br** tags is as follows:

```
"first think another Disney movie, might good, it's kids movie. watch it,
can't help enjoy it. ages love movie. first saw movie 10 8 years later still
love it! Danny Glover superb could play part better. Christopher Lloyd
hilarious perfect part. Tony Danza believable Mel Clark. can't help, enjoy
movie! give 10/10!  - review Jamie Robert Ward ("
```

Figure 7.5: The string without br tags

5. Now, we will remove all the digits from the text. This helps us reduce the size of the dataset when digits are of no significance to us:

```
string = re.sub('\d','', string)
string
```

The string without digits is shown here:

"first think another Disney movie, might good, it's kids movie. watch it, can't help enjoy it. ages love movie. first saw movie years later still love it! Danny Glover superb could play part better. Christopher Lloyd hilarious perfect part. Tony Danza believable Mel Clark. can't help, enjoy movie! give /! - review Jamie Robert Ward ("

Figure 7.6: The string without digits

6. Next, we will remove all special characters and punctuations. Depending on your problem, these could just be taking up space and not providing relevant information for the machine learning algorithms. So, we remove them with the following regex pattern:

```
string = re.sub(r'[_"\-;%()|+&=*%.,!?:#$@\[\]/]', '', string)
string
```

The string without special characters and punctuations is shown here:

"first think another Disney movie might good it's kids movie watch it can't help enjoy it ages love movie first saw movie years later still love it Danny Glover superb could play part better Christopher Lloyd hilarious perfect part Tony Danza believable Mel Clark can't help enjoy movie give review Jamie Robert Ward "

Figure 7.7: The string without special characters

7. Now, we will substitute **can't** with **cannot** and **it's** with **it is**. This helps us reduce the training time as the number of unique words reduces:

```
string = re.sub(r"can\'t", "cannot", string)
string = re.sub(r"it\'s", "it is", string)
string
```

The final string is as follows:

```
'first think another Disney movie might good it is kids movie watch it
cannot help enjoy it ages love movie first saw movie   years later still
love it Danny Glover superb could play part better Christopher Lloyd
hilarious perfect part Tony Danza believable Mel Clark cannot help enjoy
movie give   review Jamie Robert Ward '
```

Figure 7.8: The final string

8. Finally, we will calculate the length of the cleaned string:

```
len(string)
```

The output size of the string is as follows:

```
324
```

Figure 7.9: The length of cleaned string

We reduced the size of the review by 14%.

9. Now, we will use RegEx to analyze the data and get all the words that start with a capital letter:

> **Note**
>
> **`re.findall`** takes the regex pattern and the string as input and outputs all substrings that match the pattern.

This is shown in the following code:

```
re.findall(r"[A-Z][a-z]*", string)
```

The words are as follows:

```
['Disney',
 'Danny',
 'Glover',
 'Christopher',
 'Lloyd',
 'Tony',
 'Danza',
 'Mel',
 'Clark',
 'Jamie',
 'Robert',
 'Ward']
```

Figure 7.10: Words starting with capital letters

10. To find all the one- and two-letter words in the text, use the following:

```
re.findall(r"\b[A-z]{1,2}\b", string)
```

The output is as follows:

```
['it', 'is', 'it', 'it', 'it']
```

Figure 7.11: One and two letter words

Congratulations! You successfully modified and analyzed a review string using RegEx with the `re` module.

Basic Feature Extraction

Basic feature extraction helps us understand what our data consists of. This helps us select the steps to take to preprocess the dataset. Basic feature extraction consists of actions such as calculation of the average number of words and count of special characters. We will make use of the IMDB movie review dataset in this section as an example:

```
data = pd.read_csv('movie_reviews.csv', encoding='latin-1')
```

Let's see what our dataset consists of:

```
data.iloc[0]
```

The output is as follows:

```
SentimentText    first think another Disney movie, might good, ...
Sentiment                                                         1
Name: 0, dtype: object
```

Figure 7.12: SentimentText data

The **SentimentText** variable contains the actual review and the **Sentiment** variable contains the sentiment of the review. **1** represents a positive sentiment and **0** represents a negative sentiment. Let's print the first review to get a sense of the data we are dealing with:

```
data.SentimentText[0]
```

The first review is as follows:

```
"first think another Disney movie, might good, it's kids movie. watch
it, can't help enjoy it. ages love movie. first saw movie 10 8 years l
ater still love it! Danny Glover superb could play part better. Christ
opher Lloyd hilarious perfect part. Tony Danza believable Mel Clark. c
an't help, enjoy movie! give 10/10!"
```

Figure 7.13: First review

Now, we will try to understand the kind of data we are working with by getting the key statistics of the dataset.

Number of words

We can get the number of words in each review with the following code:

```
data['word_count'] = data['SentimentText'].apply(lambda x: len(str(x).
split(" ")))
```

Now, the **word_count** variable in the DataFrame contains the total number of words in the review. The **apply** function applies the **split** function to each row of the dataset iteratively. Now, we can get the average number of words for each class to see if positive reviews have more words than negative reviews.

The **mean()** function calculates the average of a column in pandas. For negative reviews, use the following code:

```
data.loc[data.Sentiment == 0, 'word_count'].mean()
```

The average number of words for a negative sentiment is as follows:

```
129.08048
```

Figure 7.14: Total number of words for negative sentiment

For positive reviews, use the following:

```
data.loc[data.Sentiment == 1, 'word_count'].mean()
```

The average number of words for a positive sentiment is as follows:

```
132.48864
```

Figure 7.15: Total number of words for positive sentiment

We can see that there isn't much difference in the average number of words for either class.

Stop words

Stop words are the most common words in a language – for example, "I", "me", "my", "yours", and "the." Most of the time, these words provide no real information about the sentence, so we remove these words from our dataset to reduce the size. The **nltk** library has a list of stop words for the English language that we can access.

```
from nltk.corpus import stopwords
stop = stopwords.words('english')
```

To get the count of these stop words, we can use the following code:

```
data['stop_count'] = data['SentimentText'].apply(lambda x: len([x for x in
x.split() if x in stop]))
```

Then, we can see the average number of stop words for each class, by using the following code:

```
data.loc[data.Sentiment == 0, 'stop_count'].mean()
```

The average number of stop words for a negative sentiment is shown here:

```
1.94104
```

Figure 7.16: Average number of stop words for a negative sentiment

Now, to get the number of stop words for a positive sentiment, we use the following code:

```
data.loc[data.Sentiment == 1, 'stop_count'].mean()
```

The output average number of stop words for a positive sentiment is shown here:

```
1.49064
```

Figure 7.17: Average number of stop words for a positive sentiment

Number of special characters

Depending on the kind of problem you are dealing with, you will want to either keep special characters such as `@`, `#`, `$`, and `*`, or remove them. To be able to do that, you first must figure out how many special characters occur in your dataset. To get the count of `^`, `&`, `*`, `$`, `@`, and `#` in your dataset, use the following code:

```
data['special_count'] = data['SentimentText'].apply(lambda x: len(re.
sub('[^\^&*$@#]+' ,'', x)))
```

Text Preprocessing

Now that we know what our data comprises, we need to preprocess it so that our machine learning algorithms can easily find patterns in the text. In this section, we will go over some of the techniques used to clean and reduce the dimensionality of the data we feed into our machine learning algorithm.

Lowercase

The first preprocessing step we perform is converting all the data into lowercase. This prevents multiple copies of the same word. You can easily convert all text to lowercase using the following code:

```
data['SentimentText'] = data['SentimentText'].apply(lambda x: " ".join(x.
lower() for x in x.split()))
```

The apply function applies the **`lower`** function to each row of the dataset iteratively.

Stop word removal

As discussed previously, stop words should be removed from the dataset as they add very little useful information. Stop words do not affect the sentiments of a sentence. We perform this step to remove any bias that stop words might introduce:

```
data['SentimentText'] = data['SentimentText'].apply(lambda x: " ".join(x for
x in x.split() if x not in stop))
```

Frequent word removal

Stop words are more general words such as 'a', 'an,' and 'the.' However, in this step, you will remove the most frequent word from the dataset you are working with. For example, the words that can be removed from a tweet dataset are `RT`, `@username`, and `DM`. First, find the most frequent words:

```
word_freq = pd.Series(' '.join(data['SentimentText']).split()).value_counts()
word_freq.head()
```

The most frequent words are:

```
/><br     50931
movie     30502
film      27399
one       20688
like      18130
dtype: int64
```

Figure 7.18: Most frequent words in tweet dataset

From the output, we get a hint: the text contains HTML tags, which can be removed to considerably reduce the dataset size. So, let's first remove all `<br />` HTML tags and then remove words such as 'movie' and 'film,' which will not have much impact on the sentiment detector:

```
data['SentimentText'] = data['SentimentText'].str.replace(r'<br />','')
data['SentimentText'] = data['SentimentText'].apply(lambda x: " ".join(x for
x in x.split() if x not in ['movie', 'film']))
```

Punctuation and special character removal

Next, we remove all the punctuations and special characters from the text as they add very little information to the text. To remove punctuations and special characters, use this regex:

```
punc_special = r"[^A-Za-z0-9\s]+"
data['SentimentText'] = data['SentimentText'].str.replace(punc_special,'')
```

The regex selects all alphanumerical characters and spaces.

Spellcheck

Sometimes, incorrect spellings of the same word causes us to have copies of the same word. This can be corrected by performing a spellcheck using the autocorrect library:

```
from autocorrect import spell
data['SentimentText'] = [' '.join([spell(i) for i in x.split()]) for x in
data['SentimentText']]
```

Stemming

Stemming refers to the practice of removing the suffixes such as 'ily', 'iest,' and 'ing.' This helps our model because variations of the same root word have the same meaning. For example, 'happy,' 'happily,' and 'happiest' all mean the same thing, so they can be replaced with 'happy.' This is helpful in cases of sentiment analysis, where the degree of happiness is not required as it will reduce the number of dimensions required to represent the data. To perform stemming, we can use the **nltk** library:

```
from nltk.stem import PorterStemmer
stemmer = PorterStemmer()
data['SentimentText'] = data['SentimentText'].apply(lambda x: "
".join([stemmer.stem(word) for word in x.split()]))
```

> **Note**
>
> Spellcheck, stemming, and lemmatization can take a lot of time to complete depending on the size of the dataset, so make sure that you do need to perform this step by looking into the dataset.

Lemmatization

> **Tip**
>
> You should prefer lemmatization to stemming as it is more effective.

Lemmatization is similar to stemming, but here, we substitute words with their root words to reduce the dimensionality of the dataset. Lemmatization is generally a more effective option than stemming. To perform lemmatization, you can use the **nltk** library:

```
lemmatizer = nltk.stem.WordNetLemmatizer()
data['SentimentText'][:5].apply(lambda x: " ".join([lemmatizer.
lemmatize(word) for word in x.split()]))
```

> **Note**
>
> We are working to reduce the dimensionality of the dataset because of the "curse of dimensionality." Datasets become sparse as their dimensionality (dependent variables) increases. This causes data science techniques to fail. This is due to the difficulty in modelling the high number of features (dependent variables) to get the correct output. As the number of features of the dataset increases, we need more data points to model them. So, to get around the curse of high-dimensional data, we need to obtain a lot more data, which in turn would increase the time required to process it.

Tokenization

Tokenization is the process of dividing either sentences into sequences of words or paragraphs into sequences of sentences. We need to do this to eventually convert the data into one-hot vectors of words. Tokenization can be performed using the **nltk** library:

```
import nltk
nltk.word_tokenize("Hello Dr. Ajay. It's nice to meet you.")
```

The tokenized list is as follows:

```
['Hello', 'Dr.', 'Ajay', '.', 'It', "'s", 'nice', 'to', 'meet', 'you',
'.']
```

Figure 7.19: Tokenized list

As you can see, it separates punctuations from words and detects complex words such as "Dr."

Exercise 55: Preprocessing the IMDB Movie Review Dataset

In this exercise, we will preprocess the IMDB Movie Review dataset to make it ready for any machine learning algorithm. The dataset consists of 25,000 movie reviews along with the sentiment (positive or negative) of the review. We want to predict sentiments using the review, so we need to keep that in mind while performing preprocessing.

1. Load the IMDB movie review dataset using pandas:

```
import pandas as pd
data = pd.read_csv('../../chapter 7/data/movie_reviews.csv',
encoding='latin-1')
```

2. First, we will convert all characters in the dataset into lowercase:

```
data.SentimentText = data.SentimentText.str.lower()
```

3. Next, we will write a **clean_str** function, in which we will clean the reviews using the **re** module:

```
import re
def clean_str(string):
     string = re.sub(r"https?\://\S+", '', string)
     string = re.sub(r'\<a href', ' ', string)
     string = re.sub(r'&amp;', 'and', string)
     string = re.sub(r'<br />', ' ', string)
     string = re.sub(r'[_"\-;%()|+&=*%.,!?:#$@\[\]/]', ' ', string)
     string = re.sub('\d','', string)
     string = re.sub(r"can\'t", "cannot", string)
     string = re.sub(r"it\'s", "it is", string)
     return string
```

> **Note**
>
> This function first removes any hyperlink from the text and then removes the HTML tags (**<a>** or **
). Next, it substitutes all **& with '**and,**' followed by removing all special characters, punctuations, and numbers. Finally, it substitutes '**can't**' with '**cannot**' and '**it's**' with '**it is**'.

```
data.SentimentText = data.SentimentText.apply(lambda x: clean_str(str(x)))
```

Use the apply function of pandas to perform review cleaning on the complete dataset.

4. Next, check the word distribution in the dataset using the following code:

```
pd.Series(' '.join(data['SentimentText']).split()).value_counts().head(10)
```

The occurrence of the top 10 words is as follows:

```
movie     43558
film      39095
it        30659
one       26509
is        20355
like      20270
good      15099
the       13913
time      12682
even      12656
dtype: int64
```

Figure 7.20: Top 10 words

5. Remove stop words from the reviews:

> **Note**
>
> This will be done by first tokenizing the reviews and then removing the stop word loaded from the **nltk** library.

6. We add '**movie**,' '**film**,' and '**time**' to the stop words as they occur very frequently in the reviews and don't really contribute much to understanding what the review sentiment is:

```
from nltk.corpus import stopwords
from nltk.tokenize import word_tokenize,sent_tokenize

stop_words = stopwords.words('english') + ['movie', 'film', 'time']
stop_words = set(stop_words)
remove_stop_words = lambda r: [[word for word in word_tokenize(sente) if
word not in stop_words] for sente in sent_tokenize(r)]
data['SentimentText'] = data['SentimentText'].apply(remove_stop_words)
```

7. Next, we convert the tokens back into sentences and drop the reviews where all the text was stop words:

```
def combine_text(text):
    try:
        return ' '.join(text[0])
    except:
        return np.nan

data.SentimentText = data.SentimentText.apply(lambda x: combine_text(x))
data = data.dropna(how='any')
```

8. The next step is to convert the text into tokens and then numbers. We will be using the Keras Tokenizer as it performs both the steps for us:

```
from keras.preprocessing.text import Tokenizer

tokenizer = Tokenizer(num_words=250)
tokenizer.fit_on_texts(list(data['SentimentText']))
sequences = tokenizer.texts_to_sequences(data['SentimentText'])
```

9. To get the size of the vocabulary, use the following:

```
word_index = tokenizer.word_index
print('Found %s unique tokens.' % len(word_index))
```

The number of unique tokens is as follows:

```
Found 77348 unique tokens.
```

Figure 7.21: Number of unique tokens

10. To reduce the training time of our model, we will cap the length of our reviews at 200 words. You can play around with this number to find out what gives you the best accuracy.

> **Note**
>
> Rows where there are less characters will get padded with 0s. You can increase or decrease this value depending on the accuracy and training time of the model.

```
from keras.preprocessing.sequence import pad_sequences
reviews = pad_sequences(sequences, maxlen=200)
```

11. You should save the tokenizer so that you can convert the reviews back to text:

```
import pickle
with open('tokenizer.pkl', 'wb') as handle:
            pickle.dump(tokenizer,
                        handle,
                        protocol=pickle.HIGHEST_PROTOCOL)
```

To preview a cleaned review, run the following command:

```
data.SentimentText[124]
```

A cleaned review looks like this:

```
"perfect example divides people groups get joke n't people usually att
ack n't understand comic style charm unparalleled since great comedy g
reat romance perfect date perfect someone wants good lighthearted laug
h perspective tense maybe n't may need counseling injustice paramount
kept shelf since early 's never seen light day dvd yet feel urban vers
ion honeymooners good idea find odd two alltime favorite romantic come
dies never released dvd gene wilder 's world 's greatest lover fox sat
since early 's well yet justin kelly nearly every video store country
justice world maybe took bash enjoy justin kelly 'm sure one watered e
nough get sometimes age people lose sense humor sometimes goes stale f
ind comic satisfaction reruns full house"
```

Figure 7.22: A cleaned review

To get the actual input to the next step of the process, run the following command:

```
reviews[124]
```

The input to the next step for the **reviews** command will look something like this:

```
array([  0,   0,   0,   0,   0,   0,   0,   0,   0,   0,   0,   0,   0,
         0,   0,   0,   0,   0,   0,   0,   0,   0,   0,   0,   0,   0,
         0,   0,   0,   0,   0,   0,   0,   0,   0,   0,   0,   0,   0,
         0,   0,   0,   0,   0,   0,   0,   0,   0,   0,   0,   0,   0,
         0,   0,   0,   0,   0,   0,   0,   0,   0,   0,   0,   0,   0,
         0,   0,   0,   0,   0,   0,   0,   0,   0,   0,   0,   0,   0,
         0,   0,   0,   0,   0,   0,   0,   0,   0,   0,   0,   0,   0,
         0,   0,   0,   0,   0,   0,   0,   0,   0,   0,   0,   0,   0,
         0,   0,   0,   0,   0,   0,   0,   0,   0,   0,   0,   0,   0,
         0,   0,   0,   0,   0,   0,   0,   0,   0,   0,   0,   0,   0,
         0,   0,   0,   0,   0,   0,   0,   0,   0,   0,   0,   0,   0,
         0,   0,   0,   0,   0,   0,  16,  15,   2,  16,   2, 129,  20,
       106,  20, 170,   5, 168,   2,  97, 238, 129,   1,  36,  31, 139,
       167, 138, 126, 197,   5, 210,  71,  29,  36, 167,   1,  76,   1,
       129,   1,  11, 138,  75,  76, 168, 244,  54, 142,   3,  93,  15,
        16, 172, 157,  71, 196])
```

Figure 7.23: Input for next step to the cleaned review

Congratulations! You have successfully preprocessed your first text dataset. The review data is now a matrix of 25,000 rows, or reviews, and 200 columns, or words. Next, we will learn how we can convert this data into embedding to make it easier to predict the sentiment.

Text Processing

Now that we have cleaned our dataset, we will convert it into a form that machine learning models can work with. Recall *Chapter 5*, *Mastering Structured Data*, where we discussed how neural networks cannot process words, so we need to represent words as numbers to be able to process them. Therefore, to be able to perform tasks such as sentiment analysis, we need to convert text into numbers.

So, the very first method we discussed was one-hot encoding, which performs poorly in the case of words, because words have certain relationships between them and one-hot encoding makes it so that the words are computed as if they were independent of each other. For example, let us assume we have three words: 'car,' 'truck,' and 'ship.' Now, 'car' is closer to 'truck' in terms of similarity, but it still has some similarity to 'ship.' One-hot encoding fails to capture that relationship.

Word embeddings too are vector representations of words, but they capture the relationship of each word with another word. The different ways of getting word embedding are explained in the following section.

Count Embedding

Count embedding is a simple vector representation of the word depending on the amount of times it appears in a piece of text. Assume a dataset where you have *n* unique words and M different records. To get the count embedding, you create an N *x* M matrix, where each row is a word and each column is a record. The values of any *(n,m)* location in the matrix will contain a count of the number of times a word *n* occurs in a record *m*.

TF-IDF Embedding

TF-IDF is a way to obtain the importance of each word in a collection of words or document. It stands for term frequency-inverse document frequency. In TF-IDF, the importance of a word increases proportionally to the frequency of the word, but this importance is offset by the number of documents that have that word, thus helping to adjust for certain words that are used more frequently. In other words, the importance of a word is calculated using the frequency of the word in one data point of the training set. This importance is increased or decreased depending on the occurrence of the word in other data points of the training set.

Weights generated by TF-IDF consist of two terms:

- **Term Frequency** (**TF**): The frequency of a word in the document, as shown in the following figure:

$$TF(w) = \frac{Number\ of\ times\ w\ appears\ in\ a\ document}{Total\ number\ of\ words\ in\ the\ document}$$

Figure 7.24: The term frequency equation

where w is the word.

- **Inverse Document Frequency** (**IDF**): The amount of information the word provides, as shown in the following figure:

$$IDF(w) = \log_e \frac{Total\ number\ of\ documents}{Number\ of\ documents\ with\ w\ in\ it}$$

Figure 7.25: The inverse document frequency equation

The weight is the product of these two terms. In case of TF-IDF, we replace the count of the word with this weight in the N *x* M matrix that we used in the count embedding section.

Continuous bag-of-words embedding

Continuous bag-of-words (**CBOW**) works by using neural networks. It predicts a word when the input is its surrounding words. The input to the neural network is the one-hot vector of the surrounding words. The count of input words is selected using the window parameter. The network has only one hidden layer and the output layer of the network is activated using the softmax activation function to get the probability. The activation function between the layers is linear, but the method of updating the gradients is the same as normal neural networks.

The embedding matrix of the corpus is the weight between the hidden layer and the output layer. Thus, this embedding matrix will be of the N *x* H dimension, where N is the number of unique words in the corpus and H is the number of hidden layer nodes. CBOW works better than the two methods discussed previously due to its probabilistic nature and low memory requirements.

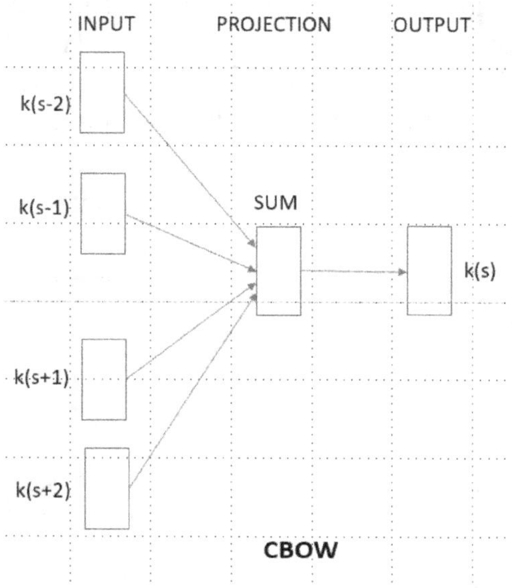

Figure 7.26: A representation of CBOW network

Skip-gram embedding

Using a neural network, skip-gram predicts the surrounding words given an input word. The input here is the one-hot vector of the word and the output is the probability of the surrounding words. The number of output words is decided by the window parameter. Much like CBOW, this method uses a neural network with a single hidden layer and the activations are all linear except for the output layer, where we use the softmax function. One big difference though is how the error gets calculated: different errors are calculated for the different words being predicted and then all are added together to get the final error. The error for each individual word is calculated by subtracting the output probability vector with the target one-hot vector.

The embedding matrix here is the weight matrix between the input layer and the hidden layer. Thus, this embedding matrix will be of the $H \times N$ dimension, where N is the number of unique words in the corpus and H is the number of hidden layer nodes. Skip-gram works much better than CBOW for less frequent words, but is generally slower:

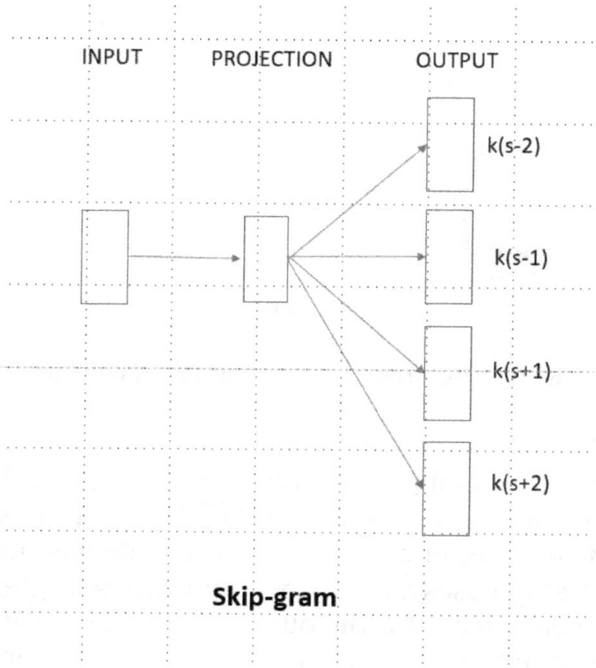

Figure 7.27: A representation of skip-gram network

> **Tip**
>
> Use CBOW for datasets with less words but a high number of samples. Use skip-gram when working with a dataset with more words and a low number of samples.

Word2Vec

The **Word2Vec** model is a group of CBOW and skip-gram that is used to produce word embedding. Word2Vec helps us obtain the word embedding of a corpus easily. To implement the model and obtain word embedding, we will make use of the **gensim** library:

```
model = gensim.models.Word2Vec(
          tokens,
          iter=5
          size=100,
          window=5,
          min_count=5,
          workers=10,
          sg=0)
```

To train the model, we need to pass the tokenized sentences as arguments to the **Word2Vec** class of **gensim**. **iter** is the number of epochs to train for, and **size** refers to the number of nodes in the hidden layer and decides the size of the embedding layer. **window** refers to the number of surrounding words that are considered when training the neural network. **min_count** refers to the minimum frequency required for a word to be considered. **workers** is the number of threads to use while training and **sg** refers to the training algorithm to be used, 0 for CBOW and 1 for skip-gram.

To get the number of unique words in the trained embedding, you can use the following:

```
vocab = list(model.wv.vocab)
len(vocab)
```

Before we use these embeddings, we need to make sure that they are correct. To do that, we find the similar words:

```
model.wv.most_similar('fun')
```

The output is as follows:

```
[('entertaining', 0.8260140419006348),
 ('lighten', 0.825722336769104),
 ('laughs', 0.8177958726882935),
 ('enjoy', 0.790296733379364),
 ('enjoyable', 0.7853423357009888),
 ('plenty', 0.7833274602890015),
 ('comedy', 0.7706939578056335),
 ('funny', 0.7564221620559692),
 ('definitely', 0.7507157325744629),
 ('guaranteed', 0.7493278980255127)]
```

Figure 7.28: Similar words

To save your embeddings to a file, use the following code:

```
model.wv.save_word2vec_format('movie_embedding.txt', binary=False)
```

To load a pretrained embedding, you can use this function:

```
def load_embedding(filename, word_index , num_words, embedding_dim):
    embeddings_index = {}
    file = open(filename, encoding="utf-8")
    for line in file:
        values = line.split()
        word = values[0]
        coef = np.asarray(values[1:])
        embeddings_index[word] = coef
    file.close()


    embedding_matrix = np.zeros((num_words, embedding_dim))
    for word, pos in word_index.items():
        if pos >= num_words:
            continue
        print(num_words)
        embedding_vector = embeddings_index.get(word)
        if embedding_vector is not None:
            embedding_matrix[pos] = embedding_vector
    return embedding_matrix
```

The function first reads the embedding file **filename** and gets all the embedding vectors present in the file. Then, it creates an embedding matrix that stacks the embedding vectors together. The **num_words** parameter limits the size of the vocabulary and can be helpful in cases where the training time of the NLP algorithm is too high. **word_index** is a dictionary with the key as unique words of the corpus and the value as the index of the word. **embedding_dim** is the size of the embedding vectors as specified while training.

> **Tip**
>
> There are a lot of really good pretrained embeddings available. Some of the popular ones are GloVe: https://nlp.stanford.edu/projects/glove/ and fastText: https://fasttext.cc/docs/en/english-vectors.html

Exercise 56: Creating Word Embeddings Using Gensim

In this exercise, we will create our own Word2Vec embedding using the **gensim** library. The word embedding will be created for the IMDB movie review dataset that we have been working with. We will take off from where we left in *Exercise* 55.

1. The reviews variable has reviews in the token form but they have been converted into numbers. The **gensim** Word2Vec requires tokens in the string form, so we backtrack to where we converted the tokens back to sentences in step 6 of *Exercise* 55.

   ```
   data['SentimentText'] [0]
   ```

   The tokens of the first review are as follows:

   ```
   [['first',
     'think',
     'another',
     'disney',
     'might',
     'good',
     'kids',
     'watch',
     'help',
   ```

   Figure 7.29: Tokens of first review

2. Now, we convert the lists in each row into a single list using the **apply** function of pandas, using the following code:

```
data['SentimentText'] = data['SentimentText'].apply(lambda x: x[0])
```

3. Now, we feed this preprocessed data into Word2Vec to create the word embedding:

```
from gensim.models import Word2Vec
model = Word2Vec(
        data['SentimentText'],
        iter=50,
        size=100,
        window=5,
        min_count=5,
        workers=10)
```

4. Let us check how well the model performs by viewing some similar words:

```
model.wv.most_similar('insight')
```

The most similar words to '**insight**' in the dataset are:

```
[('insights', 0.7341898679733276),
 ('perspective', 0.7136699557304382),
 ('understanding', 0.6958176493644714),
 ('humanity', 0.6425720453262329),
 ('complexity', 0.6353663206100464),
 ('overwhelming', 0.6318362951278687),
 ('courage', 0.6294285655021667),
 ('ambiguity', 0.6231480836868286),
 ('appreciation', 0.6217454671859741),
 ('importance', 0.6216951012611389)]
```

Figure 7.30: Similar words to 'insight'

5. To obtain the similarity between two words, use:

```
model.wv.similarity(w1='violent', w2='brutal')
```

6. The output similarity is shown here:

```
0.8172468019549712
```

Figure 7.31: Similarity output

The similarity score ranges from **0** to **1**, where **1** means that both words are the same, and **0** means that both words are completely different and not related in any way.

7. Plot the embedding on a 2D space to understand what words are found to be similar to each other.

   First, convert the embedding into two dimensions using PCA. We will plot only the first 200 words. (You can plot more if you like.)

```
from sklearn.decomposition import PCA
word_limit = 200
X = model[model.wv.vocab][: word_limit]
pca = PCA(n_components=2)
result = pca.fit_transform(X)
```

8. Now, plot the result on a scatter plot using **matplotlib**:

```
import matplotlib.pyplot as plt
plt.scatter(result[:, 0], result[:, 1])
words = list(model.wv.vocab)[: word_limit]
for i, word in enumerate(words):
    plt.annotate(word, xy=(result[i, 0], result[i, 1]))
plt.show()
```

Your output should look like the following:

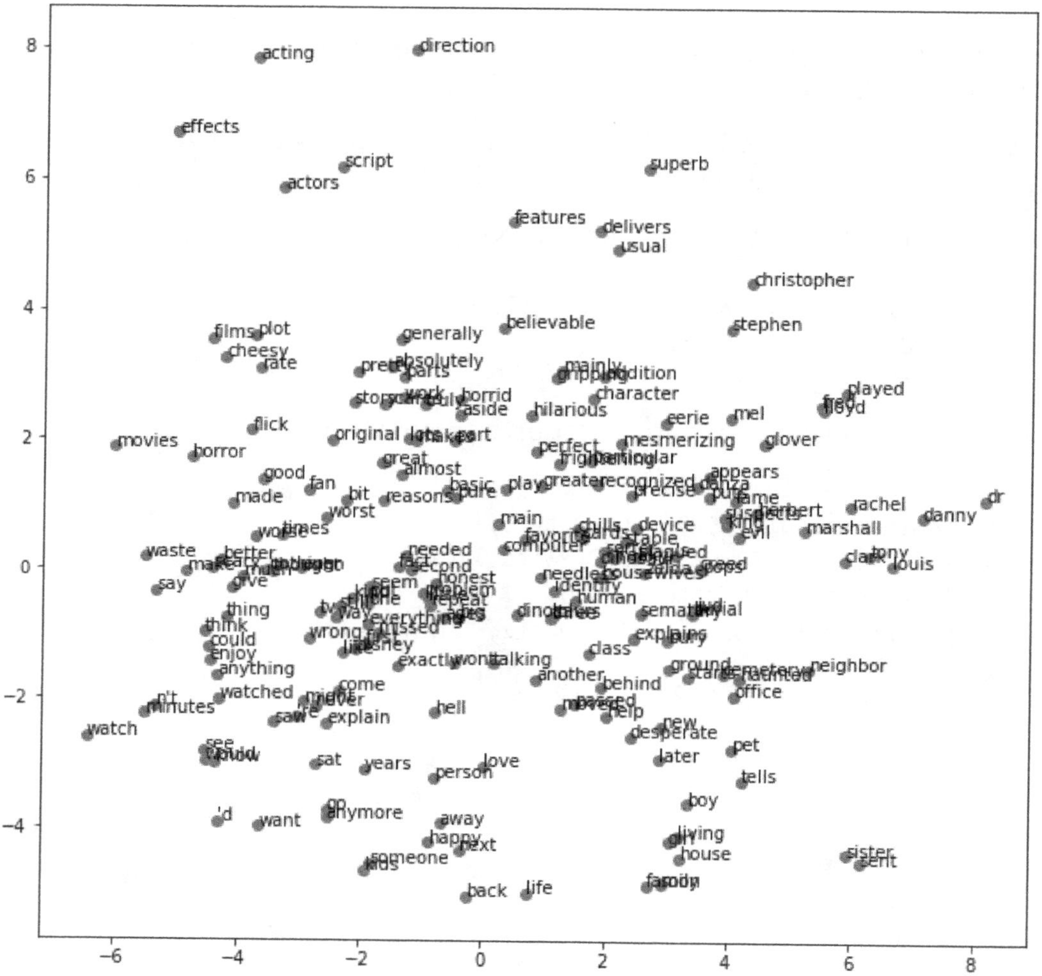

Figure 7.32: Representation of embedding of first 200 words using PCA

> **Note**
>
> The axes do not mean anything in the representation of word embedding. The representation simply shows the closeness of different words.

9. Save the embedding to a file so that you can retrieve it later:

```
model.wv.save_word2vec_format('movie_embedding.txt', binary=False)
```

Congratulations! You just created your first word embedding. You can play around with the embedding and view the similarity between different words.

Activity 19: Predicting Sentiments of Movie Reviews

In this activity, we will attempt to predict sentiments of movie reviews. The dataset (https://github.com/TrainingByPackt/Data-Science-with-Python/tree/master/Chapter07) comprises 25,000 movie reviews sourced from IMDB with their sentiment (positive or negative). Let's look at the following scenario: You work at a DVD rental company, which has to predict the number of DVDs to create of a certain movie depending on how it is being perceived by the reviewers. To do this, you create a machine learning model that can analyze reviews to figure out how the movie is being perceived.

1. Read and preprocess the movie reviews.
2. Create the word embedding of the reviews.
3. Create a fully connected neural network to predict sentiments, much like the neural network models we created in *Chapter 5: Mastering Structured Data*. The input will be the word embedding of the reviews and the output of the model will be either `1` (positive sentiment) or `0` (negative sentiment).

> **Note**
>
> The solution for this activity can be found on page 378.

The output is a little cryptic because stop words and punctuations have been removed, but you can still understand the general sense of the review.

Congratulations! You just created your first NLP module. You should find that the model gives an accuracy of of around 76% which is quite low. This is because it is predicting sentiments based on individual words; it has no way of figuring out the context of the review. For example, it will predict "not good" as a positive sentiment as it sees the word 'good.' If it could look at multiple words, it would understand that this is a negative sentiment. In the next section, we will learn how to create neural networks that can retain information of the past.

Recurrent Neural Networks (RNNs)

Until now, none of the problems we discussed had a temporal dependence, which means that the prediction depends not only on the current input but also on the past inputs. For example, in the case of the dog vs. cat classifier, we only needed the picture of the dog to classify it as a dog. No other information or images were required. Instead, if you want to make a classifier that predicts if a dog is walking or standing, you will require multiple images in a sequence or a video to figure out what the dog is doing. RNNs are like the fully connected networks that we talked about. The only change is that an RNN has memory that stores information about the previous inputs as states. The outputs of the hidden layers are fed in as inputs for the next input.

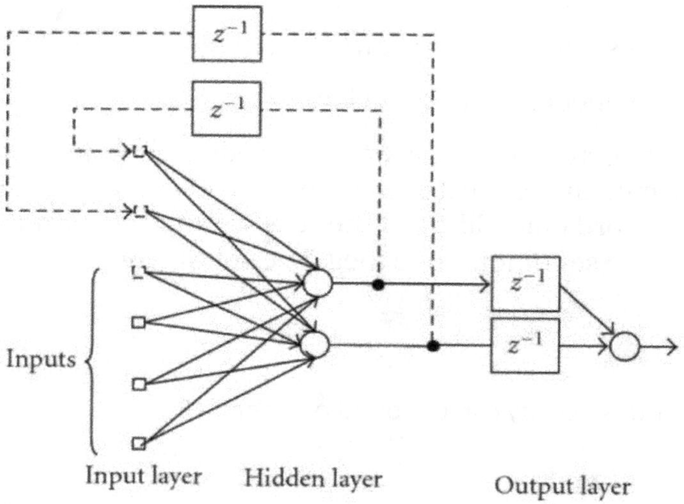

Figure 7.33: Representation of recurrent neural network

From the image, you can understand how the outputs of the hidden layers are used as inputs for the next input. This acts as a memory element in the neural network. Another thing to keep in mind is that the output of a normal neural network is a function of the input and weights of the network.

his allows us to randomly input any data point to get the right output. However, this is not the case with RNNs. In the case of RNNs, our output depends on the previous inputs, so we need to feed in the input in the correct sequence.

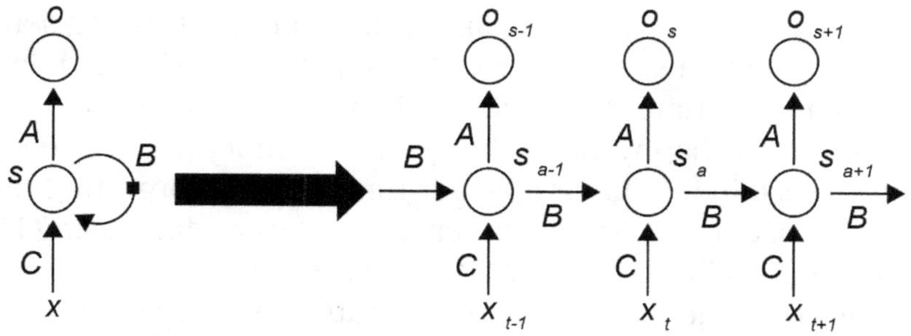

Figure 7.34: Representation of recurrent layer

In the preceding image, you can see a single RNN layer on the left in the "folded" model. U is the input weight, V is the output weight, and W is the weight associated with the memory input. The memory of the RNN is also referred to as state. The "unfolded" model on the right shows how the RNN works for the input sequence [xt-1, xt, xt+1]. The model differs based on the kind of application. For example, in case of sentiment analysis, the input sequence will require only one output in the end. The unfolded model for this problem is shown here:

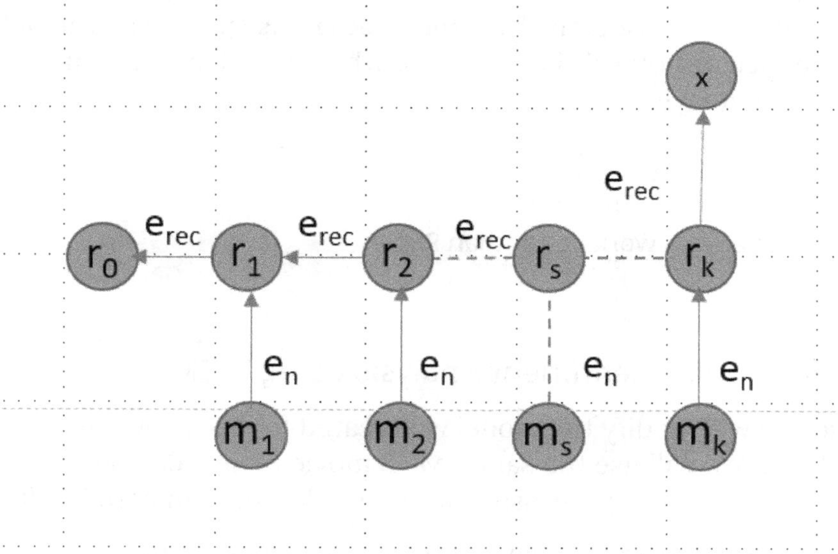

Figure 7.35: Unfolded representation of a recurrent layer used to perform sentiment analysis

LSTMs

Long short-term memory (**LSTM**) cell is a special kind of RNN cell, capable of retaining information over long-term periods of time. Hochreiter and Schmidhuber introduced LSTMs in 1997. RNNs suffer from the vanishing gradient problem. They lose information detected over long periods of time. For example, if we are performing sentiment analysis on a text and the first sentence says "I am happy today" and then the rest of the text is devoid of any sentiments, the RNN will not do a good job of detecting that the sentiment of the text is happy. Long short-term memory (LSTM) cells overcome this issue by storing certain inputs for a longer time without forgetting them. Most real-world recurrent machine learning implementations are done using LSTMs. The only difference between RNN cells and LSTM cells is the memory states. Every RNN layer takes an input of the memory state and outputs a memory state, whereas every LSTM layer takes a long-term and a short-term memory as the input and outputs both the long and the short-term memories. The long-term memory allows the network to retain information for a longer time.

LSTM cells are implemented in Keras, and you easily can add an LSTM layer into your model:

```
model.add(keras.layers.LSTM(units, activation='tanh', dropout=0.0, recurrent_
dropout=0.0, return_sequences=False))
```

Here, **`units`** is the number of nodes in the layer, **`activation`** is the activation function to use for the layer. **`recurrent_dropout`** and **`dropout`** are the dropout probability for the recurrent state and input respectively. **`return_sequences`** specifies if the output should contain the sequence or not; this is made **`True`** when you plan to use another recurrent layer after the current layer.

> **Note**
>
> LSTMs almost always work better than RNNs.

Exercise 57: Performing Sentiment Analysis Using LSTM

In this exercise, we will modify the model we created for the previous activity, to make it use an LSTM cell. We will use the same IMDB movie review dataset that we have been working with. Most of the preprocessing steps are like those in *Activity* 19.

1. Read the IMDB movie review dataset using pandas in Python:

```
import pandas as pd
data = pd.read_csv('../../chapter 7/data/movie_reviews.csv',
encoding='latin-1')
```

2. Convert the tweets to lowercase to reduce the number of unique words:

```
data.text = data.text.str.lower()
```

3. Clean the reviews using RegEx with the **clean_str** function:

```
import re
def clean_str(string):

    string = re.sub(r"https?\://\S+", '', string)
    string = re.sub(r'\<a href', ' ', string)
    string = re.sub(r'&amp;', '', string)
    string = re.sub(r'<br />', ' ', string)
    string = re.sub(r'[_"\-;%()|+&=*%.,!?:#$@\[\]/]', ' ', string)
    string = re.sub('\d','', string)
    string = re.sub(r"can\'t", "cannot", string)
    string = re.sub(r"it\'s", "it is", string)
    return string
data.SentimentText = data.SentimentText.apply(lambda x: clean_str(str(x)))
```

4. Next, remove stop words and other frequently occurring unnecessary words from the reviews. This step converts strings into tokens (which will be helpful in the next step):

```
from nltk.corpus import stopwords
from nltk.tokenize import word_tokenize,sent_tokenize
stop_words = stopwords.words('english') + ['movie', 'film', 'time']
stop_words = set(stop_words)
remove_stop_words = lambda r: [[word for word in word_tokenize(sente) if
word not in stop_words] for sente in sent_tokenize(r)]
data['SentimentText'] = data['SentimentText'].apply(remove_stop_words)
```

5. Combine the tokens to get a string and then drop any review that does not have anything in it after the stop-word removal:

```
def combine_text(text):
    try:
        return ' '.join(text[0])
    except:
        return np.nan

data.SentimentText = data.SentimentText.apply(lambda x: combine_text(x))
data = data.dropna(how='any')
```

6. Tokenize the reviews using the Keras Tokenizer and convert them into numbers:

```
from keras.preprocessing.text import Tokenizer
tokenizer = Tokenizer(num_words=5000)
tokenizer.fit_on_texts(list(data['SentimentText']))
sequences = tokenizer.texts_to_sequences(data['SentimentText'])
word_index = tokenizer.word_index
```

7. Finally, pad the tweets to have a maximum of 100 words. This will remove any words after the 100-word limit and add 0s if the number of words is less than 100:

```
from keras.preprocessing.sequence import pad_sequences
reviews = pad_sequences(sequences, maxlen=100)
```

8. Load the previously created embedding to get the embedding matrix using the **load_embedding** function discussed in the *Text Processing* section, by using the following code:

```
import numpy as np
def load_embedding(filename, word_index , num_words, embedding_dim):
    embeddings_index = {}
    file = open(filename, encoding="utf-8")
    for line in file:
        values = line.split()
        word = values[0]
        coef = np.asarray(values[1:])
        embeddings_index[word] = coef
    file.close()

    embedding_matrix = np.zeros((num_words, embedding_dim))
    for word, pos in word_index.items():
        if pos >= num_words:
            continue
        embedding_vector = embeddings_index.get(word)
        if embedding_vector is not None:
            embedding_matrix[pos] = embedding_vector
    return embedding_matrix

embedding_matrix = load_embedding('movie_embedding.txt', word_index,
len(word_index), 16)
```

9. Split the data into training and testing sets with an 80:20 split. This can be modified to find the best split:

```
from sklearn.model_selection import train_test_split
X_train, X_test, y_train, y_test = train_test_split(reviews, pd.get_
dummies(data.Sentiment), test_size=0.2, random_state=9)
```

10. Create and compile the Keras model with one LSTM layer. You can experiment with different layers and hyperparameters:

```
from keras.models import Model
from keras.layers import Input, Dense, Dropout, BatchNormalization,
Embedding, Flatten, LSTM
inp = Input((100,))
embedding_layer = Embedding(len(word_index),
                    16,
                    weights=[embedding_matrix],
                    input_length=100,
                    trainable=False)(inp)
model = Dropout(0.10)(embedding_layer)
model = LSTM(128, dropout=0.2)(model)
model = Dense(units=256, activation='relu')(model)
model = Dense(units=64, activation='relu')(model)
model = Dropout(0.3)(model)
predictions = Dense(units=2, activation='softmax')(model)
model = Model(inputs = inp, outputs = predictions)

model.compile(loss='binary_crossentropy', optimizer='sgd', metrics =
['acc'])
```

11. Train the model on the data for 10 epochs to see if it performs better than the one in *Activity* 1, by using the following code:

```
model.fit(X_train, y_train, validation_data = (X_test, y_test), epochs=10,
batch_size=256)
```

12. Check the accuracy of the model:

```
from sklearn.metrics import accuracy_score
preds = model.predict(X_test)
accuracy_score(np.argmax(preds, 1), np.argmax(y_test.values, 1))
```

The accuracy of the LSTM model is:

```
0.7692
```

Figure 7.36: LSTM model accuracy

13. Plot the confusion matrix of the model to get a proper sense of the model's prediction:

```
y_actual = pd.Series(np.argmax(y_test.values, axis=1), name='Actual')
y_pred = pd.Series(np.argmax(preds, axis=1), name='Predicted')
pd.crosstab(y_actual, y_pred, margins=True)
```

Predicted	0	1	All
Actual			
0	1922	531	2453
1	623	1924	2547
All	2545	2455	5000

Figure 7.37: Confusion matrix of the model (0 = negative sentiment, 1 = positive sentiment)

14. Check the performance of the model by seeing the sentiment predictions on random reviews using the following code:

```
review_num = 110
print("Review: \n"+tokenizer.sequences_to_texts([X_test[review_num]])[0])
sentiment = "Positive" if np.argmax(preds[review_num]) else "Negative"
print("\nPredicted sentiment = "+ sentiment)
sentiment = "Positive" if np.argmax(y_test.values[review_num]) else
"Negative"
print("\nActual sentiment = "+ sentiment)
```

The output is as follows:

```
Review:
warning spoilers really stupid group young italy find warrior souls one w
ears becomes possessed spirit demon killing several friends die blade dem
on corpse waste viewers fine young ladies leave clothes gore ludicrous be
st acting terrible perfect bad script

Predicted sentiment = Negative

Actual sentiment = Negative
```

Figure 7.38: A negative review from the IMDB dataset

Congratulations! You just implemented an RNN to predict sentiments of a movie review. This network works a little better than the previous network we created. Play around with the architecture and hyperparameters of the network to improve the accuracy of the model. You can also try using pretrained word embedding from either fastText or GloVe to improve the accuracy of the model.

Activity 20: Predicting Sentiments from Tweets

In this activity, we will attempt to predict sentiments of a tweet. The provided dataset (https://github.com/TrainingByPackt/Data-Science-with-Python/tree/master/Chapter07) contains 1.5 million tweets and their sentiments (positive or negative). Let's look at the following scenario: You work at a big consumer organization, which recently created a Twitter account. Some of the customers who have had a bad experience with your company are taking to Twitter to express their sentiments, which is causing a decline in the reputation of the company. You have been tasked to identify these tweets so that the company can get in touch with them to provide better support. You do this by creating a sentiment predictor, which can determine whether the sentiment of a tweet is positive or negative. Before using your new sentiment predictor on actual tweets about your company, you will test it on the provided tweets dataset.

1. Read the data and remove all unnecessary information.
2. Clean the tweets, tokenize them, and finally convert them into numbers.
3. Load GloVe Twitter embedding and create the embedding matrix (https://nlp.stanford.edu/projects/glove/).

4. Create an LSTM model to predict the sentiment.

> **Note**
>
> The solution for this activity can be found on page 383.

Congratulations! You just created a machine learning module to predict sentiments from tweets. You can now deploy this using Twitter API to perform real-time sentiment analysis on tweets. You can play around with different embeddings from GloVe and fastText and see how much improvement you can get on your model.

Summary

In this chapter, we learned how computers understand human language. We first learned what RegEx is and how it helps data scientists analyze and clean text data. Next, we learned about stop words, what they are, and why they are removed from the data to reduce the dimensionality. Next, we next learned about sentence tokenization and its importance, followed by word embedding. Embedding is a topic that we covered in *Chapter 5: Mastering Structured Data*; here, we learned how to create word embedding to boost our NLP model's performance. To create better models, we looked at a RNNs, a special type of neural network that retains memory of past inputs. Finally, we learned about LSTM cells and how they are better than normal RNN cells.

Now that you have completed this chapter, you are capable of handling textual data and creating machine learning models for NLP. In the next chapter, you will learn how to make models faster using transfer learning and a few tricks of the craft.

8

Tips and Tricks of the Trade

Learning Objectives

By the end of this chapter, you will be able to:

- Create better deep learning models faster with the help of transfer learning
- Utilize and work with better models through the help of separate train, development and test datasets
- Work with real life datasets
- Make use of AutoML to find the most optimal network with little to no work
- Visualize neural network models
- Use training logs better

This final chapter shall describe concepts of transfer learning and show you how to use training logs effectively.

Introduction

Now that we have covered almost every topic that you need to be able to kick-start your data science journey, we will introduce you to some tools and tricks that data scientists use to become more efficient and create better machine learning systems. You will first learn about transfer learning, which helps you train models even when there is a lack of data. Then, we will move on to important tools and tricks that you can make use of to become a better data scientist.

Transfer Learning

Training a complex neural network is hard and time-consuming due to the amount of data required for training. Transfer learning helps data scientists transfer part of the knowledge gained by one network to another. This is similar to how humans transfer knowledge from one person to another so that everyone does not have to start learning every new thing from scratch. Transfer learning helps data scientists train neural networks faster and with fewer data points. There are two ways to perform transfer learning depending on the situation. They are as follows:

- **Use a pre-trained model**: In this approach, we use a pre-trained neural network model and use it to solve the problem at hand. A pre-trained model is a neural network that has been created for a different purpose to the one at hand, has been trained on some other dataset, and has been saved for future reuse. The pre-trained model must be trained on a similar or same dataset to get reasonable accuracy.
- **Create a model**: In this approach, we train the neural network model on a dataset that is like the problem at hand. We then use this model to perform the same steps as those for the pre-trained model approach. This is helpful when the actual dataset is small and we are unable to create an acceptable model.

As discussed in *Chapter 6*, *Decoding Images*, different layers of a neural network learn different features of an image. For example, the first layer might learn to recognize horizontal lines, and a few layers later, the network might learn to recognize eyes. This is the reason why transfer learning works for images; the feature extractor that we get can be used to extract information from new images of the same distribution. Now, you must be wondering why we don't use transfer learning for every problem we have.

Let's try to understand this with the following diagram. Here, original dataset refers to the dataset used to train the network we will transfer knowledge from:

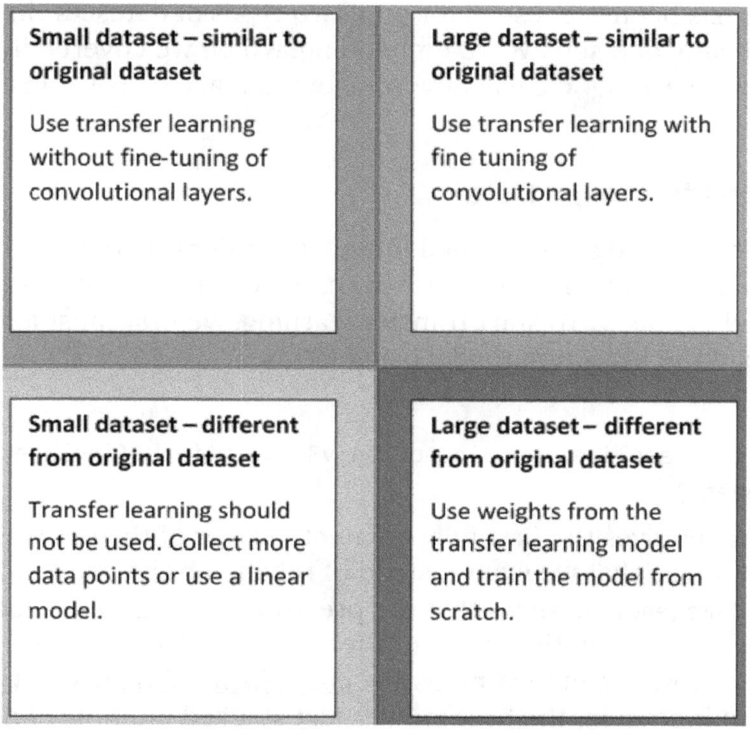

Figure 8.1: Steps to take for transfer learning in different conditions

In the diagram, there are four regions:

- **Small dataset** (similar the original dataset): This is the most common case and the case where transfer learning helps the most. Due to the similarity of the current dataset and the dataset that was used to train the pre-trained model, we can use the layers from the pre-trained model and just change the final dense layer part depending on the kind of problem.
- **Large dataset** (similar to the original dataset): This is the most optimal situation. Due to the availability of data, it is suggested that you train the model from scratch, and to speed up the learning, we can use the weights from the pre-trained model to act as a starting point.
- **Small dataset** (different from original dataset): This is the worst situation in terms of transfer learning as well as deep learning. The only solution in this situation is to find a dataset like the current dataset and train a model on it, and then use transfer learning.
- **Large dataset** (different from original dataset): Due to the large size of the dataset, we can train the model from scratch. To make the training faster, the weights from a pre-trained model can be taken as the starting point, but this is not recommended.

Transfer learning has been successful for only two types of datasets–image and natural language (textual data) datasets. Word embedding, which we covered in *Chapter 7*, is an example of transfer learning. We will now see how to make use of transfer learning for image data.

Transfer Learning for Image Data

In this section, we will load a pre-trained model using Keras and perform transfer learning. You will learn how to handle the two cases where the dataset is like the pre-trained model's dataset. To start transfer learning, we first must load a pre-trained model. We will load the Inception model using Keras:

```
import keras

base_model = keras.applications.inception_v3.InceptionV3(include_top=False,
weights='imagenet')
```

`include_top=False` removes the first fully connected layer of the network, allowing us to input images of any size that we want instead of relying on the image size of the original dataset. **`weights='imagenet'`** assures that the pre-trained weights are loaded. If none is passed to **`weights`**, then the initialization of the weights will be random. The Inception model was a huge improvement over existing **convolutional neural network** (**CNN**) classifiers. Prior to Inception, the best models just stacked multiple convolution layers, hoping to get better performance. Inception, on the other hand, was complex as it used a lot of tricks to push performance both in terms of the accuracy and the time taken to predict.

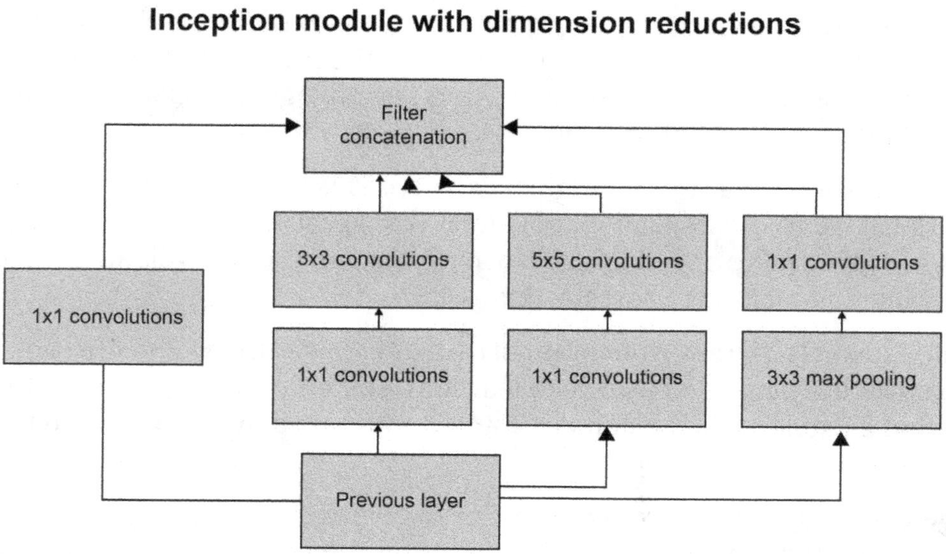

Figure 8.2: Single cell of the Inception network

The first case we will look at is a small dataset that is similar to the original dataset. In this case, we need to first freeze the layers of the pre-trained model. To do this, we simply make all the layers of this base model untrainable:

```
for layer in base_model.layers:
    layer.trainable = False
```

The next case is a large dataset that is similar to the original dataset. In this case, we need to train the model by taking the pre-trained weights to be the starting point. In this case, we do not make any modifications and simply train the whole model, which is a combination of **base_model** along with some additional dense layers depending on our problem. For example, if the problem is a two class classification problem we need to have the last dense layer to have 2 outputs. Another thing that we can do in this case is freeze the weights of the first few layers so that the training happens faster. Freezing the first few layers is helpful as these layers learn simple shapes, which can be applicable in any kind of problem. To freeze the first five layers in Keras, use the following code:

```
for layer in base_model.layers[:5]:
   layer.trainable = False
```

Exercise 58: Using InceptionV3 to Compare and Classify Images

In this exercise, we will make use of the InceptionV3 model provided by Keras to perform classification between cats and dogs. We will use the same dataset (https://github.com/TrainingByPackt/Data-Science-with-Python/tree/master/Chapter08) we used in *Chapter 6*, *Decoding Images* and compare our results. We will freeze the Inception convolutional layers so that we do not have to retrain them:

1. First, create functions to read the image and its label from the filename. Here, the **PATH** variable contains the path to the training dataset:

```
from PIL import Image
def get_input(file):
    return Image.open(PATH+file)
def get_output(file):
    class_label = file.split('.')[0]
    if class_label == 'dog': label_vector = [1,0]
    elif class_label == 'cat': label_vector = [0,1]
    return label_vector
```

2. Set the size and channel of the images:

```
SIZE = 200
CHANNELS = 3
```

3. Then, create a function to preprocess the images:

```
def preprocess_input(image):

    # Data preprocessing
    image = image.resize((SIZE,SIZE))
    image = np.array(image).reshape(SIZE,SIZE,CHANNELS)

    # Normalize image
    image = image/255.0

    return image
```

4. Now create a generator function that reads the images and labels and processes the images:

```
import numpy as np

def custom_image_generator(images, batch_size = 128):

    while True:
        # Randomly select images for the batch
        batch_images = np.random.choice(images, size = batch_size)
        batch_input = []
        batch_output = []

        # Read image, perform preprocessing and get labels
        for file in batch_images:
            # Function that reads and returns the image
            input_image = get_input(file)
            # Function that gets the label of the image
            label = get_output(file)
            # Function that pre-processes and augments the image
            image = preprocess_input(input_image)

            batch_input.append(image)
            batch_output.append(label)

        batch_x = np.array(batch_input)
        batch_y = np.array(batch_output)

        # Return a tuple of (images,labels) to feed the network
        yield(batch_x, batch_y)
```

5. Next, we will read the validation data. Create a function to read the images and their labels:

```
from tqdm import tqdm
def get_data(files):
    data_image = []
    labels = []
    for image in tqdm(files):
        label_vector = get_output(image)

        img = Image.open(PATH + image)
        img = img.resize((SIZE,SIZE))

        labels.append(label_vector)
        img = np.asarray(img).reshape(SIZE,SIZE,CHANNELS)
        img = img/255.0
        data_image.append(img)

    data_x = np.array(data_image)
    data_y = np.array(labels)

    return (data_x, data_y)
```

6. Read the validation files:

```
from random import shuffle
files = os.listdir(PATH)
random.shuffle(files)
train = files[:7000]
test = files[7000:]
validation_data = get_data(test)
```

7. Plot a few images from the dataset to see whether you loaded the files correctly:

```
import matplotlib.pyplot as plt
plt.figure(figsize=(20,10))
columns = 5
for i in range(columns):
    plt.subplot(5 / columns + 1, columns, i + 1)
    plt.imshow(validation_data[0][i])
```

The sample images are as follows:

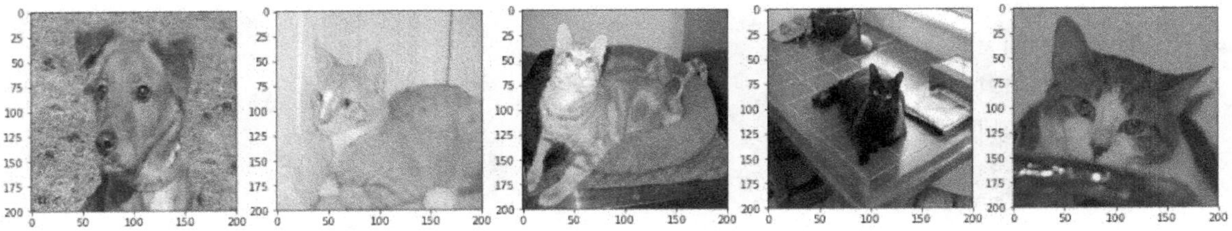

Figure 8.3: Sample images from the loaded dataset

8. Load the Inception model and pass the shape of the input images:

```
from keras.applications.inception_v3 import InceptionV3
base_model = InceptionV3(weights='imagenet', include_top=False, input_
shape=(200,200,3))
```

9. Freeze the Inception model layers so that training is not performed on them:

```
for layer in base_model.layers:
    layer.trainable = False
```

10. Now add the output dense layer according to our problem. Here **keep_prob** is the ratio of nodes to be kept while training. So, the dropout rate will be **1 - keep_prob**:

```
from keras.layers import GlobalAveragePooling2D, Dense, Dropout
from keras.models import Model
x = base_model.output
x = GlobalAveragePooling2D()(x)
x = Dense(256, activation='relu')(x)
keep_prob = 0.5
x = Dropout(rate = 1 - keep_prob)(x)
predictions = Dense(2, activation='softmax')(x)

model = Model(inputs=base_model.input, outputs=predictions)
```

11. Next, compile the model to make it ready for training:

```
model.compile(loss='categorical_crossentropy',
              optimizer='adam',
              metrics = ['accuracy'])
```

And then perform training of the model:

```
EPOCHS = 5
BATCH_SIZE = 128

model_details = model.fit_generator(custom_image_generator(train, batch_
size = BATCH_SIZE),
                    steps_per_epoch = len(train) // BATCH_SIZE,
                    epochs = EPOCHS,
                    validation_data= validation_data,
                    verbose=1)
```

12. Evaluate the model and get the accuracy:

```
score = model.evaluate(validation_data[0], validation_data[1])
print("Accuracy: {0:.2f}%".format(score[1]*100))
```

The accuracy is as follows:

```
Accuracy: 97.83%
```

Figure 8.4: The accuracy of the model

As you can see earlier, the model gets an accuracy of 97.8%, which is much higher than the 73% accuracy we achieved in *Chapter 6*, *Decoding Images*. You can play around with the model we appended to the Inception model to see whether you can improve the accuracy. You can plot the incorrectly predicted images to get a sense of how well the model performs.

```
y_pred = model.predict(validation_data[0])

incorrect_indices = np.nonzero(np.argmax(y_pred,axis=1) !=
np.argmax(validation_data[1],axis=1))[0]

labels = ['dog', 'cat']

image = 5

plt.imshow(validation_data[0][incorrect_indices[image]].reshape(SIZE, SIZE,
CHANNELS),  cmap=plt.get_cmap('gray'))

plt.show()

print("Prediction: {0}".format(labels[np.argmax(y_pred[incorrect_
indices[image]])]))
```

The incorrectly predicted image is as follows:

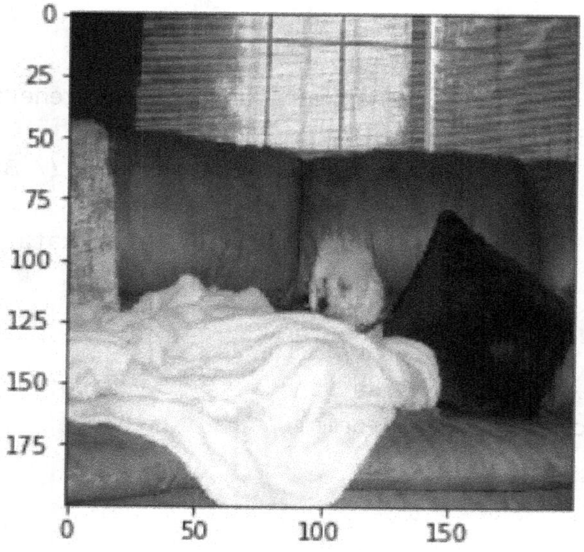


```
Prediction: cat
```

Figure 8.5: The incorrectly predicted sample

Activity 21: Classifying Images using InceptionV3

In this activity, we will make use of the InceptionV3 model provided by Keras to perform classification between cats and dogs. We will use the same dataset we used in *Chapter 6, Decoding Images* and compare our results. Here we will train the whole model, but we will make use of the weights that are present in the Inception pre-trained model as a starting point. This is similar to the exercise we just covered, but without freezing layers.

1. Create a generator to get the images and labels.
2. Create a function to get the labels and images. Then, create a function to preprocess the image and augment it.
3. Load the validation dataset, which will not be augmented.
4. Load the Inception model and add the final dense layers to it. Train the entire network.

You should see that this model gets us an accuracy of 95.4%, which is much higher than the 73% accuracy we achieved in *Chapter 6, Decoding Images*.

You must have noticed the preceding code was similar to *Exercise* 58, but here we did not freeze the layers. The model definitely benefited from taking the weights from the Inception model as the starting point. You can plot the incorrectly predicted images to get a sense of how well the model performs:

```
y_pred = model.predict(validation_data[0])

incorrect_indices = np.nonzero(np.argmax(y_pred,axis=1) !=
np.argmax(validation_data[1],axis=1))[0]

labels = ['dog', 'cat']

image = 5

plt.imshow(validation_data[0][incorrect_indices[image]].reshape(SIZE, SIZE,
CHANNELS),  cmap=plt.get_cmap('gray'))

plt.show()

print("Prediction: {0}".format(labels[np.argmax(y_pred[incorrect_
indices[image]])]))
```

> **Note**
>
> The solution for this activity can be found on page 387.

The incorrectly predicted image is as follows:

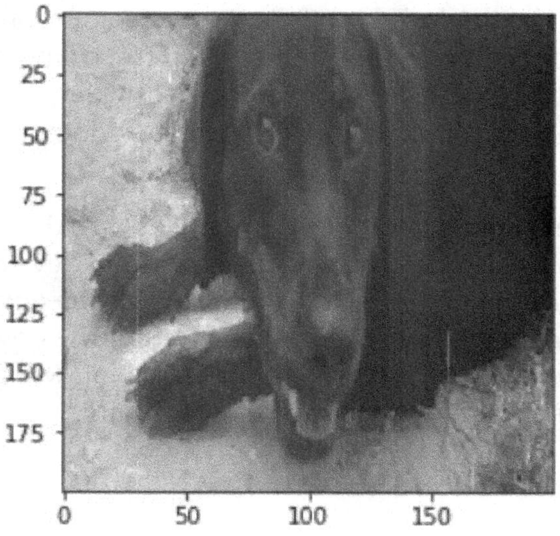

Prediction: cat

Figure 8.6: The incorrectly predicted sample from the dataset

Useful Tools and Tips

In this section, you will first learn the importance of different splits of the dataset. After that, you learn some tips that will come handy when you start working on datasets that haven't been processed before. Then come tools such as pandas profiling and TensorBoard, which will make your life easier by providing easy access to information. We will take a look at AutoML and how it can be used to get high-performance models without much manual effort. Finally, we will visualize our Keras model and export the model diagram to a file.

Train, Development, and Test Datasets

We briefly talked about train, development, and test datasets in the previous chapters. Here, we will delve deeper into the topic.

The training, or train set is a sample from the dataset, and we use this to create our machine learning models. The development, or dev set (also known as validation set), is a sample that helps us tune the hyperparameters of the created model. The testing or test set is the sample that we use to finally evaluate the model. Having all three sets is important for model development.

Distribution of the sets

The development and testing sets should be from the same distribution and should represent the data that you expect your model to get in the future. If the distribution is different, the model will be tuned to a distribution that will not be seen by the model in the future, impacting the deployed model's performance. Your model could perform poorly due to the difference in distribution between the training and testing/dev sets. To rectify this, you can take some data points from test/dev set and introduce them into the training set. Make sure that the original images dominate their respective sets to prevent incorrect results.

If the distribution of the training and development sets are different, we cannot identify whether the model is overfitting; in this case, a new train-dev set should be introduced to check for overfitting of the model. The training and train-dev set must have the same distribution. If there is a huge difference in the errors of the dev and train-dev sets, then there is a data mismatch problem. To rectify this, you will have to carry out manual error analysis, and in most cases, collect more data points.

> **Note**
>
> The dev set is the same as the validation set we have been using all this time, we sometimes referred to it as the test set but that was only to get you started. It should also be noted that we train our model only on the training dataset.

Size of the sets

The size of the dev and test sets should be determined based on the overall size of the dataset. If the size was 10,000 data points, then a 60%/20%/20% split would work well as the test and dev sets would have enough data points to accurately measure the performance of the model. On the other hand, if the dataset had 1,000,000 data points, then a split of 98%/1%/1% would suffice as 10,000 is more than enough data points to gauge the performance of the model.

The sample of the data of the three sets should remain the same, so that we evaluate all the models in the same environment. To do this, you can set a "seed" when creating random samples. Setting the random number seed helps us get the same random split of the data every time we run the experiment.

Working with Unprocessed Datasets

When you start working on more complex and less processed datasets, you will realize that most of the time you won't have all the data that you need to create a satisfactory model. To tackle this, you need to identify external datasets that can help you in creating a competent model. The additional data that you use can be of the following two types:

- **More data points for the same data**: This is helpful when the model is overfitting due to the small size of the dataset. If it is impossible to get more data points, you can use a simpler model–either a neural network with fewer layers or a linear model.
- **Additional data from different sources**: Sometimes there is some data missing from the dataset; for example, the state or country of the cities listed in the dataset, or the macroeconomic factors of the countries listed in the dataset, such as GDP and per-capita income. This data can be easily found on the internet and can be used to improve the model that you create.

A best practice is to always start with **exploratory data analysis** (**EDA**). EDA helps us become intimately familiar with the dataset. It helps identify the best model as well as the variables that can be used for machine learning. Another important aspect of EDA is to check the data for anomalies. This helps us to ensure that the data reached us without any errors. The results of EDA can be shared with the stakeholders to confirm the validity of the data. Data scientists might need to revisit the EDA step multiple times while working on a project.

Another thing to keep in mind is the application of your model. It is important to know whether your model will perform real-time processing or batch processing. This will help you choose your tools and models accordingly. For example, if real-time processing is a priority, then you would probably use a model that will produce results in less than a second, whereas if the application requires batch processing, then you can use complex neural network models that take more than a couple seconds to produce the predictions.

Next, we will look into some best practices for handling training and performing hyperparameter tuning. Always shuffle your data before splitting it into training and testing sets. Another thing that can help converge faster is shuffling the training data during training. The `fit` function of Keras has a handy parameter called **shuffle**, which accepts a Boolean input which can be set to `True` to shuffle the training data before every epoch. An important parameter to keep in mind is the random number seed; This helps data scientists create reproducible results even with the random shuffles and splits. To set the seed for Keras, use the following:

```
from numpy.random import seed
seed(1)
from tensorflow import set_random_seed
set_random_seed(1)
```

The first two lines set the random seed for NumPy, and the next two lines set the seed for TensorFlow, which is the backend Keras uses.

If you are working with a large dataset, start with a subset of data and create the model. Try to overfit this model by making the network deeper or more complex. You can use regularization to limit the model from overfitting the data. When you are confident with the model, use the complete training data and tweak the created model to improve the performance of the model.

Dropout is a very powerful regularizer; you should experiment with different dropout rates as the optimal dropout rate varies from dataset to dataset. If the dropout probability is too low, there will be no effect. On the other hand, if it is too high, the model will start to underfit. Dropout rates between 20% and 50% usually perform the best.

The learning rate is an important hyperparameter. Having a high learning rate will lead to the model overshooting the optimal solution, while having a low learning rate will cause the model to learn very slowly. As mentioned in *Chapter 5, Mastering Structured Data*, we can start with a high learning rate and reduce the learning rate after a few steps.

This helps us reach the optimal point faster and due to the reduction in step size preventing the model from overshooting the solution. To perform this reduction in the learning rate, we can use the **ReduceLROnPlateau** callback from Keras. The callback reduces the learning rate by a predefined factor if the selected metric stops improving.

> **Note**
>
> To learn further on the dataset, refer to the documentation at https://keras.io/callbacks/#reducelronplateau.

```
from keras.callbacks import ReduceLROnPlateau
ReduceLROnPlateau(monitor='val_loss', factor=0.1, patience=10, min_
delta=0.0001, min_lr=0)
```

We pass the quantity to be monitored into the **monitor** parameter. The **factor** refers to the factor by which the learning rate must be reduced; the new learning rate will be equal to the learning rate multiplied by the factor. **patience** is the number of epochs the callback will wait before changing the learning rate. **min_delta** refers to the threshold for measuring the improvement of the model on the monitored metric. **min_lr** refers to the lower bound on the learning rate.

pandas Profiling

In the initial chapters, you learned different ways to explore structured datasets. EDA plays an important role when it comes to creating models for structured data. The steps used to perform EDA, such as null value identification, correlation, and counting unique values, rarely change, so it is better to create a function that will do all this for us without writing a lot of code. The pandas profiling library does just that: it takes a dataframe and performs analysis on the data and presents the results in an interactive output.

The output contains the following information for the relevant columns:

- **Essentials**: This contains information on the type of the variable, the unique values, and the missing values.
- **Quantile statistics**: This contains information on the minimum value, Q1, the median, Q3, the maximum, the range, and the interquartile range.
- **Descriptive statistics**: This contains information on the mean, the mode, the standard deviation, the sum, the median absolute deviation, and the coefficient of variation.

- **Most frequent values**: This contains information on the most common value count along with the frequency in percentage.
- **Histogram:** This contains information on a plot of the frequency of values of different features of the dataset.
- **Correlations**: These highlight highly correlated variables and suggests removal.

To use pandas profiling, simply pass a data frame to the **`pandas_profiling`** object. Use the following code:

```
import pandas_profiling
pandas_profiling.ProfileReport(df)
```

The following screenshot displays a part of the pandas profiling output for the telecom churn dataset we worked on in *Chapter 5, Mastering Structured Data*

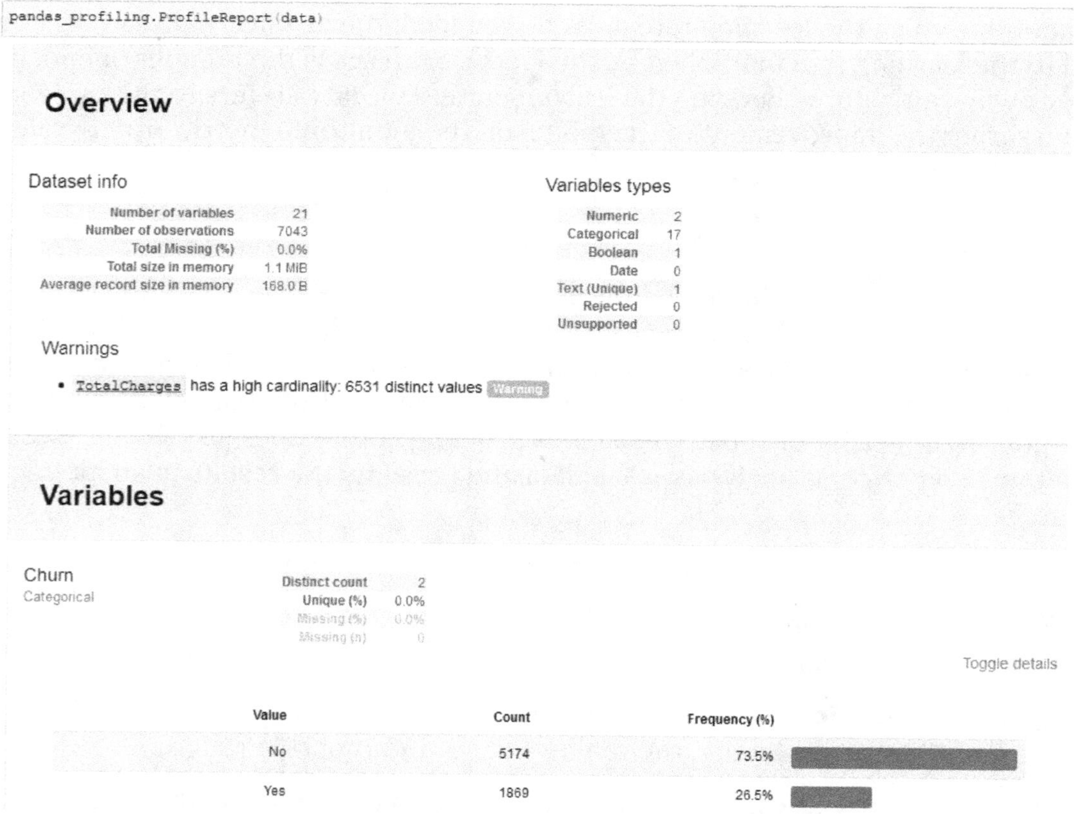

Figure 8.7: A screenshot of the pandas profiling output

You can use this to explore datasets we worked on in the previous chapters. pandas profiling offers interactive output, so you are encouraged to go ahead and play around with the output.

TensorBoard

TensorBoard is a web app that can be used to view training logs and visualize your model's accuracy and loss metrics. It was originally created to work with TensorFlow, but we can make use of TensorBoard using the **TensorBoard callback** in Keras. To start visualizing, create the Keras callback. Use the following code to do so:

```
import keras

keras.callbacks.TensorBoard(log_dir='./logs', update_freq='epoch')
```

Keep a note of the log directory that you specify here; you will need this later. You can pass '**batch**', '**epoch**', or an integer in **update_freq**; this refers to how often the logs should be written. The next step is to start TensorBoard; to do that, open a terminal and run the following command:

```
tensorboard --logdir logs --port 6607
```

Now start training. Do not forget to pass the callback to the **fit** function. The first tab of TensorBoard shows the training logs of the model. You can create multiple folders inside the log folder to get the logs of different models on the same graph for comparison:

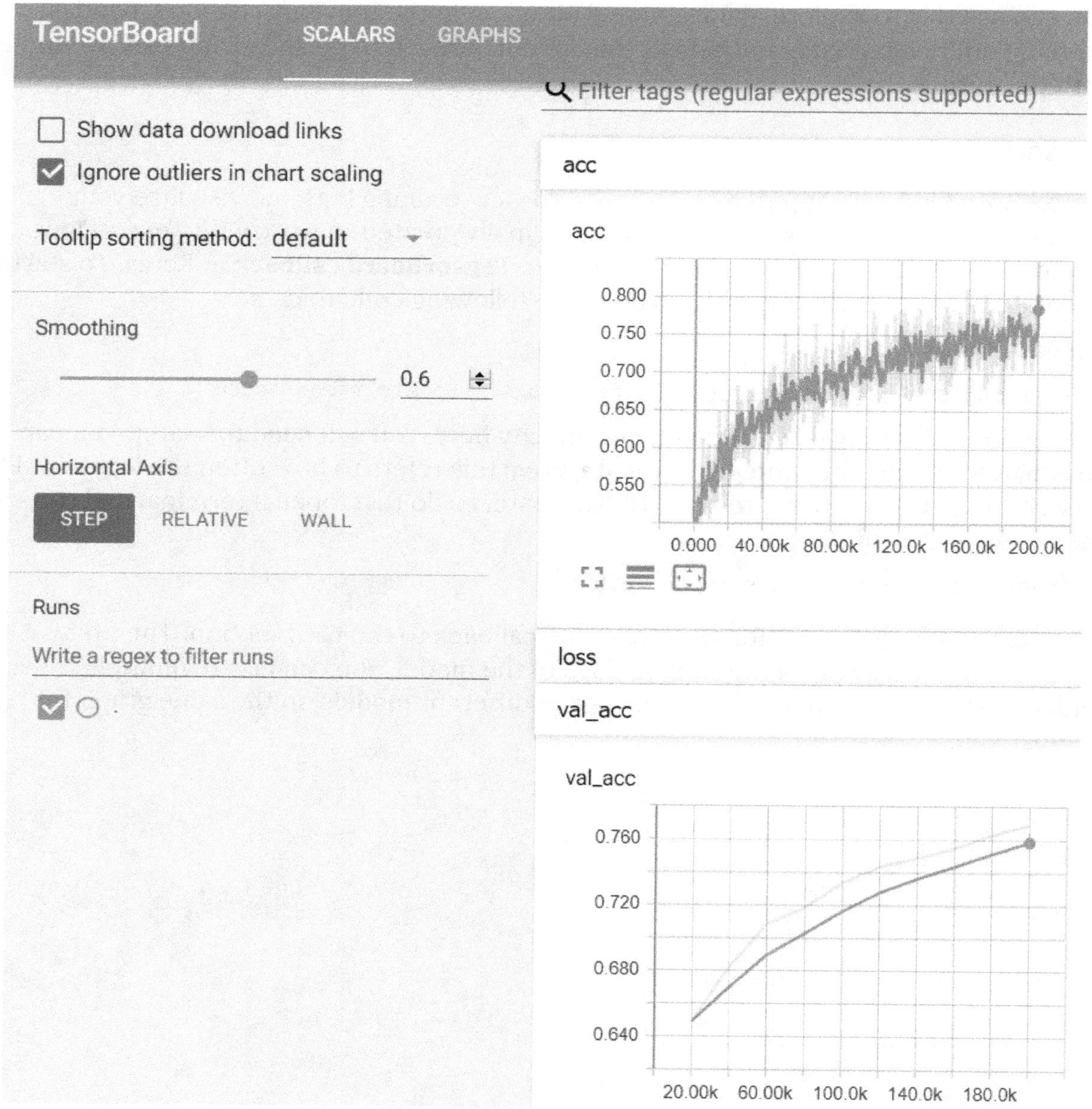

Figure 8.8: A screenshot showing the TensorBoard dashboard

In the second tab, you can visualize the model that you have created. The following figure shows the model that we created in the first activity of the previous chapter:

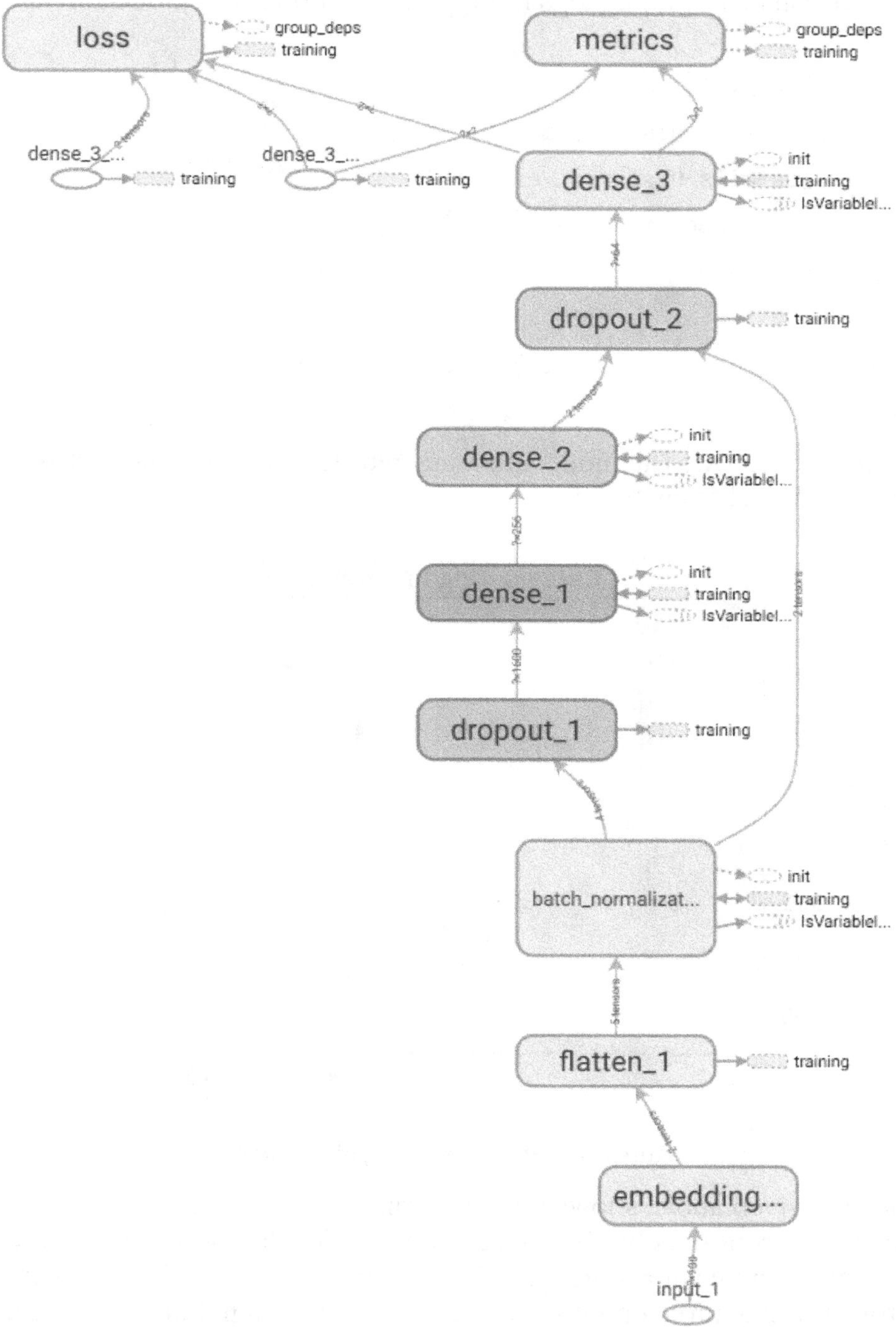

Figure 8.9: The model as interpreted by Keras

Another way to visualize training logs in Jupyter Notebook is to plot them using Matplotlib:

```
import matplotlib.pyplot as plt
plt.plot(model_details.history['acc'])
plt.plot(model_details.history['val_acc'])
plt.title('Cats vs. Dogs model accuracy')
plt.ylabel('Accuracy')
plt.xlabel('Epoch')
plt.legend(['Train set', 'Dev set'], loc='upper left')
plt.show()
```

The following figure shows the model accuracy plot for the train and test set for our cats versus dogs model from *Activity* 1:

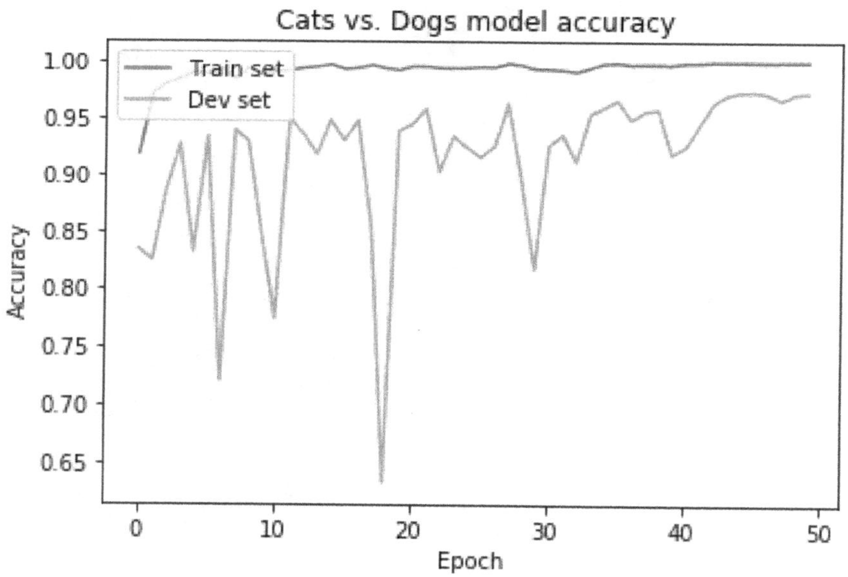

Figure 8.10: The accuracy log of the model

The accuracy log given above shows how the training and development set accuracy increased over different epochs. As you can see, the development set accuracy is more volatile than the training set accuracy. This is because the model hasn't seen these examples, towards the initial epochs this volatility will be high but as we create a robust model after having trained it for a larger number of epochs, the accuracy will become less volatile.

```
plt.plot(model_details.history['loss'])
```

```
plt.plot(model_details.history['val_loss'])
plt.title('Cats vs. Dogs model loss')
plt.ylabel('Loss')
plt.xlabel('Epoch')
plt.legend(['Train set', 'Test set'], loc='upper left')
plt.show()
```

The following figure shows the model loss plot for the train and test set for our cats-versus-dogs model from *Activity 21*:

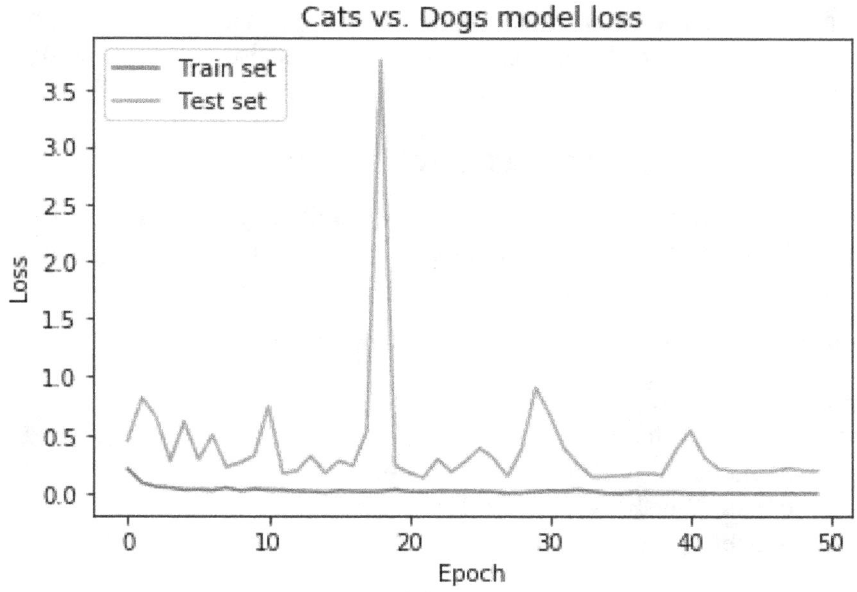

Figure 8.11: Loss log of the model

Similar to the accuracy log, the loss log given above shows how the training and development set loss decreased over different epochs. The spike near epoch 19 suggests that a really bad model which was overfit to the training set was created but, eventually the model started stabilizing and gave better results on the development set as well.

If you are only concerned with the model logs, then you can use the code given earlier to plot the model logs after the training is over. If, however, you are training a model that takes a long time to train, it would be wise to use TensorBoard, as it provides a real-time plot of the training loss and accuracy.

AutoML

Now that you have created multiple neural network models, you understand that there are two main components that go into creating well-performing networks. They are as follows:

- The architecture of the neural network
- The hyperparameters of the neural network

Depending on the problem, it could take tens of iterations to get to the best possible network. So far, we have been creating architectures and tuning the hyperparameters manually. AutoML can help us perform these tasks. It searches for the most optimal network and parameters for the dataset at hand. Auto-Keras is an open source library that helps us implement AutoML on Keras. Let's learn about how to use Auto-Keras with the help of an exercise.

Exercise 59: Get a Well-Performing Network Using Auto-Keras

In this exercise, we will make use of the Auto-Keras library to find the most optimal network and parameters for the cats-vs-dogs dataset (https://github.com/TrainingByPackt/Data-Science-with-Python/tree/master/Chapter08).

1. First, create a function to load the image labels:

```
def get_label(file):
    class_label = file.split('.')[0]
    if class_label == 'dog': label_vector = 0
    elif class_label == 'cat': label_vector = 1
    return label_vector
```

2. Set **SIZE** which is the dimension of the square image input.

```
SIZE = 50
```

3. Then create a function that reads images and their labels. Here **PATH** variable contains the path to the training dataset.

```
import os
from PIL import Image
import numpy as np
from random import shuffle
def get_data():
    data = []
    files = os.listdir(PATH)
```

```
    for image in tqdm(files):
        label_vector = get_label(image)

        img = Image.open(PATH + image).convert('L')
        img = img.resize((SIZE,SIZE))

        data.append([np.asarray(img),np.array(label_vector)])

    shuffle(data)
    return data
```

4. Load the data and divide it into train and test sets:

```
data = get_data()
train = data[:7000]
test = data[7000:]
x_train = [data[0] for data in train]
y_train = [data[1] for data in train]
x_test = [data[0] for data in test]
y_test = [data[1] for data in test]
x_train = np.array(x_train).reshape(-1,SIZE,SIZE,1)
x_test = np.array(x_test).reshape(-1,SIZE,SIZE,1)
```

5. Now, let's start with AutoML

   First, create an array with the training time for autokeras. It will terminate the process of finding the best possible model once this time is elapsed:

```
TRAINING_TIME = 60 * 60 * 1 # 1 hour
```

   We will give autokeras an hour to find the best possible method.

6. Create an image classifier model using autokeras and perform training for the time specified in the previous step:

```
import autokeras as ak
model = ak.ImageClassifier(verbose=True)
model.fit(x_train, y_train, time_limit=TRAINING_TIME)
model.final_fit(x_train, y_train, x_test, y_test, retrain=True)
```

7. The output will be as follows:

```
Saving Directory: /tmp/autokeras_SXTBBX
Preprocessing the images.
Preprocessing finished.

Initializing search.
Initialization finished.


+----------------------------------------------+
|              Training model 0                |
+----------------------------------------------+

No loss decrease after 5 epochs.


Saving model.
+--------------------------------------------------------------------------+
|        Model ID        |          Loss          |      Metric Value      |
+--------------------------------------------------------------------------+
|           0            |   2.409887635707855    |   0.6744000000000001   |
+--------------------------------------------------------------------------+


+----------------------------------------------+
|              Training model 1                |
+----------------------------------------------+
Epoch-1, Current Metric - 0:  39%|                  | 20/51 [04:51<05:04,  9.81s/
batch]Time is out.
```

Figure 8.12: Image classifier model

8. Next, we save our model so that we can use it again:

```
model.export_autokeras_model("model.h5")
```

9. Load the trained model and perform predictions using it:

```
from autokeras.utils import pickle_from_file
model = pickle_from_file("model.h5")
predictions = model.predict(x_test)
```

10. Evaluate the accuracy of the model created by autokeras:

```
score = model.evaluate(x_test, y_test)
print("\nScore: {}".format(score))
```

11. The accuracy of the model is as follows:

```
Score: 0.7186
```

Figure 8.13: Model final accuracy

12. We successfully made use of autokeras to create an image classifier that detects if the provided image is of a cat or a dog. The accuracy that we get with this model is 72% after an hour of running it which is pretty good considering that we got a 73% accuracy for the model that we created in *Chapter 6*, *Decoding Images*, *Activity 22*. This shows the power of autoML but, sometimes we do not get good enough results in an acceptable time frame.

Model Visualization Using Keras

So far, we have created a bunch of neural network models but haven't visualized any of them. Keras has a very handy utility function that plots any model. To create a plot first define the model, we will take the model created in *Chapter 6*, *Decoding images*, as shown in the following code:

```
model = Sequential()


model.add(Conv2D(48, (3, 3), activation='relu', padding='same', input_
shape=(50,50,1)))
model.add(Conv2D(48, (3, 3), activation='relu'))
model.add(MaxPool2D(pool_size=(2, 2)))
model.add(BatchNormalization())
model.add(Dropout(0.10))


model.add(Flatten())


model.add(Dense(512, activation='relu'))
model.add(Dropout(0.5))


model.add(Dense(2, activation='softmax'))


model.summary()
```

And then save the model as an image using **plot_model**, as shown in the following code.

```
from keras.utils import plot_model
plot_model(model, to_file='model.png', show_shapes=True)
```

The **show_shapes** argument gives the visualization the input and output shapes of the layers. The saved image is as follows:

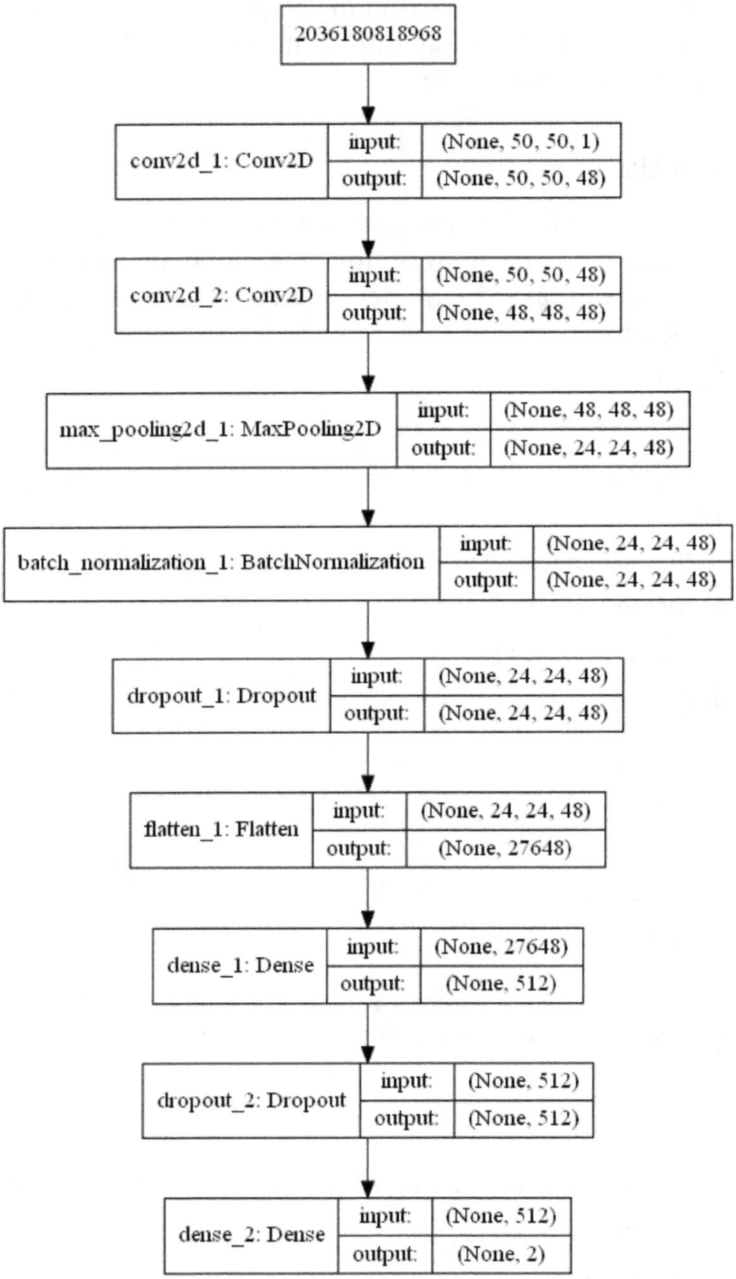

Figure 8.14: Model visualization created by Keras

Activity 22: Using Transfer Learning to Predict Images

We will create a project where you perform transfer learning to predict whether a given picture is of a dog or a cat. The model that you will be using as a baseline will be InceptionV3. We will fine-tune this model to our dataset and thus modify the model to distinguish between cats and dogs. We will use TensorBoard to monitor the training metrics in real time and use the best practices discussed in this chapter. Make sure that the results are reproducible:

1. Repeat everything you did in *Step* 1 from the previous activity.
2. Load the development and test datasets, which will not be augmented.
3. Load the Inception model and add the final dense layers to it. Train the entire network.
4. Make use of all useful callbacks.
5. Visualize the training using TensorBoard.

> **Note**
>
> The solution for this activity can be found on page 391.

You can plot the incorrectly predicted images to get a sense of how well the model performs using the following snippet:

```
y_pred = model.predict(test_data[0])


incorrect_indices = np.nonzero(np.argmax(y_pred,axis=1) != np.argmax(test_
data[1],axis=1))[0]
labels = ['dog', 'cat']
image = 5
plt.imshow(test_data[0][incorrect_indices[image]].reshape(SIZE, SIZE,
CHANNELS),  cmap=plt.get_cmap('gray'))
plt.show()
print("Prediction: {0}".format(labels[np.argmax(y_pred[incorrect_
indices[image]])]))
```

The incorrectly predicted image is as follows:

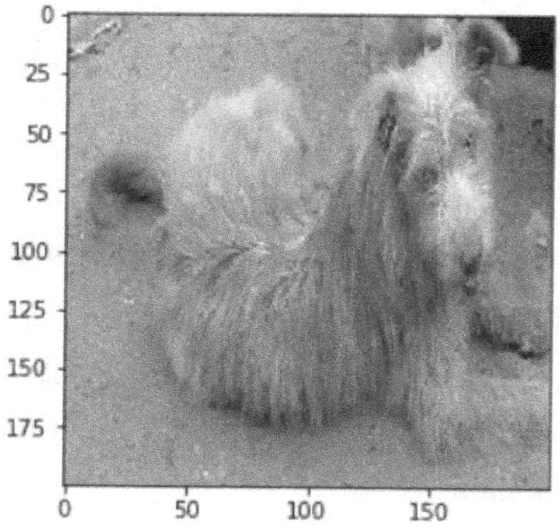


```
Prediction: cat
```

Figure 8.15: The incorrectly predicted sample

Summary

In this chapter, we covered transfer learning and leveraged it to create deep learning models faster. We then moved on to learn the importance of separate training, development, and test datasets, followed by a section on dealing with real-life, unprocessed datasets. After that, we talk about what AutoML is and how we can find the most optimal network with little to no work. We learned how to visualize neural network models and training logs.

Now that you have completed this chapter, you are now capable of handling any kind of data to create machine learning models.

Finally, having completed this book, you should now have a strong understanding of the concepts of data science, and should be able to use the Python language to work with different datasets to solve business-case problems. The different concepts that you have learned, including those of preprocessing, data visualization, image augmentation, and human language processing, should have helped in providing you with an overall grasp of how to work with data.

Appendix

About

This section is included to assist you in performing the activities present in the book. It includes detailed steps that are to be performed by the students to complete and achieve the objectives of the book.

Chapter 1: Introduction to Data Science and Data Preprocessing

Activity 1: Pre-Processing Using the Bank Marketing Subscription Dataset

Solution

Let's perform various pre-processing tasks on the **Bank Marketing Subscription** dataset. We'll also be splitting the dataset into training and testing data. Follow these steps to complete this activity:

1. Open a Jupyter notebook and add a new cell to import the pandas library and load the dataset into a pandas dataframe. To do so, you first need to import the library, and then use the **pd.read_csv()** function, as shown here:

```
import pandas as pd

Link = 'https://github.com/TrainingByPackt/Data-Science-with-Python/blob/
master/Chapter01/Data/Banking_Marketing.csv'

#reading the data into the dataframe into the object data
df = pd.read_csv(Link, header=0)
```

2. To find the number of rows and columns in the dataset, add the following code:

```
#Finding number of rows and columns
print("Number of rows and columns : ",df.shape)
```

The preceding code generates the following output:

```
Number of rows and columns :  (41199, 21)
```

Figure 1.60: Number of rows and columns in the dataset

3. To print the list of all columns, add the following code:

```
#Printing all the columns
print(list(df.columns))
```

The preceding code generates the following output:

```
['age', 'job', 'marital', 'education', 'default', 'housing', 'loan', 'contact', 'month', 'day
_of_week', 'duration', 'campaign', 'pdays', 'previous', 'poutcome', 'emp_var_rate', 'cons_pri
ce_idx', 'cons_conf_idx', 'euribor3m', 'nr_employed', 'y']
```

Figure 1.61: List of columns present in the dataset

4. To overview the basic statistics of each column, such as the count, mean, median, standard deviation, minimum value, maximum value, and so on, add the following code:

```
#Basic Statistics of each column
df.describe().transpose()
```

The preceding code generates the following output:

	count	mean	std	min	25%	50%	75%	max
age	41197.0	40.023812	10.434966	1.000	32.000	38.000	47.000	104.000
duration	41192.0	258.274762	259.270089	0.000	102.000	180.000	319.000	4918.000
campaign	41199.0	2.567514	2.769719	1.000	1.000	2.000	3.000	56.000
pdays	41199.0	962.485206	186.886905	0.000	999.000	999.000	999.000	999.000
previous	41199.0	0.172941	0.494859	0.000	0.000	0.000	0.000	7.000
emp_var_rate	41199.0	0.081900	1.570971	-3.400	-1.800	1.100	1.400	1.400
cons_price_idx	41199.0	93.575650	0.578845	92.201	93.075	93.749	93.994	94.767
cons_conf_idx	41199.0	-40.502002	4.628524	-50.800	-42.700	-41.800	-36.400	-26.900
euribor3m	41199.0	3.621336	1.734431	0.634	1.344	4.857	4.961	5.045
nr_employed	41199.0	5167.036455	72.249592	4963.600	5099.100	5191.000	5228.100	5228.100
y	41199.0	0.112648	0.316166	0.000	0.000	0.000	0.000	1.000

Figure 1.62: Basic statistics of each column

5. To print the basic information of each column, add the following code:

```
#Basic Information of each column
print(df.info())
```

The preceding code generates the following output:

```
<class 'pandas.core.frame.DataFrame'>
RangeIndex: 41199 entries, 0 to 41198
Data columns (total 21 columns):
age               41197 non-null float64
job               41199 non-null object
marital           41199 non-null object
education         41199 non-null object
default           41199 non-null object
housing           41199 non-null object
loan              41199 non-null object
contact           41193 non-null object
month             41199 non-null object
day_of_week       41199 non-null object
duration          41192 non-null float64
campaign          41199 non-null int64
pdays             41199 non-null int64
previous          41199 non-null int64
poutcome          41199 non-null object
emp_var_rate      41199 non-null float64
cons_price_idx    41199 non-null float64
cons_conf_idx     41199 non-null float64
euribor3m         41199 non-null float64
nr_employed       41199 non-null float64
y                 41199 non-null int64
dtypes: float64(7), int64(4), object(10)
memory usage: 6.6+ MB
```

Figure 1.63: Basic information of each column

In the preceding figure, you can see that none of the columns contains any null values. Also, the type of each column is provided.

6. Now let's check for missing values and the type of each feature. Add the following code to do this:

```
#finding the data types of each column and checking for null
null_ = df.isna().any()
dtypes = df.dtypes
sum_na_ = df.isna().sum()
info = pd.concat([null_,sum_na_,dtypes],axis = 1,keys = 
['isNullExist','NullSum','type'])
info
```

Have a look at the output for this in the following figure:

	isNullExist	NullSum	type
age	True	2	float64
job	False	0	object
marital	False	0	object
education	False	0	object
default	False	0	object
housing	False	0	object
loan	False	0	object
contact	True	6	object
month	False	0	object
day_of_week	False	0	object
duration	True	7	float64
campaign	False	0	int64
pdays	False	0	int64
previous	False	0	int64
poutcome	False	0	object
emp_var_rate	False	0	float64
cons_price_idx	False	0	float64
cons_conf_idx	False	0	float64
euribor3m	False	0	float64
nr_employed	False	0	float64
y	False	0	int64

Figure 1.64: Information of each column stating the number of null values and the data types

7. Since we have loaded the dataset into the **data** object, we will remove the null values from the dataset. To remove the null values from the dataset, add the following code:

```
#removing Null values
df = df.dropna()
#Total number of null in each column
print(df.isna().sum())# No NA
```

Have a look at the output for this in the following figure:

```
age               0
job               0
marital           0
education         0
default           0
housing           0
loan              0
contact           0
month             0
day_of_week       0
duration          0
campaign          0
pdays             0
previous          0
poutcome          0
emp_var_rate      0
cons_price_idx    0
cons_conf_idx     0
euribor3m         0
nr_employed       0
y                 0
```

Figure 1.65: Features of dataset with no null values

8. Now we check the frequency distribution of the **education** column in the dataset. Use the **value_counts()** function to implement this:

```
df.education.value_counts()
```

Have a look at the output for this in the following figure:

```
university.degree      12167
high.school             9516
basic.9y                6045
professional.course     5242
basic.4y                4176
basic.6y                2292
unknown                 1731
illiterate                18
Name: education, dtype: int64
```

Figure 1.66: Frequency distribution of the education column

9. In the preceding figure, we can see that the **education** column of the dataset has many categories. We need to reduce the categories for better modeling. To check the various categories in the **education** column, we use the **unique()** function. Type the following code to implement this:

```
df.education.unique()
```

The output is as follows:

```
array(['basic.4y', 'unknown', 'university.degree', 'high.school',
       'basic.9y', 'professional.course', 'basic.6y', 'illiterate'],
      dtype=object)
```

Figure 1.67: Various categories of the education column

10. Now let's group the **basic.4y**, **basic.9y**, and **basic.6y** categories together and call them **basic**. To do this, we can use the **replace** function from pandas:

```
df.education.replace({"basic.9y":"Basic","basic.6y":
"Basic","basic.4y":"Basic"},inplace=True)
```

11. To check the list of categories after grouping, add the following code:

```
df.education.unique()
```

```
array(['Basic', 'unknown', 'university.degree', 'high.school',
       'professional.course', 'illiterate'], dtype=object)
```

Figure 1.68: Various categories of the education column

In the preceding figure, you can see that **basic.9y**, **basic.6y**, and **basic.4y** are grouped together as **Basic**.

12. Now we select and perform a suitable encoding method for the data. Add the following code to implement this:

```
#Select all the non numeric data using select_dtypes function
data_column_category = df.select_dtypes(exclude=[np.number]).columns
```

The preceding code generates the following output:

```
Index(['job', 'marital', 'education', 'default', 'housing', 'loan', 'contact',
       'month', 'day_of_week', 'poutcome'],
      dtype='object')
```

Figure 1.69: Various columns of the dataset

13. Now we define a list with all the names of the categorical features in the data. Also, we loop through every variable in the list, getting dummy variable encoded output. Add the following code to do this:

```
cat_vars=data_column_category

for var in cat_vars:
    cat_list='var'+'_'+var
    cat_list = pd.get_dummies(df[var], prefix=var)
    data1=df.join(cat_list)
    df=data1
df.columns
```

The preceding code generates the following output:

```
Index(['age', 'job', 'marital', 'education', 'default', 'housing', 'loan',
       'contact', 'month', 'day_of_week', 'duration', 'campaign', 'pdays',
       'previous', 'poutcome', 'emp_var_rate', 'cons_price_idx',
       'cons_conf_idx', 'euribor3m', 'nr_employed', 'y', 'job_admin.',
       'job_blue-collar', 'job_entrepreneur', 'job_housemaid',
       'job_management', 'job_retired', 'job_self-employed', 'job_services',
       'job_student', 'job_technician', 'job_unemployed', 'job_unknown',
       'marital_divorced', 'marital_married', 'marital_single',
       'marital_unknown', 'education_basic.4y', 'education_basic.6y',
       'education_basic.9y', 'education_high.school', 'education_illiterate',
       'education_professional.course', 'education_university.degree',
       'education_unknown', 'default_no', 'default_unknown', 'default_yes',
       'housing_no', 'housing_unknown', 'housing_yes', 'loan_no',
       'loan_unknown', 'loan_yes', 'contact_cellular', 'contact_telephone',
       'month_apr', 'month_aug', 'month_dec', 'month_jul', 'month_jun',
       'month_mar', 'month_may', 'month_nov', 'month_oct', 'month_sep',
       'day_of_week_fri', 'day_of_week_mon', 'day_of_week_thu',
       'day_of_week_tue', 'day_of_week_wed', 'poutcome_failure',
       'poutcome_nonexistent', 'poutcome_success'],
      dtype='object')
```

Figure 1.70: List of categorical features in the data

14. Now we neglect the categorical column for which we have done encoding. We'll select only the numerical and encoded categorical columns. Add the code to do this:

```
#Categorical features
cat_vars=data_column_category

#All features
data_vars=df.columns.values.tolist()

#neglecting the categorical column for which we have done encoding
to_keep = []
for i in data_vars:
    if i not in cat_vars:
        to_keep.append(i)

#selecting only the numerical and encoded catergorical column
data_final=df[to_keep]

data_final.columns
```

The preceding code generates the following output:

```
Index(['age', 'duration', 'campaign', 'pdays', 'previous', 'emp_var_rate',
       'cons_price_idx', 'cons_conf_idx', 'euribor3m', 'nr_employed', 'y',
       'job_admin.', 'job_blue-collar', 'job_entrepreneur', 'job_housemaid',
       'job_management', 'job_retired', 'job_self-employed', 'job_services',
       'job_student', 'job_technician', 'job_unemployed', 'job_unknown',
       'marital_divorced', 'marital_married', 'marital_single',
       'marital_unknown', 'education_Basic', 'education_high.school',
       'education_illiterate', 'education_professional.course',
       'education_university.degree', 'education_unknown', 'default_no',
       'default_unknown', 'default_yes', 'housing_no', 'housing_unknown',
       'housing_yes', 'loan_no', 'loan_unknown', 'loan_yes',
       'contact_cellular', 'contact_telephone', 'month_apr', 'month_aug',
       'month_dec', 'month_jul', 'month_jun', 'month_mar', 'month_may',
       'month_nov', 'month_oct', 'month_sep', 'day_of_week_fri',
       'day_of_week_mon', 'day_of_week_thu', 'day_of_week_tue',
       'day_of_week_wed', 'poutcome_failure', 'poutcome_nonexistent',
       'poutcome_success'],
      dtype='object')
```

Figure 1.71: List of numerical and encoded categorical columns

15. Finally, we split the data into train and test sets. Add the following code to implement this:

```
#Segregating Independent and Target variable
X=data_final.drop(columns='y')
y=data_final['y']

from sklearn. model_selection import train_test_split
X_train, X_test, y_train, y_test = train_test_split(X, y, test_size=0.2,
random_state=0)

print("FULL Dateset X Shape: ", X.shape )
print("Train Dateset X Shape: ", X_train.shape )
print("Test Dateset X Shape: ", X_test.shape )
```

The output is as follows:

```
FULL Dateset X Shape:  (41187, 61)
Train Dateset X Shape:  (32949, 61)
Test Dateset X Shape:  (8238, 61)
```

Figure 1.72: Shape of the full, train, and test datasets

Chapter 2: Data Visualization

Activity 2: Line Plot

Solution:

1. Create a list of 6 strings for each month, January through June, and save it as x using:

```
x = ['January','February','March','April','May','June']
```

2. Create a list of 6 values for '**Items Sold**' that starts at 1000 and increases by 200, so the final value is 2000 and save it as y as follows:

```
y = [1000, 1200, 1400, 1600, 1800, 2000]
```

3. Plot y ('**Items Sold**') by x ('**Month**') with a dotted blue line and star markers using the following:

```
plt.plot(x, y, '*:b')
```

4. Set the x-axis to '**Month**' using the following code:

```
plt.xlabel('Month')
```

5. Set the y-axis to '**Items Sold**' as follows:

```
plt.ylabel('Items Sold')
```

6. To set the title to read '**Items Sold has been Increasing Linearly**', refer to the following code:

```
plt.title('Items Sold has been Increasing Linearly')
```

Check out the following screenshot for the resultant output:

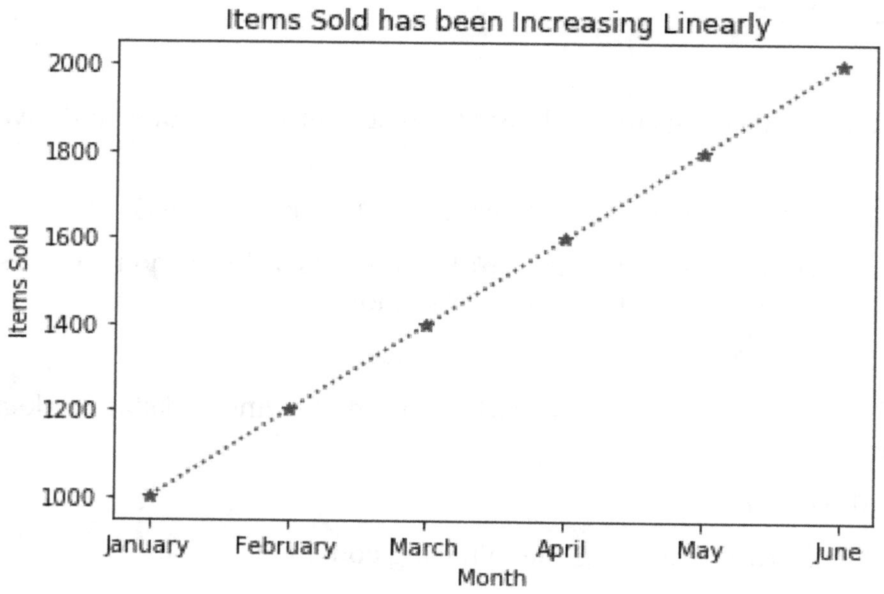

Figure 2.33: Line plot of items sold by month

Activity 3: Bar Plot

Solution:

1. Create a list of five strings for **x** containing the names of NBA franchises with the most titles using the following code:

```
x = ['Boston Celtics','Los Angeles Lakers', 'Chicago Bulls', 'Golden State
Warriors', 'San Antonio Spurs']
```

2. Create a list of five values for **y** containing values for '**Titles Won**' that correspond with the strings in **x** using the following code:

```
y = [17, 16, 6, 6, 5]
```

3. Place **x** and **y** into a data frame with the column names '**Team**' and '**Titles**', respectively, as follows:

```
import pandas as pd

df = pd.DataFrame({'Team': x,
                   'Titles': y})
```

4. To sort the data frame descending by 'Titles' and save it as df_sorted, refer to the following code:

```
df_sorted = df.sort_values(by=('Titles'), ascending=False)
```

> **Note**
>
> If we sort with **ascending=True**, the plot will have larger values to the right. Since we want the larger values on the left, we will be using **ascending=False**.

5. Make a programmatic title and save it as title by first finding the team with the most titles and saving it as the **team_with_most_titles** object using the following code:

```
team_with_most_titles = df_sorted['Team'][0]
```

6. Then, retrieve the number of titles for the team with the most titles using the following code:

```
most_titles = df_sorted['Titles'][0]
```

7. Lastly, create a string that reads '**The Boston Celtics have the most titles with 17**' using the following code:

```
title = 'The {} have the most titles with {}'.format(team_with_most_
titles, most_titles)
```

8. Use a bar graph to plot the number of titles by team using the following code:

```
import matplotlib.pyplot as plt

plt.bar(df_sorted['Team'], df_sorted['Titles'], color='red')
```

9. Set the x-axis label to '**Team**' using the following:

```
plt.xlabel('Team')
```

10. Set the y-axis label to '**Number of Championships**' using the following:

```
plt.ylabel('Number of Championships')
```

11. To prevent the x tick labels from overlapping by rotating them 45 degrees, refer to the following code:

```
plt.xticks(rotation=45)
```

12. Set the title of the plot to the programmatic **title** object we created as follows:

```
plt.title(title)
```

13. Save the plot to our current working directory as '**Titles_by_Team.png**' using the following code:

```
plt.savefig('Titles_by_Team)
```

14. Print the plot using **plt.show()**. To understand this better, check out the following output screenshot:

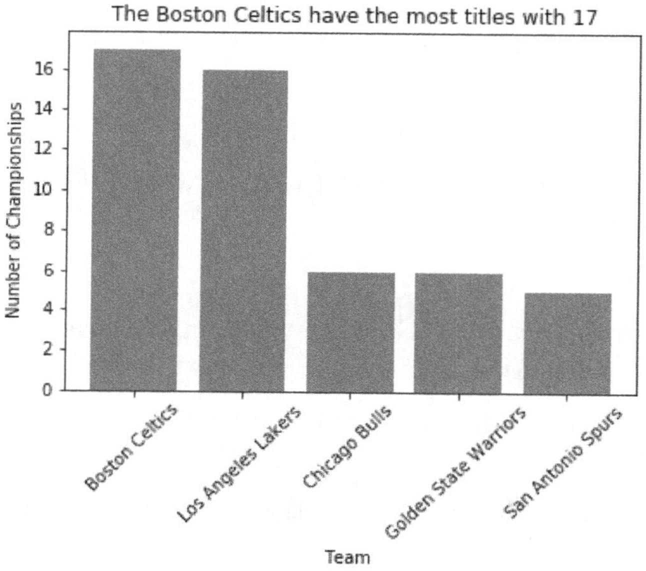

Figure 2.34: The bar plot of the number of titles held by an NBA team

> **Note**
>
> When we print the plot to the console using **plt.show()**, it appears as intended; however, when we open the file we created titled '**Titles_by_Team.png**', we see that it crops the x tick labels.

The following figure displays the bar plot with the cropped x tick labels.

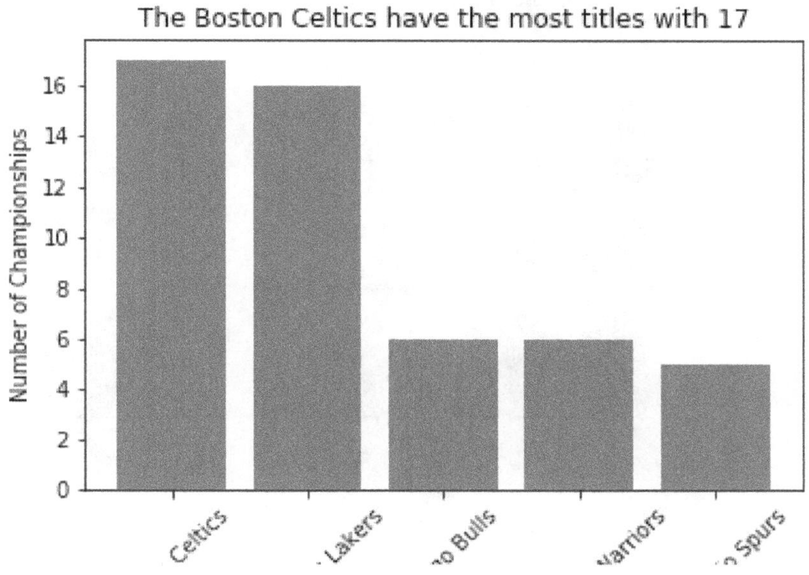

Figure 2.35: 'Titles_by_Team.png' with x tick labels cropped

15. To fix the cropping issue, add **`bbox_inches='tight'`** as an argument inside of **`plt.savefig()`** as follows:

```
plt.savefig('Titles_by_Team', bbox_inches='tight')
```

16. Now, when we open the saved '**`Titles_by_Team.png`**' file from our working directory, we see that the x tick labels are not cropped.

Check out the following output for the final result:

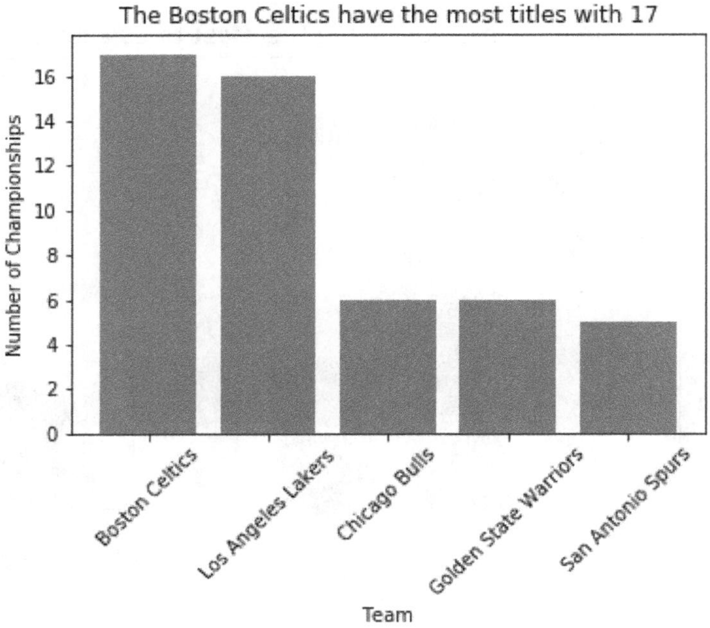

Figure 2.36: 'Titles_by_Team.png' without cropped x tick labels

Activity 4: Multiple Plot Types Using Subplots

Solution:

1. Import the '**Items_Sold_by_Week.csv**' file and save it as the **Items_by_Week** data frame object using the following code:

```
import pandas as pd

Items_by_Week = pd.read_csv('Items_Sold_by_Week.csv')
```

2. Import the '**Weight_by_Height.csv**' file and save it as the **Weight_by_Height** data frame object as follows:

```
Weight_by_Height = pd.read_csv('Weight_by_Height.csv')
```

3. Generate an array of 100 normally distributed numbers to use as data for the histogram and box-and-whisker plots and save it as y using the following code:

```
y = np.random.normal(loc=0, scale=0.1, size=100)
```

4. To generate a figure with six subplots organized in three rows and two columns that do not overlap refer to the following code:

```
import matplotlib.pyplot as plt

fig, axes = plt.subplots(nrows=3, ncols=2)
plt.tight_layout()
```

5. Set the respective axes' titles to match those in Figure 2.32 using the following code:

```
axes[0,0].set_title('Line')
axes[0,1].set_title('Bar')
axes[1,0].set_title('Horizontal Bar')
axes[1,1].set_title('Histogram')
axes[2,0].set_title('Scatter')
axes[2,1].set_title('Box-and-Whisker')
```

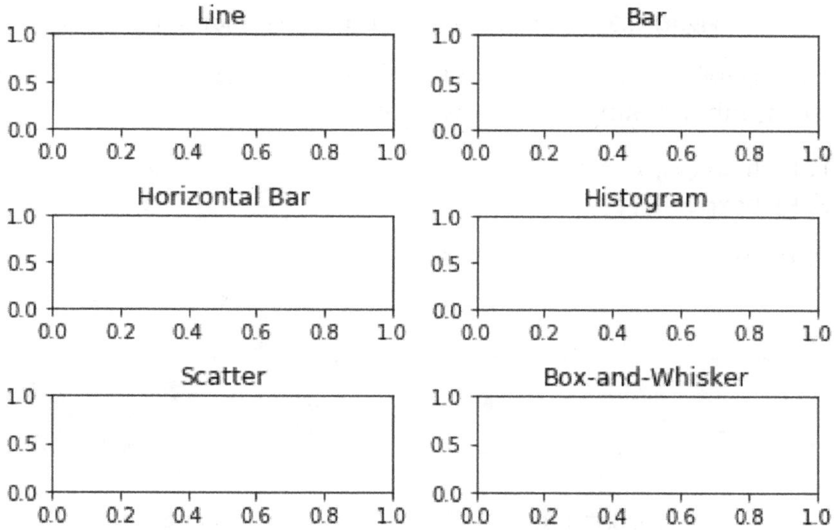

Figure 2.37: Titled, non-overlapping empty subplots

6. On the '**Line**', '**Bar**', and '**Horizontal Bar**' axes, plot '**Items_Sold**' by '**Week**' from '**Items_by_Week**' using:

```
axes[0,0].plot(Items_by_Week['Week'], Items_by_Week['Items_Sold'])
axes[0,1].bar(Items_by_Week['Week'], Items_by_Week['Items_Sold'])
axes[1,0].barh(Items_by_Week['Week'], Items_by_Week['Items_Sold'])
```

See the resultant output in the following figure:

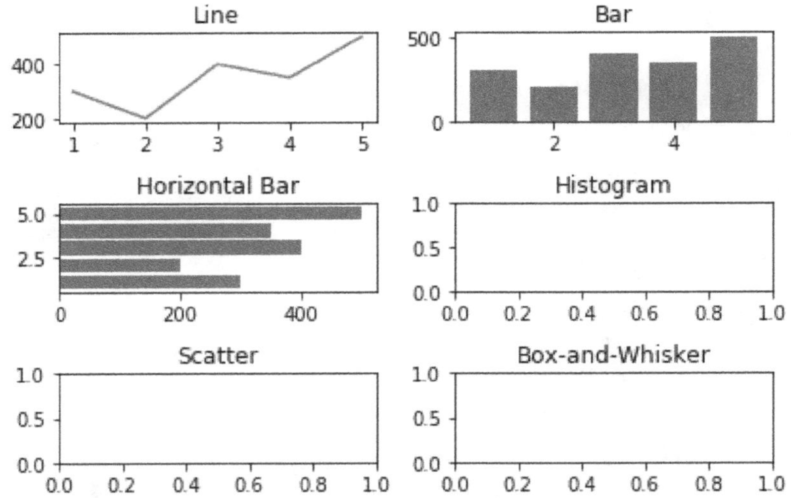

Figure 2.38: Line, bar, and horizontal bar plots added

7. On the '**Histogram**' and '**Box-and-Whisker**' axes, plot the array of 100 normally distributed numbers using the following code:

```
axes[1,1].hist(y, bins=20)
axes[2,1].boxplot(y)
```

The resultant output is displayed here:

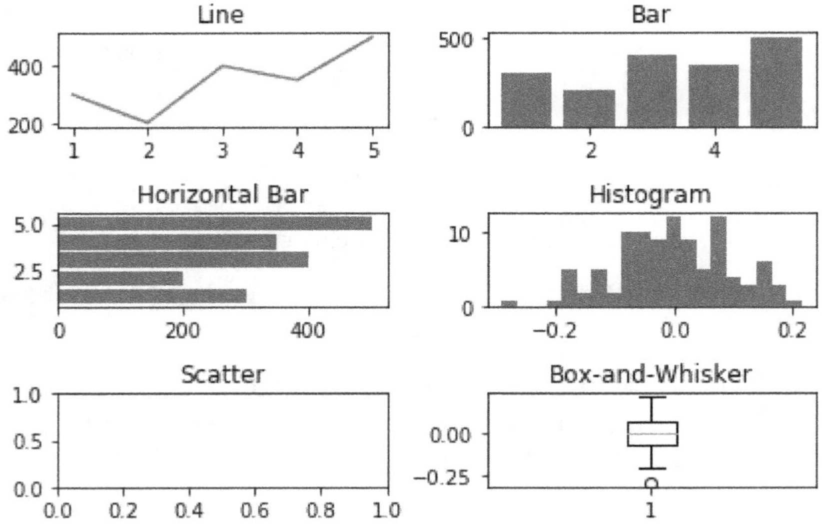

Figure 2.39: The histogram and box-and-whisker added

8. Plot '**Weight**' by '**Height**' on the '**Scatterplot**' axes from the '**Weight_by_Height**' data frame using the following code:

```
axes[2,0].scatter(Weight_by_Height['Height'], Weight_by_Height['Weight'])
```

See the figure here for the resultant output:

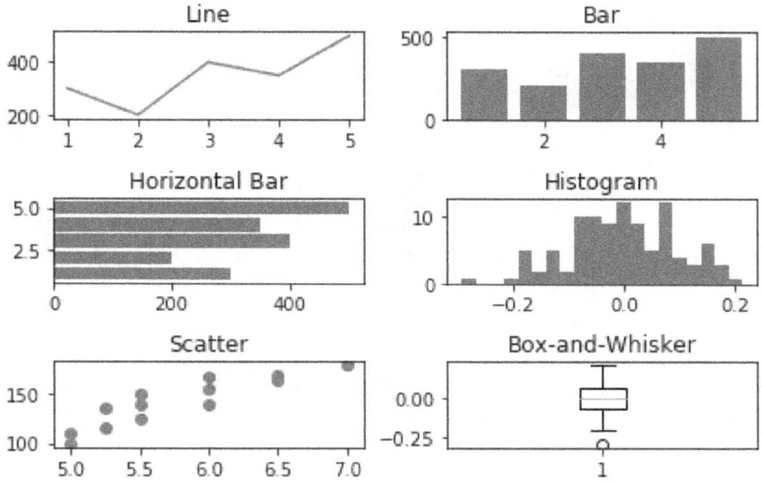

Figure 2.40: Scatterplot added

9. Label the x- and y-axis for each subplot using **axes[row, column].set_xlabel('X-Axis Label')** and **axes[row, column].set_ylabel('Y-Axis Label')**, respectively.

See the figure here for the resultant output:

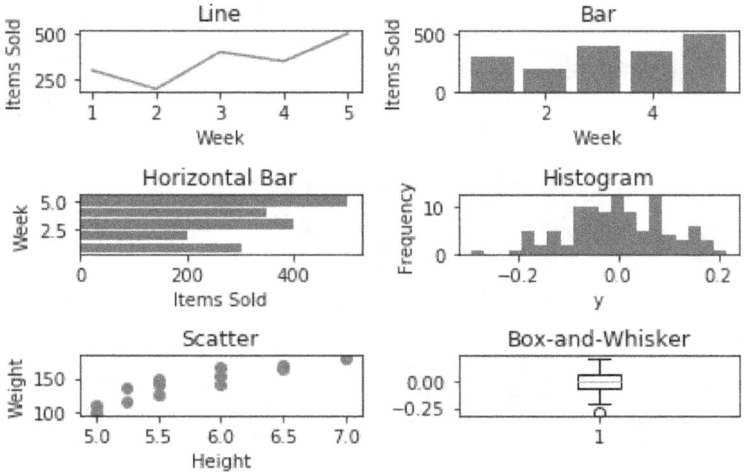

Figure 2.41: X and y axes have been labeled

10. Increase the size of the figure with the **figsize** argument in the subplots function as follows:

```
fig, axes = plt.subplots(nrows=3, ncols=2, figsize=(8,8))
```

11. Save the figure to the current working directory as '**Six_Subplots**' using the following code:

```
fig.savefig('Six_Subplots')
```

The following figure displays the '**Six_Subplots.png**' file:

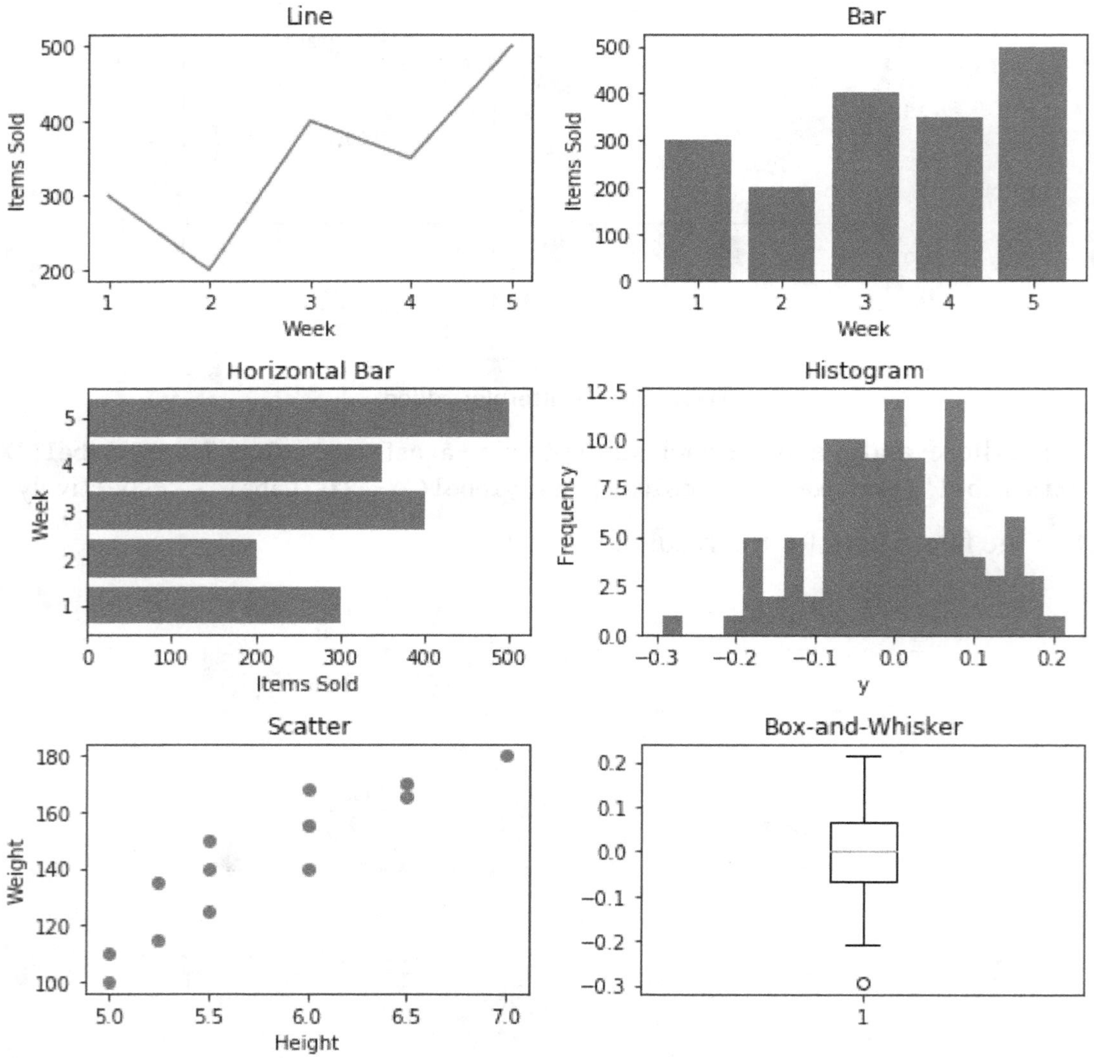

Figure 2.42: The Six_Subplots.png file

Chapter 3: Introduction to Machine Learning via Scikit-Learn

Activity 5: Generating Predictions and Evaluating the Performance of a Multiple Linear Regression Model

Solution:

1. Generate predictions on the test data using the following:

```
predictions = model.predict(X_test)
2.    Plot the predicted versus actual values on a scatterplot using the following code:
import matplotlib.pyplot as plt
from scipy.stats import pearsonr

plt.scatter(y_test, predictions)
plt.xlabel('Y Test (True Values)')
plt.ylabel('Predicted Values')
plt.title('Predicted vs. Actual Values (r = {0:0.2f})'.format(pearsonr(y_test, predictions)[0], 2))
plt.show()
```

Refer to the resultant output here:

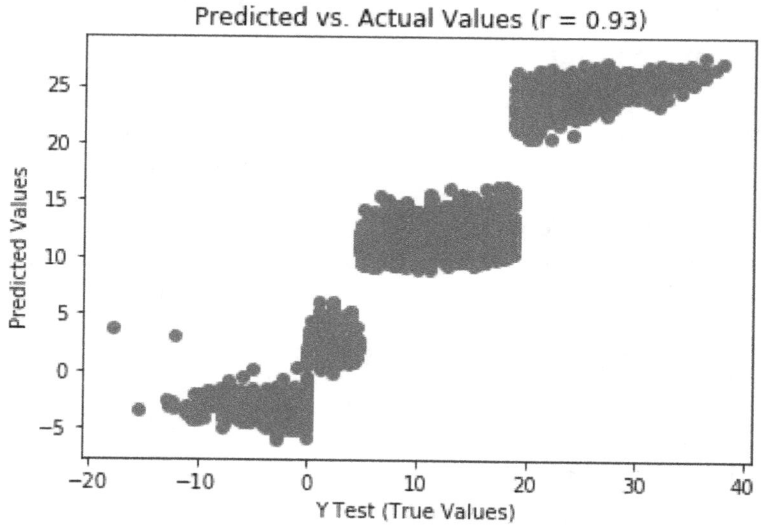

Figure 3.33: A scatterplot of predicted versus actual values from a multiple linear regression model

> **Note**
>
> There is a much stronger linear correlation between the predicted and actual values in the multiple linear regression model (r = 0.93) relative to the simple linear regression model (r = 0.62).

2. To plot the distribution of the residuals, refer to the code here:

```
import seaborn as sns
from scipy.stats import shapiro

sns.distplot((y_test - predictions), bins = 50)
plt.xlabel('Residuals')
plt.ylabel('Density')
plt.title('Histogram of Residuals (Shapiro W p-value = {0:0.3f})'.
format(shapiro(y_test - predictions)[1]))
plt.show()
```

Refer to the resultant output here:

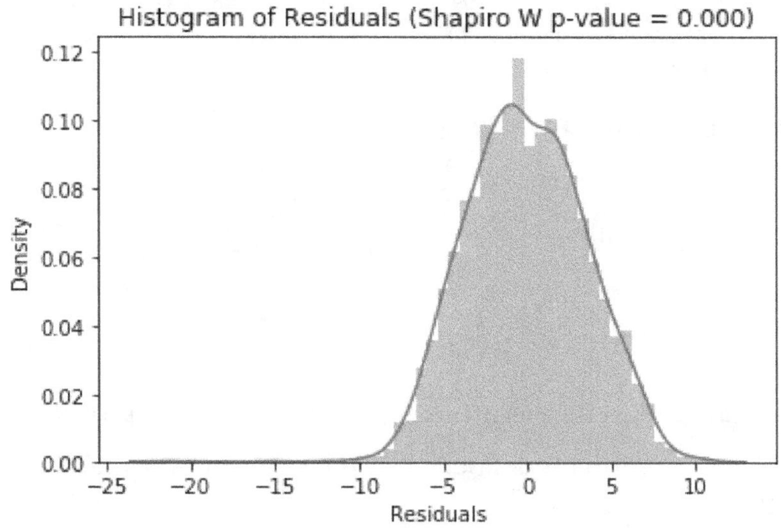

Figure 3.34: The distribution of the residuals from a multiple linear regression model

> **Note**
>
> Our residuals are negatively skewed and non-normal, but this is less skewed than in the simple linear model.

3. Calculate the metrics for mean absolute error, mean squared error, root mean squared error, and R-squared, and put them into a DataFrame as follows:

```
from sklearn import metrics
import numpy as np

metrics_df = pd.DataFrame({'Metric': ['MAE',
                                      'MSE',
                                      'RMSE',
                                      'R-Squared'],
                          'Value': [metrics.mean_absolute_error(y_test,
predictions),
                                    metrics.mean_squared_error(y_test,
predictions),
```

```
                                    np.sqrt(metrics.mean_squared_error(y_
test, predictions)),
                                    metrics.explained_variance_score(y_
test, predictions)]}).round(3)
print(metrics_df)
```

Please refer to the resultant output:

	Metric	Value
0	MAE	2.861
1	MSE	12.317
2	RMSE	3.510
3	R-Squared	0.866

Figure 3.35: Model evaluation metrics from a multiple linear regression model

The multiple linear regression model performed better on every metric relative to the simple linear regression model.

Activity 6: Generating Predictions and Evaluating Performance of a Tuned Logistic Regression Model

Solution:

1. Generate the predicted probabilities of rain using the following code:

```
predicted_prob = model.predict_proba(X_test)[:,1]
```

2. Generate the predicted class of rain using **`predicted_class = model.predict(X_test)`**.

3. Evaluate performance using a confusion matrix and save it as a DataFrame using the following code:

```
from sklearn.metrics import confusion_matrix
import numpy as np

cm = pd.DataFrame(confusion_matrix(y_test, predicted_class))
cm['Total'] = np.sum(cm, axis=1)
cm = cm.append(np.sum(cm, axis=0), ignore_index=True)
cm.columns = ['Predicted No', 'Predicted Yes', 'Total']
cm = cm.set_index([['Actual No', 'Actual Yes', 'Total']])
print(cm)
```

	Predicted No	Predicted Yes	Total
Actual No	381	2	383
Actual Yes	4	2913	2917
Total	385	2915	3300

Figure 3.36: The confusion matrix from our logistic regression grid search model

> **Note**
>
> Nice! We have decreased our number of false positives from 6 to 2. Additionally, our false negatives were lowered from 10 to 4 (see in *Exercise 26*). Be aware that results may vary slightly.

4. For further evaluation, print a classification report as follows:

```
from sklearn.metrics import classification_report

print(classification_report(y_test, predicted_class))
```

	precision	recall	f1-score	support
0	0.99	0.99	0.99	383
1	1.00	1.00	1.00	2917
micro avg	1.00	1.00	1.00	3300
macro avg	0.99	1.00	1.00	3300
weighted avg	1.00	1.00	1.00	3300

Figure 3.37: The classification report from our logistic regression grid search model

By tuning the hyperparameters of the logistic regression model, we were able to improve upon a logistic regression model that was already performing very well.

Activity 7: Generating Predictions and Evaluating the Performance of the SVC Grid Search Model

Solution:

1. Extract predicted classes of rain using the following code:

```
predicted_class = model.predict(X_test)
```

2. Create and print a confusion matrix using the code here:

```
from sklearn.metrics import confusion_matrix
import numpy as np

cm = pd.DataFrame(confusion_matrix(y_test, predicted_class))
cm['Total'] = np.sum(cm, axis=1)
cm = cm.append(np.sum(cm, axis=0), ignore_index=True)
cm.columns = ['Predicted No', 'Predicted Yes', 'Total']
cm = cm.set_index([['Actual No', 'Actual Yes', 'Total']])
print(cm)
```

See the resultant output here:

	Predicted No	Predicted Yes	Total
Actual No	326	57	383
Actual Yes	2	2915	2917
Total	328	2972	3300

Figure 3.38: The confusion matrix from our SVC grid search model

3. Generate and print a classification report as follows:

```
from sklearn.metrics import classification_report

print(classification_report(y_test, predicted_class))
```

See the resultant output here:

	precision	recall	f1-score	support
0	0.99	0.85	0.92	383
1	0.98	1.00	0.99	2917
micro avg	0.98	0.98	0.98	3300
macro avg	0.99	0.93	0.95	3300
weighted avg	0.98	0.98	0.98	3300

Figure 3.39: The classification report from our SVC grid search model

Here, we demonstrated how to tune the hyperparameters of an SVC model using grid search.

Activity 8: Preparing Data for a Decision Tree Classifier

Solution:

1. Import **weather.csv** and store it as a DataFrame using the following:

```
import pandas as pd

df = pd.read_csv('weather.csv')
```

2. Dummy code the **Description** column as follows:

```
import pandas as pd

df_dummies = pd.get_dummies(df, drop_first=True)
```

3. Shuffle **df_dummies** using the following code:

```
from sklearn.utils import shuffle

df_shuffled = shuffle(df_dummies, random_state=42)
```

4. Split **df_shuffled** into X and y as follows:

```
DV = 'Rain'
X = df_shuffled.drop(DV, axis=1)
y = df_shuffled[DV]
```

5. Split **X** and **y** into testing and training data:

```
from sklearn.model_selection import train_test_split

X_train, X_test, y_train, y_test = train_test_split(X, y, test_size=0.33,
random_state=42)
```

6. Scale **X_train** and **X_test** using the following code:

```
from sklearn.preprocessing import StandardScaler

model = StandardScaler()
X_train_scaled = model.fit_transform(X_train)
X_test_scaled = model.transform(X_test)
```

Activity 9: Generating Predictions and Evaluating the Performance of a Decision Tree Classifier Model

Solution:

1. Generate the predicted probabilities of rain using the following:

```
predicted_prob = model.predict_proba(X_test_scaled)[:,1]
```

2. Generate the predicted classes of rain using the following:

```
predicted_class = model.predict(X_test)
```

3. Generate and print a confusion matrix with the code here:

```
from sklearn.metrics import confusion_matrix
import numpy as np

cm = pd.DataFrame(confusion_matrix(y_test, predicted_class))
cm['Total'] = np.sum(cm, axis=1)
cm = cm.append(np.sum(cm, axis=0), ignore_index=True)
cm.columns = ['Predicted No', 'Predicted Yes', 'Total']
cm = cm.set_index([['Actual No', 'Actual Yes', 'Total']])
print(cm)
```

Refer to the resultant output here:

	Predicted No	Predicted Yes	Total
Actual No	327	56	383
Actual Yes	0	2917	2917
Total	327	2973	3300

Figure 3.40: The confusion matrix from our tuned decision tree classifier model

4. Print a classification report as follows:

```
from sklearn.metrics import classification_report

print(classification_report(y_test, predicted_class))
```

Refer to the resultant output here:

	precision	recall	f1-score	support
0	1.00	0.85	0.92	383
1	0.98	1.00	0.99	2917
micro avg	0.98	0.98	0.98	3300
macro avg	0.99	0.93	0.96	3300
weighted avg	0.98	0.98	0.98	3300

Figure 3.41: The classification report from our tuned decision tree classifier model

There was only one misclassified observation. Thus, by tuning a decision tree classifier model on our **weather.csv** dataset, we were able to predict rain (or snow) with great accuracy. We can see that the sole driving feature was temperature in Celsius. This makes sense due to the way in which decision trees use recursive partitioning to make predictions.

Activity 10: Tuning a Random Forest Regressor

Solution:

1. Specify the hyperparameter space as follows:

```
import numpy as np

grid = {'criterion': ['mse','mae'],
        'max_features': ['auto', 'sqrt', 'log2', None],
        'min_impurity_decrease': np.linspace(0.0, 1.0, 10),
        'bootstrap': [True, False],
        'warm_start': [True, False]}
```

2. Instantiate the **GridSearchCV** model, optimizing the explained variance using the following code:

```
from sklearn.model_selection import GridSearchCV
from sklearn.ensemble import RandomForestRegressor

model = GridSearchCV(RandomForestRegressor(), grid, scoring='explained_
variance', cv=5)
```

3. Fit the grid search model to the training set using the following (note that this may take a while):

```
model.fit(X_train_scaled, y_train)
```

See the output here:

```
GridSearchCV(cv=5, error_score='raise-deprecating',
       estimator=RandomForestRegressor(bootstrap=True, criterion='mse', max_depth=None,
           max_features='auto', max_leaf_nodes=None,
           min_impurity_decrease=0.0, min_impurity_split=None,
           min_samples_leaf=1, min_samples_split=2,
           min_weight_fraction_leaf=0.0, n_estimators='warn', n_jobs=None,
           oob_score=False, random_state=None, verbose=0, warm_start=False),
       fit_params=None, iid='warn', n_jobs=None,
       param_grid={'criterion': ['mse', 'mae'], 'max_features': ['auto', 'sqrt', 'log2', None],
'min_impurity_decrease': array([0.     , 0.11111, 0.22222, 0.33333, 0.44444, 0.55556, 0.66667,
       0.77778, 0.88889, 1.     ]), 'bootstrap': [True, False], 'warm_start': [True, False]},
       pre_dispatch='2*n_jobs', refit=True, return_train_score='warn',
       scoring='explained_variance', verbose=0)
```

Figure 3.42: The output from our tuned random forest regressor grid search model

4. Print the tuned parameters as follows:

```
best_parameters = model.best_params_
print(best_parameters)
```

See the resultant output below:

```
{'bootstrap': True, 'criterion': 'mae', 'max_features': None, 'min_impurity_decrease': 0.0, 'warm_start': True}
```

Figure 3.43: The tuned hyperparameters from our random forest regressor grid search model

Activity 11: Generating Predictions and Evaluating the Performance of a Tuned Random Forest Regressor Model

Solution:

1. Generate predictions on the test data using the following:

```
predictions = model.predict(X_test_scaled)
```

2. Plot the correlation of predicted and actual values using the following code:

```
import matplotlib.pyplot as plt
from scipy.stats import pearsonr

plt.scatter(y_test, predictions)
plt.xlabel('Y Test (True Values)')
```

```
plt.ylabel('Predicted Values')
plt.title('Predicted vs. Actual Values (r = {0:0.2f})'.format(pearsonr(y_
test, predictions)[0], 2))
plt.show()
```

Refer to the resultant output here:

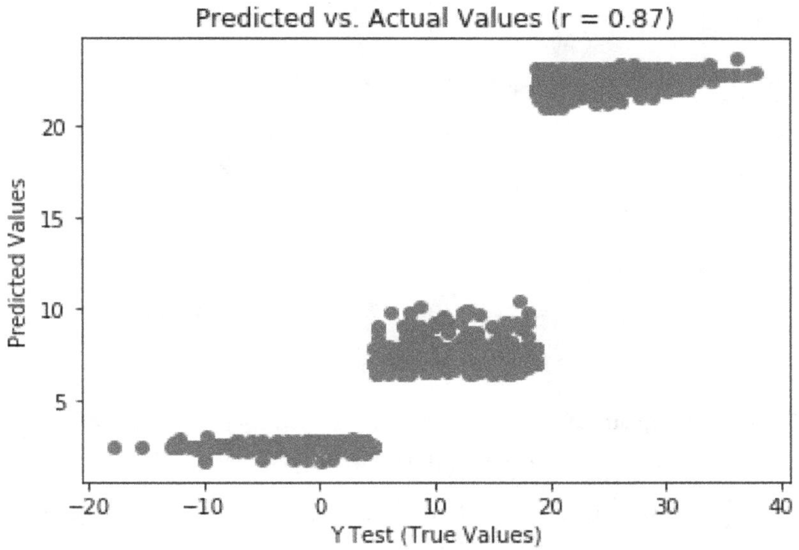

Figure 3.44: A scatterplot of predicted and actual values from our random forest regression model with tuned hyperparameters

3. Plot the distribution of residuals as follows:

```
import seaborn as sns
from scipy.stats import shapiro

sns.distplot((y_test - predictions), bins = 50)
plt.xlabel('Residuals')
plt.ylabel('Density')
plt.title('Histogram of Residuals (Shapiro W p-value = {0:0.3f})'.
format(shapiro(y_test - predictions)[1]))
plt.show()
```

Refer to the resultant output here:

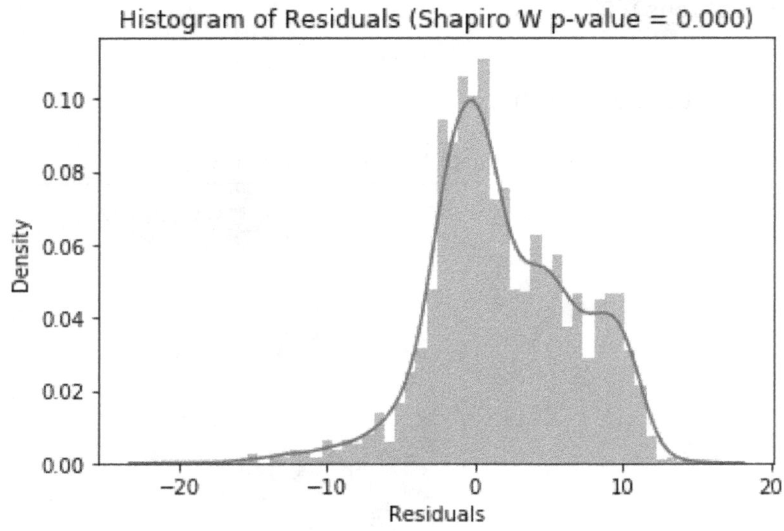

Figure 3.45: A histogram of residuals from a random forest regression model with tuned hyperparameters

4. Compute metrics, place them in a DataFrame, and print it using the code here:

```
from sklearn import metrics
import numpy as np

metrics_df = pd.DataFrame({'Metric': ['MAE',
                                      'MSE',
                                      'RMSE',
                                      'R-Squared'],
                           'Value': [metrics.mean_absolute_error(y_test, 
predictions),
                                     metrics.mean_squared_error(y_test, 
predictions),
                                     np.sqrt(metrics.mean_squared_error(y_
test, predictions)),
                                     metrics.explained_variance_score(y_
test, predictions)]}).round(3)
print(metrics_df)
```

Find the resultant output here:

	Metric	Value
0	MAE	3.974
1	MSE	26.944
2	RMSE	5.191
3	R-Squared	0.745

Figure 3.46: Model evaluation metrics from our random forest regression model with tuned hyperparameters

The random forest regressor model seems to underperform compared to the multiple linear regression, as evidenced by greater MAE, MSE, and RMSE values, as well as less explained variance. Additionally, there was a weaker correlation between the predicted and actual values, and the residuals were further from being normally distributed. Nevertheless, by leveraging ensemble methods using a random forest regressor, we constructed a model that explains 75.8% of the variance in temperature and predicts temperature in Celsius + 3.781 degrees.

Chapter 4: Dimensionality Reduction and Unsupervised Learning

Activity 12: Ensemble k-means Clustering and Calculating Predictions

Solution:

After the glass dataset has been imported, shuffled, and standardized (see Exercise 58):

1. Instantiate an empty data frame to append each model and save it as the new data frame object **labels_df** with the following code:

```
import pandas as pd
labels_df = pd.DataFrame()
```

2. Import the **KMeans** function outside of the loop using the following:

```
from sklearn.cluster import KMeans
```

3. Complete 100 iterations as follows:

```
for i in range(0, 100):
```

4. Save a KMeans model object with two clusters (arbitrarily decided upon, a priori) using:

```
model = KMeans(n_clusters=2)
```

5. Fit the model to **scaled_features** using the following:

```
model.fit(scaled_features)
```

6. Generate the labels array and save it as the labels object, as follows:

```
labels = model.labels_
```

7. Store labels as a column in **labels_df** named after the iteration using the code:

```
labels_df['Model_{}_Labels'.format(i+1)] = labels
```

8. After labels have been generated for each of the 100 models (see Activity 21), calculate the mode for each row using the following code:

```
row_mode = labels_df.mode(axis=1)
```

9. Assign **row_mode** to a new column in **labels_df**, as shown in the following code:

```
labels_df['row_mode'] = row_mode
```

10. View the first five rows of labels_df

```
print(labels_df.head(5))
```

```
   Model_1_Labels  Model_2_Labels    ...     Model_100_Labels  row_mode
0               0               0    ...                    0         0
1               1               1    ...                    1         1
2               0               0    ...                    0         0
3               0               0    ...                    0         0
4               0               0    ...                    0         0

[5 rows x 101 columns]
```

Figure 4.24: First five rows of labels_df

We have drastically increased the confidence in our predictions by iterating through numerous models, saving the predictions at each iteration, and assigning the final predictions as the mode of these predictions. However, these predictions were generated by models using a predetermined number of clusters. Unless we know the number of clusters a priori, we will want to discover the optimal number of clusters to segment our observations.

Activity 13: Evaluating Mean Inertia by Cluster after PCA Transformation

Solution:

1. Instantiate a PCA model with the value for the **n_components** argument equal to **best_n_components** (that is, remember, **best_n_components = 6**) as follows:

```
from sklearn.decomposition import PCA

model = PCA(n_components=best_n_components)
```

2. Fit the model to **scaled_features** and transform them into the six components, as shown here:

```
df_pca = model.fit_transform(scaled_features)
```

3. Import **numpy** and the **KMeans** function outside the loop using the following code:

```
from sklearn.cluster import KMeans
import numpy as np
```

4. Instantiate an empty list, **inertia_list**, for which we will append inertia values after each iteration using the following code:

```
inertia_list = []
```

5. In the inside for loop, we will iterate through 100 models as follows:

```
for i in range(100):
```

6. Build our **KMeans** model with **n_clusters=x** using:

```
model = KMeans(n_clusters=x)
```

> **Note**
>
> The value for x will be dictated by the outer loop which is covered in detail here.

7. Fit the model to **df_pca** as follows:

```
model.fit(df_pca)
```

8. Get the inertia value and save it to the object inertia using the following code:

```
inertia = model.inertia_
```

9. Append inertia to **inertia_list** using the following code:

```
inertia_list.append(inertia)
```

10. Moving to the outside loop, instantiate another empty list to store the average inertia values using the following code:

```
mean_inertia_list_PCA = []
```

11. Since we want to check the average inertia over 100 models for **n_clusters** 1 through 10, we will instantiate the outer loop as follows:

```
for x in range(1, 11):
```

12. After the inside loop has run through its 100 iterations, and the inertia value for each of the 100 models have been appended to **inertia_list**, compute the mean of this list, and save the object as **mean_inertia** using the following code:

```
mean_inertia = np.mean(inertia_list)
```

13. Append **mean_inertia** to **mean_inertia_list_PCA** using the following code:

```
mean_inertia_list_PCA.append(mean_inertia)
```

14. Print **`mean_inertia_list_PCA`** to the console using the following code:

```
print(mean_inertia_list_PCA)
```

15. Notice the output in the following screenshot:

```
[1892.8745743658694, 1272.0635708451114, 945.9585011131066, 792.9280542109909, 660.6137294703674, 542.2679610880247,
448.0582942646142, 402.0775746619672, 363.76887622845425, 330.43291214440774]
```

Figure 4.25: mean_inertia_list_PCA

Chapter 5: Mastering Structured Data

Activity 14: Training and Predicting the Income of a Person

Solution:

1. Import the libraries and load the income dataset using pandas. First, import pandas and then read the data using **read_csv**.

```
import pandas as pd
import xgboost as xgb
import numpy as np
from sklearn.metrics import accuracy_score
data = pd.read_csv("../data/adult-data.csv", names=['age', 'workclass',
'education-num', 'occupation', 'capital-gain', 'capital-loss', 'hours-per-
week', 'income'])
```

The reason we are passing the names of the columns is because the data doesn't contain them. We do this to make our lives easy.

2. Use Label Encoder from sklearn to encode strings. First, import **Label Encoder**. Then, encode all string categorical columns one by one.

```
from sklearn.preprocessing import LabelEncoder
data['workclass'] = LabelEncoder().fit_transform(data['workclass'])
data['occupation'] = LabelEncoder().fit_transform(data['occupation'])
data['income'] = LabelEncoder().fit_transform(data['income'])
```

Here, we encode all the categorical string data that we have. There is another method we can use to prevent writing the same piece of code again and again. See if you can find it.

3. We first separate the dependent and independent variables.

```
X = data.copy()
X.drop("income", inplace = True, axis = 1)
Y = data.income
```

4. Then, we divide them into training and testing sets with an 80:20 split.

```
X_train, X_test = X[:int(X.shape[0]*0.8)].values, X[int(X.shape[0]*0.8):].
values
Y_train, Y_test = Y[:int(Y.shape[0]*0.8)].values, Y[int(Y.shape[0]*0.8):].
values
```

5. Next, we convert them into DMatrix, a data structure that the library supports.

```
train = xgb.DMatrix(X_train, label=Y_train)
test = xgb.DMatrix(X_test, label=Y_test)
```

6. Then, we use the following parameters to train the model using XGBoost.

```
param = {'max_depth':7, 'eta':0.1, 'silent':1, 'objective':'binary:hinge'}
 num_round = 50
model = xgb.train(param, train, num_round)
```

7. Check the accuracy of the model.

```
preds = model.predict(test)
accuracy = accuracy_score(Y[int(Y.shape[0]*0.8):].values, preds)
print("Accuracy: %.2f%%" % (accuracy * 100.0))
```

The output is as follows:

```
Accuracy: 83.66%
```

Figure 5.36: Final model accuracy

Activity 15: Predicting the Loss of Customers

Solution:

1. Load the income dataset using pandas. First, import pandas, and then read the data using **read_csv**.

```
import pandas as pd
import numpy as np
data = data = pd.read_csv("data/telco-churn.csv")
```

2. The **customerID** variable is not required because any future prediction will have a unique **customerID**, making this variable useless for prediction.

```
data.drop('customerID', axis = 1, inplace = True)
```

3. Convert all categorical variables to integers using scikit. One example is given below.

```
from sklearn.preprocessing import LabelEncoder
data['gender'] = LabelEncoder().fit_transform(data['gender'])
```

4. Check the data types of the variables in the dataset.

```
data.dtypes
```

The data types of the variables will be shown as follows:

```
gender              int32
SeniorCitizen       int64
Partner             int32
Dependents          int32
tenure              int64
PhoneService        int32
MultipleLines       int32
InternetService     int32
OnlineSecurity      int32
OnlineBackup        int32
DeviceProtection    int32
TechSupport         int32
StreamingTV         int32
StreamingMovies     int32
Contract            int32
PaperlessBilling    int32
PaymentMethod       int32
MonthlyCharges    float64
TotalCharges       object
Churn               int32
dtype: object
```

Figure 5.37: Data types of variables

5. As you can see, **TotalCharges** is an object. So, convert the data type of **TotalCharges** from object to numeric. coerce will make the missing values null.

```
data.TotalCharges = pd.to_numeric(data.TotalCharges, errors='coerce')
```

6. Convert the data frame to an XGBoost variable and find the best parameters for the dataset using the previous exercises as reference.

```
import xgboost as xgb
import matplotlib.pyplot as plt
X = data.copy()
X.drop("Churn", inplace = True, axis = 1)
Y = data.Churn
X_train, X_test = X[:int(X.shape[0]*0.8)].values, X[int(X.shape[0]*0.8):].
values
Y_train, Y_test = Y[:int(Y.shape[0]*0.8)].values, Y[int(Y.shape[0]*0.8):].
values
train = xgb.DMatrix(X_train, label=Y_train)
test = xgb.DMatrix(X_test, label=Y_test)
test_error = {}
for i in range(20):
```

```
    param = {'max_depth':i, 'eta':0.1, 'silent':1,
'objective':'binary:hinge'}
    num_round = 50
    model_metrics = xgb.cv(param, train, num_round, nfold = 10)
    test_error[i] = model_metrics.iloc[-1]['test-error-mean']

plt.scatter(test_error.keys(),test_error.values())
plt.xlabel('Max Depth')
plt.ylabel('Test Error')
plt.show()
```

Check out the output in the following screenshot:

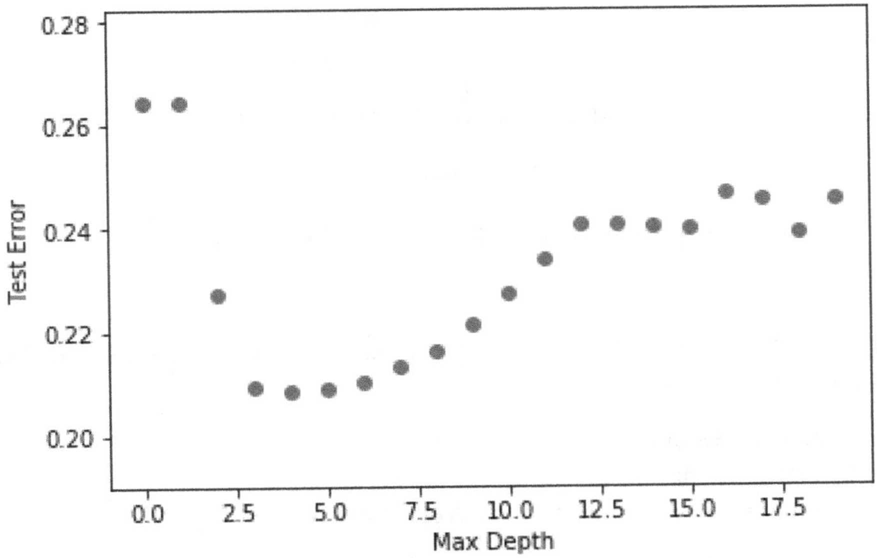

Figure 5.38: Graph of max depth to test error for telecom churn dataset

From the graph, it is clear that a max depth of 4 gives the least error. So, we will be using that to train our model.

7. Create the model using the **max_depth** parameter that we chose from the previous steps.

```
param = {'max_depth':4, 'eta':0.1, 'silent':1, 'objective':'binary:hinge'}
num_round = 100
model = xgb.train(param, train, num_round)
preds = model.predict(test)
from sklearn.metrics import accuracy_score
accuracy = accuracy_score(Y[int(Y.shape[0]*0.8):].values, preds)
print("Accuracy: %.2f%%" % (accuracy * 100.0))
```

The output is as follows:

```
Accuracy: 79.77%
```

Figure 5.39: Final accuracy

8. Save the model for future use using the following code:

```
model.save_model('churn-model.model')
```

Activity 16: Predicting a Customer's Purchase Amount

Solution:

1. Load the **Black Friday** dataset using pandas. First, import **pandas**, and then, read the data using **read_csv**.

```
import pandas as pd
import numpy as np
data = data = pd.read_csv("data/BlackFriday.csv")
```

2. The **User_ID** variable is not required to allow predictions on new user Ids, so we drop it.

```
data.isnull().sum()
data.drop(['User_ID', 'Product_Category_2', 'Product_Category_3'], axis =
1, inplace = True)
```

The product category variables have high null values, so we drop them as well.

3. Convert all categorical variables to integers using scikit-learn.

```
from collections import defaultdict
from sklearn.preprocessing import LabelEncoder, MinMaxScaler
label_dict = defaultdict(LabelEncoder)
data[['Product_ID', 'Gender', 'Age', 'Occupation', 'City_Category',
'Stay_In_Current_City_Years', 'Marital_Status', 'Product_Category_1']]
= data[['Product_ID', 'Gender', 'Age', 'Occupation', 'City_Category',
'Stay_In_Current_City_Years', 'Marital_Status', 'Product_Category_1']].
apply(lambda x: label_dict[x.name].fit_transform(x))
```

4. Split the data into training and testing sets and convert it into the form required by the embedding layers.

```
from sklearn.model_selection import train_test_split
X = data
y = X.pop('Purchase')
X_train, X_test, y_train, y_test = train_test_split(X, y, test_size=0.3,
random_state=9)

cat_cols_dict = {col: list(data[col].unique()) for col in ['Product_ID',
'Gender', 'Age', 'Occupation', 'City_Category', 'Stay_In_Current_City_
Years', 'Marital_Status', 'Product_Category_1']}
train_input_list = []
test_input_list = []

for col in cat_cols_dict.keys():
    raw_values = np.unique(data[col])
    value_map = {}
    for i in range(len(raw_values)):
        value_map[raw_values[i]] = i
    train_input_list.append(X_train[col].map(value_map).values)
    test_input_list.append(X_test[col].map(value_map).fillna(0).values)
```

5. Create the network using the embedding and dense layers in Keras and perform hyperparameter tuning to get the best accuracy.

```
from keras.models import Model
from keras.layers import Input, Dense, Concatenate, Reshape, Dropout
from keras.layers.embeddings import Embedding
cols_out_dict = {
    'Product_ID': 20,
    'Gender': 1,
    'Age': 2,
    'Occupation': 6,
    'City_Category': 1,
    'Stay_In_Current_City_Years': 2,
    'Marital_Status': 1,
    'Product_Category_1': 9
}

inputs = []
embeddings = []

for col in cat_cols_dict.keys():

    inp = Input(shape=(1,), name = 'input_' + col)
    embedding = Embedding(len(cat_cols_dict[col]), cols_out_dict[col],
input_length=1, name = 'embedding_' + col)(inp)
    embedding = Reshape(target_shape=(cols_out_dict[col],))(embedding)
    inputs.append(inp)
    embeddings.append(embedding)
```

6. Now, we create a three-layer network after the embedding layers.

```
x = Concatenate()(embeddings)
x = Dense(4, activation='relu')(x)
x = Dense(2, activation='relu')(x)
output = Dense(1, activation='relu')(x)

model = Model(inputs, output)

model.compile(loss='mae', optimizer='adam')

model.fit(train_input_list, y_train, validation_data = (test_input_list,
y_test), epochs=20, batch_size=128)
```

7. Check the RMSE of the model on the test set.

```
from sklearn.metrics import mean_squared_error
y_pred = model.predict(test_input_list)
np.sqrt(mean_squared_error(y_test, y_pred))
```

The RMSE is:

```
2769.353
```

Figure 5.40: RMSE model

8. Visualize the product ID embedding.

```
import matplotlib.pyplot as plt
from sklearn.decomposition import PCA
embedding_Product_ID = model.get_layer('embedding_Product_ID').get_
weights()[0]
pca = PCA(n_components=2)
Y = pca.fit_transform(embedding_Product_ID[:40])
plt.figure(figsize=(8,8))
plt.scatter(-Y[:, 0], -Y[:, 1])
for i, txt in enumerate(label_dict['Product_ID'].inverse_transform(cat_
cols_dict['Product_ID'])[:40]):
    plt.annotate(txt, (-Y[i, 0],-Y[i, 1]), xytext = (-20, 8), textcoords =
'offset points')
plt.show()
```

The plot is as follows:

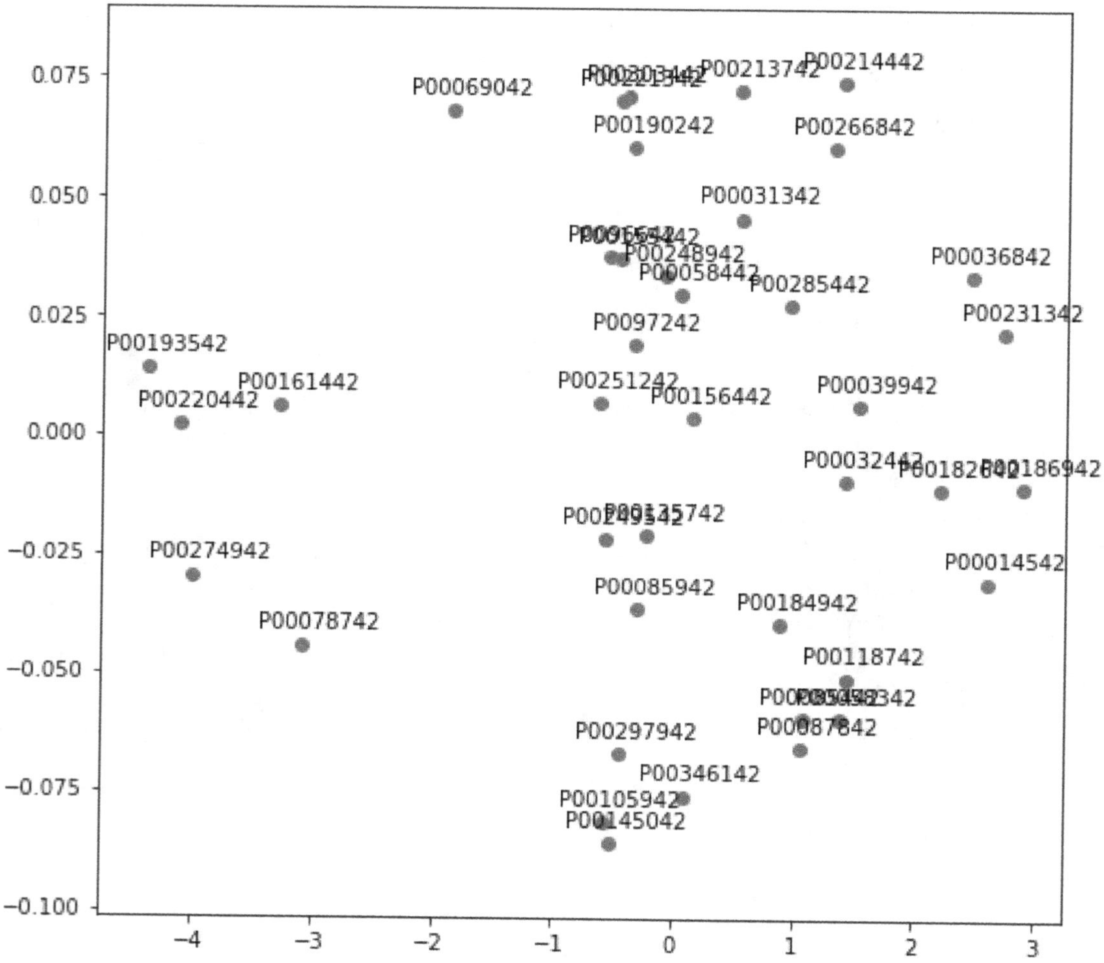

Figure 5.41: Plot of clustered model

From the plot, you can see that similar products have been clustered together by the model.

9. Save the model for future use.

```
model.save ('black-friday.model')
```

Chapter 6: Decoding Images

Activity 17: Predict if an Image Is of a Cat or a Dog

Solution:

1. If you look at the name of the images in the dataset, you will find that the images of dogs start with dog followed by '.' and then a number, for example – "dog.123.jpg". Similarly, the images of cats start with cat. So, let's create a function to get the label from the name of the file:

```
def get_label(file):
    class_label = file.split('.')[0]
    if class_label == 'dog': label_vector = [1,0]
    elif class_label == 'cat': label_vector = [0,1]
    return label_vector
```

Then, create a function to read, resize, and preprocess the images:

```
import os
import numpy as np
from PIL import Image
from tqdm import tqdm
from random import shuffle

SIZE = 50

def get_data():
    data = []
    files = os.listdir(PATH)

    for image in tqdm(files):
        label_vector = get_label(image)
        img = Image.open(PATH + image).convert('L')
        img = img.resize((SIZE,SIZE))
        data.append([np.asarray(img),np.array(label_vector)])

    shuffle(data)
    return data
```

SIZE here refers to the dimension of the final square image we will input to the model. We resize the image to have the length and breadth equal to **SIZE**.

> **Note**
>
> When running **os.listdir(PATH)**, you will find that all the images of cats come first, followed by images of dogs.

2. To have the same distribution of both the classes in the training and testing sets, we will shuffle the data.
3. Define the size of the image and read the data. Split the loaded data into training and testing sets:

```
data = get_data()
train = data[:7000]
test = data[7000:]
x_train = [data[0] for data in train]
y_train = [data[1] for data in train]
x_test = [data[0] for data in test]
y_test = [data[1] for data in test]
```

4. Transform the lists to numpy arrays and reshape the images to a format that Keras will accept:

```
y_train = np.array(y_train)
y_test = np.array(y_test)
x_train = np.array(x_train).reshape(-1, SIZE, SIZE, 1)
x_test = np.array(x_test).reshape(-1, SIZE, SIZE, 1)
```

5. Create a CNN model that makes use of regularization to perform training:

```
from keras.models import Sequential
from keras.layers import Dense, Dropout, Conv2D, MaxPool2D, Flatten, 
BatchNormalization
model = Sequential()
```

Add the convolutional layers:

```
model.add(Conv2D(48, (3, 3), activation='relu', padding='same', input_
shape=(50,50,1)))
model.add(Conv2D(48, (3, 3), activation='relu'))
```

Add the pooling layer:

```
model.add(MaxPool2D(pool_size=(2, 2)))
```

6. Add the batch normalization layer along with a dropout layer using the following code:

```
model.add(BatchNormalization())
model.add(Dropout(0.10))
```

7. Flatten the 2D matrices into 1D vectors:

```
model.add(Flatten())
```

8. Use dense layers as the final layers for the model:

```
model.add(Dense(512, activation='relu'))
model.add(Dropout(0.5))
model.add(Dense(2, activation='softmax'))
```

9. Compile the model and then train it using the training data:

```
model.compile(loss='categorical_crossentropy',
              optimizer='adam',
              metrics = ['accuracy'])
Define the number of epochs you want to train the model for:
EPOCHS = 10
model_details = model.fit(x_train, y_train,
                    batch_size = 128,
                    epochs = EPOCHS,
                    validation_data= (x_test, y_test),
                    verbose=1)
```

10. Print the model's accuracy on the test set:

```
score = model.evaluate(x_test, y_test)
print("Accuracy: {0:.2f}%".format(score[1]*100))
```

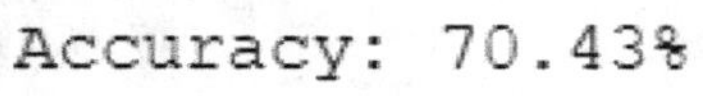

Figure 6.39: Model accuracy on the test set

11. Print the model's accuracy on the training set:

```
score = model.evaluate(x_train, y_train)
print("Accuracy: {0:.2f}%".format(score[1]*100))
```

```
Accuracy: 96.10%
```

Figure 6.40: Model accuracy on the train set

The test set accuracy for this model is 70.4%. The training set accuracy is really high, at 96%. This means that the model has started to overfit. Improving the model to get the best possible accuracy is left for you as an exercise. You can plot the incorrectly predicted images using the code from previous exercises to get a sense of how well the model performs:

```
import matplotlib.pyplot as plt
y_pred = model.predict(x_test)
incorrect_indices = np.nonzero(np.argmax(y_pred,axis=1) != np.argmax(y_test,axis=1))[0]
labels = ['dog', 'cat']
image = 5
plt.imshow(x_test[incorrect_indices[image]].reshape(50,50),  cmap=plt.get_cmap('gray'))
plt.show()
print("Prediction: {0}".format(labels[np.argmax(y_pred[incorrect_indices[image]])]))
```

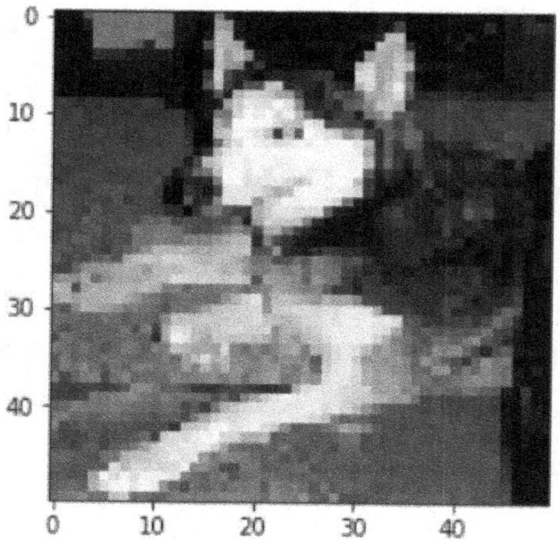


```
Prediction: cat
```

Figure 6.41: Incorrect prediction of a dog by the regularized CNN model

Activity 18: Identifying and Augmenting an Image

Solution:

1. Create functions to get the images and the labels of the dataset:

```
from PIL import Image
def get_input(file):
    return Image.open(PATH+file)

def get_output(file):
    class_label = file.split('.')[0]
    if class_label == 'dog': label_vector = [1,0]
    elif class_label == 'cat': label_vector = [0,1]
    return label_vector
```

2. Create functions to preprocess and augment images:

```
SIZE = 50
def preprocess_input(image):
    # Data preprocessing
    image = image.convert('L')
    image = image.resize((SIZE,SIZE))


    # Data augmentation
    random_vertical_shift(image, shift=0.2)
    random_horizontal_shift(image, shift=0.2)
    random_rotate(image, rot_range=45)
    random_horizontal_flip(image)

    return np.array(image).reshape(SIZE,SIZE,1)
```

3. Implement the augmentation functions to randomly execute the augmentation when passed an image and return the image with the result.

   This is for horizontal flip:

```
import random
def random_horizontal_flip(image):
    toss = random.randint(1, 2)
    if toss == 1:
        return image.transpose(Image.FLIP_LEFT_RIGHT)
    else:
        return image
```

This is for rotation:

```
def random_rotate(image, rot_range):
    value = random.randint(-rot_range,rot_range)
    return image.rotate(value)
```

This is for image shift:

```
import PIL
def random_horizontal_shift(image, shift):
    width, height = image.size
    rand_shift = random.randint(0,shift*width)
    image = PIL.ImageChops.offset(image, rand_shift, 0)
    image.paste((0), (0, 0, rand_shift, height))
    return image
def random_vertical_shift(image, shift):
    width, height = image.size
    rand_shift = random.randint(0,shift*height)
    image = PIL.ImageChops.offset(image, 0, rand_shift)
    image.paste((0), (0, 0, width, rand_shift))
    return image
```

4. Finally, create the generator that will generate images batches to be used to train the model:

```
import numpy as np
def custom_image_generator(images, batch_size = 128):
    while True:
        # Randomly select images for the batch
        batch_images = np.random.choice(images, size = batch_size)
        batch_input = []
        batch_output = []

        # Read image, perform preprocessing and get labels
        for file in batch_images:
            # Function that reads and returns the image
            input_image = get_input(file)
            # Function that gets the label of the image
            label = get_output(file)
            # Function that pre-processes and augments the image
            image = preprocess_input(input_image)

            batch_input.append(image)
            batch_output.append(label)
```

```
        batch_x = np.array(batch_input)
        batch_y = np.array(batch_output)

        # Return a tuple of (images,labels) to feed the network
        yield(batch_x, batch_y)
```

5. Create functions to load the test dataset's images and labels:

```
def get_label(file):
    class_label = file.split('.')[0]
    if class_label == 'dog': label_vector = [1,0]
    elif class_label == 'cat': label_vector = [0,1]
    return label_vector
```

This **get_data** function is similar to the one we used in *Activity* 1. The modification here is that we get the list of images to be read as an input parameter, and we return a tuple of images and their labels:

```
def get_data(files):
    data_image = []
    labels = []
    for image in tqdm(files):

        label_vector = get_label(image)


        img = Image.open(PATH + image).convert('L')
        img = img.resize((SIZE,SIZE))


        labels.append(label_vector)
        data_image.append(np.asarray(img).reshape(SIZE,SIZE,1))

    data_x = np.array(data_image)
    data_y = np.array(labels)

    return (data_x, data_y)
```

6. Now, create the test train split and load the test dataset:

```
import os
files = os.listdir(PATH)
random.shuffle(files)
train = files[:7000]
test = files[7000:]
validation_data = get_data(test)
```

7. Create the model and perform training:

```
from keras.models import Sequential
model = Sequential()
```

Add the convolutional layers

```
from keras.layers import Input, Dense, Dropout, Conv2D, MaxPool2D,
Flatten, BatchNormalization
model.add(Conv2D(32, (3, 3), activation='relu', padding='same', input_
shape=(50,50,1)))
model.add(Conv2D(32, (3, 3), activation='relu'))
```

Add the pooling layer:

```
model.add(MaxPool2D(pool_size=(2, 2)))
```

8. Add the batch normalization layer along with a dropout layer:

```
model.add(BatchNormalization())
model.add(Dropout(0.10))
```

9. Flatten the 2D matrices into 1D vectors:

```
model.add(Flatten())
```

10. Use dense layers as the final layers for the model:

```
model.add(Dense(512, activation='relu'))
model.add(Dropout(0.5))

model.add(Dense(2, activation='softmax'))
```

11. Compile the model and train it using the generator that you created:

```
EPOCHS = 10
BATCH_SIZE = 128
model.compile(loss='categorical_crossentropy',
              optimizer='adam',
              metrics = ['accuracy'])
```

```
model_details = model.fit_generator(custom_image_generator(train, batch_
size = BATCH_SIZE),
                        steps_per_epoch = len(train) // BATCH_SIZE,
                        epochs = EPOCHS,
                        validation_data= validation_data,
                        verbose=1)
```

The test set accuracy for this model is 72.6%, which is an improvement on the model in *Activity 21*. You will observe that the training accuracy is really high, at 98%. This means that this model has started to overfit, much like the one in *Activity 21*. This could be due to a lack of data augmentation. Try changing the data augmentation parameters to see if there is any change in accuracy. Alternatively, you can modify the architecture of the neural network to get better results. You can plot the incorrectly predicted images to get a sense of how well the model performs.

```
import matplotlib.pyplot as plt

y_pred = model.predict(validation_data[0])

incorrect_indices = np.nonzero(np.argmax(y_pred,axis=1) !=
np.argmax(validation_data[1],axis=1))[0]

labels = ['dog', 'cat']


image = 7

plt.imshow(validation_data[0][incorrect_indices[image]].reshape(50,50),
cmap=plt.get_cmap('gray'))

plt.show()

print("Prediction: {0}".format(labels[np.argmax(y_pred[incorrect_
indices[image]])]))
```

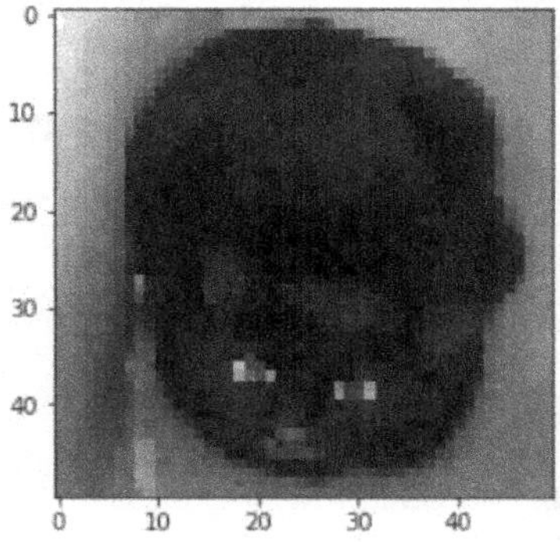

Prediction: dog

Figure 6.42: Incorrect prediction of a cat by the data augmentation CNN model

Chapter 7: Processing Human Language

Activity 19: Predicting Sentiments of Movie Reviews

Solution:

1. Read the IMDB movie review dataset using pandas in Python:

```
import pandas as pd
data = pd.read_csv('../../chapter 7/data/movie_reviews.csv',
encoding='latin-1')
```

2. Convert the tweets to lowercase to reduce the number of unique words:

```
data.text = data.text.str.lower()
```

> **Note**
>
> Keep in mind that "**Hello**" and "**hellow**" are not the same to a computer.

3. Clean the reviews using RegEx with the **clean_str** function:

```
import re
def clean_str(string):

    string = re.sub(r"https?\://\S+", '', string)
    string = re.sub(r'\<a href', ' ', string)
    string = re.sub(r'&amp;', '', string)
    string = re.sub(r'<br />', ' ', string)
    string = re.sub(r'[_"\-;%()|+&=*%.,!?:#$@\[\]/]', ' ', string)
    string = re.sub('\d','', string)
    string = re.sub(r"can\'t", "cannot", string)
    string = re.sub(r"it\'s", "it is", string)
    return string
data.SentimentText = data.SentimentText.apply(lambda x: clean_str(str(x)))
```

4. Next, remove stop words and other frequently occurring unnecessary words from the reviews:

> **Note**
>
> To see how we found these, words refer to *Exercise 51*.

5. This step converts strings into tokens (which will be helpful in the next step):

```
from nltk.corpus import stopwords
from nltk.tokenize import word_tokenize,sent_tokenize
stop_words = stopwords.words('english') + ['movie', 'film', 'time']
stop_words = set(stop_words)
remove_stop_words = lambda r: [[word for word in word_tokenize(sente) if
word not in stop_words] for sente in sent_tokenize(r)]
data['SentimentText'] = data['SentimentText'].apply(remove_stop_words)
```

6. Create the word embedding of the reviews with the tokens created in the previous step. Here, we will use genism Word2Vec to create these embedding vectors:

```
from gensim.models import Word2Vec
model = Word2Vec(
        data['SentimentText'].apply(lambda x: x[0]),
        iter=10,
        size=16,
        window=5,
        min_count=5,
        workers=10)
model.wv.save_word2vec_format('movie_embedding.txt', binary=False)
```

7. Combine the tokens to get a string and then drop any review that does not have anything in it after stop word removal:

```
def combine_text(text):
    try:
        return ' '.join(text[0])
    except:
        return np.nan

data.SentimentText = data.SentimentText.apply(lambda x: combine_text(x))
data = data.dropna(how='any')
```

8. Tokenize the reviews using the Keras Tokenizer and convert them into numbers:

```
from keras.preprocessing.text import Tokenizer
tokenizer = Tokenizer(num_words=5000)
tokenizer.fit_on_texts(list(data['SentimentText']))
sequences = tokenizer.texts_to_sequences(data['SentimentText'])
word_index = tokenizer.word_index
```

9. Finally, pad the tweets to have a maximum of 100 words. This will remove any words after the 100-word limit and add 0s if the number of words is less than 100:

```
from keras.preprocessing.sequence import pad_sequences
reviews = pad_sequences(sequences, maxlen=100)
```

10. Load the created embedding to get the embedding matrix using the **load_embedding** function discussed in the *Text Processing* section:

```
import numpy as np

def load_embedding(filename, word_index , num_words, embedding_dim):
    embeddings_index = {}
    file = open(filename, encoding="utf-8")
    for line in file:
        values = line.split()
        word = values[0]
        coef = np.asarray(values[1:])
        embeddings_index[word] = coef
    file.close()

    embedding_matrix = np.zeros((num_words, embedding_dim))
    for word, pos in word_index.items():
        if pos >= num_words:
            continue
        embedding_vector = embeddings_index.get(word)
        if embedding_vector is not None:
            embedding_matrix[pos] = embedding_vector
    return embedding_matrix

embedding_matrix = load_embedding('movie_embedding.txt', word_index,
len(word_index), 16)
```

11. Convert the label into one-hot vector using pandas' **get_dummies** function and split the dataset into testing and training sets with an 80:20 split:

```
from sklearn.model_selection import train_test_split
labels = pd.get_dummies(data.Sentiment)
X_train, X_test, y_train, y_test = train_test_split(reviews,labels, test_
size=0.2, random_state=9)
```

12. Create the neural network model starting with the input and embedding layers. This layer converts the input words into their embedding vectors:

```
from keras.layers import Input, Dense, Dropout, BatchNormalization,
Embedding, Flatten
from keras.models import Model
inp = Input((100,))
embedding_layer = Embedding(len(word_index),
                    16,
                    weights=[embedding_matrix],
                    input_length=100,
                    trainable=False)(inp)
```

13. Create the rest of the fully connected neural network using Keras:

```
model = Flatten()(embedding_layer)
model = BatchNormalization()(model)
model = Dropout(0.10)(model)
model = Dense(units=1024, activation='relu')(model)
model = Dense(units=256, activation='relu')(model)
model = Dropout(0.5)(model)
predictions = Dense(units=2, activation='softmax')(model)
model = Model(inputs = inp, outputs = predictions)
```

14. Compile and train the model for 10 epochs. You can modify the model and the hyperparameters to try and get a better accuracy:

```
model.compile(loss='binary_crossentropy', optimizer='sgd', metrics =
['acc'])
model.fit(X_train, y_train, validation_data = (X_test, y_test), epochs=10,
batch_size=256)
```

15. Calculate the accuracy of the model on the test set to see how well our model performs on previously unseen data by using the following:

```
from sklearn.metrics import accuracy_score
preds = model.predict(X_test)
accuracy_score(np.argmax(preds, 1), np.argmax(y_test.values, 1))
```

The accuracy of the model is:

```
0.7634
```

Figure 7.39: Model accuracy

16. Plot the confusion matrix of the model to get a proper sense of the model's prediction:

```
y_actual = pd.Series(np.argmax(y_test.values, axis=1), name='Actual')
y_pred = pd.Series(np.argmax(preds, axis=1), name='Predicted')
pd.crosstab(y_actual, y_pred, margins=True)
```

Check the following

Predicted	0	1	All
Actual			
0	1774	679	2453
1	504	2043	2547
All	2278	2722	5000

Figure 7.40: Confusion matrix of the model (0 = negative sentiment, 1 = positive sentiment)

17. Check the performance of the model by seeing the sentiment predictions on random reviews using the following code:

```
review_num = 111
print("Review: \n"+tokenizer.sequences_to_texts([X_test[review_num]])[0])
sentiment = "Positive" if np.argmax(preds[review_num]) else "Negative"
print("\nPredicted sentiment = "+ sentiment)
sentiment = "Positive" if np.argmax(y_test.values[review_num]) else
"Negative"
print("\nActual sentiment = "+ sentiment)
```

Check that you receive the following output:

```
Review:
love love love another absolutely superb performance miss beginning end o
ne big treat n't rent buy

Predicted sentiment = Positive

Actual sentiment = Positive
```

Figure 7.41: A review from the IMDB dataset

Activity 20: Predicting Sentiments from Tweets

Solution:

1. Read the tweet dataset using pandas and rename the columns with those given in the following code:

```
import pandas as pd
data = pd.read_csv('tweet-data.csv', encoding='latin-1', header=None)
data.columns = ['sentiment', 'id', 'date', 'q', 'user', 'text']
```

2. Drop the following columns as we won't be using them. You can analyze and use them if you want when trying to improve the accuracy:

```
data = data.drop(['id', 'date', 'q', 'user'], axis=1)
```

3. We perform this activity only on a subset (400,000 tweets) of the data to save time. If you want, you can work on the whole dataset:

```
data = data.sample(400000).reset_index(drop=True)
```

4. Convert the tweets to lowercase to reduce the number of unique words. Keep in mind that "`Hello`" and "`hellow`" are not the same to a computer:

```
data.text = data.text.str.lower()
```

5. Clean the tweets using the `clean_str` function:

```
import re
def clean_str(string):
    string = re.sub(r"https?\://\S+", '', string)
    string = re.sub(r"@\w*\s", '', string)
    string = re.sub(r'\<a href', ' ', string)
    string = re.sub(r'&amp;', '', string)
    string = re.sub(r'<br />', ' ', string)
    string = re.sub(r'[_"\-;%()|+&=*%.,!?:#$@\[\]/]', ' ', string)
    string = re.sub('\d','', string)
    return string

data.text = data.text.apply(lambda x: clean_str(str(x)))
```

6. Remove all the stop words from the tweets, as was done in the **Text Preprocessing** section:

```
from nltk.corpus import stopwords
from nltk.tokenize import word_tokenize,sent_tokenize
stop_words = stopwords.words('english')
stop_words = set(stop_words)
remove_stop_words = lambda r: [[word for word in word_tokenize(sente) if
word not in stop_words] for sente in sent_tokenize(r)]
data['text'] = data['text'].apply(remove_stop_words)

def combine_text(text):
    try:
        return ' '.join(text[0])
    except:
        return np.nan

data.text = data.text.apply(lambda x: combine_text(x))

data = data.dropna(how='any')
```

7. Tokenize the tweets and convert them to numbers using the Keras Tokenizer:

```
from keras.preprocessing.text import Tokenizer
tokenizer = Tokenizer(num_words=5000)
tokenizer.fit_on_texts(list(data['text']))
sequences = tokenizer.texts_to_sequences(data['text'])
word_index = tokenizer.word_index
```

8. Finally, pad the tweets to have a maximum of 50 words. This will remove any words after the 50-word limit and add 0s if the number of words is less than 50:

```
from keras.preprocessing.sequence import pad_sequences
tweets = pad_sequences(sequences, maxlen=50)
```

9. Create the embedding matrix from the GloVe embedding file that we downloaded using the **load_embedding** function:

```
import numpy as np
def load_embedding(filename, word_index , num_words, embedding_dim):
    embeddings_index = {}
    file = open(filename, encoding="utf-8")
    for line in file:
        values = line.split()
        word = values[0]
```

```
            coef = np.asarray(values[1:])
            embeddings_index[word] = coef
        file.close()

        embedding_matrix = np.zeros((num_words, embedding_dim))
        for word, pos in word_index.items():
            if pos >= num_words:
                continue
            embedding_vector = embeddings_index.get(word)
            if embedding_vector is not None:
                embedding_matrix[pos] = embedding_vector
        return embedding_matrix

    embedding_matrix = load_embedding('../../embedding/glove.twitter.27B.50d.
    txt', word_index, len(word_index), 50)
```

10. Split the dataset into training and testing sets with an 80:20 spilt. You can experiment with different splits:

```
from sklearn.model_selection import train_test_split
X_train, X_test, y_train, y_test = train_test_split(tweets, pd.get_
dummies(data.sentiment), test_size=0.2, random_state=9)
```

11. Create the LSTM model that will predict the sentiment. You can modify this to create your own neural network:

```
from keras.models import Sequential
from keras.layers import Dense, Dropout, BatchNormalization, Embedding,
Flatten, LSTM
embedding_layer = Embedding(len(word_index),
                            50,
                            weights=[embedding_matrix],
                             input_length=50,
                             trainable=False)
model = Sequential()
model.add(embedding_layer)
model.add(Dropout(0.5))
model.add(LSTM(100, dropout=0.2))
model.add(Dense(2, activation='softmax'))


model.compile(loss='binary_crossentropy', optimizer='sgd', metrics =
['acc'])
```

12. Train the model. Here, we train it only for 10 epochs. You can increase the number of epochs to try and get a better accuracy:

```
model.fit(X_train, y_train, validation_data = (X_test, y_test), epochs=10,
batch_size=256)
```

13. Check how well the model is performing by predicting the sentiment of a few tweets in the test set:

```
preds = model.predict(X_test)
review_num = 1
print("Tweet: \n"+tokenizer.sequences_to_texts([X_test[review_num]])[0])
sentiment = "Positive" if np.argmax(preds[review_num]) else "Negative"
print("\nPredicted sentiment = "+ sentiment)
sentiment = "Positive" if np.argmax(y_test.values[review_num]) else
"Negative"
print("\nActual sentiment = "+ sentiment)
```

The output is as follows:

```
Tweet:
wishes everyone happy mother 's day

Predicted sentiment = Positive

Actual sentiment = Positive
```

```
Tweet:
google actually didnt solve problem

Predicted sentiment = Negative

Actual sentiment = Negative
```

Figure 7.42: Positive (left) and negative (right) tweets and their predictions

Chapter 8: Tips and Tricks of the Trade

Activity 21: Classifying Images using InceptionV3

Solution:

1. Create functions to get images and labels. Here **PATH** variable contains the path to the training dataset.

```
from PIL import Image
def get_input(file):
    return Image.open(PATH+file)
def get_output(file):
    class_label = file.split('.')[0]
    if class_label == 'dog': label_vector = [1,0]
    elif class_label == 'cat': label_vector = [0,1]
    return label_vector
```

2. Set **SIZE** and **CHANNELS**. **SIZE** is the dimension of the square image input. **CHANNELS** is the number of channels in the training data images. There are 3 channels in a RGB image.

```
SIZE = 200
CHANNELS = 3
```

3. Create a function to preprocess and augment images:

```
def preprocess_input(image):

    # Data preprocessing
    image = image.resize((SIZE,SIZE))
    image = np.array(image).reshape(SIZE,SIZE,CHANNELS)

    # Normalize image
    image = image/255.0

    return image
```

4. Finally, develop the generator that will generate the batches:

```
import numpy as np
def custom_image_generator(images, batch_size = 128):

    while True:
        # Randomly select images for the batch
        batch_images = np.random.choice(images, size = batch_size)
        batch_input = []
        batch_output = []

        # Read image, perform preprocessing and get labels
        for file in batch_images:
            # Function that reads and returns the image
            input_image = get_input(file)
            # Function that gets the label of the image
            label = get_output(file)
            # Function that pre-processes and augments the image
            image = preprocess_input(input_image)

            batch_input.append(image)
            batch_output.append(label)

        batch_x = np.array(batch_input)
        batch_y = np.array(batch_output)

        # Return a tuple of (images,labels) to feed the network
        yield(batch_x, batch_y)
```

5. Next, we will read the validation data. Create a function to read the images and their labels:

```
from tqdm import tqdm
def get_data(files):
    data_image = []
    labels = []
    for image in tqdm(files):
        label_vector = get_output(image)

        img = Image.open(PATH + image)
        img = img.resize((SIZE,SIZE))

        labels.append(label_vector)
```

```
            img = np.asarray(img).reshape(SIZE,SIZE,CHANNELS)
            img = img/255.0
            data_image.append(img)

        data_x = np.array(data_image)
        data_y = np.array(labels)

        return (data_x, data_y)
```

6. Read the validation files:

```
import os
files = os.listdir(PATH)
random.shuffle(files)
train = files[:7000]
test = files[7000:]
validation_data = get_data(test)
7.    Plot a few images from the dataset to see whether you loaded the
files correctly:
import matplotlib.pyplot as plt
plt.figure(figsize=(20,10))
columns = 5
for i in range(columns):
    plt.subplot(5 / columns + 1, columns, i + 1)
    plt.imshow(validation_data[0][i])
```

A random sample of the images is shown here:

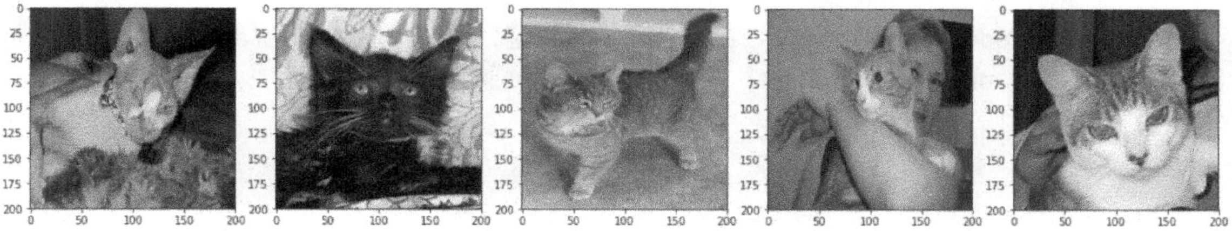

Figure 8.16: Sample images from the loaded dataset

7. Load the Inception model and pass the shape of the input images:

```
from keras.applications.inception_v3 import InceptionV3
base_model = InceptionV3(weights='imagenet', include_top=False, input_
shape=(SIZE,SIZE,CHANNELS))
```

8. Add the output dense layer according to our problem:

```
from keras.layers import GlobalAveragePooling2D, Dense, Dropout
from keras.models import Model
x = base_model.output
x = GlobalAveragePooling2D()(x)
x = Dense(256, activation='relu')(x)
x = Dropout(0.5)(x)
predictions = Dense(2, activation='softmax')(x)

model = Model(inputs=base_model.input, outputs=predictions)
```

9. Next, compile the model to make it ready for training:

```
model.compile(loss='categorical_crossentropy',
              optimizer='adam',
              metrics = ['accuracy'])
And then perform the training of the model:
EPOCHS = 50
BATCH_SIZE = 128

model_details = model.fit_generator(custom_image_generator(train, batch_
size = BATCH_SIZE),
                    steps_per_epoch = len(train) // BATCH_SIZE,
                    epochs = EPOCHS,
                    validation_data= validation_data,
                    verbose=1)
```

10. Evaluate the model and get the accuracy:

```
score = model.evaluate(validation_data[0], validation_data[1])
print("Accuracy: {0:.2f}%".format(score[1]*100))
```

The accuracy is as follows:

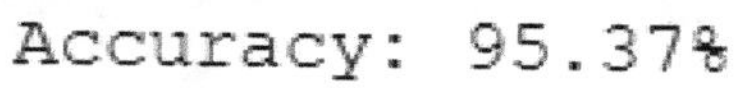

Figure 8.17: Model accuracy

Activity 22: Using Transfer Learning to Predict Images

Solution:

1. First, set the random number seed so that the results are reproducible:

```
from numpy.random import seed
seed(1)
from tensorflow import set_random_seed
set_random_seed(1)
```

2. Set **SIZE** and **CHANNELS**

SIZE is the dimension of the square image input. **CHANNELS** is the number of channels in the training data images. There are 3 channels in a RGB image.

```
SIZE = 200
CHANNELS = 3
```

3. Create functions to get images and labels. Here **PATH** variable contains the path to the training dataset.

```
from PIL import Image
def get_input(file):
    return Image.open(PATH+file)
def get_output(file):
    class_label = file.split('.')[0]
    if class_label == 'dog': label_vector = [1,0]
    elif class_label == 'cat': label_vector = [0,1]
    return label_vector
```

4. Create a function to preprocess and augment images:

```
def preprocess_input(image):

    # Data preprocessing
    image = image.resize((SIZE,SIZE))
    image = np.array(image).reshape(SIZE,SIZE,CHANNELS)

    # Normalize image
    image = image/255.0

    return image
```

5. Finally, create the generator that will generate the batches:

```
import numpy as np
def custom_image_generator(images, batch_size = 128):

    while True:
        # Randomly select images for the batch
        batch_images = np.random.choice(images, size = batch_size)
        batch_input = []
        batch_output = []

        # Read image, perform preprocessing and get labels
        for file in batch_images:
            # Function that reads and returns the image
            input_image = get_input(file)
            # Function that gets the label of the image
            label = get_output(file)
            # Function that pre-processes and augments the image
            image = preprocess_input(input_image)

            batch_input.append(image)
            batch_output.append(label)

        batch_x = np.array(batch_input)
        batch_y = np.array(batch_output)

        # Return a tuple of (images,labels) to feed the network
        yield(batch_x, batch_y)
```

6. Next, we will read the development and test data. Create a function to read the images and their labels:

```
from tqdm import tqdm
def get_data(files):
    data_image = []
    labels = []
    for image in tqdm(files):

        label_vector = get_output(image)
```

```
            img = Image.open(PATH + image)
            img = img.resize((SIZE,SIZE))


            labels.append(label_vector)
            img = np.asarray(img).reshape(SIZE,SIZE,CHANNELS)
            img = img/255.0
            data_image.append(img)

        data_x = np.array(data_image)
        data_y = np.array(labels)

        return (data_x, data_y)
```

7. Now read the development and test files. The split for the train/dev/test set is **70%/15%/15%**.

```
    import random
    random.shuffle(files)
    train = files[:7000]
    development = files[7000:8500]
    test = files[8500:]
    development_data = get_data(development)
    test_data = get_data(test)
```

8. Plot a few images from the dataset to see whether you loaded the files correctly:

```
    import matplotlib.pyplot as plt
    plt.figure(figsize=(20,10))
    columns = 5
    for i in range(columns):
        plt.subplot(5 / columns + 1, columns, i + 1)
        plt.imshow(validation_data[0][i])
```

Check the output in the following screenshot:

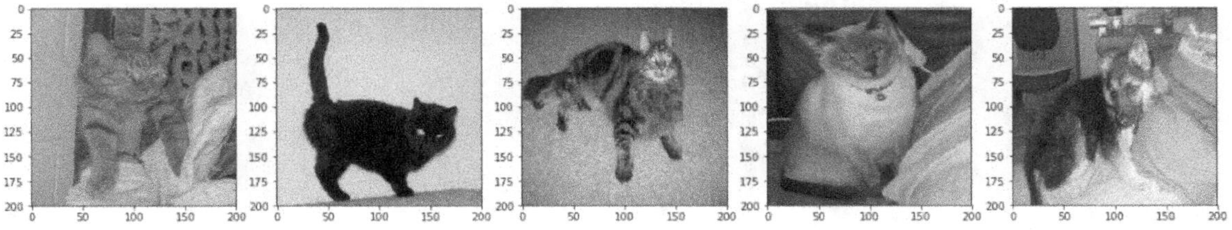

Figure 8.18: Sample images from the loaded dataset

9. Load the Inception model and pass the shape of the input images:

```
from keras.applications.inception_v3 import InceptionV3
base_model = InceptionV3(weights='imagenet', include_top=False, input_
shape=(200,200,3))
10.  Add the output dense layer according to our problem:
from keras.models import Model
from keras.layers import GlobalAveragePooling2D, Dense, Dropout
x = base_model.output
x = GlobalAveragePooling2D()(x)
x = Dense(256, activation='relu')(x)
keep_prob = 0.5
x = Dropout(rate = 1 - keep_prob)(x)
predictions = Dense(2, activation='softmax')(x)

model = Model(inputs=base_model.input, outputs=predictions)
```

10. This time around, we will freeze the first five layers of the model to help with the training time:

```
for layer in base_model.layers[:5]:
    layer.trainable = False
```

11. Compile the model to make it ready for training:

```
model.compile(loss='categorical_crossentropy',
              optimizer='adam',
              metrics = ['accuracy'])
```

12. Create callbacks for Keras:

```
from keras.callbacks import ModelCheckpoint, ReduceLROnPlateau,
EarlyStopping, TensorBoard
callbacks = [
    TensorBoard(log_dir='./logs',
                update_freq='epoch'),
    EarlyStopping(monitor = "val_loss",
                  patience = 18,
                  verbose = 1,
                  min_delta = 0.001,
                  mode = "min"),
```

```
    ReduceLROnPlateau(monitor = "val_loss",
                      factor = 0.2,
                      patience = 8,
                      verbose = 1,
                      mode = "min"),
    ModelCheckpoint(monitor = "val_loss",
                   filepath = "Dogs-vs-Cats-InceptionV3-{epoch:02d}-{val_
loss:.2f}.hdf5",
                   save_best_only=True,
                   period = 1)]
```

> **Note**
>
> Here, we are making use of four callbacks: **TensorBoard**, **EarlyStopping**, **ReduceLROnPlateau**, and **ModelCheckpoint**.

Perform training on the model. Here we train our model for 50 epochs only and with a batch size of 128:

```
EPOCHS = 50
BATCH_SIZE = 128
model_details = model.fit_generator(custom_image_generator(train, batch_
size = BATCH_SIZE),
                   steps_per_epoch = len(train) // BATCH_SIZE,
                   epochs = EPOCHS,
                   callbacks = callbacks,
                   validation_data= development_data,
                   verbose=1)
```

The training logs on TensorBoard are shown here:

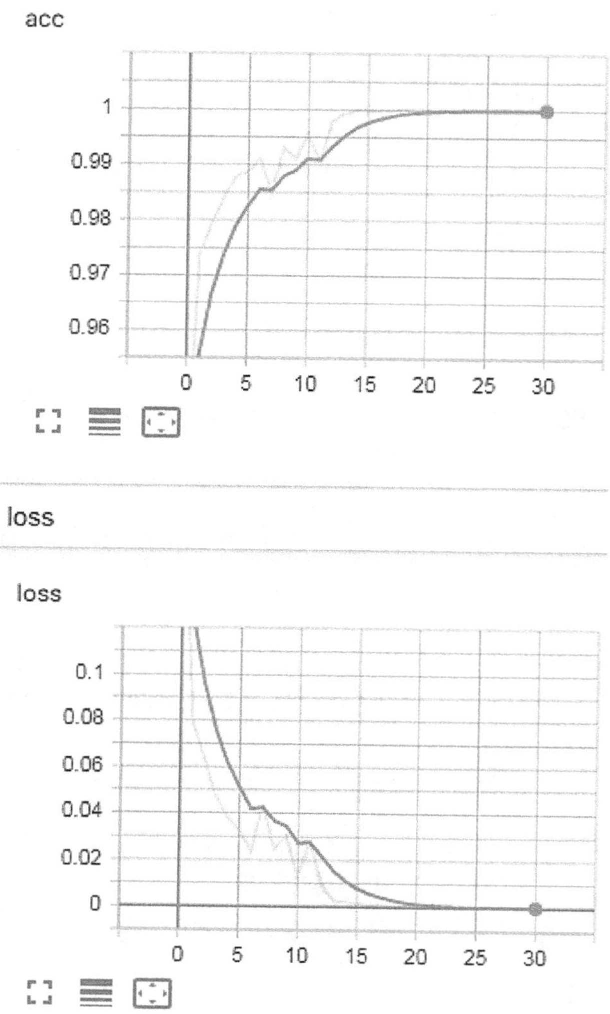

Figure 8.19: Training set logs from TensorBoard

13. You can now fine-tune the hyperparameters taking accuracy of the development set as the metric.

    The logs of the development set from the TensorBoard tool are shown here:

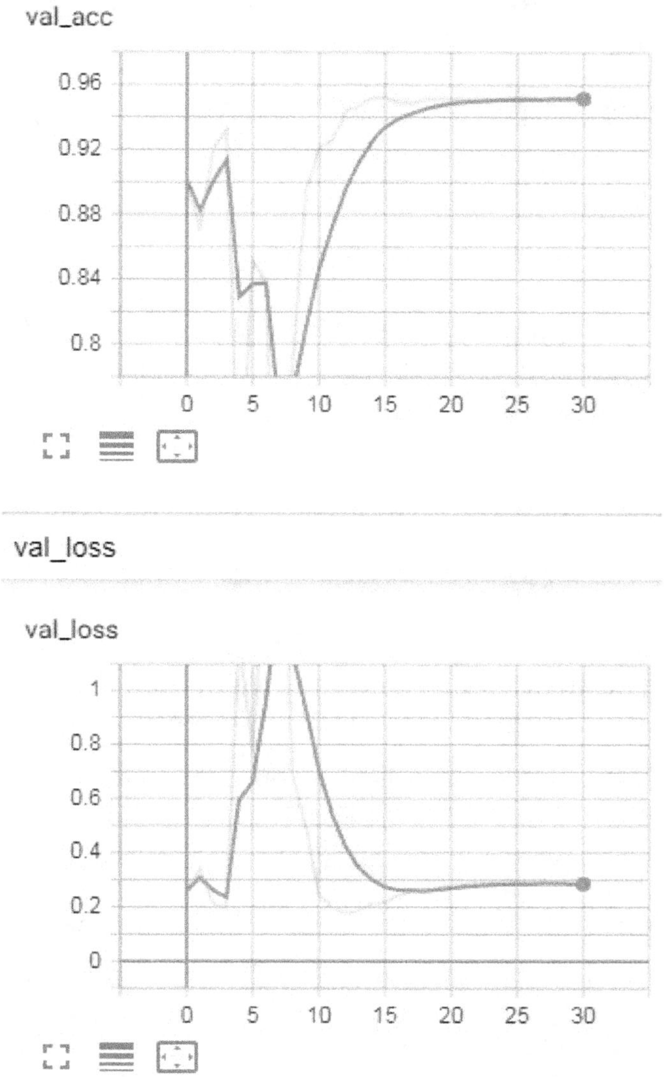

Figure 8.20: Validation set logs from TensorBoard

The learning rate decrease can be observed from the following plot:

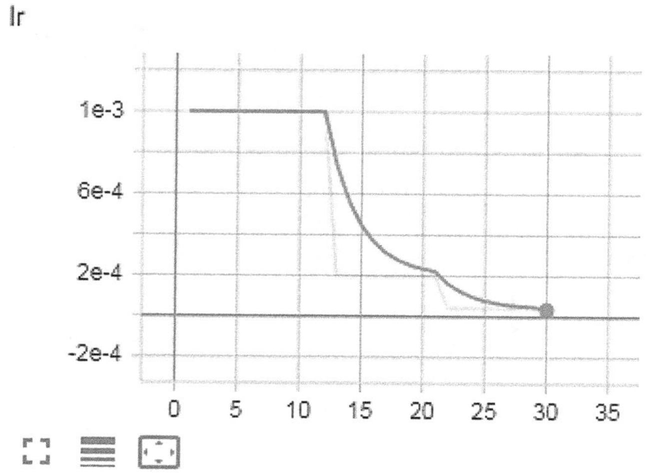

Figure 8.21: Learning rate log from TensorBoard

14. Evaluate the model on the test set and get the accuracy:

```
score = model.evaluate(test_data[0], test_data[1])
print("Accuracy: {0:.2f}%".format(score[1]*100))
```

To understand fully, refer to the following output screenshot:

```
Accuracy: 93.60%
```

Figure 8.22: The final accuracy of the model on the test set

As you can see, the model gets an accuracy of 93.6% on the test set, which is different from the accuracy of the development set (93.3% from the TensorBoard training logs). The early stopping callback stopped training when there wasn't a significant improvement in the loss of the development set; this helped us save some time. The learning rate was reduced after nine epochs, which helped training, as can be seen here:

```
Epoch 9/50
54/54 [==============================] - 41s 763ms/step - loss: 0.0270 - acc: 0.9913 - val_loss: 0.7472 - val_acc: 0.
7720

Epoch 00009: ReduceLROnPlateau reducing learning rate to 0.00020000000949949026.
Epoch 10/50
54/54 [==============================] - 41s 759ms/step - loss: 0.0183 - acc: 0.9942 - val_loss: 0.2650 - val_acc: 0.
9133
```

Figure 8.23: A snippet of the training logs of the model

Index

About

All major keywords used in this book are captured alphabetically in this section. Each one is accompanied by the page number of where they appear.

O

P

R

S

T

V

W

X

Z

CPSIA information can be obtained
at www.ICGtesting.com
Printed in the USA
FSHW020834051119
63747FS

9 781838 552862